FROM THE FALLEN TREE

FRONTIER NARRATIVES,
ENVIRONMENTAL POLITICS,
AND THE ROOTS OF
A NATIONAL PASTORAL,
1749–1826

FROM THE

Fallen Tree

THOMAS HALLOCK

The University of North Carolina Press   CHAPEL HILL & LONDON

© 2003 The University of North Carolina Press
All rights reserved
Manufactured in the United States of America

Designed by Kristina Kachele
Set in Monotype Walbaum with Serlio and Johann Sparkling display
by Tseng Information Systems, Inc.

The paper in this book meets the guidelines for permanence and durability of the Committee on Production Guidelines for Book Longevity of the Council on Library Resources.

Library of Congress Cataloging-in-Publication Data
Hallock, Thomas.
From the fallen tree : frontier narratives, environmental politics, and the roots of a national pastoral, 1749–1826 / Thomas Hallock.
p. cm.
Includes bibliographical references (p.) and index.
ISBN 0-8078-2820-3 (cloth : alk. paper) —
ISBN 0-8078-5491-3 (pbk. : alk. paper)
1. Frontier and pioneer life—United States—Historiography. 2. Frontier and pioneer life—West (U.S.)—Historiography. 3. United States—Description and travel. 4. United States—Historiography. 5. West (U.S.)—Historiography. 6. Environmental policy—United States—History. 7. Environmental policy—West (U.S.)—History. 8. Frontier and pioneer life in literature. 9. Pastoral literature, American—History and criticism. 10. Environmental literature—History and criticism. I. Title.
E179.5 .H186 2004
973'.07'2—dc21   2003007967

cloth 07 06 05 04 03   5 4 3 2 1
paper 07 06 05 04 03   5 4 3 2 1

THIS BOOK WAS DIGITALLY PRINTED.

FOR MY PARENTS, MIMI AND PETER HALLOCK,
AND FOR JULIE

Contents

Preface xi
Chronology xvii
Introduction: Closing the Wilderness, Opening the Frontier 1

PART I: THE WESTERN TEXT
1 The Imagined West: Lewis Evans 29
2 The Contested West: John Filson's *Kentucke* 56

PART II: IMPROVEMENT
3 Textual Boundaries, Discursive Control:
  Stories of the Land in the Susquehanna Valley 77
4 Jefferson's Nature and the Trans-Appalachian West:
  Notes on the State of Virginia 96

PART III: PROTÉGÉS
5 Collaboration, Incorporation, and Environmental Discourse:
  Lewis and Clark, Jane Colden 121
6 On the Borders of a New World: William Bartram's *Travels* 149

PART IV: SETTLEMENT AND APPROPRIATION
7 Reversing the Revolution through Nature:
  Anne Grant, Timothy Dwight 177
8 Disappearance and Romance: Cooper's *The Pioneers* 196

Coda: Parallel Republics 217
Notes 227   Bibliography 261   Index 285

Illustrations

I.1   Seal of the Northwest Territory *10*
I.2   Map outlining federal territories proposed in the draft of the Ordinance of 1784 *11*
I.3   Thomas Hutchins's "Plat of the Seven Ranges of Townships" (1788) *13*
1.1   Lewis Evans's "Map of Pensilvania, New-Jersey, New-York, and the Three Delaware Counties" (1749) *35*
1.2   Lewis Evans's "A General Map of the Middle British Colonies in America" (1755) *40*
1.3   Page from Lewis Evans and Benjamin Franklin's *Analysis of a General Map of the Middle British Colonies in America* (1755) *42*
1.4   Reconstruction by G. Malcolm Lewis of Neolin's "Great Book of Writing" *46*
1.5   Thomas Pownall's "A Design to represent the beginning and completion of an American Settlement or Farm" *51*
2.1   The state of Franklin in Joseph Purcell's "A Map of the States of Virginia, North Carolina, South Carolina and Georgia" (1789) *60*
2.2   John Filson's "Map of Kentucke" (1784) *62*
2.3   Reconstruction of John Filson's "Map of Kentucke" (1784) highlighting watermark of a plow and the motto "Work & Be Rich" *63*
3.1. Map of Crèvecoeur's route in "Susquehanna" and territories disputed by Connecticut and Pennsylvania *80*
4.1   "A comparative View of the Quadrupeds of Europe and America," from Thomas Jefferson's *Notes on the State of Virginia* (1787) *106*
5.1   William Clark, "A Map of Lewis and Clark's Track, Across the Western Portion of North America" (1810) *130*

5.2 Route map of Lewis and Clark Expedition, May 31–June 13, 1805, depicting forks of the Missouri and Marias Rivers *131*

5.3 Engraving from a portrait of Meriwether Lewis by Charles B. J. F. Saint-Mémin (1807) *137*

5.4 Drawings from Jane Colden's "Botanic Manuscript" *140*

6.1 Routes of John and William Bartram's travels *152*

6.2 John and William Bartram's portrayals of sinkholes *156*

6.3 William Bartram's sketch of a diamondback rattlesnake *162*

6.4 William Bartram's "View of Alatchua Savanah" *171*

6.5 William Bartram's "The Great Alachua Savanna" *172*

7.1 "Map of the Flats Above Albany," from Anne Grant's *Memoirs of an American Lady* (1808) *183*

7.2. Map of Hudson River islands, from Anne Grant's *Memoirs of an American Lady* (1808) *184*

I have written it briefly, stating everything in as few words as possible which will take less writing and reading, and will probably be better understood.
—SPENCER RECORDS

PREFACE

THIS BOOK SUGGESTS a basis for reading environmental and frontier literature from the early republic. I begin with the mid–eighteenth century, when colonial settlements began moving inland and British American writers developed forms of writing that prescribed new uses for backcountry space. I close with the advent of literary nationalism in the United States, which paralleled attenuating Indian policies and found authors pitching their veneration for wilderness alongside elegies for *things disappeared*. Between these two eras, the backcountry was cast mainly as underutilized or empty, and both the interior and its human population were seen as experiments in European progress. But narratives of nature took complicated turns, as they were forged upon still open frontiers. Writings about place unfolded against the claims of different groups, against tribal identities that were themselves in flux, and against native conceptions of and uses for overlapping resources. They were written alongside the various agendas of different empires and regions as well as ethnic and class bodies. Eventually, this fluid milieu would crystallize into a national pastoral (indeed prematurely so), with early-nineteenth-century authors drawing upon ideas of wilderness to rhetorically stabilize their otherwise fractious settings. But the elegies for nature and natives—and let's not forget squatters who ride into the sunset—were not just the harbingers of removal: In a longer view, they continued a negotiation between the environment and social structures that had been transacted over the last half century. What the romantics used to suggest closure was in fact what others before them had sought, a basis for one's claims to interior resources.

The title of this book, *From the Fallen Tree*, is from the seal of the Northwest Territory, the area west of the Appalachian Mountains that Congress zoned in 1787. Although I sometimes think that the title refers to the reams of paper that I consumed while trying to pull my thoughts together, it is indeed the loose translation of *meliorem lapsa locavit*—a succinct statement of the early republic's environmental politics. This motto, "a better one has replaced it," recognizes that attitudes and claims toward nature were implicit sources of conflict. How then do we read nature writing in this milieu? My purpose is to emphasize the social tensions that were embedded in a pastoral tradition and to provide a map for reading the still neglected body of earlier work. Despite a continued interest in environmental literature, critics have been slow to examine the colonial and revolutionary periods, simplifying the material into a one-sided story of ecological imperialism before moving to fully realized pastorals. I suggest instead that these texts, especially when read against the political dynamics that framed them, offer rich subjects in and of themselves. To make that case, I set the literature against the various groups that met on a middle ground. I should emphasize that my aims are not those of a frontier or native American historian. As should be evident, my argument draws heavily from recent scholarship in those areas, but the focus usually returns to canonical authors. Indeed, one lesson from writing this book has been recognizing where disciplines divide. As literary criticism, this book covers a rather short span of time. And while historians have the luxury of focusing on specific geographic areas, this book moves across several frontiers. But as scholarship in American environmental literature continues to address the human history that is embedded in nature, the need for a more deeply historicized ecocriticism should be apparent. I jump around geographically as a result.

The structure of this book is roughly chronological. For readers who might get lost in the contextual thicket, a chronology is provided. (The time line is meant as a handrail only, and it does not pretend to be comprehensive.) My introduction outlines theoretical concerns, weighing the differences and the potential for collaboration between literary criticism and frontier history through the example of Ohio. Part 1, on the geographer Lewis Evans and John Filson's *Kentucke*, draws from sources familiar to historians but reflects a critic's concern with narration. Part 2 revisits the settings of the previous section with discussions of J. Hector St. John de Crèvecoeur and Thomas Jefferson. By linking literary narratives with specific contact points on the frontier, I show how revolutionary prescriptions for "improvement" were negotiated against liminal zones. Part 3 argues in a different vein and—through the protégés Meriwether Lewis, Jane

Colden, and William Bartram—demonstrates how any understanding of place involved interactions with the resident populations. These three naturalists combined belletristic or metropolitan modes of writing with local knowledge and experiences in the field. Part 4 sets the emergence of literary romanticism against the politics of Indian removal as well as class and regional tensions that challenged the solidifying base of power in the early United States. I raise the question, to what ends was the *natural* being deployed? While establishing their own group as landed, authors such as Anne Grant, Timothy Dwight, Washington Irving, and James Fenimore Cooper would use nature (or their perceptions of it) as the foundation for a social order. But the push to become indigenous to the continent did not equate automatically with dispossession. For even as authors imagined a "disappearing Indian" (giving elegies for the wilderness a human face), native Americans remained at the center of national debate and continued to reinvent themselves vis-à-vis changing environs. This book closes with a discussion, or coda, on the journalist Elias Boudinot, who drafted conventional rhetoric to make his own argument for a Cherokee republic.

One source of confusion while writing this book has been in the names for various groups. Contemporary terms often conflict with eighteenth-century ones. Euroamerican authors defined themselves as "native," with writers such as Crèvecoeur lamenting "all that hath befallen our native country." From our present-day perspective, the colonial archive appears to muddy distinctions. To further complicate matters, "nativism" (meaning a pan-Indian movement) was often advanced by people who shared European descent, and these boundaries were crossed with mixed parentage, friendships, war, and adoption, and in countless other ways. Euroamerican leaders, who understood the frontier much more clearly than contemporary scholars do, made distinctions not racially but geographically. The colonial agent John Stuart, for example, reminded a British colleague that "you must . . . be careful to distinguish between the Northern and Western Indians and their views."[1] As Stuart might further suggest, even groups such as the League of Six Nations or Cherokees would split internally, often along regional lines. With these cautions in mind, this book generally uses "native" in reference to the aboriginal people of America, and when possible, I refer to specific tribal or national groups. I generally avoid the word "Indian," except in reference to Euroamerican perceptions of native Americans, policies or political appointments (superintendent of Indian affairs), or in the context of native American history (often called "Indian history").

For the sake of consistency, I use lowercase letters when referring to "native" and "white" Americans. In short, the divisions by tribe, race, or nation do not necessarily provide an accurate reflection of lived experiences on the frontier—be those frontiers from the past or from our own time. The question of naming has no easy solution, I conclude, because race was being invented alongside nature during this crucial period in United States history.

This book evolved slowly, and I have acquired many debts; the reward of a long research project, I have learned, comes in working with remarkable people. Kenneth Silverman, Pamela Schirmeister, Walter Johnson, and the late James W. Tuttleton read my dissertation and offered valuable directions for turning it into a book. Dustin Griffin gave me a home in eighteenth-century studies at New York University, and my dissertation buddy Susan Goulding generously slogged through the earliest drafts. Many friends, colleagues, and mentors read selections and offered critiques or simple encouragement. Among them are Todd Gibson, Doreen Alvarez Saar, Peter Onuf, Rich Fusco, Mike Branch, Barbara Pittman, James Kessenides, Stephanie Volmer, Mary McAleer Balkun, and Nancy Hoffmann. Members of the Bartram Trail Conference have generously shared their knowledge of southeastern flora, fauna, culture, and history—while providing much-needed companionship along the way. Amy Winans helped contextualize this study by raising questions about my selection of authors, and Gary E. Cooper (a proud Tar Heel) scrupulously edited the manuscript to ensure that it was worthy of his alma mater's press. Fredonia Woolf read selected chapters and left pinecones at my door. Sian Hunter saw potential in a prospectus and gave me the motivation to finish. My understanding of nature writing and the frontier, finally, benefited from the conversations with many fine students at Valdosta State University; I have particular debts to Tracy Brooking and William Nesbitt, whose scholarship came to inform my own.

The core of the research was through a Gordon Ray Fellowship at NYU, which allowed me to spend a couple of months at the John Carter Brown Library. A grant from the Northeast Modern Language Association brought me to the library of the American Philosophical Society, where Roy E. Goodman always had a friendly greeting, research tip, or Franklin anecdote. During a time when this book might have languished on the vine, the McNeil Center for Early American Studies provided me with a pass to the Van Pelt Library at the University of Pennsylvania. Summer grants from Valdosta State University paid for trips to the Houghton Library at Harvard University, Sterling Library at Yale University, and (what will always be my home as a reader) the New York Public Library. Denise Montgomery and Deborah Davis gave legs to the small collection at Valdosta State's Odum Library, largely through that modern miracle called ILL. Portions of this book have appeared in different form elsewhere, and I am indebted to the editors and reviewers for the *Virginia Quarterly Review*, *American Studies*, and *South Atlantic Review*. Edward Watts and Wayne Franklin read drafts of the manuscript for the University of North Carolina Press and offered invaluable suggestions for revision, and my dealings with the press have been a true pleasure.

The most significant debts are personal. My parents, Peter and Mimi Hallock, paid for my college education and never once asked what I planned to do with it. For their faith in me (and in learning for its own sake), I am enormously grateful. My sister Elizabeth and my brothers Matthew and Steven always took an interest in this project, while reminding me that there is more to life than research and writing. And my biggest shout out goes to Julie Buckner Armstrong, who is a remarkable editor, traveler, scholar, and friend. In our eight years together, we have covered most of the landscapes in this book: from the Connecticut River valley, to the Missouri River, to the head of the St. John's. May new journeys together now begin.

CHRONOLOGY

1743   Lewis Evans, Conrad Weiser, John Bartram, and Shickellamy traveled to Onondaga, the Iroquois council seat. The journey would provide material for Evans's "Map of Pensilvania, New-Jersey, New-York, and the Three Delaware Counties" (1749) and John Bartram's *Observations* (1751).

1754   Albany Congress between representatives of the Six Nations and seven British colonies. The Mohawk representatives registered land frauds, and British delegates drafted a "Plan of Union," later rejected. At Albany, the Susquehannah Company made an illegal purchase for a tract on the Susquehanna River, which would become the basis for Crèvecoeur's "Susquehannah."

1755   Lewis Evans published "A General Map of the Middle British Colonies in America," with an accompanying *Analysis*. Jane Colden reportedly completed the "Botanic Manuscript." Failed British campaign to take Fort Duquesne (Fort Pitt) began the French and Indian (or Seven Years') War in America. William Johnson appointed Crown superintendent of Indian affairs.

1763   Britain and France reached peace while Pontiac led "rebellion" from the Great Lakes region. Proclamation of 1763 reorganized British frontier policy and established the boundary of Euroamerican settlement at the Appalachian Mountains.

1768   Treaty of Fort Stanwix redrew the 1763 boundary to include Pennsylvania's Susquehanna Valley and most of Kentucky.

1774   Dunmore's War fought when the governor of Virginia (John Murray, Earl of Dunmore) led troops into Kentucky. Widespread criticism of the campaign resulted in an apocryphal speech by

	Tahgahjute (or Logan), which would be reprinted in Thomas Jefferson's *Notes on the State of Virginia* (1787).
1778	The Battle of Wyoming, or "Wyoming Massacre," punctuated hostility over settlements in the Susquehanna Valley when patriot troops suffered a convincing defeat at the hand of British Rangers, native Americans, and loyalist settlers. The battle would be described in Crèvecoeur's "Susquehannah."
1784	Congress passed the Ordinance of 1784, the first in a series of plans for territorial government in the trans-Appalachian West. Thomas Jefferson chaired a committee that drafted the report used as the foundation for the ordinance. Thomas Pownall revised his 1776 *Topographical Description of North America*, a geographic essay based upon Evans's *Analysis*. John Filson published *The Discovery, Settlement And present State of Kentucke*.
1785	Congress passed a land ordinance that led to the first federal survey of the trans-Appalachian West. Beginning from present-day Ohio, the survey initiated a grid system that would come to characterize the American landscape.
1787	The Northwest Ordinance passed, culminating a long effort to establish territorial government in the newly created national reserve. The Ohio Company would settle Marietta, at the confluence of the Ohio and Muskingum Rivers, one year later. Thomas Jefferson published *Notes on the State of Virginia* in Paris. A literary response to the western ordinances and a landmark in early national environmental thought, this book would also provide a blueprint for Indian policies over the next thirty years.
1789	Henry Knox, secretary of war in the Washington administration, drafted a federal Indian policy maintaining that the United States should encourage native Americans to adopt Euroamerican cultural values and agriculture.
1791	William Bartram published *Travels through North & South Carolina, Georgia, East & West Florida, the Cherokee Country, the Extensive Territories of the Muscogulges, or Creek Confederacy, and the Country of the Chactaws*, which recounted a 1773–77 tour. Vermont admitted into the union as the fourteenth state, culminating a forty-year controversy during which the territory had been claimed by New Hampshire and New York and (for a

	brief time) became an independent republic. Closing a similar jurisdictional crisis, Kentucky would enter the union in 1792.
1794	The confederacy of Ohio nations, after a string of victories against the United States, suffered defeat at the Battle of Fallen Timbers, marking a turning point in the settlement of Ohio.
1803	The Louisiana Purchase ceded French claims in the Mississippi Valley and tripled the territorial boundaries of the United States. Jefferson commissioned the Lewis and Clark Expedition (1804–6). *History of the Expedition under the command of Captains Lewis and Clark* would be published in 1814.
1808	Anne Grant published *Memoirs of an American Lady*, recounting her childhood in colonial New York and land controversies in Vermont.
1821–22	Timothy Dwight's *Travels in New England and New York* is published, detailing his tours throughout the Northeast over several decades.
1823	James Fenimore Cooper published *The Pioneers*.
1826	Elias Boudinot published "An Address to the Whites," an indirect response to the calls for Cherokee removal.

FROM THE FALLEN TREE

By writing stories about environmental change, we divide the causal relations of an ecosystem with a rhetorical razor that defines included and excluded, relevant and irrelevant, empowered and disempowered.
—WILLIAM CRONON

Yet one day the demons of America must be placated, the ghosts must be appeased, the Spirit of Place atoned for. Then the true passionate love for American Soil will appear. As yet, there is too much menace in the landscape.
—D. H. LAWRENCE

INTRODUCTION

CLOSING THE WILDERNESS, OPENING THE FRONTIER

IN EARLY APRIL 1789, not far from the banks of a swelling and cold Ohio River, the citizens of Marietta gathered to celebrate the one-year anniversary of the Northwest Territory. Having founded the first federal town west of the Appalachian Mountains, the Mariettans saw the mere existence of their community as a symbol of progress for an expanding nation. They hailed the occasion ceremoniously, visiting the ancient mounds near their fort, Campus Martius, and marking the day with a speech by Solomon Drowne, a New England physician who never settled in the region but whose education gave him the stock of knowledge necessary to embellish life at a frontier outpost. Drowne would toast the "firm band" that faced "the great business of unbarring a secluded wilderness and rendering it the fit abode of man." He offers precedents for this experiment, citing Virgil's *Georgics*, *The Seasons* by James Thomson, and "the illustrious Jefferson." But his allusions also give the oration a vacated quality, as Drowne appears to speak more to the hopes of a new nation than to the people in front of him. He asks a question to the women in the audience that could only have been rhetorical: "Are we, indeed, in a wilderness?—The contemplation of the scene before me, would almost lead me to distrust my senses. No wonder the gentle *Spenser* feigned such mingled beauty and elegance, by virtue benighted, could make 'a sunshine in the shady grove.'"[1]

The answer to this question presumably was "no," despite the need to ask it. The region's promoters imagined a new civilization emerging from the existing country, and this led them to understate more immediate drawbacks. They chose the site of Marietta carefully, laying out a town near the confluence of the Ohio and Muskingum Rivers, believing that commerce and farms would spread from that point through the seven ranges of townships that Congress had recently zoned. With his copy of *Notes on the State of Virginia* close at hand, Solomon Drowne would remind his listeners that "cultivators of the earth are the most virtuous and independent citizens," and he promises churches and universities, along with great strides in botany and archaeology. Evidence of this region's potential could be found in the Indian mounds nearby. The remains of a bygone civilization, these memorials suggested a promise in the physical place. City planners had left the old graves intact (they still stand there today), provided them with classical names, and organized the Marietta street grid around them. One empire presumably would replace another; yet Solomon Drowne, like his compatriots, also believed that the native people then living in the Ohio Valley were incapable of constructing such monuments. He naively glides over the tensions that the new settlement had created. His oration overlooks the threat of attack and suggests that these fears would disappear along with the other inconveniences of frontier life—snakes, poison ivy, gnats, isolation, property disputes, starvation, the cold.[2]

A public and private view left Solomon Drowne divided about the trans-Appalachian West. In his polished pronouncements before others, he would equate the Northwest Territory with a continental library: The founding of Marietta was the "first page" in a "history," and "no foul blot" (again in a Jeffersonian strain) should "stain the important volume which time is unfolding in this western world." A footnote to his speech (which was published by the Massachusetts printer Isaiah Thomas) insists that those who see "country life [as] repugnant to politeness, are surely much mistaken"; a letter to London, likewise, predicts that "the American wilderness shall bloom like the rose." Yet a couplet running throughout Drowne's diary suggests why this worldly physician never settled in the "blooming" wilderness: "He who can live in peace at home / Abroad for pleasure need not roam." And the glowing reports of "great progress" sound hollow when read against private complaints like "disagreeable time on the whole." Even the promises to his wife Betsy that they will "contemplate the wonders of nature" on the Ohio River falter before confessions of homesickness. It should come as no surprise that she never moved to Marietta. The news of Indian raids in Ohio had reached her home state, and these reports lament that "robbing, scalping and murder" deterred "bold and courageous" settlers "from adventuring into this delightful country."[3] The Drownes made it as far as Morgantown, lived there for a few years, and finished out their days back in Rhode Island.

About the same time, a Boston-based trader named John May learned a similar lesson about how border life eroded lofty expectations and rhetoric. In a 1788 diary of his commercial ventures, he claims that the "banks of the delightful Muskingum" answer "the best description I have ever heard of it," and he seems confident that "the foundations of a mighty empire" had been established. The trader had his worries, of course—he grumbles about the "savage nations" who "roar and yell" outside Campus Martius—but those fears pale beside praise for a New England community that had transplanted itself in distant environs. He glories in a congregation of three hundred that sings the shape note music of William Billings "to perfection." Business prospects would sour the next year, however, and the tone of May's journal shifts accordingly. The river dropped, hostility between natives and whites persisted, and pioneers bartered for trade instead of using cash. After his second season on the Ohio, May sensed failure and would push his own boat upriver "to rid myself of this howling wilderness." One year later, May was dead—scalped by natives who resented white settlements beyond the Ohio River.[4] These accounts indicate that while the territory qualified as a subject for belletristic prose, the textualized wilderness and the real one conflicted. Visitors who described Marietta as a civilization in its first stages could explain away hardship with a recourse to the future, but the public optimism masked often violent realities. Even as John May sang Billings "to perfection," he still slept with a rifle next to his head.

Fears of dissolution or invasion almost always surface in the early descriptions of the Northwest Territory. Authors sought to accommodate the trappings of civilization to wilderness, but as often as these attempts broke down, writers would adjust their stories. Cycles of optimism, collapse, and revision recur throughout the literature. In 1788, J. Hector St. John de Crèvecoeur lent his words to a promotional pamphlet for the Ohio Company, the group that founded Marietta. Although the ruined author of *Letters from an*

American Farmer would seem to be an unlikely celebrant of the revolutionary frontier, his revised and expanded *Lettres d'un cultivateur Américain* had taken a considerably more optimistic view, making it suitable for commercial interests. One of the published extracts from the French edition describes the Ohio Valley as the "most fertile country [that] Europeans have heretofore discovered and peopled." Sounding a lot like Solomon Drowne, Crèvecoeur looks to the future: "I saw those beautiful shores ornamented with decent houses, covered with harvests and well cultivated fields; on the hills exposed to the north, I saw orchards regularly laid out in squares; on the others vine-yard plats, plantations of mulberry trees, acacias, &c." He anticipates "activity, industry, culture and commerce" in the territory, which he predicts will yield the "force, riches, and the future glory of the United States." The degree of terror that one expects to counter this optimism, however, keeps changing. In the more widely read version, the traveler drifts too far beyond the surveyed zones and risks losing control of himself. The journey closes with a prairie fire: "What a spectacle does this vast conflagration offer! It is at once interesting and terrible!" The "whirlwinds of dark and thick smoke" threaten to suffocate him, and Crèvecoeur cannot sketch a "great picture of destruction without being penetrated with an involuntary dread."[5] Yet a second version, which appears only in a rare pamphlet, replaces smoke and fire with the more benign description of storks rising in a circle. The overlap in images is striking. The storks "raise themselves slowly," moving like flame in "a kind of circular ascent," creating "large spirals in their flight."[6] The descriptions shift as the author weighs out his hopes and fears for the interior, as he continually revises his strategy for grafting culture onto the land.

A great deal of the literature in the early United States was vested in this process of making one's home in a wilderness, and the narratives often take unexpected — on the surface, contradictory — turns as they grapple with the paradoxes of expansion. The more sophisticated authors especially recognized the need for something beyond belletrism or colonial cant; it was not enough to quote Edmund Spenser. They struggled to establish a genuine link between culture and the physical terrain, while accounting for the social conflicts that interior settlements engendered. Crèvecoeur's name appears again and again in this process of accommodation. Almost fifteen years after the extracts were were used by the Ohio Company, he published a forgotten classic of American pastoral writing, *Voyage dans la Haute Pennsylvanie et dans l'Etat de New-York*. Crèvecoeur's semifictional travelogue departs from the 1782 *Letters* by taking a more retrospective turn, and it balances the spread of European agriculture against a growing conservation sense. A typical chapter finds the narrator (identified only as an adopted member of the Oneida tribe) and his companion Gustave Herman slogging through some bottomlands in the Wyotucing River valley when they hear the chime of a town clock. The two friends can scarcely contain their delight over a "cornfield, a young orchard," and a small cabin with "four casement windows." All appears to be civility. "Welcome gentlemen," their host asks. "Aren't you perhaps lost?" The affable Mr. Herman replies, "One is never lost" when he has "the good fortune to meet a fine colonist like you."[7]

What follows is an introduction to republican landscapes. Moving beyond the jubilant predictions for Ohio, Crèvecoeur frames Euroamerican expansion through contrasts. The host, an émigré named Nadowisky, compares his past hardships in Poland to prosperity in the New World. Nadowisky describes how he acquired property and part ownership in a seine at the nearby river; he extols the values of citizenship, and he criticizes pioneers who labor only two days a week; he emphasizes the importance of a stable, representative government. That evening, Mrs. Nadowisky spreads across the table goods that she and her husband obtained through trade and the sweat of their brow: beef, shad, cakes, jam from their orchards, sugar from maple sap, and tea exchanged with the Chinese for ginseng gathered in the Pennsylvania woods. This episode chronicles the steps through which settlers transformed space into place, into surroundings they could recognize and appreciate; it suggests how Euroamericans turned an unknown and therefore undesirable country into one that reflected their own uses, needs, tastes, and individual biographies.[8] As the clock provides the wilderness travelers with a welcome landmark, the genteel pioneer would steadily create a more familiar environment over time. "My ambition," Nadowisky explains, "is to have some day many meadows and fields" from marshes on his property, and "in just a few years the most uncultivated land will burst forth with flowers, fruits, and harvests." Like countless other farmers, he will fence his boundaries, girdle trees, and burn the understory; he will straighten the riverbanks and introduce new crops and stock. These alterations, at the same time, awaken an appreciation for old-growth forests. Clear-cutting and disruptions to the water table had already ruined several mills in the area, Nadowisky observes. He laments the disappearing old-growth stands and sagely predicts that the cost of firewood will continue to rise with deforestation. The coming "generation will regret bitterly that their fathers destroyed so much," Nadowisky concludes, for in these woods "everything bears the compelling imprint of magnificence and enduring time."[9]

A clock strikes in the wilderness. A trader sings church hymns to perfection. A philosophe's tour shuffles from prairie fires to a flock of storks. Twelve years later, travelers on the upper Wyotucing encounter a home with casement windows, and they register the progress of civilization against ecological loss. Stretched over a thirteen-year period, from 1788 to 1801, these examples indicate the range of environmental writing that was produced during a time of profound social and ecological change. Postrevolutionary culture demanded viable stories of place, bases for claiming the land. The resulting narratives would construct a national subject over the interior; that is, they would assert a federal presence over the border regions. At the same time, the frontier demanded resilience and accommodation. What emerged was a body of work that, when read together and in deep historical context, takes surprising turns of narrative. This book builds upon earlier studies of eighteenth-century environmentalism to outline a poetics for wilderness writing from the early republic. I draw from some fine models. Cecelia Tichi traces how early national authors cast the interior as a "new earth," a wilderness redeemed through "improvement," and Myra Jehlen observes that national identity grounded ideology in the physical fact of the land. Annette Kolodny argues that this drive exhibited a violent desire; John Seelye and Robert Lawson-Peebles trace the fate of Enlightenment models on the land, noting that the "beautiful machine," or emasculated verbal order, inevitably collapsed.[10] But these discussions invite continued reading, particularly within the context of colonialism and the search for place. The praise for a "new earth," after all, did not always end with scalped heads and rhetorical failure. The examples of Drowne, May, and Crèvecoeur indicate a certain fluidity in environmental and frontier narratives. Writers such as Drowne or May imagined a future civilization expanding across the interior, but the realities of border life tempered their lofty rhetoric. Narratives adjusted accordingly and took on new forms. The recognition of vanishing habitats and local knowledge would appear alongside prescriptions for change, and plans for improvement would be accommodated to suit local landscapes. As the 1801 *Voyage* suggests, authors could find room for negotiation between transformation and loss.

What remains constant is the construction of nature against race, ethnicity, region, and class to form what Carroll Smith-Rosenberg calls the "republican subject." The interior of America offered a field against which early national culture defined itself, and the political work of stories about the land is the topic of this book. While emphasizing the politics of frontier and environmental writing, I combine the "new western history" and ecological criticism to demonstrate how contests over wilderness crystallized into verbal forms. What narratives emerged, in other words, from the vexed or partial attempts to create place from space? As Edward Countryman has powerfully argued, Revolutionary plans for empire were "bound up with both the self-constitution of a sovereign American people and that people's redefinition of the appropriate usage for the space where it claimed sovereignty. One social order that had filled the whole of that space gave way to another, vastly more suited than its predecessor to the democratic capitalist energy that we now see as the Revolution's product." In the texts produced by this effort to channel "capitalist energies," politics were defined through an understanding of the terrain. The "social order" necessary for an "empire of liberty," to put matters simply, could chafe against those of the existing populations. A response to Countryman by Philip J. Deloria, indeed, may serve as my own starting point: Deloria notes that historians of the West have "transformed the question of region to one of 'space,' focusing on the ways in which people moving through a landscape redefine other people's 'places.'" The ideological geography of the new republic formulated itself upon an unstable social milieu: one where cultures collided and converged and over habitats that were themselves in transition.[11] The cant used by Solomon Drowne or John May invariably collapsed or contradicted itself. But other accounts from very fluid border regions, particularly those by more skilled authors, bent as often as they collapsed, and place-oriented meditations would appear alongside the usual rhetoric of change. Eventually, an identification with native habitats and people (in an unfortunate equation) would lay the groundwork for a national pastoral; elegies for things disappeared would provide authors with a medium that was flexible enough to establish a republican citizenry as indigenous to the continent. At the center of this narrative paradox was an ecological sense, an awareness that invasion altered habitats, and this growing sentimentality gave authors what they needed to orchestrate the unlikely dialogue between possession and art.[12] These often buried politics were at the root of a pastoral tradition. But the natural, even in its incarnation as a vacated wilderness, emerged from a still populated frontier.

Meliorem Lapsa Locavit

One of the best sites for understanding the links between nature, narrative, border politics, and nation building is the Northwest Territory. Second only in importance to the Constitution, the legislation that zoned the Ohio Valley provided an opportunity for the republic to articulate its own identity. The drafts and disagreements were legendary—one bored delegate grumbled about enough ink spilled to "fill forty volumes"—and the art and literature that followed the lawmaking show how ideas of nature squared (or failed to do so) against the actual frontier. Historians generally tell two stories about the trans-Appalachian West. The first emphasizes the region's fluidity. It was a border country—a country of villages, Richard White explains, where provisional identities were forged through the interactions between many different groups. The Delawares migrated and the Shawnees returned to the Ohio Valley in order to escape the pressures of expansion, but only after they had learned to live in a colonial world. Along with others, they developed a hybrid culture that was neither white nor native but a mixture between races.[13] A second story involves consolidation, with the Middle West providing a "testing ground" or "blueprint" for an expanding "empire of liberty." The Continental Congress could not control immigration, especially as this region was contested already, and the "irregular manner" of land settlement subverted one-sided exercises of white authority. The end of the American Revolution brought a need "to nationalize and discipline the chaotic social forces" in Ohio, as Eric Hinderaker notes, but the overarching plans would "come up against the complicated social patterns and tangled histories" that were already in place.[14]

Images of nature, which suggested how the land should be used, presumed to establish a grounds for possession where little existed. Nature most commonly equals the raw material that prefigures "civilization." A 1787 poem in *American Museum*, "Address to the armies of the united states of America," illustrates how lawmakers in the early republic would imagine entitlement to backcountry resources. Written by David Humphreys (George Washington's aide-de-camp), this two-part georgic staples a patriot history onto a distant setting. Part 1 mourns revolutionary heroes who fell in battle, and part 2 urges former soldiers to settle where the river "rolls his amber tide / And nature blossoms in her virgin pride." The poet invites them to cash in on the bounties they received for their service:

Make the fair villa in full splendors smile,
And robe with verdure all the genial soil.
Then shall rich commerce court the fav'ring gales,
And wond'ring wilds admire the passing sails.

Humphreys's acknowledgment of the region's existing history is notably thin. With no allowance for the ways in which this land was being used (or claimed) already, he describes a "seat of bliss, and last retreat of man"; the general's aide-de-camp casts the backcountry as a zone awaiting Euroamerican agriculture and trade.[15] This transfer from the local to an idealized setting, from the actual landscape to a vision of progress across space, surfaces again and again in the literature and informs other pieces of legislation, scientific writing, social planning, and the arts. The seal of the Northwest Territory captures the republic's environmental imagination (figure I.1). An image in the center depicts an apple tree growing from a prostrate oak. A fruit-bearing import takes root from the decaying soil of the existing tree; around this image, the motto declares *meliorem lapsa locavit*—"a better one has replaced it," or "from the fallen tree, a new one has grown."[16] Following the plans expressed by the framers of a territorial government, poets would declare that a new empire should take root in the humus left by a vanished people.

Before that civilization could take root, however, Congress would have to exert some form of control over the Ohio Valley—and in the process, order itself. The most immediate source of contention came from native Americans who, having been ignored in the 1783 treaty that ended the Revolution, rejected claims by the United States in the trans-Appalachian West. Squatters showed similar contempt for federal authority; notoriously indifferent to legal titles, these "lawless banditti" threatened to usurp what Congress saw as revenue. The region served as a hothouse for political schemes of all stripes. Backwoods self-promoters declared their own sovereign states, and as their rogue ventures were rejected by Congress, threatened allegiance to England or Spain. The end of the war, to make matters worse, left the union with antiquated charters that in some cases dated back to the seventeenth century. The old boundaries stifled the "mutual good" of the republic and, in the words of one delegate, threatened "our very existence as a sovereign and independent people." The more egregious claims strike one today as inconceivable, but they were all too real to members of the Continental Congress:

Figure I.1. Seal of the Northwest Territory with the motto *meliorem lapsa locavit*—loosely, "a better one has replaced it." The earliest mention of the seal was in 1788. Courtesy Ohio Historical Society Archives/Library.

New York claimed tracts of territory into Tennessee through the "defeated" Iroquois, Connecticut held a reserve in Pennsylvania as well as in present-day Ohio, and Virginia technically reached to the Pacific Ocean. These internal disputes, further exacerbated by private land companies, undermined the first calls for a federal domain.[17]

The attempt to solidify a national presence loosely follows a plot from political idealism to expediency. For European radicals and like-minded patriots, the West suggested a blank space that the government could fill with principle: The continent was as a "prospect of future peace and happiness," an "improveable territory" that could redeem a fallen Europe.[18] A congressional committee chaired by Jefferson offered a well-known report that used geography as the field for Enlightenment ideals, and this report

Figure I.2. Map outlining federal territories proposed in the draft of the Ordinance of 1784. The "hard names" are Jefferson's. Courtesy Princeton University Press.

became the basis for the Ordinance of 1784. As the map that accompanied the ordinance suggests, the framers were more beholden to theory than to the physical terrain (figure I.2). A "ladder" of longitudes would structure the territory, and while the meridians were drawn from specific landmarks (the shoals of the Ohio at Louisville, the mouth of the Kanawha River), the actual contours of the land were subsumed by a Euclidian order. More important, the Jeffersonian plan failed to offer practical solutions to pressing problems. The 1784 ordinance offered some "hard names"—Cherronesus,

Sylvania, Metropotamia, Pelisipia, Polypotamia—but neither stability nor a "a national fund . . . equal to our debt."[19]

In 1785, Congress passed a land ordinance that was more specifically addressed to the generation of property and therefore capital. By squaring the West into neat parcels (to follow Edward Countryman's terms), Congress would channel "democratic capitalist energy" into federal coffers and lay the basis for a Euroamerican political economy over the wilderness. The geographer Thomas Hutchins was dispatched to Ohio, where he was to lay out thirteen "ranges," or columns of land; in 1788, he published the results as a "Plat of the Seven Ranges of Townships" (figure I.3). On the surface, his map epitomized the Enlightenment rage for order. But the map and the story behind it were two different things. The federal survey had symbolic and almost quaint beginnings: It was to have thirteen ranges for thirteen states, with each state sending a delegate to supervise the division of wilderness into orderly blocks. Yet the "straight lines and squared corners" belied the complications that came with execution. To begin with, Congress had issued Hutchins an impossible task. The grid relied upon meridians to ensure an even division of land; because meridians converge as they move north, however, these lines could never match the measurements determined by surveyors' chains. The "new earth" was thus riddled from the outset by an incompatibility between topography and the terrain, between the abstracted and the physical place. Second, the very presence of a compass in the Ohio Valley could put one's life at risk. Hutchins's company as a result worked under a military escort. The ensign for one surveying team reported of one squatter who, "determined to hold possession," had to be escorted forcefully to Wheeling. The Shawnees expressed particular contempt toward the survey: "We do not understand measuring out the lands," council leaders objected; "it is all ours." This resistance from several levels forced Hutchins to reduce the scale of his commission. Citing problems with the "mirey Swamps," the rugged terrain, and the "ill temper of the Indians," he abandoned the initial goal of thirteen ranges and completed only seven. In the long run, the Land Ordinance of 1785 proved to be unsuccessful. Only a few tracts sold in Hutchins's lifetime, the returns would not finance even a year of the public debt, and a baseline for the entire map was off by a half mile. An aerial view of the seven ranges today shows that the grid had little effect on the land.[20]

It finally took the combination of political lobbying and corporate investment to direct federal settlement into the Ohio Valley, and in 1787, Congress

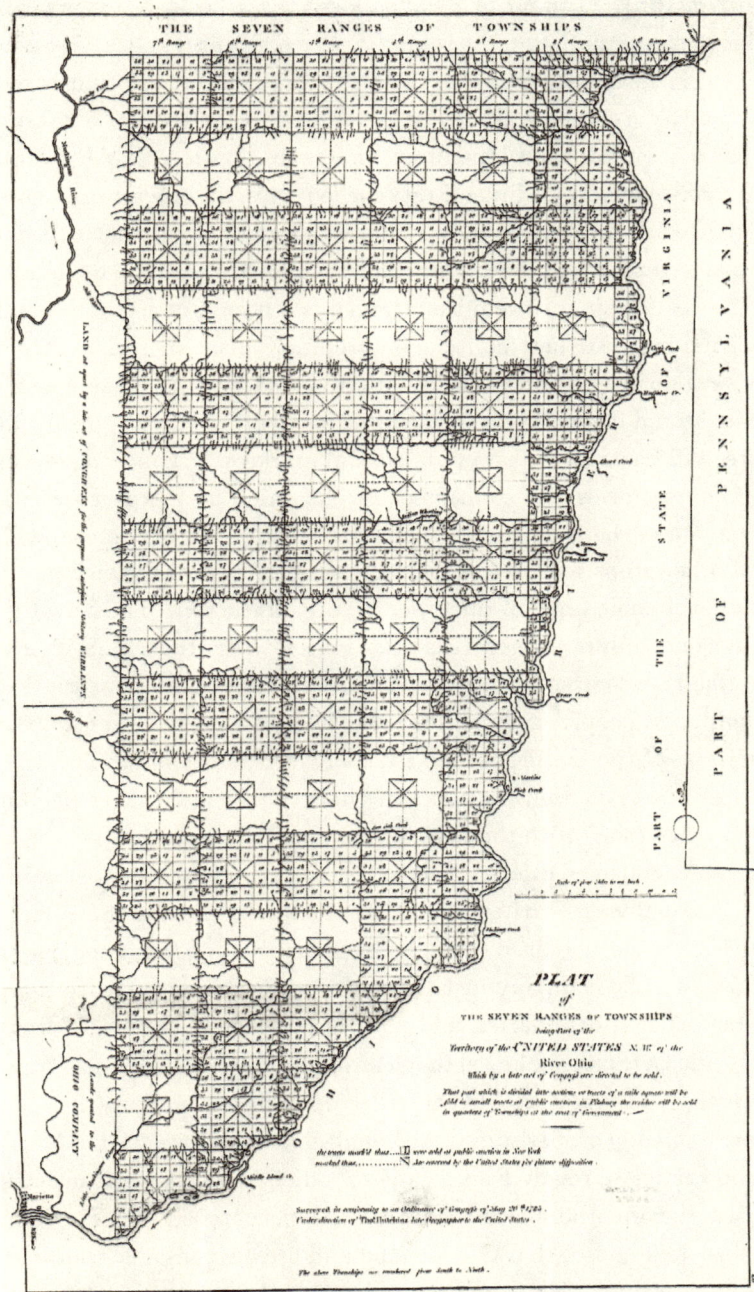

Figure 1.3. Thomas Hutchins's "Plat of the Seven Ranges of Townships" (1788), following the survey ordered by the Ordinance of 1785. Courtesy John Carter Brown Library, Brown University.

passed the Northwest Ordinance, which offered the necessary "measure of preparation" for speculation in the region. Spurring Congress to action was Manasseh Cutler, a Congregationalist minister who, with the Boston-based Ohio Company, purchased a tract just beyond the seventh range (taking advice from none other than Hutchins). In keeping with a New England influence, the Northwest Ordinance established a system of territorial government that was more conservative than its prototype and that tied expansion to an Atlantic-based economy and balance of power.[21] The details of the Northwest Ordinance require no rehearsal here, but a promotional tract by Cutler suggests how political environmentalism shaped the Ohio Company's rhetoric. Cutler's pamphlet often appeared with Crèvecoeur's extracts and would depict rivers in terms of navigability, land in terms of agriculture, and trade for its benefit to coastal markets. In Cutler's view of the West, the territories are "connected," so the union may expect an "immense intercourse" between them; wetlands become "natural meadows"; cotton and other crops will be grown "in great perfection"; the rich game offers "unquestionable proof of the great fertility of the soil." The New England lobbyist not only outlines future trade routes, where the Ohio will provide "raw materials for manufacturers," but predicts that a territory "settled by an enlightened people" may become the "seat of empire"—indeed the future capital—of the United States. Like Crèvecoeur, Solomon Drowne, and countless others, Cutler grafts politics onto nature and makes habitat disruption synonymous with the federal republic.[22]

The literature reflected a desire by the Ohio Company to cultivate "civilization" in the Northwest Territory, bringing changes not just to the wilderness but to the people who lived there. Even as the rhetoric remained out of sync with reality, the company insisted that settlers should improve their property, honor legal boundaries, and plant profit-yielding crops.[23] Members of the Ohio Company believed that a new nation would take root "from the fallen tree," and that it should capitalize upon resources that (they believed) were not being properly used. Although evidence suggests that Marietta was sometimes "a rowdy frontier town," official reports were at pains to distinguish it from other border communities. Settlers left New England with prefabricated houses that they framed and finished on-site. Their village had a six-acre garden within three weeks, a bridge over the Muskingum two weeks later, and before the end of summer, a school, common green, and church. Travelers contrasted the new settlements with those on the other side of the river, noting that the Ohioans cleared stumps from their fields and penned their livestock. The Mariettans built fences, not split rails; they glazed windows, while most backwoods folk in Kentucky settled for greased paper. Pioneers in the Northwest Territory gathered for patriotic holidays, where they toasted pompous orations by the likes of Solomon Drowne.[24]

This fixation with progress set the Ohio Company at odds with the existing population, as prevailing ideas for environmental and social change would not accommodate forms of land use that fell outside an Enlightenment schema. Leaders attempted to direct the region's civic life, and while shares in the Ohio Company generated slight returns, complaints about the "white savages" abounded.[25] "Run not into [Indian] customs and habits," Governor Arthur St. Clair implored, "but endeavor to induce them to yours." Conservatives like St. Clair had little use for the common culture that characterized the colonial period. His "Indians" (and the pioneers that resembled them) were either the subjects for improvement or an obstacle — at any rate, an Other. Maybe, if "persuaded" to farm as well as to read and write, a British traveler observed, "they might soon be civilized"; patriot commentators held a more aggressive position, that the "tribes of Indians ... will decease faster" with the quickening pace of settlement.[26] Public policy straddled a paradox between benevolent progress and (what would become) Manifest Destiny. The Northwest Ordinance provided a blueprint for expansion, and while seeming to preserve the republic's lofty intentions, it anticipated dispossession in a single, conciliatory clause. "The utmost good faith shall always be observed" toward the natives, reads article 3 of the ordinance, "and property shall never be taken from them without their consent. . . . They never shall be invaded or disturbed, unless in just and lawful wars authorised by Congress; but laws founded in justice and humanity shall from time to time be made, for preventing wrongs being done to them, and for preserving peace and friendship with them." As the concession "from time to time" reveals, officials responded to a contradiction by looking toward the future. The United States failed to provide solutions for that immediate moment. The Northwest Ordinance treated native people only in Euroamerican terms: as either the subjects for improvement or the counterweights to progress but not as people who possessed their own legitimate uses for backcountry space.[27]

Literary responses to the ordinances echo this paradox. In celebrations of an expanding civilization, natives hold a tenuous position — one that authors would recognize even as they sought to explain it away. Philip Freneau's "On the emigration to America, and peopling the western country" (from the same magazine where Humphreys's doggerel appeared) provides a representative example. On one hand, Freneau's Ohio serves as the topos for national ascendancy. It is a landscape of hope, dripping in classicism and receptive to market potential:

> To western woods and lonely plains,
> Palemon from the crowd departs,
> Where nature's wildest genius reigns,
> To tame the soil, and plant the arts—
> What wonders there shall freedom shew!
> What mighty states successive grow!

The image of "lonely plains" casts the country as a vacated space awaiting humanity. The grafting of the natural and artificial replicates the message of *meliorem lapsa locavit*, where a nation exploits the vital but still dormant force of nature. Agriculture domesticates the wild; it can "tame the soil," so that civil society may "plant the arts." The "genius" suggests some local spirit, some Ariel trapped in the oak, that republican economy would release. The assumption that "forests bloom'd but to decay," however, forces the poet to bid farewell to the existing inhabitants of the same country. Slinking into the shadows of the text, Freneau writes,

> Th' unsocial Indian far retreats
> To make some other clime his own—
> Where other streams, less pleasing flow,
> And darker forests round him grow.[28]

This "unsocial Indian" (tellingly reduced to a singular type) offers little more than the tawny reflection of a new agricultural order.

The poem suggests at least two conclusions that I will explore further in this book. The first is how projections of environmental change carried the seeds of conflict. Carolyn Merchant notes that "the history of spatial changes is a history of power changes," and texts like Freneau's depict one side of a struggle for resources. The motto *meliorem lapsa locavit* was not just an exercise in classical training; it offered an implicit case for dispossession.[29] (As the trader John May speculated before he got scalped, "whenever a new country is settled, the natives must flee or die.") Still, I must qualify my position against previous literary studies. Scholars of American literature argue forcefully that textual removals anticipate real ones, and Freneau sometimes plays a leading role in what might be called "dispossession studies." But taking Freneau at his word (and assuming that the "unsocial Indian" vanished before an imperial imagination) glosses the more immediate context of the Ohio Valley. A confederacy of native warriors, this "unsocial Indian," resisted expansion and handed the United States disastrous losses in 1790 and 1792. The Ohio confederacy held the advantage through most of this period. Indeed, by the end of the second campaign, the Kaskasian Ducoigne would consider his position strong enough to demand a boundary at the Ohio River: "It is best that the white people live in their Country," he explained, "and we live in ours." It finally took a massive campaign (consuming 80 percent of the federal budget for 1794) and the failure of England to back its native allies to defeat this confederacy.[30] The United States claimed victory with the Battle of Fallen Timbers in 1794, but even then, one might overemphasize the impact of military might. After the 1794 campaign, many soldiers decided to stay, and as they cleared farms and imported new species, habitat disruption accelerated.[31] The field of battle in Ohio was not so much lost as ruined.

My second conclusion is actually a series of questions: How did writings about place register the interests of native peoples? Can native perspectives be drawn from a literature predicated upon environmental change? Years after leading the rout of 1792, the Miami chief Little Turtle met the French geologist and philosophe Constantin-François Chasseboeuf, the Comte de Volney. Little Turtle, as presented through a text that was translated by Charles Brockden Brown, contends that the past war was over land use:

> A white man gathers from a field, a few times bigger than his room, bread enough for a whole year. If he adds to this a small field of grass, he maintains beasts . . . while we must have a great deal of ground to live upon. A deer will serve us a couple of days, and a single deer must have a great deal of ground to put him in good condition. If we kill two or three hundred a year, 'tis the same as to eat all the wood and grass of the land they live on and that is a great deal. No wonder the whites drive us every year further before them from the sea to the Mississippi. They spread like oil on a blanket; we melt like snow before the sun.[32]

Obviously, several indicators here suggest that this speech projects a white perspective through the native's voice. The talk of melting "like snow" and "oil on a blanket" casts Euroamerican expansion as an inevitability; it indulges a romantic nostalgia to exculpate a society's conscience and supports a dichotomy between agriculture and hunting that did not exist. White emigrants commonly sought out native American farms. Yet the text also points to some rather believable sources of tension. Native relations with the United States fared poorly in the Ohio Valley because Euroamerican settlement (as opposed to trade) threatened existing habitats and therefore cultures of the land. As Little Turtle explains (if these are indeed his words), expansion became an issue when the country could not support an adequate population of deer. Even though the Battle of Fallen Timbers conventionally marks a turning point for this region, one should not let the story end with ascendancy and mournful defeat. (Historians such as Richard White trace the conflict to Tecumseh and the War of 1812.) I would note how the written text registers a struggle for natural resources and emphasize that descriptions of the backcountry set authors into dialogue with an Other. With writers inventing both human and natural cultures, ideas of nature were forged upon a populated frontier. Ideas of the land were being imagined, as were the intersecting and crosshatched relations between native and white peoples.

Ideas of Nature

The exchange between Volney and Little Turtle raises critical issues as well for the canon of American environmental literature. Despite the emergence of pastoral or ecological criticism in the last decade, the eighteenth century remains largely uncharted territory. This probably is due to the attention that many ecocritics pay to the "nonhuman," with less attention to still populated landscapes. If native people occupy this landscape, by the same thinking, it is because their culture is noninvasive—further supporting that unsubstantiated myth that Shepard Krech calls the "Ecological Indian." A study in early national frontier and environmental writing therefore might challenge ahistorical conceptions of the environment and move beyond a mournful rhetoric of loss. Raymond Williams has famously observed that ideas of "nature" contain "an extraordinary amount of human history," and his observations bear deep relevance to a national cult that (for reasons of political expediency) fetishizes wilderness as the last "untouched" space. Scholarship in literary ecology, or ecocriticism, has been slow to recognize how cultures invent, share, and fight over wilderness—except in preservation battles. As a result, the colonial roots of a later tradition (where authors cast the interior as a commodity or future possession) suffer simplification or remain ignored. Roderick Nash offers a status quo reading in his monumental *Wilderness and the American Mind* when he argues that authors imaginatively transformed their "untamed" surroundings out of fear. Wilderness was an obstacle. By Nash's account, this fear progressed to romantic veneration and eventually would lead to the twentieth-century concept of refuge.[33] But ecocritics need a broader tradition to move beyond pat explanations. To imply that the "nature" of this continent was ever vacant (or inhabited by unchanging civilizations that did not impact the land) bypasses what one frontier historian calls the "longer, grimmer, but more interesting story" of the American West.[34]

Before proceeding further, then, some key terms (particularly "wilderness" and "frontier") need to be examined and reintroduced. In the eighteenth century, wilderness commonly meant land before white settlement. Pioneers from the Ohio Valley would complain of having "ventured their lives in a Wild uncultivated part"; to be "in a state of nature," on the other hand, meant living without "law government or protection." American thought has evolved from this dichotomy, changing only to reverse the terms. A conservation sense that dates back at least to Thoreau's *Walden* seeks to avoid the passage of time through the study of isolated habitats. This view would carry into the twentieth century through such writers as Aldo Leopold, who famously argued that "a thing is right when it tends to preserve the integrity, stability, and beauty of the biotic community. It is wrong when it tends otherwise." Following Leopold, green cultural studies would initially dismiss republican writing as anthrocentric or as evidencing an immature ethos. The earlier authors saw the surrounding countryside as capital, as sites for future empire—not as parks—and the tradition that was defined for the United States emphasized figures who valued aesthetics over commerce. The usual taxonomy for the United States begins with the unrepresentative William Bartram or (even more incongruously) the English ornithologist Gilbert White and then extends "to America through Henry Thoreau, John Burroughs, John Muir," and into the present. If the revolutionaries receive mention, it is for their influence on later, more important works.[35] The scholarship on this line more recently has come under criticism, however, for failing to acknowledge issues of gender, race, and ethnicity. Joni Adamson Clarke calls for a "transformative ecocriticism," one that recognizes "the connections between the oppressions of certain peoples and places" and opens itself to the links between community and country. David Mazel discusses "environ" as a verb, not as a fixed entity, and interrogates the construction of a white male subject through canonical landscapes.[36]

Such interventions to the usual stable of authors catch up with the work of environmental historians and postcolonial thinkers who have argued convincingly that wilderness exists primarily in the American imagination. The terms have been complicated considerably since Congress defined wilderness in 1964 as "an area where the earth and its community of life are untrammeled by man, where man is a visitor who does not remain." That idea of nature as "untrammeled," articulated shortly after Frederick Jackson Turner declared the West "closed," ignores the ways in which humans shape their surroundings. The Aboriginal Australian Fabienne Bayet notes that the view from the United States represents "yet another form of paternalism and dispossession" when exported around the globe. Arturo Goméz-Pompa and Andrea Kraus make a similar case from Latin America. "The inhabitants of rural areas," they counter, "have different views of the areas that urbanites designate as wilderness, and they base their land-use and resource management practices on these alternative visions. Indigenous groups in the tropics, for example, do not consider the tropical forest environment to be wild; it is their home."[37] Even in colonial America (where a mythology of wilderness took on biblical proportions), a pristine "biotic community" never existed. William Cronon sums up the historical consensus when he notes there is "no climax forest in permanent stasis"; all human groups, his frequent collaborator Richard White adds, "change their environment to some extent." The idea of an untouched zone that precedes development, born in the late nineteenth century, does the nation's political work. "Only to the white man was nature a 'wilderness,'" the Lakota Standing Bear protested in 1933; while many native rituals and mythologies acknowledge liminal spaces as sacred, the twentieth-century idea of parks evolved in the wake of Manifest Destiny. Recent scholarship accordingly focuses on how people imagine and define other people's spaces, and frontier historians especially have shifted their attention to the relationships between unstable habitats and people. James H. Merrell shows how the Catawbas, for example, addressed changes in the Carolina Piedmont. Although "generations of natives had inscribed their own versions of ordered landscape," creating place from space in effect, Euroamericans put their own mark on the country. The Catawbas responded by adapting white practices themselves, by violently resisting, by negotiating, or by leaving. Merrell's account complicates what was a simple narrative of conquest, inevitability, and regret; he shows how changes in both social and natural landscapes forced people to rethink their relation to the environment and to one another.[38]

An ethic that dates its beginnings from Thoreau continues what Patricia Nelson Limerick calls a "legacy of conquest," and two avenues of inquiry need to be followed in order to develop a "transformative ecocriticism." The first, as Joni Adamson Clarke suggests, involves a deeper mapping of the relations between subaltern groups and the land. A second step, and a basis for this book, is to interrogate the links between imperialism and the canonical pastoral tradition. How did authors invent the wilderness, and how would they define their ideas vis-à-vis border conflicts? In what ways did descriptions of the backcountry register (even if to subsume) different forms of land use? How were native Americans constructed along with the interior, particularly as white pioneers provided a foil for "Indianness"? Finally, upon what terms would Euroamerican authors seek to establish republican culture as indigenous to a place? By recasting wilderness as a contested (rather than emptied) space, colonial and early national texts become not only readable but essential to understanding a nation's literary heritage and self-definition. The rhetoric and legislation of Ohio overwhelmingly demonstrates that the early republic saw border regions in terms of commercial potential. Nature provided the raw material for an "empire of liberty," and the language would rhetorically yoke topography to a republican vision of progress. In Philip Freneau's imagination, the arts are to "plant" and the soil is "tamed." Politicians, propagandists, and utilitarian as well as belletristic authors imagined an expanding civilization, one that shed its rays over the continent and that explained Indians away to "some other clime." But writers would still have to acknowledge somehow the existing populations on the frontier. Skilled authors such as Crèvecoeur negotiated this problem by manipulating class antagonism and identifying with (prematurely) extinct tribes. His hybrid narrator casts native American decline as a "melancholy fact" decades before removal became widespread and presents his own group as the "natural" legatees over a less refined white population.[39] This effort to reconcile, revise, or ignore prior claims to and uses for the wilderness—whether by natives or pioneers—creates what might be called the political unconscious of an environmental imagination.

I belabor this position because, to date, the dialogue between ecocriticism and western history has been surprisingly slight. By ecocriticism, I mean the attention to nature as an active component in the text and, arguably, a disproportionate concern for "unpeopled" settings. The focus upon an imagined wilderness has directed literary scholars away from imperial legacies; meanwhile, new western historians have excused themselves for different reasons. The latter have focused on demythologizing their field, and the desire to sweep out the old narratives—in all but select cases— has left little room for analyzing the business of storytelling. Foundational works by Patricia Nelson Limerick and Richard White conclude with chapters that flatly debunk the "imagined West." White expresses misgivings with symbols or narrative designs (other than his own) that shape the frontier to suit the needs of national identity. He writes that environmental historians "are uncomfortable with easy references to symbols that govern our perceptions"; these stories "lose the absolute reference points" and escape fact. Such a hard-nosed dismissal, as one critic in American studies has noted, attests to the enduring assumption that narratives of the past be "anchored in something real." But a grail quest for fact has driven White and Limerick around the questions that make literary study worth pursuing: Limerick maintains that the "process of invasion, conquest, and colonization was the very kind of activity that provoked shiftiness in verbal activity." Anyone interested in narrative would, of course, say, "Yes—start here." But Limerick does not. She dodges a sticking point by reducing literary frontiers to Henry Nash Smith (whose book *Virgin Land* was then forty years old) and complaining about dime Westerns. Rather than offering a useful point of departure, she piously concludes that the task of separating history from cant involves finding "order, pattern, and meaning in a swirl of perplexing events and perspectives."[40]

Authors on the eighteenth-century frontier obviously did exactly what Limerick describes—if from a different vantage point. And the attempt to understand how "order, pattern, and meaning" came from a shifting ground is what makes these texts so interesting. My task, then, is to read from the "fluid and perplexing" context that the new western history describes. These texts require more attention than the standard canon of pastoral writing has demanded of them but more nuanced interpretation than contemporary historians are wont to offer. They should be seen as accounts of contested space negotiated within what Mary Louise Pratt calls the "contact zone," that area where "disparate cultures meet, clash, and grapple with each other, often in highly asymmetrical relations of domination and subordination." Annette Kolodny argues that when approaching narratives from this "cultural contact," readers should interrogate "language—especially as hybridized style, trope, story or structure—for the complex intersections of human encounters with the physical environment." The pastoral tradition that was received by the nineteenth century evolved through engagement with the very groups that earlier writers sought to silence or dismiss. The links between the rhetoric and the social context thus become essential to understanding the literature, even as the "myths" hide as much as they reveal. Rather than weighing in with the facts or essentializing identity, as Frank Shuffelton argues, one may study "the generation of signs with which groups negotiate relationships variously hostile and accommodating with their neighbors."[41] Nature provides an especially rich point of intersection. The fluidity in relations, both between human groups and the land and with one another, forced authors into positions of linguistic improvisation. As writers described the backcountry, they would have to recognize in some way how other inhabitants used the same resources. Even the imagined "wilderness," therefore, could become a contested space; at the very least, narratives from the frontier record in subtle ways the struggle for a certain kind of environment.

My concern is primarily with spatialized accounts, with what I call cartographic texts, and how these texts negotiated their position on already claimed country. This focus upon narrative design (what Limerick or White might dismiss as myth) stays close to the site of conflict—even if in memory. The texts survive as artifacts from encounters that authors saw through a clouded lens or sought to efface altogether. Peter Hulme argues in *Colonial Encounters* that by laying a narrative canvas over stretchers, the thin spots of ideology (where power was constructed) are betrayed. Interrogation reveals the cruces where "the text stutters in its articulation, and which can therefore be used as levers to open out the ideology of colonial discourse, to spread it out in this text, in an act of explication. The venture, it should be said, is archaeological: no smooth history emerges, but rather a series of fragments which, read speculatively, hint at a story that can never be fully recovered." Hulme offers a cautious point of entry for any poststructural exegesis, one that is both rigorous and compelling in what it claims not to provide. (Here the work of literary criticism and history diverges.) His critical method exposes the traces of "resistance" in a narration, presumably bringing the text to reveal itself under a brutal cross-questioning. The critic may demonstrate where the account slips—or says what one wants it to say. Intense scrutiny forces acknowledgment, without so much as hearing (and this distinction is critical) an Other in the written accounts. An imposition upon text that is almost perverse in its pressure demonstrates where narratives efface the conflict that inevitably followed the construction of ideology; however, the model yields mixed results. On one hand, these exposed traces of a prehistory offer Hulme an exit from hermetically sealed readings. On the other hand, if these unmercifully dense "interrogations" force the text to "speak more than it knows," then what exactly could the account have said? Hulme leaves open the poignant question of whether his critique uncovers anything at all. Having ceded that colonial discourse constitutes signification, he searches for alternative stories to imperial myths.[42]

The matter of disappearance raises some theoretical reservations that, to be quite candid, I sometimes resist. Literary scholars have written at length about textual removals. Postcolonial critic Terry Goldie notes that "our image of the indigene" has functioned "as a constant source for semiotic reproduction in which each textual image refers back to those offered before"; attempts to disclose the referent, in other words, only slip back to images. Read in the context of United States history, literary removals can be shown to anticipate the real removals—to the point that critics might focus on little else. Scholars such as Lucy Maddox, Helen Carr, Renée L. Bergland, and Susan Scheckel show how a nation was imagined through "Indians" but with those Indians tucked safely in the past. It goes without question that natives "haunt" American culture; the focus upon "ghosts" only, however, leads to a simplified narrative of native-white relations. It reduces history to a morality play in which patriotic myths get debunked and "Indians" provide the voice for a contemporary critic's conscience.[43] One advantage that comes from breaking off this study in the 1820s is that it enables me to focus upon the relations between different groups (rather than removal). Authors from the colonial and early national periods forged their impressions of the physical environment against still populated frontiers. Eventually, land greed would lead to an aesthetic of dispossession, as became painfully clear for the Cherokees, and the incipient Manifest Destiny in authors such as Washington Irving and James Fenimore Cooper is unmistakable. What critics have not explored, however, is the literature that these authors inherited—modes of writing that were as much artifacts of social exchange as the precursors of dispossession.

One way around this matter of disappearance, I would suggest, is to focus upon how writings about place also negotiated cross-cultural relations. A useful model for this book comes from Joshua David Bellin, who argues for an "intercultural" criticism: an examination of the "complex, intricate, and even indeterminate interrelationships among" various groups.[44] Describing a method similar to that of Kolodny, Pratt, and Shuffelton, Bellin may allow for the violence and inequality that came to characterize federal Indian policies, yet he retains the interpretative agility necessary for understanding the eighteenth-century frontier. As the product of a contact zone, Crèvecoeur might cast himself as "Oneida," while backwoods pioneers were derided as "white savages." Enlightenment categories of race were not necessarily biological; or if they were, biology was not the sole concern. The prevailing schema in this literature remained "civilization" or "progress." Indeed, a certain permeability allowed Euroamerican writers to establish themselves as "indigenous" to the continent—and project their "natural" or "native" rights against a different class of settlers. In a literature of invention, then, identities remain especially fluid, and impressions of the land unfold through the interactions with an Other. This book charts how ideas of nature unfolded in an "intercultural" context. Only after recognizing an Other, after all, could authors develop convincing terms for their paper claims to place.

PART I

The Western Text

Thus say the Indians, speaking to the European Land-workers, You take a deal of Pains to spoil a good World.
—THOMAS POWNALL

THE IMAGINED WEST

LEWIS EVANS

AS THE LITERATURE describing the Northwest Territory suggests, one role that eighteenth-century American writing served was to offer terms for belonging on the continent. Revolutionary authors would struggle to define an identity over the land, to fix not only geographic borders but a cultural presence over still contested realms. The proclamations, promotional tracts, sermons, territorial seals, and journals predict new turns for a country that, to their authors, lacked a prior history. Poetic tributes by Philip Freneau, David Humphreys, and others begin from the land and then imagine a civilization unfolding there, bespeaking an ideological geography that was pervasive throughout the early republic. Evidence of the spatial orientation of early national culture exists in the many prospect poems written at this time; one after another, authors climb a nearby hilltop to forecast a future for the still unstable United States. Joel Barlow's epic *Vision of Columbus* (1787) begins with a woebegone Christopher Columbus who relieves his despair through the imagined survey of an evolving New World. Timothy Dwight's *Greenfield Hill* (1794) moves from the panorama of his Connecticut parish and through the region's Puritan past to conclude with great hopes for a nation rooted in New England authority. Sarah Wentworth Morton organizes *Beacon Hill* (1797), a verse history of the Revolution that spans the thirteen states, around her Boston home. By Morton's time the views were already getting crowded. She apologizes for ignoring nearby Bunker Hill, as this "consecrated ground" had been surveyed already by another poet. A spatial or geographic sense informs most works of environmental writing during this period, particularly the prose. Crèvecoeur, Jefferson, Cooper, and others make reference to the organizing premise of a map; as the critic Martin Brückner observes, geography was "a literal reading practice for early republicans."[1]

But where did this spatial imagination come from? Around the mid-eighteenth century, a combination of forces would boost the demand for accurate data about the continent's interior. Most notably, the century-long rivalry with France culminated with the Seven Years' (or French and Indian) War, which led to a spike in cartographic activity and scientific exploration. Economic expansion also played a role: As metropolitan centers on the Atlantic coast began to swell, settlers moved increasingly to the interior. The resulting changes in demographics fed a market for writing that equated land with opportunity and that anticipated the revolutionaries' environmental imagination. Specific genres emerged.[2] The draftsman Lewis Evans and Benjamin Franklin collaborated on the *Analysis of a General Map of the Middle British Colonies in America* to accompany Evans's "General Map of the Middle British Colonies in America" (1755), and together they produced an early example of the topographical description. Before surveying the seven ranges of Ohio, Thomas Hutchins penned *A Topographical Description of Virginia, Pennsylvania, Maryland, and North Carolina* (1778) and later *An Historical Narrative and Topographical Description of Louisiana, and West Florida* (1784). Any number of authors used maps and surveys or statements of geographic boundaries to organize narrative. William Stork's *An Account of East Florida* (1766) begins in typical fashion with a chapter on "Boundaries and Extent," situating Florida's longitude and latitude in order to describe the region's soil, climate, flora and fauna, and potential for plantations. Works that were not primarily geographic often had a cartographic frame: essays in law and natural philosophy like Jefferson's *Notes on the State of Virginia* (1787); medical reports like David Ramsay's *A Sketch of the Soil, Climate, Weather and Diseases of South-Carolina* (1796); or radical treatises like *A Topographical Description of the*

Western Territory (1797), by Gilbert Imlay (better known as Mary Wollstonecraft's lover).

A similar spatial imperative informed the many literary natural histories that, like the map-based texts, were both protean and ubiquitous. Except in an imperial context (what Mary Louise Pratt calls "planetary consciousness"), the field defies easy classification. Natural histories were at once for hard-nosed exploitation and for disinterested, or "curious," collectors. The literature was by turns static, verbless, and evolutionary; scientific, self-promoting, taxonomic, or devotional; as apt to focus upon a branch of knowledge as it was a species of life or a given corner of the planet. What might be said to hold this catholic body of texts together (and I am suggesting no single paradigm) is the effort to construct place, the desire to expand imperial realms through the charting of nature and natural processes. A journal by John Bartram, the preeminent botanist of his time, might therefore appear alongside Stork's promotional tract, *A Description of East-Florida* (1769); John Filson would use the same conventions to peddle frontier property in *The Discovery, Settlement And present State of Kentucke* (1784). James Edward Smith of London would offer his book on butterflies, *The Natural History of the Rarer Lepidopterous Insects of Georgia* (1797), as a tribute to Linnaeus, while William Dandridge Peck would stick to the more pedestrian purposes of the Massachusetts Agricultural Society with *Natural History of the Slug Worm* (1799). Again, what holds this literature together? For one, an awareness of European expansion and a cultivation of environmental change. The concern with constructing "place" may explain why examples of natural history and geography so often intersected. Where one branch of knowledge defined a region and suggested how resources might be used, the other helped bring about those transformations.[3]

Part 1 of this book accordingly reviews how Euroamerican authors constructed a textualized West against specific acts of colonial expansion. I begin at the mid–eighteenth century and trace images of the middle colonies through the Seven Years' War and then examine the Ohio Valley (specifically Kentucky) before the Revolution. My point is to destabilize the ideological geography that republican authors inherited and show how that ideology emerged from contested grounds. The projection of a future for any given landscape equals or assumes an exercise of power (academic geographers call this process "structuration"), and the genres used to codify space in early America as a result would capture both the efforts to order the land and the conflicts that invariably followed.[4] In both the topographical description (the prose form accompanying maps) and the natural histories, authors would have to position their plans for the backcountry against an existing population. The interior thus becomes a subject for invention. The maps and the surveys of flora and fauna would yield a story; at the same time, those stories would betray a resistance that no author could fully co-opt. The Philadelphia geographer Lewis Evans provides an ideal point for examining this vexed process of textualization. Evans was supported by Parliament and the Pennsylvania Assembly, and his work passed through several editions over an extended period of time (between 1749 and 1784). Produced as the colonies began moving beyond coastal cities and as the rivalry with France intensified, his maps made the case for expanding civilization through the engagement with native people. This paradox in the Evans maps was indicative of a paradox in the political culture: As colonial officials looked to the wilderness for improvement (and to French Canada as a threat), they relied upon indigenous groups. Evans would suggest a center and a periphery, or "front" and "back," while attempting to gloss the highly unstable relations between native and white Americans.

Because Evans provided one of the more fully realized expressions of how public officials viewed the interior, finally, he may be used to resituate the cartographic text in the context of expansionist politics. His example raises a series of questions that I will return to throughout this book: What narrative forms evolved from the attempt to claim interior lands? How would the standard frames used for portraying the interior recognize an Other? In what ways did colonizers register, even as they sought to efface, native ties to and uses for the same country? The imperial role of maps has never been lost on commentators. Samuel Johnson called geography "a branch of political action," and contemporary scholars have examined in depth how maps expressed both actual and perceived power relations.[5] A paradigm commonly followed by literary critics focuses upon an imagined country coming to replace the real one. Benedict Anderson, for example, speculates that invented boundaries come to be accepted as a given when replicated in print. The imposed lines of state define an area from which a new history would unfold; from within the redrawn boundaries, a "political-biographical narrative of the realm" materializes. This notion of an imagined realm supplanting the real one resembles what literary critic Eric Cheyfitz sees in acts of translation. Drawing from the classical definition of metaphor (semantically tied to the Greek root, "carry across"), Cheyfitz argues that translation "severs" the "figurative" from the literal, carrying across the native body into a "foreign" realm.⁶ The imposition of metaphor, the governing through a map, would equate with dispossession. In a manner that Anderson describes, the geographer would define the territory. But this one-way tautology also needs to be qualified; after all, native Americans were not simply vaporized by text. Even as their maps "translated" or reinvented a territory, colonial officials would rely upon native groups. Evans's work accordingly unfolds through often complicated engagements between front and back, center and periphery, Self and Other. The written accounts accompanying his maps show how new "property-histories" (to borrow Anderson's term) were imagined over territories that were—as whites obviously knew—already inhabited.

A Path Taken Together: Lewis Evans and the Iroquois

To better understand how Evans defined both geographic and cultural boundaries, one might begin with diplomacy. On the western frontiers of New York and Pennsylvania, political decisions revolved around the Iroquois Confederacy, or League of Six Nations. Known to themselves as the People of the Haudenosaunee, the Iroquois met through a formidable Grand Council that was established in the fifteenth century and that united the Seneca, Cayuga, Oneida, Onondaga, Mohawk, and (after 1722) Tuscarora nations under a "Great Tree of Peace." Several "dependent" nations, notably the Shawnees and Delawares, also took shade under this "Great Tree." In their dealings with whites, meanwhile, the Iroquois exploited the uneasy balance between the French in Canada and the British colonies in America. As the Six Nations leveraged their own interests, any number of different groups and individuals felt the influence of Iroquois decisions.⁷ But this cohesive indigenous empire was both projected and real by Evans's time—it was a shared fiction that native as well as Euroamericans sought to shape. On one hand, the "play off" system between England and France secured an edge in an unstable world; on the other hand, the Iroquois nations had come to depend upon a balance of European power, and they might present the illusion of cohesion although the confederacy was splitting along its east and west axes.⁸ The Mohawks and Onondagas would frequently court the British in council, for example, while the Senecas were more inclined to deal with the French. Even as colonial records often present dramatic posturing by council sachems, these records simplify a more complicated process of deliberation: one that involved different clans, men's and women's councils, and decisions that were made geographically rather than tribally.

The people whose names appeared in treaty minutes would direct how the Six Nations were portrayed, and in a society where authority was consensual rather than hierarchical, the question of who could speak for whom becomes essential.

The story of Evans's maps begins from this complicated political milieu. In 1749, he published a "Map of Pensilvania, New-Jersey, New-York, and the Three Delaware Counties" (figure 1.1), a work that provides a baseline for later geographies. Superficially, the text would reflect a split between known territory and terra incognita.[9] The Appalachian Mountains cut diagonally across the frame, with the bottom right marked in some detail, while the western country remains empty except for prose filler. The exception is the Susquehanna River, which reaches with telling accuracy toward the interior; Evans's knowledge of this river came from a path that British and Iroquois people took together. He first explored the Susquehanna as part of a 1743 diplomatic envoy to Onondaga—the Iroquois council fire, near present-day Syracuse. The cause of the misunderstanding that led to his trip does not really matter for my purposes (a group of Virginians had a scrape with a traveling party of Iroquois), but the result attests to the centrality of the Six Nations in frontier diplomacy. To settle the "heart burnings" from the Virginia affair, the Pennsylvania Assembly sent a delegation to Onondaga, what then might be called the "capital" of Iroquoia. Lewis Evans joined the translator and diplomat Conrad Weiser, the botanist John Bartram, an Oneida ward over the Susquehanna Valley named Shickellamy, and Shickellamy's son. The basis for this tour was diplomatic, not cartographic. With the approach of King George's War (1745–48), the Iroquois needed to be recognized, lest England lose the Six Nations and their allies in the struggle against France.[10] Pennsylvania needed its native neighbors more than the natives needed them.

In the written records of the tour that remain, one can see how a British empire was being imagined across space and through contact with Shickellamy, his son, and indigenous people from Pennsylvania to Onondaga. Bartram, Evans, and Weiser all kept journals, and Evans published his map six years later. These texts suggest where worlds came together, where they came apart, and how different ideas about the land would come to compete. The map itself presents a known domain on one side and a textualized realm on the other, capturing a view of the middle colonies that typified public discourse. A ship hugs the south shore of Long Island, while another approaches the Delaware Bay; emphasizing commerce, tidal readings mark

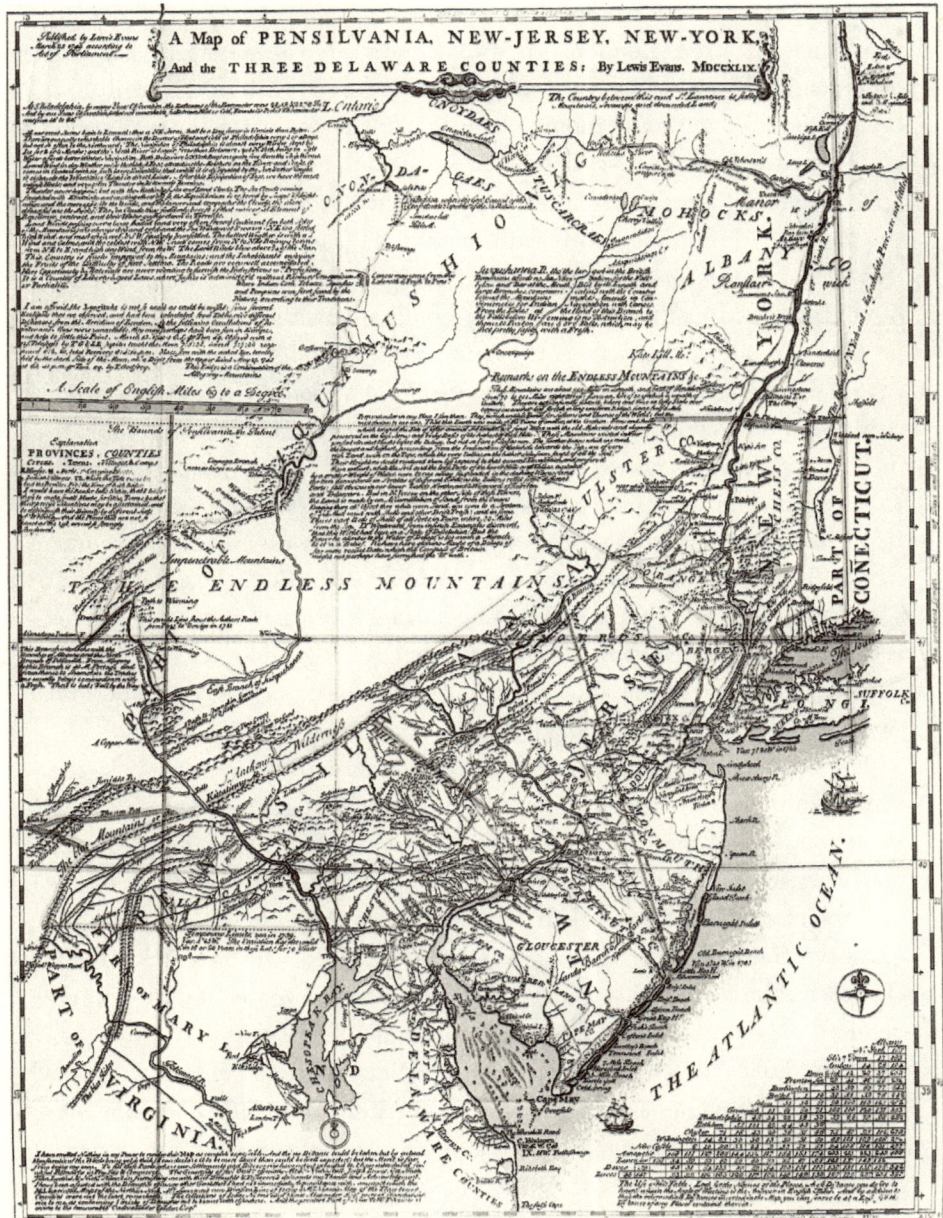

Figure 1.1. Lewis Evans's "Map of Pensilvania, New-Jersey, New-York, and the Three Delaware Counties" (1749). Notes on Ogarechny Mountain appear near the top of the Susquehanna's East Branch. Courtesy Historical Society of Pennsylvania (HSP Of 500 1749 E).

the ports. The top and bottom provide two longitudes—one from Philadelphia, the other from London—as if to acknowledge an emerging but still provincial metropolis. The perceived emptiness of the interior, by contrast, brings about invention. Graphic symbols identify the better-known areas, while prose fills in the rest. The latter is considerably more ambiguous and open ended, as Evans speculates where he is less sure of the terrain. He calls the Endless Mountains "confusedly scattered" (meaning he saw no logic there), and the blank sheet prompts his thoughts on geology. John Bartram, by contrast, would offer a more direct account of how the backcountry could be used—and how natives saw the land already—in his journal, published in 1751 as *Observations on the Inhabitants, Climate, Soil, Rivers, Productions, Animals, and other matters worthy of Notice. Made by Mr. John Bartram, In his Travels from Pensilvania to Onondago, Oswego and the Lake Ontario in Canada.* Internal evidence suggests that *Observations* would accompany the 1749 map; Bartram supplements the image of the west-reaching Susquehanna River and outlines the prospects for structuration, the allocation of space and resources that is linked to geographic work. He variously rates the soil as "poor and stoney," "midling," "fruitful," "good level rich," "excellent," producing "plumbs and excellent grapes"; he describes "a rich bottom [with] high grass" and "excellent soil on a charming vale."[11]

The contact with native Americans, at the same time, would expose the Philadelphians to indigenous markers of place. Along a path that brought two groups together, Shickellamy or his son would point out features of both the physical and cultural landscape. Indigenous geographies figure into the colonial text as a result. The white travelers learn about the religious associations with low-lying wetlands, "haunted" woods, and hillsides. One sacred landmark that generated comment was Ogarechny Mountain, believed to be the source of Iroquois staple crops. The Evans map notes that the "the Natives" first found "Corn, Tobacco, Squashes and Pompions" there, and Bartram includes a longer version of the story. An "*Indian (whose wife had eloped)* came hither to hunt," Bartram writes, "and with his skins to purchase another" woman, the jilted husband,

> espied a young sqaw alone at the hill; going to her, and enquiring where she came from, he received for answer, that she came from heaven to provide sustenance for the poor *Indians*, and if he came to that place twelve months after he should find food there. He came accordingly and found corn, squashes and tobacco, which were propagated from thence

and spread through the country, and this silly story is religiously held for truth among them.[12]

The legend accounts for two of the "three sisters" of Iroquois agriculture (corn, squash, and beans), a combination of crops that covered basic nutritional needs, while having a low impact on the soil. Yet where Bartram acknowledges the importance of Ogarechny Mountain and native American agriculture, his tone is dismissive. He recites the legend but adds the awkward-sounding clause "this silly story is religiously held for truth among them." A tension between white and native American environmentalism in this way gives shape to the *Observations*, betraying a dependence of Pennsylvania upon the Six Nations that is readable in the language. A vexed spirit of cooperation was behind the diplomatic envoy. Cultures came together, both in council and when describing the land—yet authors would seek to distance themselves from the initial points of contact that produced their accounts.

The 1743 tour prompts several conclusions about cartography and map-based writing. First, the texts suggest how different groups converged in the construction of Euroamerican writings about place. Despite the recognition of native landmarks and beliefs about nature, the "Map of Pensilvania, New-Jersey, New-York, and the Three Delaware Counties" and Bartram's *Observations* present a largely colonial view of the interior. Evans defines a "front" and "back," or center and periphery, depicting one side of his map empirically, while using the other as a field for invention; Bartram rates the soil, imagining new settlements in areas that were already being farmed. Second, the transactions between verbal and spatial texts, and the innate need to ground one's environs in culturally bound perceptions, would signal the need for distinct forms of writing. European authors since Columbus, of course, had told stories to accompany a map, but by the mid–eighteenth century, distinct genres would link the cartographic and narrative modes. Writers from William Stork to Thomas Hutchins to Sarah Wentworth Morton would combine geography and description to articulate what should be done with the continent. The trip to Onondaga produced an early example of a textualized West (even if that West was still close to Philadelphia). Most important, frontier writing would begin from specific points of cultural contact. Although John Bartram and Lewis Evans imply a new "political-biographical narrative of the realm," their stories started from a path taken with an Oneida guide to the Iroquois council fire. Bartram might remark upon "excellent soil on a charming vail" and presumably eye that soil for colonization, but he would note native landmarks as well. The cartographic text in America would unfold from this very tension between an ideological geography and the experiences on a still open frontier.

Lewis Evans and the Imagined West

The 1743 journey provides a model and point of comparison for reading later, more famous backcountry accounts. In 1755, Lewis Evans completed "A General Map of the Middle British Colonies in America," the work by which he is best known and a landmark in colonial geography. He and Benjamin Franklin collaborated on an accompanying essay, *Analysis of a General Map of the Middle British Colonies in America*, that was published by Franklin and advances the idea of a civilization defined by its borders. Native sites such as Ogarechny Mountain, in a telling contrast, disappear from the text. Yet the "General Map" remains every bit as indebted as its predecessor to a middle ground. Evans would expand upon what he learned on the Onondaga tour, credit a "very intelligent Indian called The Eagle," and draw from traders whose information came from native sources. A change in emphasis would simply give the text a different turn. The coming Seven Years' War, and the belief that the colonies could best secure the border regions through frontier settlements, would lead Evans to focus upon "the value of the now contested lands" and depict the interior through the lens of an expanding civilization.[13]

Despite the widened gap between an ideological geography and the middle ground, however, the 1755 map was at least initially the result of fractures in Iroquois diplomacy. The scenes had changed just slightly. Through the late 1740s, the principal axis between British America and the Six Nations had moved from Onondaga and Pennsylvania to the Mohawks and New York. The Albany trader turned baronet William Johnson had been remarkably successful in cultivating friendship with the "eastern door of the Iroquois" (he had a Mohawk wife), and his collaboration with the Mohawks became a focal point in white-native relations. The shift would lead Johnson's collaborator, a sachem known to the English as Hendrick, to approach the governor of New York in 1753 about encroachments on tribal lands. Hendrick threatened to break the Covenant Chain, a century-old metaphor for friendship, and delivered a carefully calculated message that produced direct results: "We will send up a Belt of Wampum to our Brothers the 5 Nations to acquaint them the Covenant Chain is broken between you and us. So brother you are not to expect to hear of me any more, and Brother we desire to hear no more of you."[14] Whether the Mohawks could speak for the other "5 Nations" notwithstanding, Hendrick would prompt action through the threat of a united Iroquois front. The Lords Commissioners of Trade and Plantations, or Board of Trade charged with administering colonial affairs, had been primed already by pamphlets criticizing abuses overseas, and they instructed Crown officials in America to settle the issue. "When we consider of how great consequence the friendship and alliance of the Six Nations is," the earl of Halifax warned, "we cannot but be greatly concern'd and surprized" that New York had been so inattentive. Halifax ordered a renewal of the chain "in his Majes^{ty's} name," and delegates from seven states and the Iroquois (with the Mohawks in front) met at Albany the following summer.[15]

The details of the Albany Congress lie beyond the scope of this discussion, but the public debates that followed gave shape to Evans's work, and the arguments that circulated through the northern colonies are essential to understanding his strategies of representation. At Albany, the Mohawks aired their grievances with New York, delegates drafted a plan for union, and (while officials called for fair dealings with the natives) land grabbers dealt "in the bushes" for new cessions from the Iroquois who were present.[16] The pamphlets that followed the Albany Congress raise three general themes involving the backcountry: a conception of the empire from the borders, a need to protect the less settled parts against France, and the essential but liminal status of the Six Nations. Franklin's "A Plan for Settling Two Western Colonies" would call the "great country back of the Apalachian mountains . . . one of the finest in North America," and he promises returns for agriculture and trade. The interior appears to be an untapped economic infrastructure, one that William Clarke describes as "capable of supporting as many Inhabitants at least as any Kingdom in Europe." The status of the Six Nations, meanwhile, would shift with political winds. Franklin would argue in 1747 that the "French know the Power and Importance of the Six Nations, and spare no Artifice, Pains or Expence, to gain them to their Interest"; in 1755, the Iroquois again would appear to be potential partners and allies. The New York councilman Archibald Kennedy would claim in 1751 that "the Preservation of the whole continent depends upon a proper regulation of the Six Nations," but the end of the Seven Years' War in 1763 would prompt different assessments of the natives. With apprehensions about the

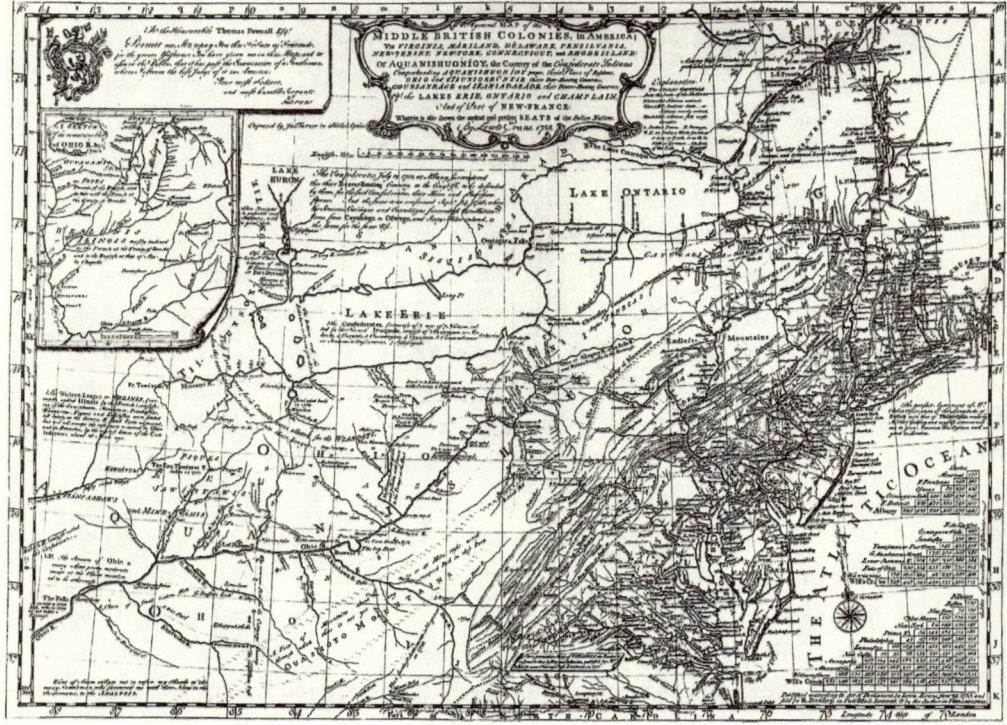

Figure 1.2. Lewis Evans's "A General Map of the Middle British Colonies in America" (1755). Courtesy Historical Society of Pennsylvania (HSP Of 360 1755 E).

French removed, the agent William Johnson would apologize, "our Principles of negotiating with the Indians are quite changed." John Bartram (who had shown some restraint in his *Observations*) would write after the war that "unless we bang the Indians stoutly," they will "never keep peace long with us." The native population is now an impediment to expansion, Franklin would explain; they are "savages" who "massacre our planters" and cause "the certain diminution of our people and the contraction of our settlements."[17] The statements are contradictory, but the logic is clear. Anticipating the paradox of the Northwest Ordinance, whites forged an expansionist policy against relations with the existing population.

The same calculus involving an ideological geography and the dependence upon native Americans would shape the "General Map" (figure 1.2). Evans provided cartographic ammunition for a pamphlet war that paralleled the Albany Congress, and as Franklin and others would argue for colonies in Ohio, Evans would shift his focus over the Appalachians. The Great

Lakes and Fort Duquesne replace the Endless Mountains as the focal point; Philadelphia is the anchor, and the country south of the Great Lakes is cast as a peripheral region that the Crown should claim. An implicit historical narrative, one that moved the empire onto new territories, created the need for the genre of a topographical description. As a supplement to the map, the *Analysis* would provide the textual room—not available elsewhere—to develop a chronological axis. The collaboration between Evans and Franklin, a draftsman and a printer, would result in a system that would link spatial and narrative modes. Typographic symbols connect the prose to geographic coordinates, allowing Evans to plot the same future that Franklin did in his pamphlets. Their task would lead to a westering argument that was made through a strange hybrid of typefaces: "The Settlements made by the *English* ... may be considered as extended to No. 4.|| * on Connecticut River, and thence to Saretoga† on Hudson's River, and to Case's§ on the Mohock's River; thence back, by the Lakes ¶, at the Head of Susquehanna, to the Head of Delaware, and thence down the last mentioned River to the Mouth of Legheiwacksein|| ☞," and so on (figure 1.3). Structurally, the passage moves from the Susquehanna to the Juniata River, to the last "scattered Settlements thence to Ohio," to the outer reaches of Virginia and Carolina. The description progresses, at the same time, from the better- to lesser-known parts: from the Northeast to the South, to "our remotest Settlements." Evans defines an area cartographically, while projecting the border regions into a possible future; the back parts of Virginia and Carolina "yet remain undisturbed." The typographic symbols meanwhile provide a point of intersection between the "General Map" and the *Analysis*. A footnote to the latter explains: "Carry your Eye from the Capital Westward till you come into the Square, under the small Letter, and there you will find the Place referred to."[18] However strange this format may appear to modern readers, it supports what a topographical description is supposed to do. It presents the spatially defined realm as a field for narrative, mediating between prose and map, while drawing the backcountry into a framework of European time.

In Evans's hands, the continent appears to be a vacancy that awaits narrative history. Five "Stages" in his *Analysis* divide the country: the "Lower Plains" along the coast, the "small Mountains," the Piedmont, the "Endless Mountains," and the "Upper Plains" south of the Great Lakes. Evans periodically enters the account to suggest how that country could be filled, emphasizing always the tactical importance of the trans-Appalachian West

The Extent of the English Settlements and Trade.

The Extent of the British Settlements.

THE Settlements made by the *English* are bounded on one Side by the Ocean, and on the other by no certain Line or Distance; for in some Places they are not above 30 or 40 Miles from the Heads of Tide, and in others 150 or 200. In general, they may be considered as extended to No. 4 ‖ * on Connecticut River, and thence to Saretoga † on Hudson's River, and to Cafe's § on the Mohock's River; thence back, by the Lakes ¶, at the Head of Susquehanna, to the Head of Delaware, and thence down the last mentioned River to the Mouth of Legheiwackſein ‖ ☞; from whence to include those of Penſilvania, you cross over to Susquehanna River § by the Purchaſe Line laid down in the Map; and further along Westward, so as to include the Southern Branches of Juniata, Frank's Town †, and Ray's Town ¶. The ſcattered Settlements thence to Ohio along Yoghiogani ‖ and Monaungahela ‖ are lately broke up by the Incroachments of the French in that Quarter. Thoſe on Green Briar § and its Branches, and downward to the Fork, and thence Southward by Stahlmakers ¶, at the Head Fork of Holſton River, to the Line dividing Virginia and Carolina, complete the Line, and yet remain undiſturbed. This may be ſuppoſed to include our remoteſt Settlements; but for many Miles in Breadth, they are very widely ſcattered; not ſo much for want of People to improve and plant, but Schemes in almoſt every Colony to prevent them.

Margin keys:
‖ C b
† C e
§ C d ¶ D d
‖ E d
§ F f
† F h
¶ G h
‖ F j & G j
§ H k
¶ K l

Trade much farther ſettled.

THERE have been Britiſh Subjects ſcattered over many Places, beſides thoſe above-mentioned, eſpecially on Ohio, Wawyaghtas, and the Branches of Cherokee River to the Weſt; and the Lake Ontario Northward; but they cannot with any Propriety be ſaid to be *Settlers*, becauſe they have not acquired *Titles to the Soil under their King*, nor *cultivated the Land by Huſbandry*; two Things abſolutely neceſſary to denominate a Settlement.

§ G q
¶ G p
‖ H o

AT the *Wawyaghtas* §, the Engliſh Tuſchtanwi Town ¶, Lower Shawane Town ‖, and many Places on Ohio and Lake Erie, our Traders have occaſionally ſettled a Trade, and purchaſed Ground for their Houſes; and tho' they might not be deemed *Settlers* as Planters or Coloneſt, they may with the greateſt Propriety be ſuch as *Traders*.

Longitude computed from Philadelphia and London.

THE Longitude at the Top is computed from Philadelphia; at Bottom from London, according to the late Mr. THOMAS GODFREY's Obſervations and my own at Philadelphia. And I was induced to give theſe the Preference

to

---

* The Letters in the Margin point out a ready Way of finding a Place in the Map. In the Eaſt Margin is a Row of Capitals; at Top, another of ſmall Letters, in each Degree of Latitude and Longitude. Carry your Eye from the Capital Weſtward till you come into the Square, and there you will find the Place referred to.

☞ In the Letter-preſs Printing I am obliged, for want of proper Characters, to ſubſtitute *gh* in the Indian Words to expreſs a certain Sound that the Italians, French and Engliſh are deſtitute of; and that other modern Nations, who have it, are not agreed to expreſs by any ſettled Character. The Hollanders uſe *g*, the Iriſh *gh*, the Welch and Germans *ch*. In the Engraving, I have revived the antient Greek Character which was uſed to expreſs the ſame Sound.

Figure 1.3. Page from Lewis Evans and Benjamin Franklin's *Analysis of a General Map of the Middle British Colonies in America* (1755). Courtesy Library Company of Philadelphia.

(south of the Great Lakes to present-day Tennessee). "If we secure the Country back of Carolina in Time," he explains, "we shall yet defeat the very Point that it is the French Interest to pursue." In this contested space between England and France, the Ohio Valley appears to be held in a kind of escrow by the Six Nations. Example after example overrates the Iroquois's influence in the border regions in order to support colonial ambitions. Canadian "Beaver-Hunting Country" belongs to the English, the map states; the Ohio lands are "by the Confederates allotted for the Wiandots"; Pennsylvania appears unoccupied except for the Delawares. The *Analysis* still more blatantly constructs the interior around an Iroquois hierarchy. "The Notion that every little society [in Ohio] is a separate Nation," Evans misleadingly argues, is "without the least Foundation"; the Shawnees "have been subdued by the Confederates, and the Country since become their Property"; the Delawares are "entirely subdued." These suggestions simply did not square with more reliable reports, which indicated that the Ohio people wanted both England and France out of the region and that groups like the Shawnees were in "Defiance of the Six Nations." Evans constructs at best a workable fiction, an imagined hierarchy that could justify British interests and that eventually looks past the need for native alliances altogether.[19]

It is this invented West, a West that was imagined over inevitable resistance, that would come to characterize the cartographic text. The *Analysis* suggests English strength through an Iroquois hegemony and then dissolves whatever claims the confederacy purportedly held. In a closing argument for settling the country south of the Great Lakes, Evans looks beyond even the pretense of native place-holders. "Were there nothing at Stake between the Crowns of Britain and France," he maintains,

> we may reckon it as great a Prize, as has ever yet been contended for, between two Nations; but if we further observe, that this is scarce a Qu[a]rter of the valuable Land, that is contained in one continued Extent, and the Influence that a State, vested with all the Wealth and Power [t]hat will naturally arise from the Culture of so great an Extent of good Land, in a happy Climate, it will make so great an Addition to that Nation which wins it, where there is no third State to hold the Ballance of Power, that the Loser must inevitably sink under his Rival. It is not as two Nations at War, contending the one for the other's Habitations; where the Conquered, on Submission, would be admitted to partake of the Privileges of the Conquerors; but for a vast Country, ex-

ceeding in Extent and good Land all the European Dominions of Britain, France and Spain, almost destitute of Inhabitants, and will as fast as the Europeans settle become more so of its former Inhabitants.

As the written account establishes an imperial history over mapped space, it removes other claims from that imagined zone. The territory appears to be "almost destitute of Inhabitants," the "prize" between two European powers. Evans suggests that "there is no third State"; the Iroquois matter to him only in a war for empire, while their dependents are "subdued." It is important to note that Evans's contemporaries dismissed his conclusions as egregious.[20] These criticisms focused, in part, upon points where Evans strained his own credibility. For the projections into the future would distance him from an imperial contest in which success or failure rested upon native alliances.

The *Analysis* shows signs of weakness, in short, when seeking to dissolve the very middle ground that produced it. What the conclusion reveals is the process of invention—the "carrying across," if you will—that Eric Cheyfitz likens to imperial "translation." This translation would involve several steps and a few ironies of its own. Evans most significantly simplifies the relations between native groups through a false hierarchy of tribes. He continues the process of "carrying across" that had begun the previous decade; what gets marginalized, however, is his own text. For while Evans leveraged his ideological geography through the Iroquois, he would overlook more realistic reports that probably were available to him. Even Evans himself must make occasional allowances for fractures in the Iroquois hegemony. Take as an example how he portrays affairs in the Illinois Valley. The *Analysis* contends that the Illinois nation acknowledged the "Superiority" of the confederacy and that it was "in close Friendship to the English."[21] An insert in the upper-left corner of the map, however, describes a more ambivalent status, "mostly inclined with the French at the Treaty of Utrecht and to the English of Aix la Chapelle." The contradiction brings the narrative to a crux, and the representation deconstructs itself in the exaggeration of a hierarchy. In order to bring the Illinois River valley (which feeds into the Mississippi) into the existing frame (and into the sphere of Iroquois control), Evans creates the illusion of one sheet of paper superimposed upon the other. False shadows distinguish the insert from the larger map. But his assessment of tribal relations did not fit with reality, any more than the insert fit within the space being described. A corner of the upper image rolls away to reveal the claim that "these parts were by the Confederates allotted for the Wiandots, when they were lately admitted into their League," an observation that is readable only through the artifice. The illusion locates the source of authority in little beyond the map itself. The false shadows and curling corner suggest that an Iroquois hegemony was also a fiction imposed upon the country. These slips define a genre: Like the two sheets separating the Illinois and Ohio Valleys, the story of a landscape and the actual country (as well as its inhabitants) occupy separate planes. A trick to reading Lewis Evans lies in understanding where those planes no longer meet.

Thomas Pownall: Revising the Imagined West

The differences between the 1749 and 1755 maps suggest how emphases could shift from a record of the middle ground to a more one-sided ideological geography, and this comparison becomes especially valuable as the latter defines an empire from its borders rather than through cultural contact. The "General Map" depicts the interior as a contested zone between England and France, and the Six Nations appear to be the temporary "place keepers" in that zone. This alignment marginalizes the supposedly "dependent" tribes. Evans would cast the Shawnees and Delawares as "subdued," and he would maintain that the western groups followed the Confederacy as one body. Yet considerable evidence suggests a sense of betrayal by Covenant Chain politics and particular suspicion toward the British after the Seven Years' War. These misgivings inform the way that many natives envisioned the postwar political landscape for themselves. In 1762, a Delaware prophet named Neolin experienced a vision for survival in the colonial world, and he began spreading his gospel against the backdrop of British expansion, ecological change, and societal stress. To demonstrate his point, Neolin drew a map that connected this world and the afterlife, showing how native Americans could pass from one realm to the other (figure 1.4). The inner square (representing the afterlife) previously had two doors, but exposure to Europeans had blocked one door, so the dead would have to use the more distant and dangerous portal. A concern for the land anchored his message: "The land on which you are," the Great Spirit had instructed Neolin, "I have made for you not for others; Wherefore do you suffer the whites to dwell upon your lands? Can you not do without them?"[22] The map circulated widely. Neolin used it throughout his far-ranging lectures, and it was reproduced on deer skins so that it might hang in homes. The message would also correspond

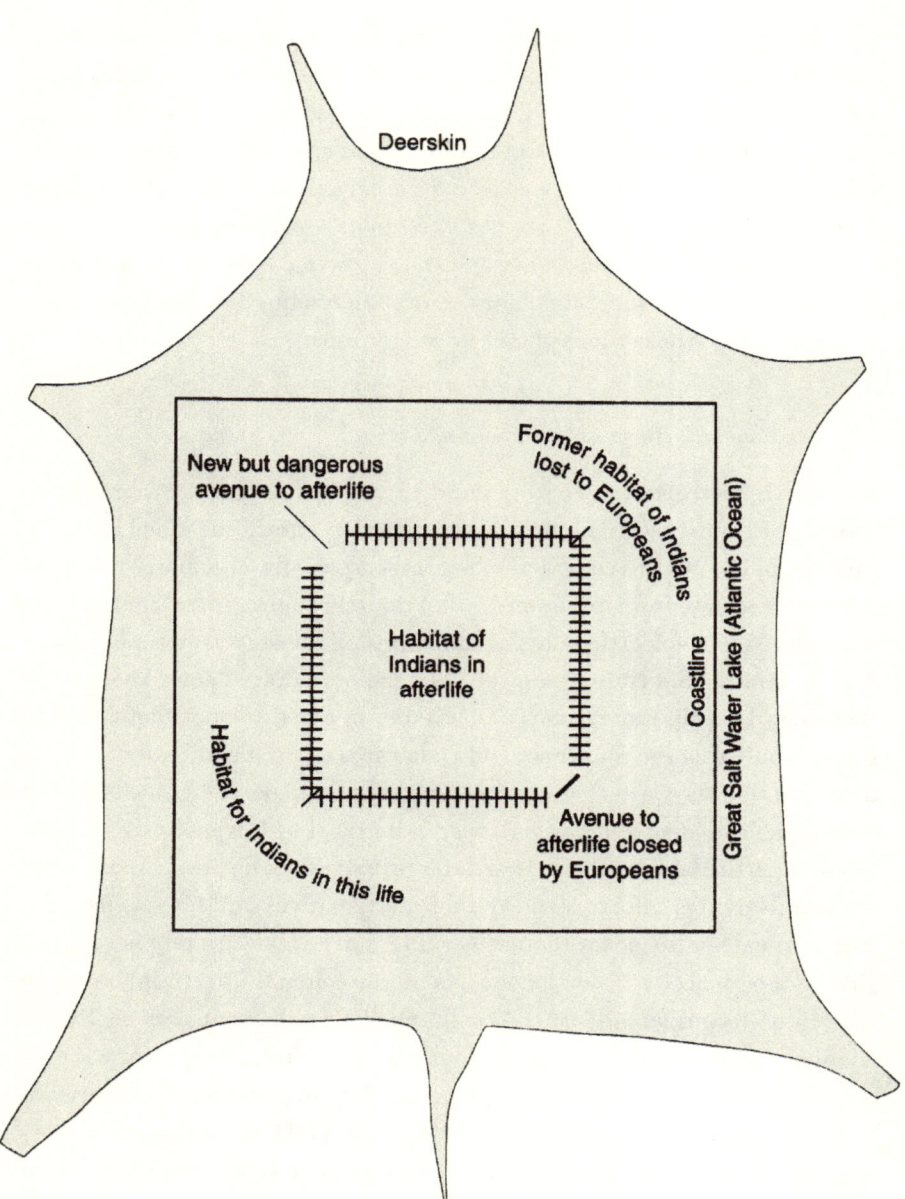

Figure 1.4. Reconstruction by G. Malcolm Lewis of Neolin's "Great Book of Writing," which circulated originally on deer skins. From David Woodward and G. Malcolm Lewis, eds., *Cartography in the Traditional African, American, Arctic, Australian, and Pacific Societies*, The History of Cartography, vol. 2, bk. 3 (Chicago: University of Chicago Press, 1998). Courtesy University of Chicago Press.

with the nativist uprising led by Pontiac in 1763–64. Whatever Lewis Evans might suggest, the "dependent" groups would develop their own ideas of possession and sovereignty.

As a colonial map would come to represent its own reality, meanwhile, imperial narratives would focus less on existing property-histories, political tensions, and markers of place. In the years following Neolin's vision and Pontiac's western "rebellion," white elites would cast the border regions as a new earth, as wilderness redeemed through "civilization." Maps would provide the field for new turns of literary geography, and Evans's work in this light entered a third stage. Following the process that Benedict Anderson describes, the "General Map" was reprinted, consulted, pirated, corrected, revised, and appropriated.[23] A benchmark for other portrayals of the interior, it provided as well the vehicle for reflecting upon colonial expansion. The standard account would contrast sharply with the map-framed message that Neolin brought. In perhaps the most famous revision of Evans's work, the Massachusetts governor Thomas Pownall would use the "General Map" as a template for *A Topographical Description of North America* (1776, revised 1784). Pownall would provide an odd example of belletristic geography, collating into one account long passages from the *Analysis*, notes from his own explorations, and the journals of other travelers. The result is not just an account of the land but the realization of an emotive landscape, a poeticized tribute to a civilization expanding across space. This act of translation, one must recall, was built upon a map first drawn after a diplomatic envoy.

Politics and an artistic temperament nominated Pownall as the one to mine the literary potential of a utilitarian form (and distance the cartographic text from the middle ground that produced it). Pownall landed in America in 1754, attended the Albany Congress, and over the next decades held a series of posts that put him at the center of imperial affairs; he speculated in land, wrote Whiggish apologies for colonial growth, and established himself as an authority on British relations with the New World. The *Topographical Description*, by and large, offers a geographic contribution to the debates about empire that preceded the Revolution. The book describes changes in the land as "Matters of curious Antiquity" and treats the continent itself as a field for literary expression. The idea of America as a rising empire finds this colonial Edward Gibbon shifting from English to Latin. "Many Tracks" on the "western Parts of the Map," Pownall explains in a preface, were,

> mere Indian or Traders Paths through the Wilderness,
> .... per avia quâ Sola nunquam
> Trita rotis ....
>
> but are now in the Course of a very few Years become great Waggon Roads, & are here mark'd as such.
> Et modo quae fuerat Semita, facta via.[24]

The theme being the construction of place, Pownall nominates himself as master compiler. He explains how he "never travelled without a Compass and a little level," how he sketched scenes that impressed him and formed a "Set of Instructions" for military officers venturing into lesser-known parts. In the account that results, one landscape replaces another. "A View in which a Country whose Face [is] changing everyday," he writes, "will become in this short space a matter of curiosity"; even in forests "we see Woods of a different Species," trees that are "aliens," which "from a new power of Vegetation [are] springing up and possessing the Land." The language, in short, captures the attempt to turn one group's space into another's place. As he explains how human (or botanic) "Aliens" would make the country their own, at the same time, the window into competing attitudes toward the environment closes. The text alludes with telling obscurity to an unnamed native who observes, "you take a deal of Pains to spoil a good World."[25]

The shift in emphasis from the earlier accounts, beginning in 1749, would reflect changes in British policy, for Pownall revised Evans during a period when officials increasingly based decisions upon a fictional hierarchy and an invented frontier. From the Albany Congress to the years just prior to the Revolution, Iroquois and British council discourse relied upon a projected hegemony that simply did not exist. The Board of Trade had rejected the famous Plan of Union from 1754 and chose instead to consolidate relations through William Johnson, who was appointed "Colonel of the Six Nations." But the Seven Years' War showed that while Johnson's effectiveness depended upon a unified Confederacy, the League lacked its celebrated influence or cohesion. His voluminous correspondence suggests that the Confederacy had split along a geographic axis, and Iroquois authority (fronted by the Mohawks) did not cross into the trans-Appalachian West; French intelligence indeed would note that England relied upon a "chimera." Johnson admitted during needy moments that the League's reputed power "may exceed the reality," and that it would take "a considerable sum of money" to secure the friendship of the entire Six Nations, not to mention their "dependents." The outcome of the Seven Years' War only deepened suspicions among the latter group. The nativism led by Pontiac and Neolin, which was rooted in the land, would suggest that the "dependent" nations had become "Jealous" of Britain's "growing power," fearful (in Johnson's biased assessment) that the colonies should "surround them on every side & at length Extirpate them."[26]

The continued demand for land in British America, which had previously been checked by France, would fuel the expansionist energies of investors and public officials (who were often one and the same). Although England had established a boundary of settlement at the Appalachian Mountains with the Proclamation of 1763, speculators and settlers began chipping away at the line almost immediately. One prominent Virginian called the Proclamation Line a "temporary expedient," and lobbyists flooded the Board of Trade with petitions for new developments; the western nations meanwhile grumbled that the "white people covet the Land and Eat them [the natives] by inches." The land hunger would reach Franklin, Pownall, and William Johnson through a Philadelphia investment group sometimes called the "Suffering Traders" (they actually had several names), and Johnson began promising "an Advantagious Grant" for them around 1766.[27] His opportunity came two years later, when the Crown issued orders to clarify and close gaps in the 1763 Proclamation Line. At the Treaty of Fort Stanwix that followed (in western New York), Iroquois sachems offered territory to the south and west, hoping to relieve pressure closer to home, while receiving considerable compensation for a region over which they had no legitimate claim. They tabled a huge tract: The proposed boundary cut diagonally across Pennsylvania to the Ohio River and then down the Ohio to include most of Kentucky. By Johnson's own admission, the treaty went "more favorably than was proposed by the Crown," and with the deal, a fictive hegemony was used as the means to expand an imperial realm. The Iroquois maintained their position at the front of British-native relations, parted with the responsibility for country that they knew they could not control, hoped to direct land speculation elsewhere, and went home with a considerable "tribute." Obviously the groups who stood to lose these lands resisted the Fort Stanwix Treaty (I will discuss the outcome further in reference to Kentucky), but the meeting suggests how Johnson and the circle involved with the Evans map would negotiate through an imagined hierarchy for a textualized West.[28]

More directly to my point: The gap between the invented and actual frontier would set the stage for literature, and against a drama of dispossession that privileged fiction over frontier realities, Pownall would revise Lewis Evans. *A Topographical Description of North America* chronicles the construction of Euroamerican place and the author's own role in the processes of structuration. Presenting himself as the editor of a map, Pownall recounts his arrival at New York harbor in 1754, recalling the vivid smell of burning cedar chips in Manhattan; he catalogs exceptional features of a new country, such as New England's "Interval Lands" and leaf season; he weighs the potential for commerce against existing resources by cataloging native flora—thick-skinned grapes that resist the heat, wild rye, hemp, and sugar maple. Ever the antiquarian, Pownall takes heart in "Paths through the Wilderness" that have become "great Waggon Roads." The country that Evans mapped provides the setting for a new earth, and Pownall shuttles breathlessly between past, present, and future: "This is not Poetry but fact, and a Natural Operation," he reminds readers. The poetic language accordingly leaps from the duty-bound terms of a topographical description and into the heady realm of possibility. "As the Eye is lead on from Reach to Reach," he writes during a characteristically effusive moment, "the Imagination is in a perpetual Alternative of curious Suspense and new Delight." The prospect is completed with a prediction for the land: "But while the Eye is thus catching new Pleasures from the Landscape, with what an overflowing Joy does the Heart melt, while one views the Banks where rising Farms, new Fields, or flowering Orchards begin to illuminate this Face of Nature; nothing can be more delightful to the Eye, nothing go with more penetrating Sensation to the Heart."[29] The heart does not melt from the pleasure of viewing the terrain but from development. Farms, orchards, new fields: These typify a "completed landscape."

In a print engraved before the *Topographical Description*, but probably meant for the 1784 edition, Pownall shapes his combination of geography and history into a visual allegory. "A Design to represent the beginning and completion of an American Settlement or Farm" packs onto a single frame the colonial stage theory that explained how forests were transformed into farmland (figure 1.5). The left side shows the first seeds of a settlement, with a pioneer clearing trees around a primitive log cabin, while a mill in the foreground promises a happy future for these still dark woods. A river, the symbol of commerce, connects the scene. In the lighter distance to the right stands a framed house, outbuildings, straight rows of crops, and piles

Figure 1.5. Thomas Pownall's "A Design to represent the beginning and completion of an American Settlement or Farm." From *Six Remarkable Views in the Provinces of New-York, New-Jersey, and Pennsylvania* (1761). Courtesy John Carter Brown Library, Brown University.

of hay. This remarkable image presents the standard view that intellectuals brought to the frontier, but on a single tableau, neatly illustrating the environmental ethos that revolutionary authors would inherit. Passages from the *Topographical Description* indeed could have been written by Crèvecoeur. While traveling through the woods of eastern Pennsylvania at dusk, following a "mere track" with nightfall approaching, Pownall hears a "Trio of French-Horns playing a pleasing meloncholly Tune." The lines between belletristic and utilitarian prose fade, and the author concedes that the scene was like "an Incident in a Romance." This last outpost of Euroamerican civilization introduces him to a character who could have inhabited the "Design":

> What pleasure must this Old Man, escaped from the Sovereign Tyranny of his European Lords & while here — placida â compôstus pace quiescit — feel in the Contrast: And yet I thought the melancholly of the Musick

had a retrospective regrett of his Native Country. I asked him. He said No & yet I thought he felt yes; so are we formed. We were most hospitably received & treated & I never lay in a neater more cleanly comfortable bed in my Life.[30]

An operative word here, "Contrast," splits culture from wilderness. The anomaly of a backwoods horn concerto, every bit as odd as the shift from English to Latin, captures the gaps that appeared when attempting to show how the country was becoming something that it was still not. Pownall drains the space of its prior history and presents the interior instead as the field for a new earth.

Conclusion: Natives, Nature, and Imperial Geography

Changes across successive editions would distance a map-based account (through a slow but not inexorable process of revision) from its beginnings in a shared culture to the model for a transformed wilderness. Pownall's hopes for an expanding civilization would become commonplace to the cartographic text, but such texts, one must always remember, often originated from a middle ground, and the narratives articulated a usurpation that was intended but not complete. A recognition of these origins and limits should inform how we read a literature that seeks to define "place" (by which I mean the appropriation of space and nature). As Benedict Anderson argues (to follow up an earlier point), the reproduction of new boundaries would lead to a separate "political-biographical narrative of the realm." Circulated in print culture, maps would "translate" or "sever" (to borrow Cheyfitz's terms) the figurative landscape from a real one. The revisions to Evans's work certainly attest to the power of mechanical reproduction. But the translations did not always occur in one direction, and the surveyed realm would not automatically displace existing "property-histories." The records from a journey to Onondaga show how mapmakers incorporated indigenous sources and landmarks into their accounts. As colonial geographers redefined the terms of their relations with native groups, moreover, native Americans would draw their own maps. And while Thomas Pownall's *Topographical Description* reflected a marginalizing policy of expansion, the process of invention could also marginalize the map itself.

Consider an instance from the 1743 journey to Onondaga, if only to emphasize once again the points of contact behind cartographic activity. When venturing up the Susquehanna, Evans would visit a native home and commit a revealing faux pas. An unnamed host had given Conrad Weiser (a seasoned translator and frontier diplomat) a "double-share" of venison. As Weiser understood, eastern woodland groups such as the Iroquois did not carry much food when they traveled because hosts customarily fed their guests well. Weiser felt sick, however, and could not finish his "double-share." He passed the venison to John Bartram, his proxy. Bartram could not finish the portion either, so Evans would take a turn. According to Bartram's *Observations*, the mapmaker would finish the meal and throw the bone to some dogs. The act would insult the spirit of the slain species, and in atonement, the group's host would rescue the remains and "religiously [cover] it over with hot ashes." A proper apology would become necessary to restore the relationship between the hunter and the hunted. "This seems to be a kind of offering," Bartram explains, "perhaps first fruits to the Almighty power to crave future success in the approaching hunting season [and] celebrated with as much decency and more silence, than many superstitious ceremonies: the bigotry of the popish missionaries tempt them to compass sea and land to teach their weak Proselites what they call the christian religion." The passage captures how cultures intersected and diverged at several levels. As James H. Merrell notes, a path through the American interior could bring people together, even as it "cast in sharp relief how far apart they were." The gap in understanding is evident in the failure to recognize a "double-share." Euroamericans tended to carry everything they would eat when traveling, while natives would rely upon hunting and hospitality.[31] Differences between Christian and indigenous beliefs about nature also are revealed. As Bartram notes, the "offering" was for "future success in the approaching hunting season"; he obviously recognizes the Iroquois belief in reciprocity between the animal and human worlds. Where Euroamericans saw the environment in terms of commercial development, natives maintained spiritual ties to their surroundings (which is not to say that the spirit world and economics never intersected). Even as the Quaker Bartram would recognize this matter of faith, the language would distance him from the idea of animal spirits. He rhetorically excuses himself from the scene through a weak appositive: the awkward-sounding jab at "popish missionaries."

The syntax suggests a removal from the frontier that is common in the cartographic text. The narrative quite visibly negotiates the observer's position vis-à-vis an Other. To complicate matters, the text does not sound like

Bartram in either content or grammar (his correspondence often alludes to spirits in the natural world, and the dismissal occurs in a syntactically awkward construction). How then do we read this narrative "crux?" Eight years separated the 1743 journey to Onondaga and the publication of *Observations*; in that time, the perspective and the purpose of his text probably shifted. Unfortunately, no copy of the original journal exists, but the discrepancy between the body of the sentence and the appositive marks a gap from a middle ground to public discourse (with the latter marred by anti-Catholicism). The break in language points to a larger question of how maps and map-based texts would mediate between cultural expectations and actual experiences in the contact zone. On one hand, the behavior documented here may explain the arrogance of the later texts. If Evans were the last in his party to recognize an obvious faux pas, what turns would his published work take? What recognition would he show of indigenous markers of place, existing "property-histories," or what he learned from native informants? The person who established the space for a new "biography of the realm" would throw animal spirits to the dogs. On the other hand, Evans was deeply indebted to native Americans and to his Iroquois companions especially. His 1755 *Analysis* credits the "Eagle" and traders whose knowledge came from the middle ground; the recognition of sites like Ogarechny Mountain indicates that the colonial cartographer went to school on the Susquehanna. A recurring tension between intellectual (or literary) discourse and an open frontier would shape most environmental and cartographic texts of the period.

Evans's example, finally, illustrates how maps were central to defining the border regions but strangely peripheral to daily interactions on the frontier. In a revealing postscript to the 1743 tour, the Pennsylvania Assembly directed Conrad Weiser in 1750 to take a second journey that was to include Evans, this one to the Ohio Valley. Pennsylvania officials wanted more information about a land venture that the Virginia-based Loyal Company was planning. Evans had already prepared a memorandum that outlined his intentions: He would survey western rivers, locate the best spots for trade, and take notes on the natural resources he encountered. But Weiser refused to collaborate with Evans on this expedition. He recognized that straying from the usual paths could ruin his diplomatic mission and maybe get him killed.[32] The selective terms of their collaboration suggests how mapmaking brought worlds together, and once again, where interests divided. Geography often followed diplomacy, but sometimes the two were at cross-purposes. Three years later, Evans would advance a one-sided imperial perspective that alarmed his contemporaries. The "General Map" would provide a blueprint for expansion, and in that spirit Pownall offered revisions during a period of increased land grabbing. But the redrawn property-histories and stories of place did not equal willful alienation, any more than the cartographic text could represent a human population. The imagined West generated conflict, and at a certain point Conrad Weiser wanted nothing to do with Lewis Evans. My next example will follow one of the conflicts that this "invented West" helped create and will pick up where Weiser would not allow Evans to go: into the Ohio Valley. Speculators and public officials would continue to define the interior in terms of how land should be used, and as their justifications for possession were easily challenged, the narratives that followed would always seem uncertain. The result would be more narrative and a continued search for rhetorical position on a still open frontier. It was a tension between the textualized West and actual experiences on the border regions that would come to define writings about place in the revolutionary era.

BooNs bEst FREN
—Inscription on Daniel Boone's rifle

There must be a new wedding. But he saw and only he saw the prototype of it all, the native savage. To Boone the Indian was his greatest master. Not for himself surely to be an Indian, though they eagerly sought to adopt him into their tribes, but the reverse: to be himself in a new world, Indian-like. If the land were to be possessed it must be possessed as the Indian possessed it. Boone saw the truth of the Red Man, not an aberrant type, treacherous and anti-white to be feared and exterminated, but as a natural expression of the place, the Indian himself as "right," the flower of his world.
—WILLIAM CARLOS WILLIAMS

THE CONTESTED WEST

JOHN FILSON'S *Kentucke*

Nature, Nation, and Natural History

IN 1784, THE former schoolteacher turned frontier speculator John Filson published *The Discovery, Settlement And present State of Kentucke*, a book that grounds hopes for the newly formed United States in the physical terrain. It might also be said to begin where Lewis Evans left off. Filson presents the ideological geography that the revolutionaries would bring to Ohio, yet he does so through the literature that had materialized in the third quarter of the century. The Seven Years' War, as noted, created a demand for accurate information about the interior, and that market only grew in the years that followed. Botanists, land speculators, surveyors, veterans of military expeditions, and "restored" captives all penned accounts of the territories that France ceded with the 1763 Peace of Paris. Much of this literature, as the critic Wayne Franklin observes, was "determined by the narrow arc of 'use,'" and whatever genre they invoked, authors would emphasize the potential of supposedly "untapped" resources. William Stork's *An Account of East Florida* (1766) outlines "the climate, soil, and produce," where settlers may "take up grants from the crown"; a swamp "signifies a tract of land" that when "cleared and drained is proper for the growth of rice, hemp, and indigo." John Bartram toured Florida in 1765–66, and his botanic journal was appended to Stork's *Account* to make "known to the world the nature of the country." (Bartram's Florida tour is discussed further in chapter 6.) Thomas Hutchins, then a British officer, journeyed down the Ohio Valley and to Pensacola in 1766 and would outline his findings in *A Topographical Description of Virginia, Pennsylvania, Maryland, and North Carolina* (1778). Hutchins emphasizes what lands were "good farming" and "pleasant situations for settlements," and he offers the rich variety of game in Ohio as "unquestionable proof of the extraordinary goodness of its soil!"[1]

When Filson began describing Kentucky, then, he would have a well-established set of conventions to follow. The examples of Bartram, Hutchins, and Stork, not to mention Lewis Evans and Thomas Pownall, defined how one group's space could be portrayed as another's place. While authors sought to reinvent the backcountry, moreover, they would have to confront a region's prior history: What nations or empires already exercised claims there, and in what ways did existing communities use the resources being described? The narratives tied to Evans's maps suggest how a tension between environment and an Other could yield surprising turns of prose, especially as authors had to account for the relations between people and the land. But Filson faced an even more fraught situation. He began from the edges of a West that the geographers only imagined, yet he wrote in the years that the United States settled a peace with England. The patriotic imperative would lead him to simplify an extremely complicated milieu, and several layers of context need to be established in order to frame his response to a still open frontier. I return to the 1768 Treaty of Fort Stanwix. At a basic level, the Six Nations put their interests ahead of the "dependents" by offering to move the 1763 boundary and include most of Kentucky. The Shawnees held traditional rights there, and along with the Cherokees and Ohio nations, they used the region for hunting. The Iroquois's offer was both ambiguous and a source of later conflict. They received ample compensation at Fort Stanwix and probably saw the revised boundary as a chance of directing pressure away from their own homelands. In all likelihood, however, the Six Nations did not believe that property could be sold or transferred. Treaties traditionally ceded usufruct rights—the privilege of using land, not possessing or destroying it. The problem was doubly vexed then: Even if the Iroquois understood white conceptions of property and possession (and still it seems probable that they did by 1768), the Shawnees or western Delawares or Cherokees would not recognize the transfer of what could not be sold in the first place.[2]

The groups that were not served by the Fort Stanwix Treaty refused to recognize it, and the Shawnees led a resistance that—while involving several nations—can be explained in part through ethnography. The front was not simply united and oppositional. Historically, the Shawnees divided their time between summer farms and winter hunting grounds, and this geographic mobility made villages the center of their political life; a complex social structure that worked through interlocking clan affiliations and divisions, moreover, led to the appearance of later atomization. The nation had always been governed locally rather than collectively, and it was a "world made of fragments" (as Richard White notes) by the eighteenth century. The Shawnees were tradition bound but anxious to preserve a flow of trade goods. They shared a wariness toward the British and the Iroquois, adopted outsiders to restore their ranks, but divided over how best to protect tribal interests in the postcontact world. The adjustments to white settlements over the Appalachians would fall along the already complicated lines that organized their society. Although the usual mythology of the Shawnees emphasizes military prowess, violence was what whites were most inclined to report. War was just one means of self-protection. Faced with the encroachment on their lands, many Shawnees fled the Ohio Valley and headed further west; some forged military alliances with other tribes or with the British during the Revolution; others sought redress through council; still others fought, but not usually without warning. The pioneers in Kentucky met a confusing response: one that might result in adoption, a peaceful reminder, a threat, unforeseen military alliances, forced removal, torture, or death.[3] Their heads clouded already by land desire, few whites could reliably read how native Americans met the encroachments upon traditional hunting lands.

And Kentucky was just one front, the Shawnees just one nation. The complicated milieu that John Filson describes was in every sense a frontier. Several groups competed for overlapping resources there, changes in demographics affected local ecologies, and new identities were formed as the environment itself changed. The Ohio Valley fell outside the Iroquois hierarchy that Lewis Evans imagined, and a few dozen, different powers were constantly "ebbing and surging." William Johnson promised that the western nations "would pay all due submission" to an Anglo-Iroquois agreement, and that thinking led to the Treaty of Fort Stanwix; but as travelers through the Ohio Valley reported, "It Greives ye Indians to see ye White People Settle on these Lands & follow Hunting or Planting." The Cherokee Dragging Canoe famously declared that "there was a dark cloud" over Kentucky, and a spike in settlement after the Revolution only worsened white-native relations. According to one count, the nonnative population of the state exploded from 150 in 1775 to 12,000 in 1784 (the year that Filson's book appeared). Overhunting was rampant, the boom in demographics taxed the game population, and changes in the land generated friction between people. Settlers from Virginia and North Carolina, by one report, would kill up to six buffalo without taking enough meat to load a pack horse; game laws appeared on the books as early as 1775. For native groups, the disappearing bison would destroy what made Kentucky valuable — the slaughter of bison was cause for concern, and for young hunters especially, it equaled a declaration of war.[4] However paradoxical this may sound, the conflicts that resulted shaped new forms of culture and brought disparate groups into contact with one another, even as hostilities hardened divisions across race.

Among Euroamericans, finally, the rapid pace of settlement exacerbated class and regional tensions. Colonial leaders and investors railed against "white savages" who squatted on their legal patents, while pioneers resented speculation on land they actually worked. "We are surrounded by numerous savages," a group of petitioners would complain (the word "savage" appearing in an economic context), and the petitioners refused to honor "those whome ease and Cowardice prevent settling." Bureaucratic delays by Virginia created a recurring problem with property boundaries and titles, and an apparent political vacuum would lead whites to establish their own bases of entitlement.[5] In 1785, one year after Filson wrote *Kentucke*, settlers in present-day Tennessee formed the phantom state of Franklin. Arguing that North Carolina had ignored its frontiers, the Franklinites (or Wataugans) established their own legislature, counties, and courts, and they petitioned the Continental Congress for recognition. Franklin was eventually folded into Tennessee, but not without controversy and despite the state's occasional appearance on later maps (figure 2.1).[6]

A second, more colorful example (and one that Filson directly acknowledges) involved Transylvania, a forerunner of Kentucky that the North Carolina judge Richard Henderson founded through an obscure writ known as the Camden-Yorke decision. Camden-Yorke addressed deeds from "Indian princes or governments" (those Indians being in Asia). The pretense was

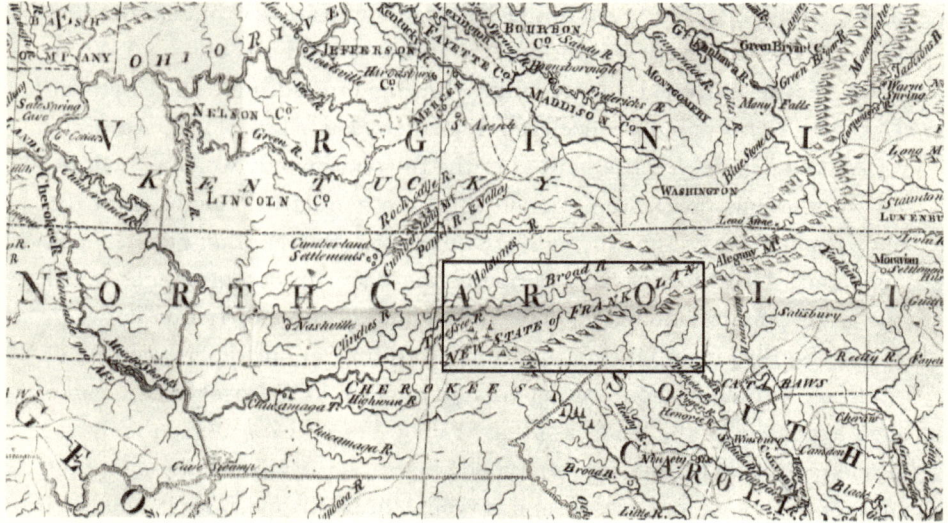

Figure 2.1. The state of Franklin, shown along the eastern boundary of present-day Tennessee, in Joseph Purcell's "A Map of the States of Virginia, North Carolina, South Carolina and Georgia" (1789). Courtesy Beinecke Rare Book and Manuscript Library, Yale University.

enough for Henderson to purchase 200,000 acres from the Cherokee "Indians" and declare Transylvania a state. And he was able to accomplish this lucky feat only through intratribal factions. The Cherokee headmen that agreed to the deal sought to smooth generational tensions outside their clans. Younger hunters, who were angry about the vanishing game in their best preserves, would receive compensation from the Henderson purchase; the council leaders, in turn, could prevent further violence as whites invaded other lands. The treaty that resulted did little to settle conflicts among the Cherokees, however, and could be said to symbolize the disintegrating authority in the colonies. A founding address shows that Henderson meanwhile was as loose with his metaphors as he was with the law: "You, perhaps, are fixing the palladium, or placing the first-cornerstone of an edifice, the height and magnificence of whose superstructure is now in the womb of futurity, and can only become great in production to the excellence of its foundation." Whether it was a cornerstone or a palladium, the foundation or a womb, competitors and officials railed against the movement. The plan failed soon enough (ironically, because Henderson ignored local factions), but the proposed state captures the opportunism that emerged from this political landscape, one where—in the face of little legitimate authority— speculators invented their own terms for occupation.[7]

John Filson would author the equivalent to a Transylvania claim: attempting to establish a rhetorical order upon a still open frontier, suggesting national prerogatives over contested lands, and providing his own version of opportunism against environmental change. The life of the author matters less than the book he wrote. Filson moved from Pennsylvania to Kentucky in the early 1780s, purchased about twelve thousand acres, and wrote up what he learned from earlier pioneers in a tract to support his investments. A Wilmington publisher printed his book and an accompanying map in 1784; Filson died a few years later—scalped while surveying in present-day Cincinnati. The cartographic text that he left, meanwhile, would establish a mythology where little grounds for occupation existed, lending a patriotic sense of mission to the still largely utilitarian literature of place. A watermark on Filson's map sums up his intent (figures 2.2 and 2.3). Under a plow, the motto reads "Work and Be Rich." The book itself is a mélange, with a natural history (really a thinly veiled promotional essay) at the center and several appendixes that follow—most famously, a biography of Daniel Boone, but also a heavily excerpted treaty, an ethnography, and a mileage table to connect the "here" and the "there." These various parts converge around a central theme—the appropriation of resources—yet to account for the vagaries of possession, he also would have to explain away the recent past. The language accordingly divides a messy frontier into polarities, swinging from a bloody struggle to promises for the future, from wilderness to civilization. In a typical manner, the conclusion locates this transition in the physical fact of the land. "This fertile region," Filson writes,

> abounding with all the luxuries of nature, stored with all the principal materials for art and industry, inhabited by virtuous and ingenious citizens, must universally attract the attention of mankind, being situated in the central part of the extensive American empire . . . where agriculture, industry, laws, arts and sciences, flourish; where afflicted humanity raises her drooping head; where springs a harvest for the poor; where conscience ceases to be a slave, and laws are no more than the security of happiness; where nature makes reparation for having created man; and government, so long prostituted to the most criminal purposes, establishes an asylum in the wilderness for the distressed.[8]

Embedded clauses and dramatic contrasts ("an asylum in the wilderness") shape a border region into the field for a new earth and rework a host of overlapping and conflicting claims into an imperial grammar: what William

Figure 2.2. John Filson's "Map of Kentucke" (1784). Courtesy John Carter Brown Library, Brown University.

Carlos Williams defined as "regenerative violence" and Richard Slotkin called "the first nationally viable statement of a myth of the frontier."[9]

Most of the book, and the natural history especially, justifies the recent past by explaining how the backcountry should be transformed. Images of nature purport to advance the tenuous rights on a still open frontier. As ecocritic David Mazel argues, American environmental discourse begins from the desire to cast wilderness as a colonial or national subject.

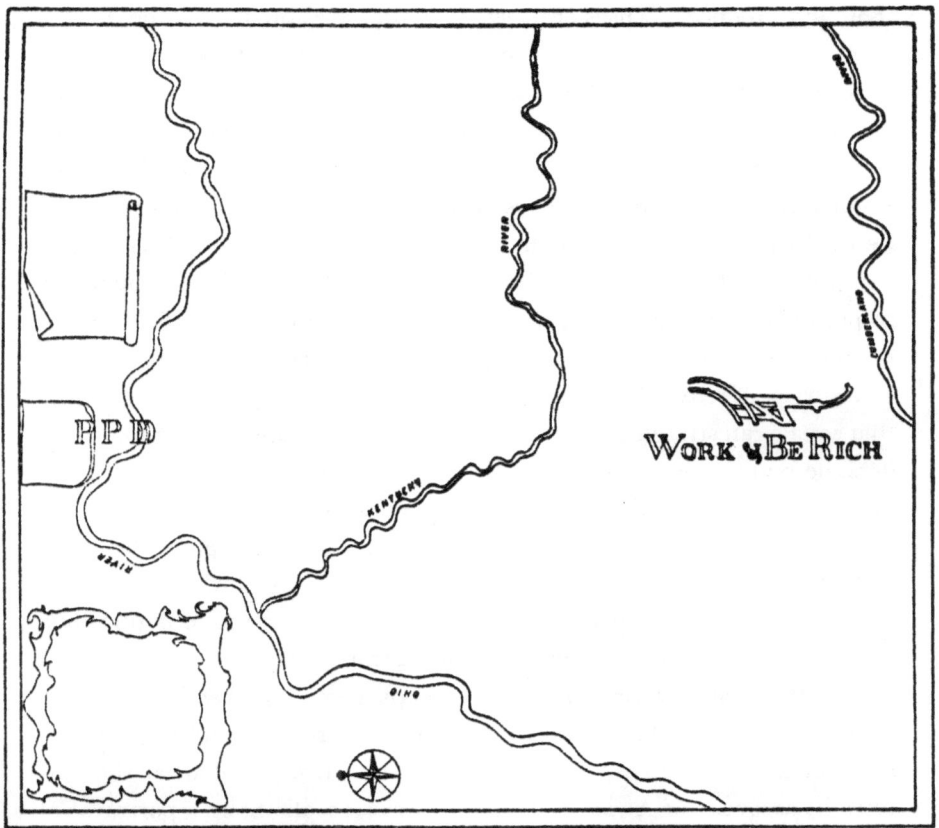

Figure 2.3. Reconstruction of John Filson's "Map of Kentucke" (1784) highlighting watermark of a plow and the motto "Work & Be Rich." Courtesy John Carter Brown Library, Brown University.

Tracing the roots of the word *environment* to its earlier verb form (to *environ*, meaning to surround), Mazel shows how early authors would codify wilderness with text and *environ* ideology through place.[10] Filson's *Kentucke* exercises that prerogative by presenting the economic as a natural, or self-evident, fact of the land. It redefines a cartographically framed realm. With the same format as Stork's *An Account of East Florida*, a section entitled "Situation and Boundaries" sets geographic parameters, which are then followed by chapters entitled "Rivers," "Nature of the Soil," "Air and Climate," "Soil and Produce," "Quadrupeds," "Inhabitants," "Curiosities," "Rights of Land," and "Trade of Kentucky." As the discussion moves from topography to the region's civil life, the descriptive also leads to economics.

"Soil and Produce" focuses entirely on commercial products; cane, for example, is described solely as fodder for cattle (23). The Ohio in the section "Rivers" might be "beautiful," but anticipated development directs how he portrays the Ohio's tributaries and branches: They "pay tribute to its glory," and the North Branch of the Kentucky collects "its silver streams" from the smaller creeks (44–49). Nor does accuracy matter (settlers described the Kentucky River as "inconveniant and Dangerous by Reasons of its Craggy and precipate Bancks").[11] This fixation upon profits, justified through the trappings of a natural history, locates the taxonomic on an implicitly temporal plane, making Euroamerican expansion a logical outcome of the terrain. In a survey of rivers, Filson envisions "channels" of commerce and argues that canals can straighten the curving Mississippi; leaping geographic borders, he reviews probable trade routes and finishes with the flat assertion "sound policy tells us the Floridas must be ours too" (47). Substituting politics and economics for the environment, he grounds ideology in the continent itself.

The construction of place, through which the literature of natural history played a decided role, would demand a transformation — some kind of change that generated conflict even as people came together. Mary Louise Pratt reminds us that natural history narrates "territorial surveillance, appropriation of resources, and administrative control," and what she outlines in accounts of Africa or South America recalls Stork's portrayal of East Florida or Filson's Ohio Valley. Given the emphasis upon contact and change, then, Filson would turn to the issue of agency and pen that became the most famous section of *Kentucke*, a biography of Daniel Boone. Boone would serve as the embodiment of change, the "translating figure" in the appropriation of a contested realm. The stylized biography follows a pattern that I will trace in other cartographic texts: As authors defined a colonial or national subject over the land, they would construct an Other as well, and the narratives that resulted would negotiate a position vis-à-vis the middle ground. The invention of place also necessitated the invention of a border self. Christoph Irmscher observes that any taxonomy — any collection, garden, cabinet, or literary natural history — tells a "good story."[12] In Filson's natural history–promotional tract, the transforming agent would make the wilderness available for agriculture; he would clear the space where the farmer could "work and be rich." (Boone is a cousin to the map reviser Thomas Pownall, who traverses the country that Lewis Evans defined.)

The transformation, at the same time, would force the author to interpret a confusing but steady resistance led by the Shawnees. The presumptions of environmental change would create the need for more narrative, for complications to the "good story" behind the tableau.

Daniel Boone and the Captive Environment

Daniel Boone himself is a mystified blank, a body over which stories of masculinity, the frontier, national identity, race, social conflict, and the land get told again and again. One version has it that the only firsthand account by Daniel Boone was lost when a canoe being piloted by his son-in-law capsized. He was reportedly soft spoken and offered opinions reluctantly. An inscription on the stock of his rifle, "BooNs bEst FREN," trades words for brute force, suggesting bloodshed as a possible surrogate for story. The legends and artifacts may be apocryphal, but the truth matters little; poets, writers, storytellers, historians, and antiquarians would take it upon themselves to compensate for the missing language. Filson offered the prototype, a thirty-two-page appendix to *Kentucke* entitled "The ADVENTURES of Col. Daniel Boon," which John Trumbull honed into a fast-paced Western. Lord Byron read Trumbull's version, and the American primitive (happiest in the "wilds of the deepest maze") would make a cameo in *Don Juan*. In the early twentieth century, William Carlos Williams would devote a chapter of *In the American Grain* to Daniel Boone and cast the backwoodsman as the first to embrace wilderness and make himself native to the continent. Boone was the first "to be *himself* in a new world, Indianlike," Williams writes; he was a "natural expression of the place."[13] As both a modernist and a regionalist poet, Williams clearly had his own agenda. In the immediate context of the revolutionary frontier, meanwhile, the life would provide a vehicle for stabilizing a contested backcountry. The 1784 biography would offer the beginnings of a national mythology, one in which racial boundaries were clear and the republic was rooted in the physical terrain. As Filson fixes an ascendant identity in the land, he in turn would remove his character from the middle ground.

A quick review of Kentucky and Boone's life suggests how the mythology would gloss tremendous changes in the culture and the physical environment through a neat textual symmetry. Colonial land hunger, as noted, put western native nations such as the Shawnees in a paradoxical position, one from which they negotiated in a variety of ways. The local bases of authority and a lateral political structure (with decisions made across clans, by war parties, village councils, and women's councils) resulted in a very complicated engagement. Certainly the Shawnees defended their hunting lands fiercely — that much Filson recognizes — but as ethnographer James H. Howard notes, they "were as warlike *as they had to be to survive* in their historical and cultural milieu."[14] Filson ignores the more peaceful ways in which native Americans defended their lands: In 1769, for example, a party escorted Boone back over the mountains, leaving him unhurt. The details of that encounter go unmentioned in *Kentucke*. Nor would Boone's life seem to fit the usual jingoistic narratives of empire. He was more accurately a product of that middle ground from which authors sought to distance their texts. Boone grew up on the border regions of Pennsylvania, where he spoke a pidgin that combined several native and European tongues. He later followed a well-traveled migration path down the Appalachian ridge and into the Yadkin Valley of North Carolina. The ability to cross linguistic as well as social divides served Boone well when he later emigrated over the Appalachian Mountains. (There he established his reputation as a guide for outfits like Henderson's Transylvania Company.) In the years before he met Filson, Boone fought in a series of territorial wars, the highlight of which was his captivity among the Shawnees, where he earned the respect of his captors because his skills resembled theirs. Like many pioneers, he would occasionally be mistaken for a native, and as one might expect, fared better in the border regions than in colonized country. Certainly he was no red man in white skin (despite what William Carlos Williams implies); Boone later served in the Virginia legislature. But when the 1780s brought a new and more litigious class of settlers and speculators over the mountains, the courts stripped him of his lands. The prototypical American frontiersman lit out for the territory because the new Kentucky defeated him, not because he needed the elbow room.[15]

The social permeability is important to recognize because Filson would attempt to cast a border figure as the progenitor of a national landscape. *Kentucke* seeks to establish a new history of the realm, one that advances Euroamerican terms on the frontier; not allowing for hybridity in a contested domain, Filson would situate his subject in universal experience. "Curiosity is natural to the soul of man," the story begins. The rest follows in a tumult of parallel clauses and dramatic contrasts that reset the middle ground on teleological terms:

> Let these influencing powers actuate, by the permission or disposal of Providence, from selfish or social views, yet in time the mysterious will of Heaven is unfolded, and we behold our conduct, from whatsoever motives excited, operating to answer the important designs of heaven. Thus we behold Kentucke, lately an howling wilderness, the habitation of savages and wild beasts, become a fruitful field; this region, so favourably distinguished by nature, now become the habitation of civilization, at a period unparalleled in history, in the midst of a raging war, and under all the disadvantages of emigration to a country so remote from the inhabited parts of the continent. Here, where the hand of violence shed the blood of the innocent; where the horrid yells of savages, and the groans of the distress, sounded in our ears, we now hear the praises and adorations of our Creator; where wretched wigwams stood, the miserable abodes of savages, we behold the foundation of cities laid, that, in all probability, will rival the glory of the greatest upon earth. (49–50)

The syntax slides past the stickier points of an earlier time. Denied a prior sense of beginnings, the reader "beholds" a landscape transformed from a "howling wilderness" to a "fruitful field." A religious tone (one that Slotkin dubiously ascribes to the Puritans) sanctions the changes that a cartographic text conventionally documents, as the plot of a "regenerative violence" distances the story from the shared culture that produced it.[16]

A plotted geographic space (the region mapped in *Kentucke*) yields a linear narrative plot, and the text establishes the imagined domain from which a new earth, that redeemed environment, might unfold.[17] In the same way that the Evans geographies would move from shared experiences among the Iroquois to imagined appropriation, Filson would rhetorically bracket the frontier, using the imagined life of Boon (I will refer to Boone without the "e" as Filson's literary persona) in an act of "carrying across" that Eric Cheyfitz describes. The point of the biography is to close a paradox established in the beginning, "where the hand of violence shed the blood of the innocent"; the "good story" in the book is the transformation of a "dark and bloody ground" into a completed natural history. Two rhetorical strategies work toward that end: a contrast of domesticity and wilderness, and a captivity narrative that redeems not just Daniel Boon from the middle ground but the land itself. The language accordingly may present "either" and "or," but it phases out that common space where the real-life Daniel Boone apparently thrived. In his first trip over the mountains, the hero witnesses the "ingenuity and industry" of nature, only to be ambushed later that night (52). Poetic contrasts dissolve the more complicated story of resistance into a simple beginning, middle, and end. A second trip finds Boon "surrounded with plenty in the midst of want," "happy in the midst of dangers," and like Adam "giving names to the different waters" (56). A gap between personal hardship and potential wealth drives the plot: He endures "long and fatiguing march[es] through an exceeding fertile country" (64). The story moves from there to a formulaic close. After many battles, captivities, and partial attempts to move his family over the mountains, the conclusion reconciles the thematic divide between wilderness and civilization. "Many dark and sleepless nights," he meditates, "have I been a companion for owls, separated from the chearful society of men, scorched by the Summer's sun, and pinched by the Winter's cold, an instrument ordained to settle the wilderness. But now the scene is changed: Peace crowns the sylvan shade" (80–81). The figure of Boon — framed by winter and summer, sunburn and shade — serves as the translating agent for a national landscape. With parting lines that anticipate a pitch to future farmers and investors, the hero finishes with a triumphant posting of the address that he created — "Daniel Boon, Fayette county, Kentucke." And so the story comes to a close.

This plot of environmental redemption would allow Filson to transform a liminal character into the defender of a family farm, into the one who secures a space where the settler might "work and be rich." Stories of male captivity, as June Namias notes, conventionally provide a vehicle for defining a national subject in the wilderness. They ask, "Who are you? What might you become? What might this land become?" Filson's myth indeed presents the new nation with a test: In this kind of account, Namias maintains, "You will see a different world, a different self, and in the process you will reevaluate the society of which you are a part."[18] For that reason, one can easily condense the plot of Boon's life to the restoration of a divided family. "It was on the first of May, in the year 1769," the story begins, "that I resigned my domestic happiness for a time . . . to wander through the wilderness . . . in quest of the country of Kentucke" (50–51). The hero remarks from the following year's captivity that "the idea of a beloved wife and family, and their anxiety upon the account of my absence and exposed situation, made sensible impressions on my heart" (54). This sentimental note is followed by the boast that his wife and daughter were "the first white women that ever stood on the banks of the Kentucke river" (60). War mounts when the "innocent husbandman was shot down"; he was, of course, "busy cultivating the soil for his family's supply" (60–61). A wrinkle in the story comes when Boon's wife and daughters flee Kentucky. But they cross the mountains again, and eventually "peace crowns the sylvan shade." In the end, any loss of kin lingers only as a bad memory. The hero makes wilderness safe for the privately owned farms, he identifies what the frontier republic might become, and he establishes the logical terminus for the trans-Appalachian West as "domestic happiness."

But the formulaic plot would leave open some important questions regarding the shared spaces of a frontier: How did the emphasis upon a domesticated wilderness rhetorically displace more believable causes and means of resistance in Kentucky? In what ways would the mythology polarize a hybrid culture? And what motivated the Shawnees? A vast body of scholarship on the captivity narrative suggests how authors used stories to reinscribe the transactions that passed between people in a fluid realm. The "whole history of the American captivity," David R. Sewell states, is the attempt to correct "a syntax of Indian-white conversation in which the imperative mode is supposed to operate in only one direction." The literature "constantly negotiates zones of contact," Michelle Burnham observes.[19] Kentucky provides a rich field of inquiry because, even more so than elsewhere, adoption had become central to native society. The region was a "world made of fragments," to use Richard White's words, where social boundaries remained open for the sake of survival. The imagined lines between civilized and savage betray the recognized fact that the Ohio nations usually assimilated outsiders successfully, and (if not scalped or tortured to death and after painful rituals of adoption) captives entered the full life of the community. A hostage taken around the same time as Daniel Boone writes that "I never knew them to make any distinction between me and themselves in any respect whatever until I left them." Mary Jemison remarks of her adopted Seneca family, "I was ever considered by them as a real sister, the same as though I had been born of their mother." Boone probably experienced the same, even in his short time. A war party captured him in 1778, and after running the gauntlet, the "Long Knife" was taken into the tribe. His scalp was plucked; his skin scrubbed; the leader Blackfish named the stocky Boone "Sheltowee," or "Big Turtle." The group assimilated the backwoodsman to the extent, in fact, that he could engineer his own escape.[20] When the Shawnees agreed to join an English siege against the fort at Boonesborough, "Sheltowee" told his captors that he was going for a hunt and then disappeared to warn the town—not without having established ties, however, to his second family.

The binaries that Filson establishes must allow for this social slippage, for the probability that one "received as good treatment as prisoners could expect from savages" (63).

Nowhere is the disparity between the reinscribed and socially fluid frontier more striking than in the attack on Boonesborough. In this episode, Filson recasts divided affections within a single-minded plot of assault and defiance. Having escaped his captors, according to historical accounts, Boone returned to the station and warned his countrymen. An eleven-day siege began. When the battle paused for negotiations, Boone joined the talks, and he showed signs of accommodation that apparently disturbed the white settlers. By one report (not Filson's), Boone welcomed his adopted father Blackfish with a hug; this may or may not be apocryphal, but by another, he stated "that they could make peace with the Indeans." The attackers extended realistic terms of surrender. In return for the fort, they would move its entire population to the British post at Detroit, off Lake Erie. (Another instance of not-so-violent resistance by natives in the trans-Appalachian West.) Boone wanted to accept the offer, a decision that had repercussions later. The pioneers chose to fight, and they weathered the assault. After the siege, many frontiersmen remained suspicious of Boone's willingness to entertain enemy demands, and those doubts came to a head with a court-martial.[21] According to the accusations, Boone struck a bargain with the commander at Detroit, and they had previously negotiated a plan to exchange the fort for protection under British forces. The charges were dropped, but they nonetheless would create a point of conflict for Filson. In the face of local memory, the author would have to reimagine how the hero negotiated racial and national boundaries. The willingness to accommodate the mixed force of attackers disappears in *Kentucke*; there is no embrace, and the tone becomes defiant. "Death was preferable to captivity," Boon declares in the autobiography, "and if taken by storm, we must inevitably be devoted to destruction." The controversy is buried under the vague antecedent "we." Tough words, alliteration, and a hickory resolve replace what could only have been a vexed decision. Filson writes, "Now, said I to their commander, who stood attentively hearing my sentiments, We laugh at all your formidable preparations. . . . Your efforts will not prevail; for our gates shall for ever deny you admittance" (68). Any signs of ambivalence disappear, and the episode closes abruptly with a flat dismissal: "Nothing worthy of a place in this account passed in my affairs for some time" (70). The narrative visibly skips over the trial. At precisely where the author intervenes, the process of mythmaking gets exposed. The evidence of an elision ("nothing worthy of notice") concedes to the construction of a story, to the task of translating the frontier upon new terms. The narrative speeds up, it bears emphasizing, at a moment where racial boundaries possibly disappeared under a common ground.

This "hiccough," to borrow Peter Hulme's term, may serve as a lesson for reading similar accounts of the backcountry, as the plot of wilderness to ecological redemption would simplify border life in instructive ways. Anxious about hybridity, Filson effaces the traces of ambivalence on a still open frontier. The point was to move a country from one stage to the next. Toward that end, the biography lumbers predictably to concluding prophecies for a new earth. With the usual avalanche of invectives and parallel clauses, Filson closes the story by reframing contrasts that had been established in the beginning: "What ardent and ceaseless thanks are due to that all-superintending Providence which has turned a cruel war into peace, brought order out of confusion, made the fierce savages placid, and turned away their hostile weapons from our country! . . . Let peace, descending from her native heaven, bid her olives spring amidst the joyful nations; and plenty, in league with commerce, scatter blessings from her copious hand" (81). Boon issues a postcard from this conquered domain: "I now live in peace and safety" and enjoy a "delightful country," he muses. The dualities fix themselves at clear poles, and an alternative story, one that describes a shared culture, appears only in concessions like "received as good treatment as prisoners could expect to receive." The work carries the prospects of Benjamin Franklin, Lewis Evans, and Thomas Pownall over the mountains, and much like the later versions of the Evans maps, it seeks distance from the shared culture that produced it. *Kentucke* also might be read as a response to the conflicts that the Treaty of Fort Stanwix helped create. The text registers the potential for discontent, one that earlier authors dismissed through an exaggerated Iroquois hierarchy (Filson writes from where Evans imagined there to be no "third state"), even as the text glosses other forms of engagement with the Shawnees. The early republic's vision of a new earth would lead Filson to tuck the bloodshed into a mythologized past, to skip episodes that intone friendship across races and loyalties to the British, and to replay Daniel Boone's life in a less ambiguous realm — the imagined space of national identity.

Conclusion: "Avail Yourselves of the Benefits of Nature"

In its rhetorical strategies and in the attempt to renegotiate the border culture from which it came, *Kentucke* provides a model for the early national environmental discourse. This view of the backcountry outlined the prospects of a new earth over a middle ground, even as that middle ground could never quite be closed. Through no coincidence, the narrative of Boone's life comes to a crux outside a stockade, for the biography takes as one of its premises the establishment of social boundaries that were spatially enforced. A textual order seeks to regulate or contain the wilderness, by the same token, but the wilderness creates fractures in the text. Early American writers, of course, had always faced this problem of narrative closure and exclusion. David Mazel notes that the Puritan captive Mary Rowlandson relies upon the Bible as a "legitimating master narrative," yet scriptural orthodoxy cannot fully distance her from a haunting past. In the final "Remove" of her story, Rowlandson remains painfully aware of the "resistances and refusals that keep open the possibility of wildness." Oral accounts from the eighteenth-century Ohio Valley show that settlers there often dreaded the world outside narrow stockade walls as well. Historian Elizabeth A. Perkins observes that the pioneers' most basic spatial perceptions were "in" and "out." John Filson might portray Kentucky as a landscape welcoming the peaceful farmer, but the people around him felt most secure inside a station or fort. An oral history by the settler Spenser Records recalls a harrowing episode that drives home this fear of exposure. While crossing the Ohio Valley wilderness, soldiers found a dead white baby. The corpse "was lying tomahawked and scalped," Records recalls, "with its mother's apron spread over it, she not being able to carry it any further and keep up with them. Perhaps she might have thought, that by spreading her apron over it, the wolves would not devour it, that they would be pursued, and that probably her child would be found, carried to the fort, and buried."[22] The image sits heavily against the more buoyant predictions for the West. An apron over the infant's flayed skull suggests a terror induced by the "outside" that no amount of mythmaking could settle or contain. Shortly after *Kentucke* was published, it should be noted, Filson suffered a similar fate. He was scalped while surveying, trying to enclose the land.

A second area of attempted closure that *Kentucke* captures was racial. Fueled in part by the violence that Spencer Records describes, the years following the Revolution saw relations between native and white Americans worsen. Dependency seemed to support accommodation, and imperial rivalries in America had demanded an attention to the interior nations. With the need to preserve an advantage in the war against France and then later in the Revolution, British colonial officials would be expected at least to consider native concerns on the border regions. But with the end of both wars, energies turned to the acquisition of land. A growing interest in the creation of property would result in simplified portrayals of the trans-Appalachian West. Texts like Filson's *Kentucke* would revel in the prospects of a "new earth," in changes to the environment and the establishment of new boundaries over unceded territories. But as historian Eric Hinderaker observes, the "clarity and simplicity for a new American empire came up against the complicated social patterns and histories of settlers, Indians, and Indian agents and officials who already occupied the region."[23] This clash of "clarity and simplicity" with a more turbulent milieu would crystallize into a selectively narrated myth. John Filson concludes his book with a neat statement of historical symmetry, one that balances a bloody past against a jubilant future. His Kentucky is "where agriculture, industry, laws, arts and sciences, flourish; where afflicted humanity raises her drooping head; where springs a harvest for the poor; where conscience ceases to be a slave," and so on (clauses piling onto one another as if there were no one to stop him). The violence that paralleled his predictions for the backcountry would be triangulated into narrative.

And so the opportunism that *Kentucke* epitomizes would lead to a third point of attempted closure: that was through politics. Representatives of the United States looked to the West for expansion, but they also feared that the region could not be easily contained. The ordinances of the 1780s marked an attempt to channel the enthusiasm and spirit of innovation that Filson captured. *Kentucke* was published the same year that Congress passed the Ordinance of 1784. One year later, Congress commissioned Thomas Hutchins (who, since 1779, had been with the United States) to begin surveying a federal reserve. Another two years brought the Northwest Ordinance and a fully realized plan for territorial government. The latter act repealed some of the more liberal measures of its predecessor and tightened an expression of liberty that was equated with the frontier. General Arthur St. Clair settled in Marietta in 1788, instituting a rigid set of laws that established a conservative presence over essentially ungovernable space. "It was always my fear that our western territory," St. Clair wrote to John Jay, would "be a source of mischief and increasing expense" for the United States. The promise of property would give "such spring to the spirit of emigration" that, while "pregnant with the most serious consequences to the Atlantic States," it could "not now be held back." Here and elsewhere, St. Clair would fret that "government does not advance with the settlers."[24] Such cautiousness contrasts starkly with the more effusive *Kentucke*, which asks Euroamericans to "Avail yourselves of the benefits of nature." Where the federalist St. Clair sees "mischief" (gendered as "pregnant"), Filson beholds opportunity. The differences between the two would define a paradox that shaped backcountry accounts through the early years of the republic. Territorial government would carry forward the vision of a new earth, but immigration necessitated channels and restraints. The need to reconcile centripetal and centrifugal forces, to divine a pattern in chaotic expansion, would lead to new terms of imagining and containing space. Yet the surveys and land grabbing brought violence that legislators could not control. Describing the same country as Evans and Filson, J. Hector St. John de Crèvecoeur and Thomas Jefferson would attempt to rhetorically contain an imagined country. As they sought to bracket the border regions through narrative, however, the purported subject of their texts would disappear. Whether in political legislation, in promotional tracts, or in literature, the recent past of a border country would not be easily enclosed.

PART II

Improvement

Western history has been an ongoing competition for legitimacy, for the right to claim for oneself and sometimes for one's group the status of legitimate beneficiary of Western resources.
—PATRICIA NELSON LIMERICK

I plainly foresee that if they increase much beyond their present Numbers they will create you infinite trouble in Pennsylvania.
—WILLIAM JOHNSON

Textual Boundaries, Discursive Control

STORIES OF THE LAND IN THE SUSQUEHANNA VALLEY

THE EXAMPLES OF the Seven Years' War and the war for Kentucky show how expansion brought Euroamericans into contact with native groups and how those relations—by turns violent and conciliatory, familiar and diplomatic—produced surprisingly subtle narrative registers. The utilitarian texts influenced better-known writers in several ways. At the level of aesthetics, genres such as the topographical description and the natural history provided a structure and a syntax for constructing the frontier. A second influence was topical. The description of border regions by Evans, Pownall, and Filson established recognizable settings against which a national ideology of nature and wilderness was defined. As sites of conflict produced parallel (but not equivalent) struggles for textual control, a set of thematic questions would emerge that now beg closer examination: How did Enlightenment models of "improvement" negotiate competing claims to and uses for backcountry space? To what extent did a rhetoric of entitlement, one that was rooted in environmental change, register a native presence? What were the dynamics between race, nature, and class? Where and when do native

77

Americans speak back? The Susquehanna River valley of eastern Pennsylvania provides a particularly useful field for addressing these questions. The land was in transition, and it was itself the subject of contest—disputed between British colonies (later American states), between white and native people, and between the native groups themselves. A dizzying social milieu yielded equally vexed narratives. J. Hector St. John de Crèvecoeur and native American treaty literature provide useful points for understanding the various stories of place, and together they offer a kind of casebook in the struggles for tactical and discursive control.

For compelling biographical reasons, Crèvecoeur offers a touchstone on Euroamerican attitudes toward the environment. He served as a French officer in the Seven Years' War, where he distinguished himself as a geographer, and he journeyed through most of the British colonies while working as a surveyor. In 1769, he purchased a plot of choice land in Orange County, New York, where he wrote, started a family, and lived the life of his prototypical character, the American farmer. Patriot hostilities forced him to uproot in 1778, however, and he returned to Europe with a trunk of manuscripts that his Whiggish editors shaped into *Letters from an American Farmer* (1782). Of the sketches not suited for his book, some were recycled into the expanded French edition, and others remained unpublished in English until the twentieth century. "Susquehannah," the longest of the "unpublished" sketches, expresses the ruin of the British American colonies as a reversal of progress-across-space. The sketch ends tragically, with the infamous Battle of Wyoming (in present-day Wilkes-Barre) in 1778. Yet the manuscript would show signs of stress as a Euroamerican view of the interior was imposed upon the actual frontier. Crèvecoeur's 1925 editors, in fact, broke the manuscript into two parts, "On the Susquehanna" and "The Wyoming Massacre," because the pieces do not cohere. Contemporary readers can identify the limits to a colonial grammar of entitlement in this fracturing, and the incoherence may be set alongside the "longer, grimmer, but more interesting" story that historians have brought to the American West.[1]

I read the narrative as an instructive, fascinating failure, although several layers of contextualization are needed to make "Susquehannah" resonate in this way. The most immediate is formal—the aesthetics of map-based writing. As a surveyor in the colonies and as one who received accolades for his "Carte des limites du Canada avec les colonies anglaises," Crèvecoeur dealt comfortably with the cartographic text. "Susquehannah" begins accordingly with the narrator unrolling a map, showing where the story will unfold (164), and the text presumes a knowledge of Pennsylvania geography (or at least that readers have a map at hand). A comparison of two settlements structures the sketch. The narrator journeys up the East and West Branches of the Susquehanna River (about seventy miles below the New York line) in 1774 and weighs the prospects for Euroamerican settlements on each branch against the physical environment there (figure 3.1). A second tour, tracing the rivalry between the two groups, seeks to explain the "Wyoming Massacre." The vehicle of geography, defined by one critic as a "spatial contrast," suggests the disinterested vantage point from which Enlightenment readers would develop a reasonable notion of what the land should become. This "spatial" frame, even in its failure, indicates the presumed ability of geography to mediate local differences.[2]

The map-based narrative indeed glosses a heated (but now obscure) jurisdictional battle, the "Yankee-Pennamite War." Although Crèvecoeur downplays this sectional crisis, it arguably epitomized the collapse of authority that accompanied the Revolution. And like Lewis Evans's "General Map," the Yankee-Pennamite affair originated at the Albany Congress. In 1754, a Connecticut-based firm called the Susquehannah Company "purchased" a tract in Pennsylvania from a group of mostly Mohawks who were in Albany for the anticipated "brightening" of the Covenant Chain. The New England group exploited a loophole in Connecticut's antiquated charter (the claim ran sea to sea, beyond New York, between the 41st and 42nd parallels) and engaged a shady trader named John Lydius, who made a deal "in the bushes" that satisfied the investors only. As one Mohawk sachem complained, Lydius got "our people Drunk & then persuaded them to Sign a Deed"; the Penns protested immediately, and a legal battle with Connecticut ensued that lasted until 1784. "Susquehannah" dismisses this crisis as "too antecedent & [perhaps] to uninteresting" for detailed discussion (165), but colonial records suggest otherwise. William Johnson reported the case to the Board of Trade in London, George III was briefed on the affair, and the Continental Congress debated the controversy ad nauseam. Native council speakers repeatedly warned colonial officials of "the fatal consequences" that would follow the purchase. The Iroquois held that the New England pioneers would bring "infinite trouble," and the powerful Delaware sachem Teedyuscung vowed ominously that the "Six Nations and their Numerous Allies & Dependants"

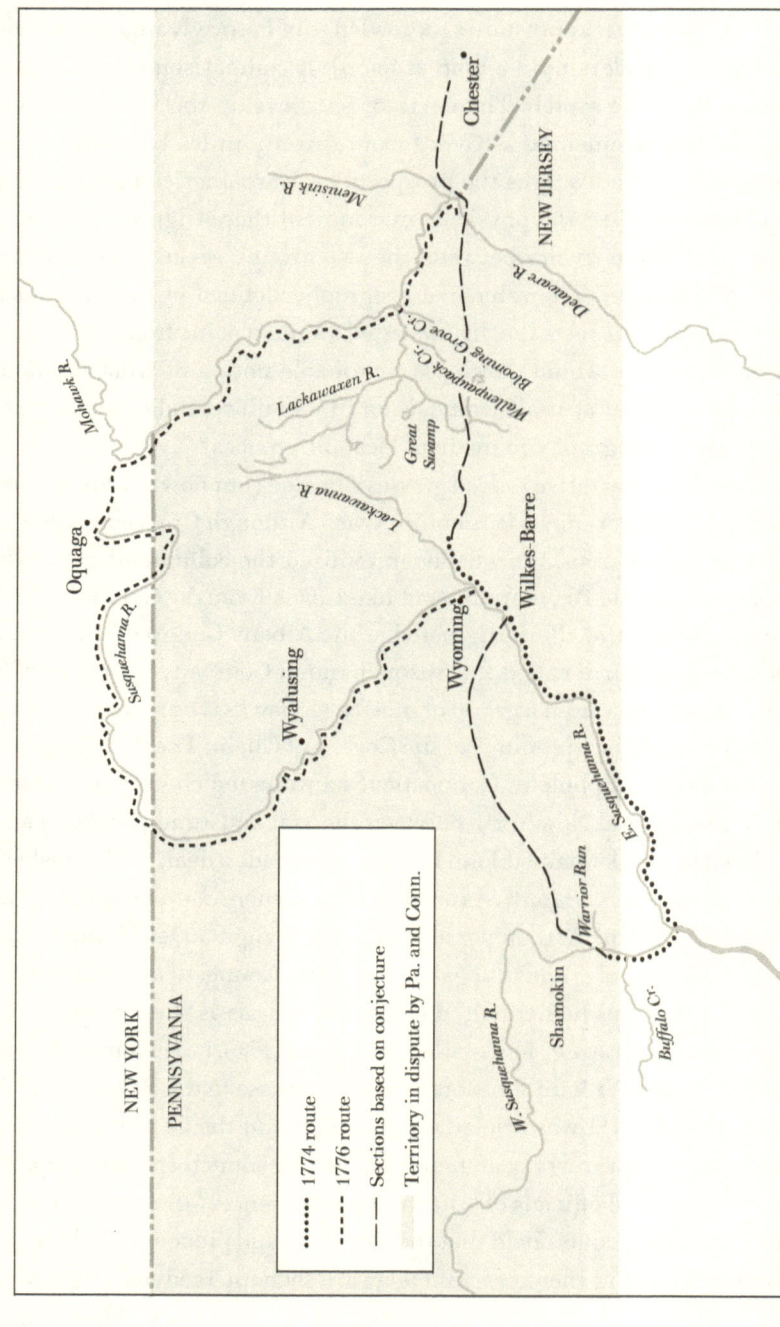

Figure 3.1. Map of Crèvecoeur's route in "Susquehanna" and territories disputed by Connecticut and Pennsylvania.

would be "irritated to fall upon" them. The "irritation" only worsened after the Seven Years' War, as the Fort Stanwix Treaty of 1768 seemed to license further settlement.[3]

Changing attitudes toward the land, however, would allow Crèvecoeur to gloss over the region's tangled environmental and social history. "Susquehannah" advances what historian Francis Jennings calls the "basic conquest myth": nature as the unused space that awaits "civilization." While unrolling the map, the narrator thus points to that "great Branch of humanity shooting up" around the "hitherto savage & wild & Entirely uncultivated" Susquehanna Valley (164). A staggering fertility appears sui generis. Grass touches the narrator's shoulders even while he is on horseback; a buttonwood tree reaches five feet in diameter; angelica is twelve feet high; wild cucumber takes root at the tops of cherry trees and strangles corn stalks within forty-eight hours. The "only Labour" farmers "are obliged to Perform is to find proper means to keep the Weeds down & to watch their growth" (176–80). Accounts written around the same time as Crèvecoeur's suggest that this was no exaggeration. But what brought about such tremendous potential? And what led authors to see the land as exclusively their own? Since about 1800 (after disease decimated the Susquehannock people), the region had supported a diverse population that thrived on a rich stock of peltry and that supported an economy in which different groups held a share. As overhunting depleted this stock, however, one form of land use replaced another. Dams from the exhausted beaver supply collapsed, which in turn exposed a "Strong healthy Slime" in the old pond beds. These bottomlands made perfect sites for agriculture (Crèvecoeur being perfectly aware of where they came from); the increased market for property, in turn, informed how the region was described. Changes in the physical environment brought changes in culture: Where the fur trade created a forum for interaction, the desire for commercial farming set peoples' interests at odds. The naturalized history of a place (the "elders higher than my head") justified a hunger for property and further eroded the prior landscape of accommodation between native and white Americans.[4]

The shift from trade to commercial agricultural helps explain why authors interpreted the Battle of Wyoming as they did and why they willed a certain blindness to the probable causes of the so-called massacre. Map-based narratives of progress across space allowed little latitude for weighing competing interests in the Susquehanna Valley. Given the region's visibility in frontier diplomacy, however, one can round out the likely motives that

Crèvecoeur buries under "natural" fertility and teary surprise. Since at least the 1740s, the Six Nations held the Susquehanna Valley as a buffer zone to the south. Shickellamy, the Oneida intermediary who joined the envoy to Onondaga (discussed in chapter 1), lived at the river forks partly with the charge of monitoring affairs. In 1758, William Johnson asked the Delawares to settle there, noting that they could "live with the Rest of your Brethren on the Waters of the Sasquehannah, which you will find safe and pleasant and have Ground enough to plant on." Besides recognizing native American agriculture (and discounting suggestions that the soil remained uncultivated), the harangue captures the region's role in preserving the League's hegemony.[5] The Iroquois who sided with the British in the Revolution protected their flank to the south, and the Battle of Wyoming stemmed from a decades-long effort to check white settlement. The same battle played in the public press as a "massacre," by contrast, as Crèvecoeur latched onto a racially enforced rhetoric of entitlement. "Our groaning country bleeds at every vein," a newspaper poet wailed in 1778, while

> New murder, rapes, fell massacres prevail;
> Who can hear this and not, with patriot zeal,
> Nobly step forth to guard their wives and children,
> And sheathe a dagger in the villain's heart
> Who'd rob us of our peace; our all, our honor!

There is evidence enough to suggest that Crèvecoeur did not witness the attack on Wyoming but that he used popular sentiment to punctuate his narrative of progress betrayed.[6] As with Filson's *Kentucke*, the sentimentalized death of pioneers connects "wives and children" to the generation of property and profit. The Yankee-Pennamite affair would provide a negative example for misguided policy on the national frontier, moreover, with the Lydius purchase epitomizing the kind of problems that geography could resolve. Crèvecoeur's contemporaries called it a "violation of publick Faith and an arrogant piece of Fraud"; a "frolic"; the cause for "heart burning," "hostility and bloodshed."[7] He seeks to remedy this "frolic" through the agency of a map; this ideological geography, in turn, moves competing ideas of space to the textual margins.

How, then, to read "Susquehannah?" I would begin with Job Chillaway, a Delaware land agent who successfully negotiated the middle ground. Of course, "Susquehannah" advances the usual rhetoric of an expanding civilization: Crèvecoeur describes "acres of the most usefull soyl which posterity has to clear" (174). But this plot of nature and progress eddies momentarily around hybrid figures such as Chillaway. Sources contemporary to Crèvecoeur note that Chillaway spoke English perfectly and (according to the Quaker John Woolman) was "acquainted with several people in and about Philadelphia." Crèvecoeur meanwhile introduces him as a "cunning old fellow" and hurries the plot forward.[8] Much as Filson glossed Daniel Boone's affection for the Shawnees, "Susquehannah" suggests a desire to repair beyond a shared culture. "Here the Soyl has a greater Mixture of clay than other spott therefore richer Pastures" runs the description of Chillaway's land. The word "therefore" nudges the country into futurity, and the transitional phrase implicitly commodifies the country, even though this soil obviously was being farmed already. Crèvecoeur continues: "There are Still Standing many good Indian Houses; was I a farmer here with pleasure I wou'd Pitch my Tent for nature in her most Indulgent hours cou'd not form an richer assemblage of all that man wants; here have I seen her dissolving into the Kindest volupty" (193). More than just nature "dissolves" in this passage, for the native land agent upsets the usual starting point of white settlement in wilderness; the portrayal of nature as "the Kindest volupty" bypasses the material demands of the "cunning old" trader. A shift rhetorically into the subjunctive case ("was I a farmer here") projects the Euroamerican stage theory over occupied property, while the syntax (parallel clauses with hurried or no transitions) pushes readers beyond a period of shared occupation. The narrator would have pioneers in a new tent rather than in "good Indian houses."

Such moments, where the narrative slides off script momentarily, reveal what the schema of progress and wilderness sought to hide. And these elisions typify early national writings about place. Frontier historians note that an "alchemy of property," justified by the promises of "improvement," marginalized native Americans and skewed the portrayal of white pioneers. The cartographic text, from which "Susquehannah" takes its cue, advanced proto-republican ideals over the backcountry and removed figures of the middle ground to the textual margins. The imaging of national space and the need to explain away an existing population was the problem upon which narratives were triangulated. As the previous section demonstrated, map-based writing would provide a vehicle for "translating" the interior upon specific terms. The Yankee-Pennamite War, moreover, was precisely the kind of crisis that geography was meant to document. Crèvecoeur's appeal to geography makes recourse to what Thomas Paine (in a slightly different context) called the "public good"; the accompanying plot of history across space naturalizes the human presence on the terrain and "dissolves" the holdings of a native land agent into the vaguely feminized "volupty." The rest of "Susquehannah" attempts to gloss or deflect similar conflicts. Patricia Nelson Limerick argues that western history "has been an ongoing competition for legitimacy," one in which individuals and groups vie to establish themselves as the "beneficiary of Western resources."[9] She underscores a struggle for narrative control that is central to Crèvecoeur. Using standard colonial tropes, "Susquehannah" begins with "savage & wild & entirely uncultivated" lands, emptying space of a prior history in order to justify new claims there. Yet even the most arrogant forms of imagined appropriation would contain the seeds of countering resistance, and signs of occupation break through the usual plot of empire.

"Mammy Where Are We Going?": The Limits of Frontier Prose in "Susquehannah"

"Susquehannah" offers an obtuse explanation to a more complicated state of affairs, which leads to an intriguing failure, one that is rife with suggestion. A comparative tour of two forks of the same river provides a vehicle for measuring the pace of progress in one corner of the backcountry, and observations made in 1774 and 1776 compare the Connecticut settlements (on the East Branch of the Susquehanna) to the Pennamite (or Pennsylvania) homesteads on the West Branch. The Connecticut group evicts the West Branch settlers in 1776, and they retreat to the upper reaches of the Delaware Valley, above the 42nd parallel (and beyond the Connecticut charter). Their remoteness leads to a loss of European manners and social decline. When the Yankee-Pennamite War bleeds into the Revolution, the once-evicted Pennamites join a British-Iroquois attack on the Connecticut patriot town of Wilkes Barre, and the battle culminates what critic John Hales calls "the tragedy of a community's geographic setting."[10] This progress-across-space theme distances the sketch from more probable causes of the Battle of Wyoming, and the manuscript's separate pieces cannot quite hold together; put differently, the sketch collapses because the premise of a topographical description offered little latitude for establishing the motives of an Other. Yet the text hardly represents a philosophical exercise over abstract space, for a negotiation between belletrism and locale (even when suppressed) actually deepens this narrative's resonance. The interests of native Americans may be reconstructed partly through colonial records, which suggest that the Iroquois who joined the British defended a buffer zone that they vocally claimed as their own. The patriots from New England, who happened to practice a more obnoxious form of land grabbing, represented a common enemy during the Revolution. "Susquehannah" represents the problematic effort to explain away this resistance.

The account begins with Enlightenment buoyancy, with the narrator greeting readers at the shore, ("When an European arrives in this Country"), and leading to some obscure point on the map. He notes soil exhaustion on the coast, and having argued for "future cultivation and prosperity" elsewhere (163), traces a path from New England to Pennsylvania. This route establishes the Yankee settlement as an ideal, encapsulating the stage theory as it moves from the less to the more "completed" towns. On the outer reaches of the West Branch, one meets the "first adventurers" from New England, who "Sat themselves down" and began the "Herculean Labours" that preceded their "Near prospect of future Ease" (168). The space-time frame allows the narrator to present nature as the antecedent of civility, so that even the swamp between the Delaware and Susquehanna watersheds may offer "a Logg house built Mid way by the New England people for the accomo[dation] of benighted or weary Travellers" (173). A first glance at the Wyoming Valley emphasizes prospects for agriculture—"Acres of the most Valuable & most usefull soyl which posterity has to clear & the benefits of which it has to enjoy"—that in turn leads to predictions of "agricolle Prosperity" (174–75). Here one finds the shoulder-high grass and the wild cucumber eighty feet in the air; one finds no mention of the history behind that fertility or of the Delaware sachem Teedyuscung, who lived in Wyoming and predicted the violence that would "fall upon" the settlers. (His new neighbors murdered him.)[11] The protocol of a topographical description glides past the violence. With an apostrophe issued mostly for the sake of formal structure, Crèvecoeur laments, "what pity, that this [branch] cannot be permanently settled" to suit the "Political Tranquillity" that "nature" seems to offer (180).

As the space-time frame compresses the events, "Susquehannah" suffers in coherence, particularly as it flattens a longer and less flattering history into clean stages.[12] Although the account begins in 1774, New Englanders actually began moving to the region after 1768. In 1769, they went so far as to hire the Paxton Boys, a notorious band of outlaws that slaughtered the peaceful Conestoga Indians six years before, to evict Pennsylvania patentees from the region. With the earlier tours mostly serving as the foil for a coming tragedy, however, the problems appear in a one-sentence paragraph: "At last some Demagagues appeared for hitherto they had been all Equal" (185). So much for the Paxton Boys! These omissions lead to a confusing chronology, and the tentative authorial decisions (evident in the manuscript) belie the effort to smooth over uglier episodes. Take as an example the insistence that the Lydius purchase was "a solemn Bargain properly ratified." A deletion in the manuscript hints toward lingering resentment over the initial treaty: "The Long delay of the Proprietors, the Ignorance, & carelessness of the first surveyors & perhaps Some fraud in the first ~~purch~~ Settlers, all these causes produced Errors ~~w~~ & horrid Mistakes cou'd not be Easily remedied" (184). The strike out, presumably of "purchase," allows for some misgivings about the 1754 cession—one where, by a previously cited account, John Lydius got "our people Drunk & then persuaded them to Sign a Deed."[13] This barely detectable but deliberate shift suggests how the public rhetoric moved key issues of white-native relations to the background. The text "hiccoughs" as it substitutes a neat historical geography over the realities of frontier politics; as Crèvecoeur simplified events elsewhere, the sketch would become almost illegible.[14]

These costs of compression become particularly apparent in the treatment of race, which is cast through the historical matrix of an expanding "civilization." The language of a new earth distances the sketch from the negotiation and conflict that characterized the frontier, and this willed amnesia bypasses one-half of a land war. As noted earlier, the Iroquois who entered the Revolution probably did so because of the continued pressure of Euroamerican expansion, and—as Crèvecoeur was undoubtedly aware—native council leaders repeatedly warned that the Connecticut settlements would lead to bloodshed.[15] But "Susquehannah" is determined to explain the Wyoming "massacre" differently: as the result of white pioneers mixing too closely with the Indians. The 1776 tour suggests that the isolated West Branch families (the Pennamites) lose "their European prejudices & Embibe those of y' Natives"; without the "opportunities of Improv^t," they become "a New breed of people neither Europeans nor yet Natives" (183). And when the Susquehannah Company evicts these families, forcing them to tracts above the 42nd parallel, they cut their ties to European society altogether. The "Power of Indian Education" creates "a new sett of people" (195). The "horrid Poyson" of the Revolution then turns the provincial Yankee-Pennamite War into an imperial conflict, and the disgruntled Pennamites join the Iroquois-British attack downriver. "Improvement" thus serves as the thematic touchstone, as the basis for plot, and race is framed against the demise of an idealized community.

This leads—or does *not* lead—to the Battle of Wyoming. The plot of progress-betrayed casts the frontier on belletristic terms and removes the account from more immediate causes of conflict. Despite the randomness with which Crèvecoeur portrays the attack on Wyoming, public officials had been registering complaints about the Connecticut pioneers for decades. And the path of "Susquehannah" cuts straight through this landscape of discontent. In 1776, the narrator visits Oquaga, a refugee community on the East Branch that happened to be a hotbed of Indian nationalism. The Oneidas in this town vocally protested the redrawn Fort Stanwix line of 1768, and Iroquois living there would join the British at Fort Niagara, where the attack on Wyoming originated. In 1775, a party from Oquaga addressed the Continental Commission on Indian Affairs about the Susquehannah Company, making the particular complaint that Lydius had "only pretended to make a purchase." The Mohawk war chief Joseph Brant visited Oquaga one year later and railed against patriots who wanted "to be sole masters of this continent."[16] The narrator of "Susquehannah" meanwhile says nothing about the simmering discontent—reporting only that he had nothing to report. After a week of conversation, he notes of the local elders: "I was greatly édyfyed at the Knowledge & sagacity they made to my many questions, I shou'd grow too diffuse, was I to Enter into further details, I must therefore quit this subject & go down to Wiomen again to contemplate the Increase of this famous settlement" (193). The pace of narration quickens with an authorial intrusion. Should one pause here, the story would grow "too diffuse," and the dissolving of a local landscape ("I must therefore quit this subject") reveals the pull of a geographical history *away* from people like Joseph Brant. The sketch moves downriver, literally steering readers away from a narrative that could address native grievances. Instead Crèvecoeur attributes the Battle of Wyoming to "Demagagues" from New England, the "Power of Indian Education," and the "horrid Poyson" of the Revolution.

This attempt to reconcile rhetoric and the frontier, to explain away conflicts that are explicable from other sources, leads to a collapse in the final battle scene. In Crèvecoeur's telling, a vastly outnumbered unit marches from the stockade and to their own slaughter.[17] The Iroquois-British force (the Pennamites having vanished from the picture) overtakes the patriot soldiers, many of whom die while trying to flee across the river. The townspeople huddle inside, listening to friends and family suffer outside the stockade walls. An emphasis upon passive immobility appeals to the reader's heart: "The aged people the Women & Children who were Inclosed in the Stockade, distinctly cou'd hear & See this dreadfull onset, the ~~conclus~~ last Scene of which had been Transacted close to the very Gates — what a Scituation these unfortunate people were in, Each wife Each father Each mother cou'd Easily distingu[ish] Husband & son as they fell" (198). But the plot cannot sustain itself, and the sketch sinks to the level of a rough draft. The narrator cries, such "dreadfull Scenes . . . I Know not how to retrace" (197), and meditates upon his own position, suggesting that "I can Easily Imagine . . . the feeling of a soldier burying the bodies of his companions" (200). These theatrical flourishes betray a general loss for words. Crèvecoeur imagines a painter "Calmly" seated amidst this chaos; at another point, he reaches for the brush himself—suggesting "a cow perhaps with hollow flanks & projecting Ribs" (202). The tentativeness, the "perhaps," means that no amount of formulaic and theatrical defeatism could bridge the gap between backcountry violence and the conventions of public letters. A nod to the topographical description is made, and an authorial note suggests Crèvecoeur considered folding in a dramatic monologue by an "undaunted Woman"— the surviving "Mrs. B" who narrates the next segment in the manuscript book.

"Mammy where are we going," a child asks after the battle. The same question could be asked of Crèvecoeur himself, who apparently was not sure how to close his own sketch. (Several options are presented, none works completely.) A splintering recourse to the sentimental underscores a divergence of views toward the interior: the colonial notion of civilization-across-space, and Iroquois assertions of a buffer in the Susquehanna Valley. Major John Butler built his forces among the Iroquois—by one report, the Onondagas, Cayugas, and Senecas—as well as some Delawares, and the British attracted these groups probably because the Crown represented the best check against colonial settlement. Crèvecoeur's appeal to readers' hearts, by contrast, marks yet one more attempt to define a national subject over wilderness, to justify the entitlement of orderly pioneers to backcountry frontier resources. Ostensibly, the sketch traces the competition between Connecticut and Pennsylvania patentees, but these separate camps more accurately represent two fronts in a larger push to alter the face of the country, to construct this "new earth" that authors continue to describe. An appeal through the cartographic text would seem to address the problem, but the conventions of a literary geography isolated the problem as between whites. The natives that enter the narrative, therefore, appear from nowhere—even as the manuscript's missteps reveal how they became marginalized during the writing process. The Iroquois and "dependents" joined Butler's Rangers in order to preserve a buffer between native country and a settlement that had been granted on corrupt terms, because the British side provided the best chance for driving back Euroamerican settlers. These motives do not register in "Susquehannah," which is exactly the point. The break in the narrative, where editors divided the text into separate sketches, reveals how partial justifications unfolded over country that Euroamericans sought to colonize.

A recognition of the implicit violence in republican environmentalism should inform how we read Crèvecoeur—and early national writings about place in general. The plot of Yankees-and-Pennamites distracts one from the more compelling problems of expansion and environmental change. A vaguely poetic identification with "savage & wild" nature begins (as Crèvecoeur well knew) with a country that native Americans had shaped for generations, often through an economy that brought people together. His vision of progress across space would establish the land as a beginning for commercial agriculture, and the comparative travelogues suggest what kind of "policy" best supported continued expansion. Yet the crosscurrents in this manuscript show how an ideological geography was forged against an open frontier. The traces of interactions with native Americans, often outside the main currents of plot, reveal how stories of the frontier were selected, crafted, reshaped, and often ignored. The narrator hurries readers away from Oquaga or directs settlers into the tents alongside (perfectly) "good Indian houses." Those people who remain outside republican discourse might be found at the margins, in other words, but that is not to say that they vanish altogether.

The "Wyomen" of Treaty Literature

A setting like the Susquehanna Valley would defy one-sided acts of co-optation, be they political or textual, so long as control for the region remained under negotiation and so long as different groups came together there. Native Americans remained at the center of the region's environmental and human history, despite their suggested "removal" in belletristic writing.

Any act of textual effacement seems particularly egregious, then, when one reads Crèvecoeur against other forms of documenting native-white relations. The vast archive of treaty minutes provides a particularly useful point of comparison for competing stories of the land. In this record of cross-cultural theater, the Iroquois Nations especially retained their advantage in an ongoing struggle for tactical and discursive control in the mid-Atlantic backcountry. Treaty literature can explain what the one-sided portrayal of a "massacre" would not, that attacks such as the Battle of Wyoming came after repeated warning, and it suggests an alternative to the usual aesthetics of usurpation. Genuine products of the encounter (though hardly representative of an authentic, indigenous voice), these transcripts show how natives forged identities in a colonialist setting to protect their own interests across physical space.[18]

A focal point in this literature was "Wyomen" in the Susquehanna Valley. In July 1742, the so-called Six Nations (only five were present) and their Delaware "dependents" traveled to Philadelphia to meet with colonial officials. For Pennsylvania, the concerns were the usual ones: land acquisition, diplomatic ties, the fears of friendly relations between the Iroquois and France, and punishment for the past seasons' crimes on the frontier. A record of the treaty was assembled in London, and Benjamin Franklin printed the proceedings in a visually striking digest entitled *The Treaty Held with the Indians of the Six Nations, at Philadelphia, in July 1742*. According to a preface written by the London naturalist John Fothergill (discussed in chapter 6), a primary purpose of the Philadelphia treaty was to reassert the Walking Purchase of 1737, an infamous swindle that robbed the Delawares of the land between the forks of the Delaware River and that had been the thorn in native-white diplomacy for decades. The printed record for this reason climaxes with the Onondaga speaker, Canasatego, protecting his position at the head of relations with Pennsylvania and ordering the Delawares off their ancestral home. Canasatego rails, "You ought to be taken by the Hair of the Head and shaked severely." He puts "petticoats" on his rebellious "cousins" and orders:

> You are Women. Take the Advice of a wise Man, and remove immediately. You may return to the other Side of *Delaware* where you came from: But we do not know whether, considering how you have demean'd yourselves, you will be permitted to live there.... We therefore assign you two Places to go, either to *Wyomen* or *Shamokin*. You may go to

either of these Places, and then we shall have you more under our Eye, and shall see how you behave. Don't deliberate; but remove away, and take this Belt of Wampum.

Several incongruities suggest that this speech was a diplomatic fiction. The use of "women" to dictate a subordinate position upholds Euroamerican ideas of gender that are inconsistent with those of the Iroquois—a clan-based, matriarchal society where women's councils shape tribal decisions. Canasatego punctuates his demand with wampum, using the traditional marker of consent as an agent of enforcement.[19] The speech (which had no lasting effect) presumes to reconstitute Indian signs in order to advance Euroamerican property claims. But to what degree did the native speaker participate in this reconfiguration of the "Indian" sign? And to what degree would his particular group gain from the misrepresentation by Pennsylvania?

By their very structure, treaty transcripts resist simple narratives of dispossession. The product of print and oral traditions (as Sandra N. Gustafson has shown), these texts capture a discursive struggle—one in which Iroquois speakers maintained a certain amount of control. In this highly figurative field, with the status of metaphor itself coming under dispute, native participants monitored the mechanics of translation with particular care. My point is to suggest how natives "talked back" even in print texts that presumed to usurp sovereignty. On one hand, translation provided the means for "carrying across" that literary critic Eric Cheyfitz describes. Cheyfitz, as noted earlier, argues that linguistic transfers from the foreign to the domestic equaled "an act of violence." John Carlos Rowe, in a similar case, maintains that it is "impossible to 'translate' oral Native American narratives without fundamentally violating the social, religious and cultural practices in which such narratives functioned." But when read against intertribal rivalries and within a field that incorporated native tradition, this syntax of (dis)possession can be shown to flow in multiple directions. Native council and Euroamerican leaders recognized alike the power of translation. The transcript reprinted by Franklin, for example, emphasizes the role of Conrad Weiser, a "go between" who was successful precisely because he was trusted on all sides. (As noted in chapter 1, John Bartram joined Weiser on his trip to Onondaga.) Pennsylvania paid Weiser one hundred pounds for his services as "go between," and Canasatego declared his similar sentiments, noting that Weiser was of "Two equal Parts"—in other words, he was successful because he was divided between cultures. Again, without question, the *Treaty Held with the Indians* summoned native voices in order to justify Indian removal. (The preface reviews the history of land claims "on both Sides of the River *Susquehannah*"; the text includes the tribute exchanged and the people in attendance; as if in the spirit of fairness, the "discourse" unfolds "according to their usual method.") Yet the text remains decidedly Iroquois in format and allusion; as the Pennsylvanians adopted a native way of doing business, moreover, they ceded an advantage that comes with the control of protocol—syntax, allusion, *story*.[20]

Historians of the Iroquois trace the protocol of meetings like the 1742 treaty to an older condolence ceremony, and colonists quickly learned that ignoring ritual could ruin attempts at negotiation. Following a long-standing custom (one that continues to this day), hosts met an approaching party outside the town, or "at wood's edge," where gifts were exchanged and the opening speeches would "wipe away tears" and "cover graves." Over the course of several days, speakers then would rehearse a common memory, using canes and belts or strings of wampum to reconstruct past transactions. The purpose of these exchanges was to establish a workable narrative of the past, a "congruence," in Richard White's term, that (whether true or not) both sides could accept as a usable narrative of the past. The skeleton to an "Indian address" was sketched out on the back of a letter written to William Johnson:

1st glad to see me at my fire & bid me Welcome Home
2d   letting me know ye leaves were so long & think they could not hear w[hat] was s[aid] at F Stanwix
3d   Clear my Eyes to see . . . Clearly & to Open my Ears—
4th. to remind me of ye old agreement.

Following the same general procedure, the events recorded from 1742 begin at James Logan's house, which serves as the "wood's edge" for this meeting. The Onondaga Canasatego, misleadingly called a "chief" because he speaks for the Iroquois, removes "Obstructions to a good understanding" and presents "condolences" for the usual frontier squabbles; Pennsylvania does the same. A week later, "*The Chiefs of the Six Nations*" meet colonial officials and review a friendship with Pennsylvania and the Indians that dates back to William Penn. The recollection of a common past brightens the "Chain of Friendship" and recalls the promise "to be one Flesh and one

People." The Iroquois who were present assure Pennsylvania about their loyalty in the coming war between England and France.[21]

These negotiations suggest that native groups actively shaped a story of native-white relations on the Pennsylvania frontier. In previous chapters, I discussed how the Six Nations constructed their own body politic against a European rivalry, and in particular, how they pursued local advantages that sometimes came at the expense of "dependent" tribes. Council speakers like Canasatego projected an image of the Confederacy that put his nation (the Onondagas) at the head of forest diplomacy; territories to the south could be leveraged, by the same token, to protect territories more valuable to a given group. This strategy was in keeping with the longer history of Iroquois relations with the British colonies. The same protectionism (as noted) was practiced by the Mohawk sachem Hendrick, who presumed to speak for all Six Nations as he threatened to dissolve the "Covenant Chain" with New York. His rhetorical gambit brought concrete results. The threat led to the Albany Congress, and attention was paid to land swindles in Mohawk country. William Johnson (the Mohawk-friendly trader) was later promoted to "Superintendent of Indian Affairs," while Hendrick's party left that summer with thirty wagonloads of gifts.[22] As different factions within the League of Six Nations vied to serve as the leading partners with the British, the 1742 meeting at Philadelphia would represent one stage in a long history of political theater. The review of a storied past, as emblematized by the "Chain of Friendship," marks the search for "congruent" interests—for a diplomatic truth that was true enough because it benefited the participating parties.

The theatrics suggest a wrinkle to cultural criticism that sees "translation" solely as a one-sided vehicle of dispossession. The rehearsal of a common past, where a narrative of the realm was "translated" between different groups, would provide native speakers with an opportunity to pursue their interests—particularly when the talks turned to land. In literary terms, speakers negotiated the metaphoric contents of an accepted past, and as the sign was "carried across" a cultural divide, each group staked its rhetorical advantage. In the 1742 *Treaty Held with the Indians*, the figure of *Onas* (or quill) puns to mean William Penn, who represents a standard of fairness against which Pennsylvania's later shortcomings could be defined. The governor of Pennsylvania, George Thomas, reminds the Iroquois of Onas's (or Penn's) treaty. Canasatego agrees: "We well remember the Treaty you mentioned . . . by which we confirmed our League of Friendship that is to last as long as the Sun and Moon endure." He then adds sarcastically, while angling for more presents, "if the Proprietor had been here himself . . . he would have made an Addition to them." Having been reconstituted through the rehearsal of a shared history, *Onas* serves as a sign through which the Iroquois advance their own ends. Canasatego and Thomas wrangle over the value of a territory undergoing environmental change, which finds the Onondaga speaker weighing his group's priorities against those of the Delawares. While noting that "Your People daily settle on" the lands west of the Susquehanna and that horses and cows "eat the Grass our Deer used to stand on," the former suggests the property values had risen since an earlier treaty; Thomas replies that "the Industry and Labour used by the white People in their Cultivation and Improvement" had increased values, and Pennsylvania refuses to make further tribute.[23] As Canasatego concedes on the point of compensation for the Delaware Valley, however, he calls attention to encroachments elsewhere. The feints, jabs, and fades show how a clear-eyed orator worked the links between the environment and the marketplace to negotiate (like Job Chillaway) specific interests in a colonial exchange.

The hegemony that the Iroquois sought and maintained through diplomacy often returned treaty literature to the Susquehanna River valley. However inconsistent Canasatego's use of the term "women" might be with Iroquois culture, his directive nonetheless suggests a strategy of local advancement in a continued imperial struggle.[24] Canasatego permits the assumption that the Walking Purchase should be upheld, in this case at the expense of the Delawares, in order to consolidate power and shield lands elsewhere. The concerns with preserving the southern flank of Iroquoia and a certain kind of environment throughout the border regions explain the rhetorical parries with the governor of Pennsylvania. The intertribal rivalry captured in this text happens to square with Pennsylvania's ambitions, which in turn gives voice to an Onondaga perspective vis-à-vis the Susquehanna Valley. The text captures a continuing and crosshatched struggle for authority in a contact zone; the transcript also may explain the Battle of Wyoming. At least back to 1742, the Iroquois pointed to "Wyomen" and "Shamokin" as a site from which hegemony to the south was maintained. The League of Six Nations divided during the War of Independence. Some Iroquois remained neutral, others sided with the British. The Iroquois that rallied against the United States did so because a continued British alliance offered the best boundary defense then available. Never a one-sided affair, colonial expansion brought different groups together in complicated ways. Representations of the Susquehanna Valley suggest that as different groups vied for territorial control, they engaged in an analogous discursive struggle. Authors like Crèvecoeur and texts like the *Treaty Held with the Indians* capture the relations that were forged (and contested) between different groups as they vied for control of a certain kind of environment—and for the boundaries of physical space. The question that remains, and one that is vital to understanding early national writings, is how any author would position the narrative against the frontier that was purportedly being described.

All discourse is textual or scriptive, and it is precisely the nature of script that it can never be scripture, fixed in its meaning as the spoken word is—erroneously, of course—claimed to be.
—ARNOLD KRUPAT

Jefferson's Nature and the Trans-Appalachian West

Notes on the State of Virginia

THE PAPER WAR between Connecticut and Pennsylvania did not end with the 1778 Battle of Wyoming but lingered into the next decade, underscoring the uncertainty of jurisdiction during the revolutionary era and the difficulty of articulating a political order across contested boundaries. What began from ambiguities in the antiquated charters snowballed into a nearly fatal crisis after the War of Independence. Unless "speedily quitted," members of Congress warned, the affair would "interrupt the Harmony and weaken the Union of the confederated Colonies." The nation needed to resolve these kinds of disputes before it could govern itself, and the problems of sovereignty were nothing if not persistent. In 1782, lawyers from the two states pleaded their cases before a congressional court of commissioners. The president of the Continental Congress, John Hanson, argued that "the peace of ... the Whole Union depends upon an amicable settlement of this dispute." Two years later, after the court had already sided with Pennsylvania, the Susquehannah Company and the Wyoming Valley settlers once again pleaded for their collective and individual rights. A petition led by Zebulon Butler (the losing officer at the Battle of Wyoming) was heard by a committee chaired by Thomas Jefferson. Describing their travails in a way that resembles "Susquehannah," the settlers maintained that they legally purchased territory from the "Native Proprietors" and made "Improvements" to country "in a Wilderness State," only to feel the "most intolerable sufferings during the late unhappy Warr." The connection between property and sentiment was reiterated: "Their Houses and Other Buildings have been Burned, and their Lands Laid waste, their Cattle Killed, and Pillaged, Many of their Fathers, Mothers, Wives and Children have been Sacraficed by the relentless fury of A Savage Enemy; Yet through all their Sufferings and distresses they have preserved An Inviolable Attachment to the Important Cause of America in which many of their nearest and Dearest friends have bled and fallen." Jefferson's committee upheld the court of commissioners' decision, and from the standpoint of an ideological geography, it represented a minor landmark in the ability of the United States to preside over countering claims. Instead of "deluging the land with human blood [and] misery," Jefferson wrote, Congress proved that the vagaries of colonial charters could be "weighed in the scales of justice." The union proved to itself, and with "the Eyes of all Europe watching," that the legal suits that accompanied expansion could be settled in a peaceful manner.[1]

The timing recalls a more famous series of acts, those involving Ohio; for the same year that Congress upheld its decision on the Yankee-Pennamite affair, a committee with two of the same members—Jefferson and Hugh Williamson—drafted a report that led to the Ordinance of 1784. This act marked a second precedent of national over sectional interests, if on a more recognizable scale. Virginia had offered to part with its paper claims on several occasions, but members of Congress, many anxious to protect their interests under colonial land companies, were slow in agreeing to terms. Almost immediately after the Virginia cession was accepted, however, the committee submitted its plan for territorial government. A revised version of the report passed one month later as the Ordinance of 1784. The western ordinance created new terms of jurisdiction over country that representatives regarded as vaguely defined, providing a check to innovations such as the Susquehannah Company or Transylvania. The squared boundaries (as Robert F. Berkhofer Jr. explains) "constituted nothing less than a ground plan for the entire trans-Appalachian" region, but this rezoned West also was a statement of dispossession. As several accounts suggest, the union had been preparing "a treaty with the late hostile tribes of Indians" in order "to settle a line or boundary for them"; Jefferson himself would explain how the union opened "treaties with the several Nations North of the Ohio, within our boundaries, for the purpose of concluding peace and buying lands." The syntax is revealing: surveys first, treaties next. Legislators would develop a political calculus that weighed social control against geography and population, and it was assumed—if not always openly expressed—that the diminishment of native claims was inevitable.[2]

Expansionist policy posed analogous philosophical questions, as I have demonstrated, and the position of native Americans in this westering "empire of liberty" piqued the civic and literary imagination of the early republic. Jefferson wrote *Notes on the State of Virginia* during the period in which the United States established its own ideological geography, and as the book summed up "the basic thinking of his age," it directly engaged some of the more disturbing trends that followed the war. The Revolution brought a rash of Indian hating (epitomized in texts such as Filson's *Kentucke*) that was softened only by enlightened projects that cast native Americans as the subjects for "improvement"—or as the counterweights of progress. (Neither view allowed room for indigenous agency or autonomy.) With an orator like Samuel Drowne calling the Ohio Valley an "important volume which time is unfolding in the western world," the region's existing population would fall to the textual margins. As the poet Philip Freneau prophesied, the new earth was one from which "Th' unsocial Indian far retreats." The republic attempted to establish colonies west of the Appalachians, as noted, with surveys first and cessions second. By the end of the 1780s, however, intellectuals would begin to address native Americans as they would the environment. Such were the beginnings of the "benevolent plan," which Secretary of War Henry Knox developed in 1789. Defined by neoclassical ideas of history and comparative civilizations, the less primitive groups (Knox maintained) would abandon their existing systems of land use for a European model—thereby rendering moot the problem of cessions. Yet this "benevolent plan" obviously would not recognize native Americans as having their own interests to protect, and they were as much the objects of experiment as they were topics for elegy—at any rate, rarely recognized in public discourse within the living present.[3] Even in its most "benevolent" moments, the narrative of a republic transforming the continent defined an Other that was secondary to a Euroamerican plot of progress across space.

A tension between race, land, and nation building explains the themes that converge around *Notes on the State of Virginia*: geography as the basis of a public order, the conception of space on a historical scale, nature, and the compulsion to be "native" to the American continent. Much in the way that "Susquehannah" operates through the persona of an enlightened traveler, Jefferson would adopt the cartographic text in order to narrate the future of a country. The book marks yet one more attempt to construct a life over the map, bringing an authorial rage for order over experience that could not be so easily contained.[4] Born from personal anguish, *Notes on the State of Virginia* projects a republican citizenry (embodied by Jefferson, the patriot intellectual) over material gathered from the middle ground. Biography alone is enough to explain this conflation of the cartographic and political self. In 1780, the diplomat François Marbois distributed a list of queries to representatives from each of the thirteen states. Jefferson began his response for Virginia during a low period in his life: shortly after the death of his daughter Lucy Elizabeth, while his wife Martha was gravely ill, and while he was recuperating from a disastrous term as Virginia's governor. As the book became more than just a mourning piece, *Notes on the State of Virginia* would fold a project of personal recovery into national events and would do so in a way that intertwined the republican subject and the physical terrain. This claim is not nearly as extraordinary as it sounds, if one considers when the book that we read today took its final shape. The manuscript (begun in 1781 as the response to a questionnaire) tripled in size after a 1783–84 revision, and in this period of revision Jefferson took his seat as a congressional delegate.[5] Unsurprisingly, the book would advance prescriptions for environmental and social change that paralleled the legislation of the period and—as if to anticipate the paradoxes of the western ordinances—provide a blueprint for Henry Knox's "benevolent plan." Questions of geography and racial identity intersect with the narrative life, and the voice that emerges as native to the continent (in a literary analogue to Knox's policies) turns out to be the author's own.

 A remarkable argument ensues, one that continues the colonizing work of a cartographic text but that raises this otherwise utilitarian mode to a new level of philosophical inquiry. The narrative is about establishing and inventing territory yet preserving the grounding in what is concrete, tactile, or measurable. Nature, or what might be defined as experience, provides the foundation for a reconstituted political realm. A "man-made world is always open to question," critic Myra Jehlen notes; by implementing settlement across "the continent's permanent contours and conditions," therefore, the narrator locates "the emerging social structures beyond debate." Yet the grounding in a survey yields problems. The textual would fix itself in the empirical, which for Jefferson was scriptural—"The continent that was the modern spirit's flesh was also its word," Jehlen observes—but this basis in the land was never as fixed as one would wish it to be. The point of departure is a map of Virginia, not the state itself. As a frontispiece for the book, Jefferson commissioned a clean engraving of the map that his father had made for a colonial land company in 1751 with Joshua Fry (it also was used by Lewis Evans), and Jefferson's initial step as an author was to rearrange Marbois's list so that "limits and boundaries" became the first of the book's twenty-three chapters, or "Queries." The argument builds accordingly upon a geographic frame, neatly encapsulated by an elaborately punctuated, single sentence:

> Virginia is bounded on the East by the Atlantic: on the North by a line of latitude, crossing the Eastern Shore through Watkin's Point, being about 37.° 57.' North latitude; from thence by a streight line to Cinquac, near the mouth of the Patowmac; thence by the Patowmac, which is common to Virginia and Maryland, to the first fountain of its northern branch; thence by a meridian line, passing through that fountain till it intersects a line running East and West, in latitude 39.° 43.' 42.4" which divides Maryland from Pennsylvania, and which was marked by Messrs. Mason and Dixon; thence by that line, and a continuation of it westwardly to the completion of five degrees of longitude from the eastern boundary of Pennsylvania, in the same latitude, and thence by a meridian line to the Ohio: On the west by the Ohio and Mississippi, to latitude 36.° 30.' North, and on the South by the line of latitude last mentioned.[6]

The plot of the book resembles the construction of a literary diorama, one in which the American philosophe imaginatively stocks the space that the opening sentence defines. The twenty-two queries that follow "Boundaries" move from topography, to "Productions Mineral, Vegetable and Animal," to "Climate," and then into Euroamerican civic and cultural life. The natural environment, by this arrangement, serves as the foundation for later statements on the state's civil history. But what tensions emerge as the intellectual model supplanted the country itself and when the author cast his own voice as local to a colonized domain? Jefferson would tellingly clarify his distinctions between Euroamericans and native Americans in a later appendix, and as I will show in the conclusion of this chapter, the need for clarification returns him to the initial conflation of abstraction and experience. A beginning from the cartographic statement (as was the case with "Susquehannah") results in the disappearance of the very subject that *Notes on the State of Virginia* purports to describe. Much in the way that Knox's "benevolent plan" would chart a course for improvement that ignored the "living Indian," Jefferson substitutes an Enlightenment model of ethnography for experience on the middle ground. Eventually the native voice — like the place itself — would be usurped by Jefferson's own version. A displacement from the terrain brings the text to an aporia that emerges against this very question of voice. Virginia and its indigenous population reveal themselves as imagined in the text, which becomes problematic because the text presumes to be grounded in concreteness at the same time.

But to focus upon the ending loses sight of the immediate issue: the effort to mediate between a map and the terrain, between ideas and experience, between discourse and place. These contraries give *Notes on the State of Virginia* its structure and resonance. The book defines new terms for constituting space, make no mistake about that. The very use of latitude and longitude in query 1 implies an act of appropriation. When reviewing the principal causes of dispute between whites and native Americans, the Iroquois agent William Johnson blamed differing systems of keeping boundaries. "I cannot but think that natural marks," Johnson wrote, "are to be greatly preferred to imaginary Lines in dealing with them."[7] At the most basic level then, Jefferson would impose new terms upon the terrain, and the plot of the book evolves from this attempt to reassemble a model from abstracted space. The main character in this intellectual drama becomes Jefferson himself, who self-consciously assumes the role of an American philosophe as he constructs the image that will attempt to — but never quite — pass for the thing itself. The mind that is "put on display," as Mitchell Robert Breitwieser notes, frequently pauses to reflect upon its own processes, to ask how one comes to know. Jefferson writes: "Ignorance is preferable to error; and he is less remote from the truth who believes nothing, than he who believes what is wrong" (33). Breitwieser argues that this early pragmatism suggests "an antithetical unity," a recourse to particulars that rejects the totality of any single system, and the effect for readers is to follow an author as he works through an admittedly partial re-creation: as he establishes provisional bases for his later opinions, while trusting only what is verifiable and concrete.[8] As with Lewis Evans and Thomas Pownall, indeed as with any cartographic text, the narration will reveal itself to be only a narration—which may not seem compelling, except that Jefferson presumes to work from particulars.

Ideological Geography and the Disappearing West

For an example of how ideology and place are conflated through authorial voice, consider query 2, entitled "Rivers." Marbois asked for a "notice" of the state's "rivers, rivulets, and how far they are navigable." The response begins with an allusion to the 1751 map by Peter Jefferson and Joshua Fry, which "will give a better idea . . . than any description in writing" (5). Immediately, Thomas Jefferson points the words to something other than the terrain, to a map that is more exact than language but representational nonetheless. The cartographic "enters his text as an ideal means of discovery and comprehension," the critic Wayne Franklin remarks, while putting the narrative "out of touch with the world which it purports to describe." Jefferson accordingly moves from discussion of length and depth and currents to trade, which in turn gives the chapter a much broader geographic scope than query 1 (on boundaries) had established. He jumps outside Virginia's immediate borders without the slightest transition:

> The Shenandoah branch interlocks with James river about the Blue ridge, and may perhaps in future be opened.
> The *Missisipi* will be one of the principal channels of future commerce for the country westward of the Alleghaney. (7)

Economic expansion has a material basis, the text suggests, as the absence of syntactical links locates Euroamerican interests beyond explanation and in the land itself.[9] The Mississippi thus opens the compass of discussion to include the sources of the Potomac and the Missouri, the trade entrepôts of Santa Fe and New Orleans, and the Ohio as well as *its* tributaries. Statistical information feeds into an ideological geography that moves across time every bit as naturally as these rivers do downstream. There are shades of Lewis Evans, Thomas Pownall, and John Filson here; indeed, the narrative springs from this slippage from actual to potential place, from this "translation" of the physical country to possible place. An Enlightenment plot of improvement would seek to incorporate economic prospects with the environment, and in doing so, it introduces political valences that eventually override the premise of describing just Virginia.

This construction of an imagined place from the real one, in turn, calls for a narrator. The previous discussion of "Susquehannah" suggested that Crèvecoeur portrayed himself as a figure journeying through the map. As Jefferson would imagine the territory, he likewise constructs narrating personae — identities to negotiate between literary discourse and the frontier, between belletristic tastes and a middle ground. The sixth chapter of his book especially, "Productions Mineral, Vegetable and Animal," casts the interior as a subject of philosophical discourse, and as Jefferson abstracted space, he also would define his own role as the American philosophe. The immediate cause for this performance was a popular but weakening argument in Europe: that the New World was inherently unhealthy and that all productions of natural and human life survived there on a smaller scale. To refute this case Jefferson would marshal evidence favoring American environs, with the more significant pieces of evidence coming from the trans-Appalachian West. A primary point of reference were the remains of a "mammoth" or mastodon that had recently been found in an Ohio Valley tar pit and whose size should suffice to "have rescued the earth it inhabited" (47). Scientific discussions look to the interior. While gathering material for his book, Jefferson asked the revolutionary general George Rogers Clark to make secure the bones and teeth of a mastodon at Fort Pitt, where they could be held for safekeeping. (The correspondence was carried by none other than Daniel Boone.).[10] In a related frontier encounter, *Notes on the State of Virginia* introduces the mastodon through an interview with native Americans. A group of Delaware warriors was in Richmond on public business, and Jefferson (then governor) would ask them about the remains of exhumed bones along the Ohio. "Their chief speaker immediately put himself into an attitude of oratory," Jefferson explains and then proceeds with a legend of the mastodon. An entire herd reportedly ranged the Middle West, but when the mastodons killed other mammals, the "Great Man" angrily struck them with a lightning bolt. Only one survived, and he fled across the Great Lakes, "where he is living at this day" (43). This episode leads into a review of other fossil deposits, a comparison of the mastodon and the elephant, and a meditation on the health of American environs versus the position of the sun.

How then does an author negotiate between metropolitan discourse and a border region? Through the mastodon, Jefferson begins an argument that registers evidence collected on the frontier but that leads him into a transAtlantic debate. The remainder of query 6 (except for a few loose pages) attacks the hypothesis that American environs were inferior to Europe due to an unequal distribution of the sun's warmth. Known as the heliotropic theory, the case for unequal climes gave the American philosophe a means for identifying with the continent that he inhabited and a point of patriotic attack against a leading naturalist of the day, George Louis Leclerc, the Comte de Buffon. Buffon apparently needed to see mastodon fossils. He had argued in his forty-four-volume *Histoire naturelle* that "La nature vivante est beaucoup moins agissante, beaucoup moins forte"—nature is less active and strong—in some parts of the globe than in others. The planet was divided into four quadrants, and the rate of dessication, or drying of the earth after the deluge, determined the pace of evolution in each quadrant. On the paucity of North American species, the French naturalist would surmise that "there must be something" in the New World "that opposes the aggrandisement of animated nature." He concedes that "when the lands are cultivated, the forests cut down, the rivers confined within proper channels, and the marshes drained," the country "will become the most fruitful, healthy and opulent in the world," but because of its later discovery, North America would lag behind Europe.[11] Buffon's readers later turned this logic to the indigenous people of America. Cornelius De Pauw's *Recherches philosophique sur les Americains* moves from horses and cows and such to the "savage," who "living in the state of nature can only be a brute, incapable of progress." The Abbé Raynal (to whom Crèvecoeur dedicated *Letters from an American Farmer*) similarly argues in his massive *Histoire des deux Indies* that native Americans are "degraded in their national constitution, in their stature, in their way of life, and in their understanding, which is but little advanced in the arts of civilization." Such arguments would shape how Euroamerican intellectuals would write about themselves and a country that had only recently declared independence from England. They argued a point of national pride. Buffon and Raynal were translated into several languages—the *Histoire des deux Indies* going through thirty-seven editions between 1770 and 1820—and the philosophes would provide the standard fodder for entire histories and geographies. The circulation of their ideas may explain Jefferson's fixation with the mastodon, with what he more appropriately calls elsewhere the "Animal Incognitum of Ohio," or for that matter, with anything big.[12]

Rather than weighing out the winners and losers of this (now thankfully obscure) scientific debate, I will suggest that the *querelle d'Amerique* (as it was known) provided Jefferson with an opportunity to define a narrative self—one who then presided over the construction of an American space through Enlightenment discourse. In a strange footnote to *Notes on the State of Virginia*, the editor William Peden takes it upon himself to defend Jefferson's cause; a lengthy review explains how with "meticulous care" Jefferson "demolished Buffon's thesis" (268n). But a closer read of query 6 against the currents of eighteenth-century intellectual debate suggests that the heliotropic theory was ready for demolition and that it provided—most immediately—a vehicle for asserting one's identity as an *American* naturalist. Scientific interests addressed provincial anxieties. Despite the continued popularity of Buffon and Raynal, the principal proponents of the heliotropic theory had already distanced themselves from their earlier statements by the time of Jefferson's attack. European perceptions of America had been improving in intellectual circles since the 1760s, and the reputation of Benjamin Franklin, the repeal of the Stamp Act, and finally the Revolution transformed the French view from condescension to near euphoria. Buffon renounced Cornelius De Pauw during the War for Independence, Raynal revised the *Histoire des deux Indies* soon after, and radicals such as Richard Price and the Marquis de Condorcet would present the continent as a potential redeemer of mankind. Many intellectuals would fix their attention to a rising nation, not a degenerate clime.[13]

The slow but visible change in European attitudes allows Jefferson to define the role of the American philosophe, and it shapes his argument in unexpected ways. The mind that gets "put on display" (to borrow Breitwieser's terms) claims to favor particulars over unifying systems. Jefferson attacks Buffon on the basis of a greater familiarity with immediate evidence. "Our only appeal to such questions is to experience," he explains of Buffon's hypothesis. Yet the effort to refute another's theory will lead to the abandonment of an empirical base. Query 6 advances fact over fancy or system, while engaging experience toward patriotic ends. As the centerpiece of his case against the *Histoire naturelle*, for example, Jefferson prepares a series of tables that compare the weights of animals in Europe and America (figure 4.1). The tables would bury the Comte de Buffon with numbers. The third (animals domesticated in both continents) measures a European cow, at 763 pounds, versus its American equivalent, a Rhode Island bullock that was slaughtered at 2,500 pounds. The wild boar, mocked as the "elephant of Europe," appears alongside the tapir, "the elephant of America" (51–57). And so on. But a blank space next to "Mammoth" at the head of his "Comparative View of the Quadrupeds of Europe and America" suggests how the

A comparative View of the Quadrupeds of Europe and of America.

I. Aboriginals of both.

	Europe. lb.	America. lb.
Mammoth		
Buffalo. Bison		*1800
White bear. Ours blanc		
Caribou. Renne		
Bear. Ours	153.7	*410
Elk. Elan. Orignal, palmated		
Red deer. Cerf	288.8	*273
Fallow deer. Daim	167.8	
Wolf. Loup	69.8	
Roe. Chevreuil	56.7	
Glutton. Glouton. Carcajou		
Wild cat. Chat sauvage		†30
Lynx. Loup cervier	25.	
Beaver. Castor	18.5	*45
Badger. Blaireau	13.6	
Red Fox. Renard	13.5	
Grey Fox. Isatis		
Otter. Loutre	8.9	†12
Monax. Marmotte	6.5	
Vison. Fouine	2.8	
Hedgehog. Herisson	2.2	
Martin. Marte	1.9 oz.	†6
Water rat. Rat d'eau	7.5	
Wesel. Belette	2.2	oz.
Flying squirrel. Polatouche	2.2	†4
Shrew mouse. Musaraigne	1.	

II. Aboriginals of one only.

EUROPE.	lb.	AMERICA.	lb.
Sanglier. Wild boar	280.	Tapir	534.*
Mouflon. Wild sheep	56.	Elk, round horned	†450.*
Bouquetin. Wildgoat		Puma	
Lievre. Hare	7.6	Jaguar	218.
Lapin. Rabbet	3.4	Cabiai	109.
Putois. Polecat	3.3	Tamanoir	109.
Genette	3.1	Tamandua	65.4
Desman. Muskrat	oz.	Cougar of N. Amer.	75.
Ecureuil. Squirrel	12.	Cougar of S. America	59.4
Hermine. Ermin	8.2	Ocelot	
Rat. Rat	7.5	Pecari	46.3
Loirs.	3.1	Jaguaret	43.6
Lerot. Dormouse	1.8	Alco	
Taupe. Mole	1.2	Lama	
Hamster	.9	Paco	
Zisel		Paca	32.7
Leming		Serval	
Souris. Mouse	.6	Sloth. Unau.	27¼
		Saricovienne	
		Kincajou	
		Tatou Kabassou	21.8
		Urson. Urchin	
		Raccoon. Raton	16.5
		Coati	
		Coendou	16.3
		Sloth. Aï	13.
		Sapajou Ouarini	
		Sapajou Coaita	9.8
		Tatou Encubert	
		Tatou Apar	
		Tatou Cachica	7.
		Little Coendou	6.5
		Opossum. Sarigue	

Figure 4.1. "A comparative View of the Quadrupeds of Europe and America," from Thomas Jefferson's *Notes on the State of Virginia* (1787). Courtesy John Carter Brown Library, Brown University.

polemic had overwhelmed Jefferson's earlier deference to "experience." On one hand, he would maintain that the "Mammoth … should have sufficed to have rescued the earth it inhabited and the atmosphere it breathed from the imputation of impotence in the conception and nourishment of animal life on a large scale"; that in the New World, "La nature vivante est beaucoup moins agissante, beaucoup moins forte" (47). As evidence, however, Jefferson provides very slight sources: a legend collected from the Delawares, a fossilized tooth, and the assumption, after Linnaeus, that an "œconomy of nature" rendered extinction impossible (53). In short, the beginning from particulars had created a point of entry for the American philosophe, but as the target against Buffon became clearer, that recourse to experience would diminish. The result is an argument for American civilization whose basis was both imagined and grounded in the scripture of empirical fact.

One finds the same process of vacating and reconstituting a subject that defined the Evans maps and the same distancing from a middle ground that riddled "Susquehannah." Jefferson may operate from an identification with the continent, but as his adopted persona simply internalizes European perceptions of the New World, the story of the continent that he provides is largely an inversion of Enlightenment models — not one rooted in nature or locale. This act of transferring the subject becomes especially clear when the subject changes from the natural environment to the continent's human population. The argument having been patriotic from the beginning (as the negligible scientific contributions of Jefferson's case against Buffon suggest), query 6 closes by comparing cultures on both sides of the Atlantic. Jefferson catalogs the early successes of the United States in government, commerce, science, and the arts, much as he would list the weights of cattle, wild boar, and elk. He predicts a rising glory in America, where the sun of "philosophy [having] crossed the channel" may shed its beams over the United States (65). Turning the same cataloging impulse to indigenous people, he cites the authority of "my own knowledge" and launches into the historical racism of the Abbé Raynal. Native Americans are brave, "affectionate," and possess a keen sensibility, Jefferson explains. Of their "address in war we have multiplied proofs," and as evidence, he cites a famous speech by an Ohio trader and war chief known as Logan, or Tahgahjute (59–62). The example of Indian oratory suggests what the race might accomplish once exposed to European models. "Before we condemn the Indians of this continent as wanting genius," Jefferson therefore reminds his readers, "we must consider that letters have not yet been introduced among them. Were we to compare them in their present state with the Europeans North of the Alps, when the Roman arms and arts first crossed those mountains, the comparison would be unequal, because at that time, those parts of Europe were swarming with numbers; because numbers produce emulation, and multiply the chances of improvement, and one improvement begets another" (63). One recalls the predictions made for the Ohio Valley by the first settlers of Marietta. Having designed their town around ancient mounds, leading citizens speculated about the continent's capacity to support a civilization there. The monuments were interpreted as evidence of an earlier great race (of course, not the one then inhabiting the Ohio Valley) that had reached a pinnacle before disappearing. The burial mounds left by an indigenous empire were evidence of a history that the United States would repeat.

This anticipation of "one improvement" begetting another qualifies *Notes on the State of Virginia*, more than any other work of its time, as the literary equivalent to the western ordinances. Both are the product of the same ideological geography. Jefferson helped draft the blueprint for an expanding republic, and he would address Buffon on the same terms—with the understanding of a civilization unfolding across space. The Ohio legislation sought to graft order onto a border region through a system that began with new surveys. Settlers were to transform forests into farmland, building states on the frontier *from the fallen tree*. The rhetorical risk of claiming the "mammoth" (or for likening animal weights to a piece of native oratory and Benjamin Franklin's scientific discoveries) would result from this desire to privilege potential over the products of the actual terrain. The timing of *Notes on the State of Virginia*, moreover, suggests how easily nationalism could supplant experience or nature. Regardless of the new evidence that Jefferson supplied, Buffon never answered his critics—he was just a few years from death—and he had recanted the heliotropic theory anyway; the attack on a naturalist at the end of his career seems almost unnecessary.[14] Yet Jefferson's contemporaries cited *Notes on the State of Virginia* widely. It articulated the ideological drive behind early national environmentalism and became a standard reference: For some, it was an easy sourcebook for attacks during Jefferson's presidential campaigns, and for genteel readers like Solomon Drowne, it was an *Opus omnigena literatura imbutuns*—a work imbued with genius of all kinds.[15] The book expressed a desire shared by lawmakers to show how the interior would accommodate a new nation, how republican principles could be grafted onto a place, how (like Thomas Pownall's incomplete surveys) abstraction removed republican plans from the physical terrain. And here lies the paradox that one finds in almost any narrative of improvement: The products and people in a backcountry setting appear to be on the constant brink of disappearance. The rhetoric of progress would eclipse the nominal subject, the "mammoth" would never materialize, and the "living Indian" would be moved to the margins. As the public narrative of "Susquehannah" removed Crèvecoeur from the very country upon which his work was purportedly set, Jefferson too would open an unsustainable exchange between discourse and locale. Query 6 assumed that the "mammoth" was still alive, even though settlers in the trans-Appalachian West had only exhumed fossils from the ground. The same argument also would make predictions for native Americans upon a reading of Roman history, while the interests of native Americans fell behind the expediencies of an overarching "benevolent plan."

Jefferson, Logan, and the Vanishing Native

The persona of the American philosophe in *Notes on the State of Virginia* at once voices national prerogatives, while assuming a rhetorical advantage through the knowledge of particulars, through a willingness to front experience. The narrative voice therefore mediates transactions between ideology and locale, and through that voice, the products of the land are recast for their political value. Nowhere is this dialogic of improvement and disappearance more visible than in the example of Logan, who in an instance of the "carrying across" that Eric Cheyfitz describes, provides evidence that native Americans could potentially equal Europeans in the verbal arts. The example is an especially rich one because it turns Jefferson to one of the principle products of the middle ground, the council speech, and the way that native American oratory gets framed in the context of query 6 provides a point for unpacking his relationship to the frontier. Ethnohistorian Nancy L. Hagedorn maintains that "the Indian conference" represented the "product *par excellence* of European contact," and as the previous chapter noted, native-white relations were freighted with the politics of translation. Colonial officials found themselves dependent upon native protocol, and success or failure rested upon their ability to adapt the language of an Other. Translators were valued on both sides, and these intermediaries, or "go betweens," could negotiate across linguistic as well as cultural divides. Documents such as the *Treaty Held with the Indians* between Pennsylvania and the Six Nations record how different interests converged in a shared forum — and where those interests could divide. Colonial savants such as Benjamin Franklin (and before Franklin, Cadwallader Colden) established a precedent for writers such as Jefferson, emphasizing the literary value of treaty documents. But as the critic Arnold Krupat notes, "Indian texts are always the product of a collaboration," making it "useful to know, as far as we can, just how they were made," and the politics of representation in forest diplomacy were especially shifty.[16] This wariness leads one to an important question: What were the circumstances of production behind Logan's speech, and upon what terms does his voice enter *Notes on the State of Virginia*?

Jefferson's account strains in the "translation" of border experience for metropolitan tastes and suggests (once again) an erosion of the middle ground in literary portrayals of the West. In terms of immediate origins, the speech came from the trans-Appalachian West, which had been opened to exploitation and abuse by the Fort Stanwix Treaty of 1768 (see chapter 1). Briefly, a party of land-hungry white frontiersmen had murdered the métis family of the Mingo (or western Seneca) Logan in 1774. The crime culminated in this purported speech. For Jefferson, however, Logan's eloquence provided an indicator of innate gifts, and following the lead that Colden and Franklin established, he would liken Logan to Demosthenes and Cicero. Query 6 quotes the speech in full. "I appeal to any man," the noble savage asks,

> if he ever entered Logan's cabin hungry, and he gave him not meat; if he ever came cold and naked, and he clothed him not. During the course of the last long and bloody war, Logan remained idle in his cabin, an advocate for peace. Such was my love for the whites, that my countrymen pointed as they passed and said, "Logan is the friend of white men." I had even thought to have lived with you, but for the injuries of one man. Col. Cresap, the last spring, in cold blood, and unprovoked, murdered all the relations of Logan, not sparing even my women and children. There runs not a drop of my blood in the veins of any living creature. This called on me for revenge. I have sought it: I have killed many: I have fully glutted my vengeance. For my country, I rejoice at the beams of peace. But do not harbour a thought that mine is the joy of fear. Logan never felt fear. He will not turn on his heel to save his life. Who is there to mourn for Logan?—Not one. (63)

The language is impassioned, powerfully measured through repetition and parallel syntax. Yet as Arnold Krupat suggests, readers should pay attention to modes of production, and this speech is no exception, especially since it probably did not come from Logan. Charges at the end of the eighteenth century revealed this to be the invention of local journalists. Before discussing the implications of Jefferson's text, however, I first must backtrack and return to Logan's frontier.

Colonial officials repeatedly note that the "Western tribes" were "exasperated" with the Iroquois after the Fort Stanwix Treaty of 1768. The Shawnees began to circulate war belts, and they were "very much alarmed at the numbers who go from Virginia . . . in pursuit of new settlements." Even while some council leaders promised peace, few could contain the war chiefs from the Ohio nations. The more militant leaders, it was reported, refused to "be kicked around Like Doggs." A border dispute between Pennsylvania and Virginia complicated matters further, as both sites claimed the forks of the Ohio River (site of Fort Pitt), and their governors were "at open War about Lands."[17] In short, the region was kindled for battle: Two rival but expanding states claimed the same territory, natives resented the advancing settlements, and authority on all sides was locally held. Rumors were flying. Into this troubled scene entered a Virginia surveyor named Michael Cresap, who received word of attacks at Wheeling, and Cresap joined a character named Daniel Greathouse to lead a retaliation party. The path of revenge took them to a trading post on Yellow Creek that was run by Logan. The village ironically was a site of the middle ground, where cultures intermingled in more peaceful ways. People from many backgrounds traded there, and several languages were spoken. Logan was of mixed parentage, the son of Weiser's native partner, Shickellamy (which would suggest he was versed in forest diplomacy), and he had taken his name from the prominent Philadelphian James Logan.[18] But Cresap and Greathouse represented a growing culture of Indian hating in a region that also was growing, and with the Wheeling rumors calling for blood, they killed thirteen innocent people. Logan sought and found retribution. He recruited a group of Shawnees and Mingos, took thirteen Virginia scalps, and then (with the calculated act of compensation complete) laid down his hatchet.

The exchange of lives meant different things to different groups. For a Seneca, retaliation was an act of mourning. The soul of a murdered individual could not find peace in the next world until some measure was taken to compensate for the loss—either in adoption, torture, or murder. For whites anxious to assert western claims, meanwhile, the scalping provided a pretense for invasion. John Murray, the Earl of Dunmore and governor of Virginia, saw the murders as an occasion to assert Virginia's presence in a region where Pennsylvania also presumed to hold a claim. (Dunmore's investments in western land probably influenced his decision, and the coming Revolution probably exacerbated the need for a diversion—the House of Burgesses had just voted to close in sympathy with the Boston Tea Party.) He donned a kilt and led an inglorious campaign into Kentucky that came to be known as Dunmore's War. The invasion ended quickly, culminating with Dunmore's victory at the Battle of Point Pleasant in 1774 and a forced cession by the Shawnees. But colonial commentators, British officials, and patriots alike recognized the war for what it was: a self-serving abuse of power that sacrificed peace for private gain. William Johnson blasted the "imbecility of American government"; the Earl of Dartmouth wrote that the war was "not only a violation of the King's right but diametrically opposed to and inconsistent with those policies that have hitherto operated against settlement in such situations." From the widespread criticism of the war came Logan's speech. Supposedly, the métis trader refused to attend the peace negotiations, delivering his words instead through an interpreter, and the address began to circulate through the colonies as an indirect critique of Virginia's colonial governor. For the revolutionaries especially, it represented a blast against Dunmore's indiscretion. Members of the Continental Congress regarded his arrogant campaign as a threat to the common good. They believed that the invasion of Kentucky (much like the Yankee-Pennamite affair) was an unneeded "jarr" to native-white relations.[19]

The example that appears in *Notes on the State of Virginia* was hardly neutral then but was embedded within the revolutionary debates about sovereignty, public discourse, and therefore space. Eighteenth-century political theorists believed that true republicanism was possible only among native Americans, with oratory serving as an exemplum and foundation of the classical ideal. James Madison, who produced the first known report of Logan's speech, bristled at the Kentucky campaign: He maintained that the Shawnees had "been grossly magnified and misrepresented" and that land companies "found their Interest" in Dunmore's War. Critical of the indiscretion (and whether by coincidence or in a direct critique), he sent Logan's speech to the Philadelphia patriot William Bradford. Bradford in turn admired the "nervous and untutor'd eloquence." He compared Logan to Pliny and passed the account on to his brother, who edited the *Pennsylvania Journal*. Publishers from New York to Virginia picked up the story from Bradford's paper, and the Logan episode was added to a growing list of grievances against the Crown.[20] Jefferson himself was silent about Dunmore's War, but as a member of the Virginia House of Delegates, he chaired a committee to reconcile the boundary dispute with Pennsylvania. A petition for amnesty that he signed anticipates his decision on the Susquehannah Company. As "representatives of two of the colonies united," the document pleads, "we think it our duty to remove ... every obstacle that may prevent her sons from co-operating" to the "great and important end" of the Revolution.[21] One such "obstacle," the ambiguity of colonial charters in the back regions, had justified the invasion of Kentucky. In this report, one can detect the emerging geographic component in Jeffersonian political thought. The assertion of state claims (which also led to Dunmore's War) undermined public order on the border regions. From the Pennsylvania-Virginia controversy to the Ordinance of 1784, Jefferson would argue for the reconciliation of a boundary dispute through a recourse to the union or to law. Over the distractions of partisanship, he advocated the creation of a federal reserve.

These efforts to legislate a geographic order over the mountains distinguished, in the revolutionary imagination at least, the new empire of liberty from the colonial era. Dunmore's War marked a low point in imperial policy and a nadir in the decline that followed the Albany Congress and the Fort Stanwix Treaty. The Earl of Hillsborough wrote that "every day discovers more and more the fatal policy of departing from the line prescribed by the proclamation of 1763"; Johnson's acceptance of the boundary that the Iroquois proposed was "inconsistent with every true principle of polity and could only have the effect to produce a general Indian war." The United States experimented with new mechanisms for territorial expansion, however, and the attempt to reconcile a new earth against native-white relations was a problem over which national identity was defined. How would the revolutionaries maintain "just and peaceful relations with the Indian tribes," as historian Francis Paul Prucha asks, while "allowing (if not encouraging) the expansion of white society from the Atlantic coast?"[22] Jefferson acted as if a solution rested in the reordering of boundaries and in economic development within those boundaries. A series of separate but related cases uphold a "common good" over colonial claims, implicitly supporting a public geography over partisanship. The response to the Virginia-Pennsylvania affair and the Susquehannah Company fiasco, as well as Jefferson's draft for the Ordinance of 1784, all make recourse to a political or legal body that could mediate local faction. These spatially grounded politics contrast starkly to Dunmore's arrogant invasion of Kentucky. Read within the context of prior abuse and presented as one more piece of evidence in a case for improvement, Logan comes to link Jefferson's political and literary activity. Oratory would provide a count against both Buffon and the colonial governor, suggesting alternatively that (with the introduction of arts and letters) native Americans would adopt European practices of civilization themselves. This sign of a capacity for literary production and therefore progress, with its basis in eighteenth-century aesthetic and political theory, provides the substitute for Dunmore's inglorious campaign.

Where, then, does that leave Logan, once he enters *Notes on the State of Virginia*? Since at least midcentury, treaty proceedings had subtly registered power relations between native and white groups. The transcripts especially would mark the terms upon which different people came together, and as the subject was often land, where their interests divided. The printed versions of an oral tradition were hybrid texts, products of a border culture that was neither indigenous nor Euroamerican but the result of an (often grudging) collaboration. For the revolutionaries, however, Logan embodied a proof of national mission because he exhibited the potential for "improvement"; he was the truly republican persona that also evidenced how the continent could support a narrative of progress across space. As the product of a widely criticized war, moreover, the speech distanced that republican ideal from imperial corruption and neglect. Yet this translation, this carrying across, played into plans for colonization as Logan became less a figure of the middle ground—a trader of mixed parentage—and more of a symbolic presence. Native Americans presumably had the innate qualities, the pathos demonstrated by a sentimental oration, to adopt European standards of civilization. As Bernard Sheehan writes, revolutionary environmental theory maintained that a native could "abandon his way of life and become a white man"; historian Rhys Isaac agrees, noting that "the story . . . of the future greatness of America as a virtuous farmer's republic silently but ruthlessly continued the story of these Indians' dispossession."[23] Neoclassical models of ecological and social change (the idea that verbal gifts would evolve with the introduction of letters) would nudge a race up the chain of creation; at the same time, this revolutionary ideology would distance whites from a recent and violent colonial past. The figure that Jefferson cites was not a real person who acted upon individual agency but a metaphor for what went wrong under Dunmore and a suggestion for what path the United States should follow. The attack on a peace-loving, noble savage epitomized why colonial expansion had run amok—and how the independent states would settle the same frontier. But as the product of a middle ground becomes the emblem of a new nation, the "living Indian" disappears from the text. This disappearance leads *Notes on the State of Virginia* to a revealing postscript.

Conclusion: "Wherefore the Forgery?"

The problem begins from the fundamentally colonial act that I have been tracing: the negotiation between metropolitan culture and a middle landscape, as one seeks to establish one's own group as the proper subject of the land. In early national environmental discourse, voices from the middle ground move to the margins or dissipate. Arnold Krupat notes of native American literature (but implicitly any text) that "all discourse is textual or scriptive, and it is precisely the nature of script that it can never be scripture, fixed in its meaning as the spoken word is—erroneously, of course— claimed to be." For Jefferson, the empirical was itself scripture (as Myra Jehlen observed, "the continent that was the modern spirit's flesh was also its word"), and the rhetorical grounding in experience would eventually collapse into figure. The word would unfix itself from place because script "can never be scripture." As Jefferson attempts to translate what is "fixed" in the land, then, his literary effort appropriately unravels in the spoken word. In a strange but predictable coda to the book, political enemies challenged the veracity of Logan's speech. The point of contention today matters little (whether blame for the massacre fell on Cresap or Greathouse), but the charges of forgery potentially invalidated Jefferson's literary model of republican expansion. What fascinates is how Jefferson dealt with those charges. He researched the controversy and collected the responses into an appendix that he published in 1801, making the flat claim that "I have given it as I have received it." In this tedious packet of affidavits (where at least one competing example was silently omitted), the need for evidence disappears and the conclusion steps around the pretense of relying upon verifiable fact.[24] Jefferson responds to the charges that white journalists made up the speech by asking, "wherefore the forgery? Whether Logan's or mine, it would still have been American. I should indeed consult my own fame if the suggestion, that this speech is mine, were suffered to be believed. He would have a just right to be proud who could with truth claim that composition. But it is none of mine; and I yield it to whom it is due" (230). In a sense Jefferson was right: Logan represented a hybrid culture that was neither Euroamerican nor native American but a synthesis of several groups. *Notes on the State of Virginia* does not concern itself with the "living Indian," however. The 1801 concession instead accedes to the wedge between theory and fact that gives the book its shape, while distancing the author from the very place and people that he purports to describe.

Experience, or nature, disappears in the attempt to base political identity in the land, and Jefferson commits his own act of usurpation by referencing a native voice. The recourse to the verifiable would mean to locate a new social order in the physical terrain; by advancing a civilization in the "continent's permanent contours and structures," as Jehlen observed, the author "places the emerging social structures beyond debate." But Jefferson's 1801 appendix abandons experience and allows for a conflation between narration and the thing itself—"wherefore the forgery?" he asks. The slip has historical resonance, as the substitution of an imagined ideal for a "living Indian" anticipates the "benevolent plan" that Henry Knox formulated around this time. Native Americans (in Knox's formulation) would recognize the virtues of Euroamerican agriculture and abandon their former systems of land management, thereby making cessions an afterthought. Bernard W. Sheehan calls this strategy "a willful failure of intellect."[25] Republican environmental and social theory failed to allow for the independent agency of an Other, and the "living Indian" disappears as a new history for the continent was imagined. Revolutionary authors did the same thing. "Susquehannah" presents the case of Job Chillaway, the Delaware intermediary who apparently fared well in a white world. Crèvecoeur's plot of progress across space, however, makes no allowance for this figure of a middle ground, and the Delaware land agent is moved to the textual margins. A similar instance occurs in Jefferson's treatment of native oratory. Logan serves as the model for a classical ideal, but the figurative import of his speech displaces the actual person of the speaker. In the final analysis, Jefferson concedes, Logan's actual existence was immaterial. The question "wherefore the forgery?" points to the inevitable dislocation as the American philosophe establishes his own voice as equally native to the continent.

In often complicated turns of narration, the authors discussed through the remainder of this book would wrestle with the problem of establishing a basis of entitlement for one's group to American natural resources. A plot of improvement across space served as the starting point for most narratives. Writers needed to reconcile the usual prescriptions for change, however, against existing conceptions of space; the rhetoric of a new earth would be negotiated against a middle ground. By portraying nature or natives as the raw material for an expanding civilization, Jefferson and Crèvecoeur distanced their accounts from the very settings they presumed to describe. But concessions like the 1801 appendix provide a textual crevice from which we may explore further the tensions of early national environmental literature vis-à-vis native peoples. Part 3 of this book explores how the standard space–time frame could sometimes veer into more complicated play between competing discourses and senses of the land. The ideological geography of the new republic did not necessarily break so much as fracture and bend, and a pastoral—relinquishment to one's physical setting—or local understandings of the environment were negotiated against the usual prescriptions for change. The effect was a literature that might dwell less on imported cultures and more upon the interactions with existing people at a given place. But even then, the idea of *place* was never as stable as authors wished it to be.

PART III

Protégés

The initial trip into that far northern landscape is perceived by the explorer as something from which one might derive prestige, money, social advantage, or notable awards and adulation. Although these intentions are not lost sight of on subsequent trips, they are never so purely held or so highly regarded as they are before the first journey begins. They are tempered by a mounting sense of consternation and awe. It is as though the land slowly works its way into the man and by virtue of its character eclipses these motives. The land becomes large, alive like an animal; it humbles him in a way he cannot pronounce.
—BARRY LOPEZ

COLLABORATION, INCORPORATION, AND ENVIRONMENTAL DISCOURSE

LEWIS AND CLARK, JANE COLDEN

Was That a Hoh-host or a Yâck-kâh?

THE DIFFERENCE BETWEEN a philosophical exercise for Thomas Jefferson and experiences in the field for Lewis and Clark were clear two years into their famous expedition, in May 1806, when a hunter brought a dead bear and two cubs into camp. Jefferson had instructed Meriwether Lewis to describe "the animals of the country," and the appearance of three specimens, each with different-colored fur, prompted an investigation into ursine taxonomy. The puzzle proved to be a welcome distraction, for members of the Corps of Discovery were bored. They had left their soggy camp on the Pacific Coast prematurely—before the salmon began to run and while snow was still blocking Lolo Pass in the Bitterroot Mountains. With little else to do, they learned about the region's environment and forged particularly close ties with the local natives, the Nez Perce, who befriended the

121

company for reasons of their own. The nearby Blackfeet Sioux and Atsinas had acquired weapons from Canadian traders, which meant that the Nez Perce needed guns to hunt and to protect their villages. Self-defense on one side, and a forced delay on the other yielded deep cultural contact: As ethnohistorian James P. Ronda notes, the shared interests "ranged from trade and medicine to sport and sex." The month-long camp proved to be a bonanza for natural history as well. Lewis and Clark described a woodpecker (killed by the hunter John Shields), a staple of the western diet known as *cous* (a root resembling the sweet potato), and the "horned" lizard or toad. The Nez Perces helped Lewis and Clark classify the varieties of western bears. Variations in fur color had thrown off the white explorers, but after consulting with his neighbors, Lewis concluded that the "Indian distinction" between a "Hoh-host" (a grizzly with longer claws) and a Yâck-kâh (a less aggressive tree climber with shorter claws) was indeed correct.[1]

The reliance upon native taxonomy indicates the amount of collaboration in even the most imperial of texts. The Lewis and Clark *Journals* epitomizes that mix of expansionism and science that Mary Louise Pratt calls the "anti-conquest." In an age when the nation literally was defining itself, a journey to the headwaters of the Missouri River (marking the extent of the Louisiana Purchase), over the western mountains, and back provided an unprecedented occasion for self-canonization on the national stage. The image of a hero-naturalist, a republican self writ over the land, survives to this day; contemporary critics, by the same token, counter the myths by treating the *Journals* as a failed exercise in rhetorical authority.[2] An accepted reading emphasizes the hopes for a Northwest Passage and notes how vain expectations preceded any real knowledge of the physical terrain. Humbled by the wilds of America, the "beautiful machine" or the "republican plan" breaks down. Yet even these readings of heroism-to-hubris limit themselves to an imperial logic. The fixation upon epic ambition (and dashed hopes) obscures how the Corps of Discovery processed and came to know their surroundings. Where many groups rejected the expedition, some pelting stones at the explorers as they passed by, others such as the Nez Perce met the invaders with an eye for self-advancement. Any conclusions about the Hoh-host and Yâck-kâh would depend upon a taxonomy that already existed.[3]

The *Journals* unfold from this paradox: negotiating Enlightenment discourse against experiences on local settings, with local people. Ideas of nature took shape against an open frontier. A slightly different story emerges, in other words, from the one I traced in previous chapters. "Susquehannah" collapsed because Crèvecoeur sought to explain a British-Iroquois attack through the plot of progress-across-space; the gap next to Jefferson's mammoth (and the question "wherefore the forgery?") revealed the rhetorical ends of an empirical pretense. Cast over a contested domain, the *natural* would seek to claim the continent as a national subject, while discourse eclipsed the populations and places that authors purported to describe. Ecocritic David Mazel regards this implicit appropriation as a cornerstone of American literary environmentalism: in his formula, "*interpretation = whiteness + masculinity = ownership.*"[4] But to emphasize only the rhetoric of improvement (and that rhetoric certainly served as a shorthand for ownership) potentially misses the various forms of social engagement that pervaded eighteenth-century environmental literature. Writers incorporated indigenous or folk knowledge as they prescribed changes in the land; they collaborated with others and triangulated what they learned against resident populations, even as they romanticized the beauty of an emptied wilderness. The negotiation between externalized textual authority and remote settings was a hallmark of Enlightenment science—and the context of empire made that negotiation still more vexed. Lewis and Clark represented the western extension of an accumulative culture, a literalization of Jefferson's prospect, and earlier protégés such as Jane Colden and William Bartram (both the children of famous naturalists) faced a similar paradox. Their texts marked the transfer between existing communities, or community-held knowledge, and an imperial scientific culture that fetishized individual achievement. Even as interpretation presumed possession, a point that Mazel rightly notes, discovery would necessitate a certain amount of relinquishment to one's immediate surroundings. The following chapters examine the element of collaboration, as well incorporation and relinquishment, in narratives that measured backcountry settings against a culture whose center was elsewhere.

The primacy of the frontier raises one final consideration. For authors in the early republic, environmental discourse unfolded alongside federal Indian policies. As the exercises in geography and natural history brought explorers into contact with native peoples, the literature would weigh representations of nature against human populations. This process in some sense began with *Notes on the State of Virginia*, a book that provided a blueprint for federal policies. As the military actions in Ohio and the obnoxious treaties that dictated one-sided demands yielded bloodshed and further expense, Secretary of War Henry Knox forged what came to be called the "benevolent plan." His aim was to continue expansion while preserving the principles upon which the republic was founded. The United States would move west and bring further "improvements" to those environs, Knox speculated, leading native Americans to make "new purchases for small considerations." Natives would willingly cede land, in this circular logic, because they would have adopted Euroamerican agriculture already.[5] The strategy failed on account of homogenization; it swept the tremendous range of indigenous cultures and interests under the rigid paradigm of "civilized" and "savage," and by the early nineteenth century, the calls for improvement were drafted into arguments of dispossession. (A "benevolent" position in the Jacksonian mind-set was to "protect" Indians from corruption by pushing them west, where they had less contact with whites, and seizing tribal lands.) While softened only by intentions, policy makers in the early republic provided a slightly different case: National identity was imagined over the continent and alongside native-white relations. Authors would therefore define their ideas and understanding of the land amid fluid, varied—sometimes welcome, often hostile—exchanges with the existing inhabitants of a middle ground.

Fractures in an Imperial Narrative

Without question, Thomas Jefferson's plans for an expedition to the headwaters of the Missouri (and beyond the jurisdiction of the Louisiana Purchase) exercised the political and cultural ambitions of the early republic. The Corps of Discovery performed a tactical exercise—establishing borders, assessing resources, scouting new avenues for trade—through a territory that was freighted with expectation. The 1803 purchase raised debates about geography and public policy that recalled the Ohio ordinances and that measured national identity on a continental scale. Conservative members of Congress criticized the covert purchase, fretting that the government could not contain an overextended republic; others expressed relief that the union had acquired a buffer against meddling European empires; still others saw a space for Indian removal. In the public press, jubilant propagandists cast the region as a "field" for the future "harvest of human happiness."[6] Meriwether Lewis shared this latter view. Since 1801, he had served as the president's personal assistant, and in preparation for the journey, Jefferson arranged a series of tutorials for him with leading minds of the American Enlightenment. Lewis studied natural and "Indian history" under Benjamin Smith Barton, astronomy under Andrew Ellicott and Robert Patterson, and medicine under Caspar Wistar and Benjamin Rush. Jefferson then penned a detailed set of instructions (playing the role of François Marbois himself) that asked for data about the region's geography, river drainage, flora and fauna, minerals, and geologic activity; and about the demographics, cultures, and commercial interests of native Americans.[7] By their return, Lewis, Clark, and the enlisted men who could write accumulated a massive archive—over one million words and almost thirty manuscript notebooks—that advanced an expanding republic by providing concrete information about the Far West.

But a problem with preconceptions, an empiricism before the fact, was manifested in the instructions that Jefferson issued to Lewis. In terms of geography, Jefferson held to a quaintly neoclassical belief that the eastern and western watersheds of America mirrored each other, thereby allowing Lewis and Clark to cross the western mountains as one might trek over the Appalachians. This simplification led to troublesome assertions about the company's route. "The object of your mission," Jefferson wrote, "is to explore the Missouri river, & such principal stream of it, as, by it's course and communication with the waters of the Pacific ocean, whether the Columbia, Oregan, Colorado or any other river may offer the most direct & practicable water communication across this continent for the purposes of commerce." The vague understanding leads to tricky syntax, with the ambiguity fudged by an ampersand. Jefferson instructs the Corps of Discovery to trace the "principal stream" of the Missouri and the most "practicable" route—which assumes that there *was* a "practicable" route and that this route (at least from the east) was the Missouri. The instructions cast an equally overoptimistic view toward native Americans. Lewis and Clark should "treat them in the most friendly & conciliatory manner which their own conduct will admit" and "satisfy" them of the expedition's "innocence." The "dispositions" of the United States were "neighborly, friendly & useful."[8] These professions of "innocence" and friendly "dispositions" recall Knox's "benevolent plan"; they assume that natives would accept any new commercial and military alliances gladly, without encumbering ties of their own. Even if the prospects for actually settling the Far West were decades away, the instructions follow a line of reasoning consistent with the early republic. Jefferson probably had only the vaguest plans for the Louisiana Territory, but he assumed—alongside Knox—that native and white American interests would intersect.

The clash of preconceptions and experience shapes how literary critics sometimes read the *Journals*. Robert Lawson-Peebles and John Seelye trace the erosion of Enlightenment optimism through Lewis's belletristic landscapes, which steadily lose their relevance as the terrain becomes more difficult to contain through standard conventions. This lesson in aesthetic limits explains as it obscures (like any critical argument) and deals selectively with an admittedly unwieldy account. A typical day's entry, this by Clark, reads: "A Cold morning. Set out early under a gentle Breeze from the S.E. by E., passed the 3rd old Village of the Mandans which has been Desd. for many years" (October 25, 1805). Bypassing tedious passages like this one, Lawson-Peebles and Seelye focus upon Lewis's mercurial writing habits—his puzzling entrances and exits and his self-fashioned persona. Lewis remains invisible through the first year of his journey and begins a daily record only when the company crosses where "the foot of civilized man has never trodden."[9] His prose soars through the high prairie of present-day South Dakota and Montana, where welcome challenges provide opportunities for self-canonization; on July 4, 1805, he surveys the ranks and notes that "we are now about to enter on the most perilous and difficult part of our voyage."[10] Far into the Bitterroots, his language echoes Jefferson's instructions: Lewis assures himself that (the "strong rapid water" aside) the route was "practicable & by no means dangerous" (July 22, 1805). As the dashed hopes for a Northwest Passage unglue the hero-naturalist, however, the mounting despair becomes readable in his prose. Clark reports of "Hills or mountains" that were "like the Side of a tree Streight up" (August 23, 1805). Lewis stops writing just three days later, his narrative breaking midsentence on August 26:

> I had nothing but a little parched corn to eat this evening.
> This morning Capt. C. and party

Only sheer boredom the following January would compel him to reenter the *Journals*. From the winter camp on the Pacific through much of their return journey, Lewis reports on the region's natural history and native culture, but even then, the narrative lacks a compelling form.[11]

The silence and later return raise a crucial question for reading the *Journals* as a literary artifact: namely, what kind of narrative was this? When Lewis enters the text again on the first day of 1806, he begins by stating his desire to move the calendar forward. The "repast of this day," he writes, "consisted principally in the anticipation of the 1st day of January 1807." The company's weather diary from this month aches with repetition:

27th	rained	moderately last	night and to day
28t	do	do do	do
29th	do	do do	do untill 7 A.M. after.

Yet the complaints about the weather and tedium in camp usually precede observations about the region's natural history and native inhabitants. Lewis grumbles on January 8, 1806, that "nothing extraordinary happened today" and then offers 150 words on how the Chinooks and Clatsops draw tobacco; January 16 ("no occurrence worthy of relation") includes notes on fishing; February 2 ("not any occurrence today worthy of notice") explains native games of chance; January 29 ("enquiring of the cook whether dinner or breakfast is ready") discusses the taxonomy of an evergreen shrub. While the company's months at a winter camp lack the built-in drama of a drive to the Pacific, in other words, Lewis and Clark follow their instructions—offering the western companion to *Notes on the State of Virginia* that Jefferson requested. Yielding three times the number of botanic discoveries from the last fall, the winter camp and slow trek back up the Columbia provide valued notes toward a natural history of the Far West. The *Journals* become an almanac of sorts. On March 7, the scarlet ruffled grouse appears and the elk sheds its antlers; a robin returns on March 15; the skunk cabbage and black alder bloom on March 24. By the beginning of April, the party is swatting mosquitoes, pulling off ticks, and so on.[12] Staying in one place would allow Lewis and Clark to better perform their assigned task—which was to introduce new objects for science and provide the rudiments of an ethnographic study.[13]

Suffice to say that this material rarely fits into readings that treat the *Journals* as a narrative of empire.[14] As literary critics are wont to observe, the textual history of the expedition would get folded into the sad story of Lewis's life. The hero-naturalist could never quite pull the strands of his own narrative together. When Lewis should have been shaping the papers for publication after his return, he procrastinated and eventually succumbed to depression, committing suicide in 1809. Only a prospectus, spurred by the news of a rival book in 1807, can hint at the intended form of his never-published account. The three-volume edition was to combine the conventions of a natural history and a belletristic tour. The first two volumes would trace the company's route, while the third would be "confined exclusively to scientific research." But Lewis died with the work barely started, and the plan never materialized. Jefferson and Clark (who did not think of himself as an author) took over, and they tapped the Philadelphia banker Nicholas Biddle to edit the first part and the naturalist Benjamin Smith Barton to organize the scientific material. Biddle dutifully saw *History of the Expedition under the command of Captains Lewis and Clark* into print by 1814, while Barton died with the work unfinished, his papers in an "immense heap."[15] Jefferson penned a memorial for the posthumous *History* that casts the suicide as a blow to the republic of letters. As his preface explains, the public lost "the benefit of recieving from his own hand the Narrative . . . of his sufferings & successes in endeavoring to extend for them the boundaries of science, and to present their knolege [of] that vast & fertile country which their sons are destined to fill with arts, with science, with freedom & happiness." It is the interpretation that survives to this day: The untimely death created a missing volume in the history of an expanding empire, a gap in the original library of America.[16]

Collaboration, Incorporation, Triangulation

This fixation upon epic ambition and thwarted achievement often leads to the neglect of the more quotidian operations of the expedition. If one may set aside the pretensions of empire for just a moment, then the *Journals* might be read as the product of collaboration, from a culture of both incorporation and "improvement"—as the triangulation between Enlightenment tastes and a middle ground. Maps provide one such window into this paradox. In a review of geographic imperatives, Martin Brückner notes how Jefferson provided a template of the continent—a semicompleted map—that served as a "master narrative" for Lewis and Clark to complete. After one winter near the Mandans and Hidatsas in present-day North Dakota, however, native geographies replaced the image developed back East. Brückner suggests a kind of student rebellion, with an indigenous view of the land confusing the imperial one; in a similar vein, the comparison of two maps underscores a constant shuttling between the republican vista and observations made on site. Biddle's 1814 *History* includes a frontispiece with "A Map of Lewis and Clark's Track," drawn by Clark and engraved by Samuel Lewis in 1810 (figure 5.1). This magisterial work of imperial geography traces the company's route with a slightly darkened line that allows readers to follow the expedition in its course across the continent. By presenting the "track" to the Pacific with the clarity of hindsight, however, the 1810 map distorts the physical terrain. The path was not always so clear during the expedition itself. A telling moment of indecision would come at the junction of the Marias and Missouri Rivers, which the published map depicts with a misleading emphasis upon the latter. In a map drawn in the field, by contrast, Clark portrays the two as about the same size (figure 5.2). The imperial narrative suggests a certainty where ideology is grounded in the continent itself, even as it misrepresents features of the terrain.[17]

The story behind this contradiction reveals how Jefferson's view of the West was emended, dismissed, and—in ways that Brückner does not fully allow—often retained. Lewis and Clark were about fifty miles below the Missouri Falls. They relied that season, through spring 1805, upon accurate directions that the natives had provided the previous winter. But the Marias posed a problem. The Mandan and Hidatsa geographies indicated that the Missouri reached well into the mountain, yet they did not seem to suggest a major fork. The Corps of Discovery paused to reconsider its route. Jefferson's instructions only complicated matters: "Explore the Missouri river, & such principal stream of it" for the "most direct & practicable water communication across this continent." But what if the "principal stream" did not provide the more "practicable" route? Lewis and Clark weighed several factors in their decision: water flow and color, size, geographic coordinates, and the various opinions of native Americans, members of the party, and Jefferson (in absentia). The captains could deduce the distance to the mountains from where they were, and they had learned from the natives that the Missouri had a waterfall. The South Branch (later recognized as the Missouri) was clear, and the North Branch (the Marias River) was silty, which would suggest that the former ran quickly through rocky soil, while the latter crossed prairie. The company's most experienced river pilot, Pierre Cruzatte, favored the North Branch, and most of the company agreed with him. So Lewis and Clark divided the party and sent two groups ahead; whichever river led to a waterfall, it stood to reason, would be the Missouri. On June 13, Lewis discovered a cascade on the South Branch (famously described in the *Journals*) that settled "all further doubts as to the Missouri." So they went left. Still, the path of empire brought its own ironies. A later survey revealed the Marias (the North Branch) to be an easier route to the Pacific.[18] Although he technically would not have followed the Missouri,

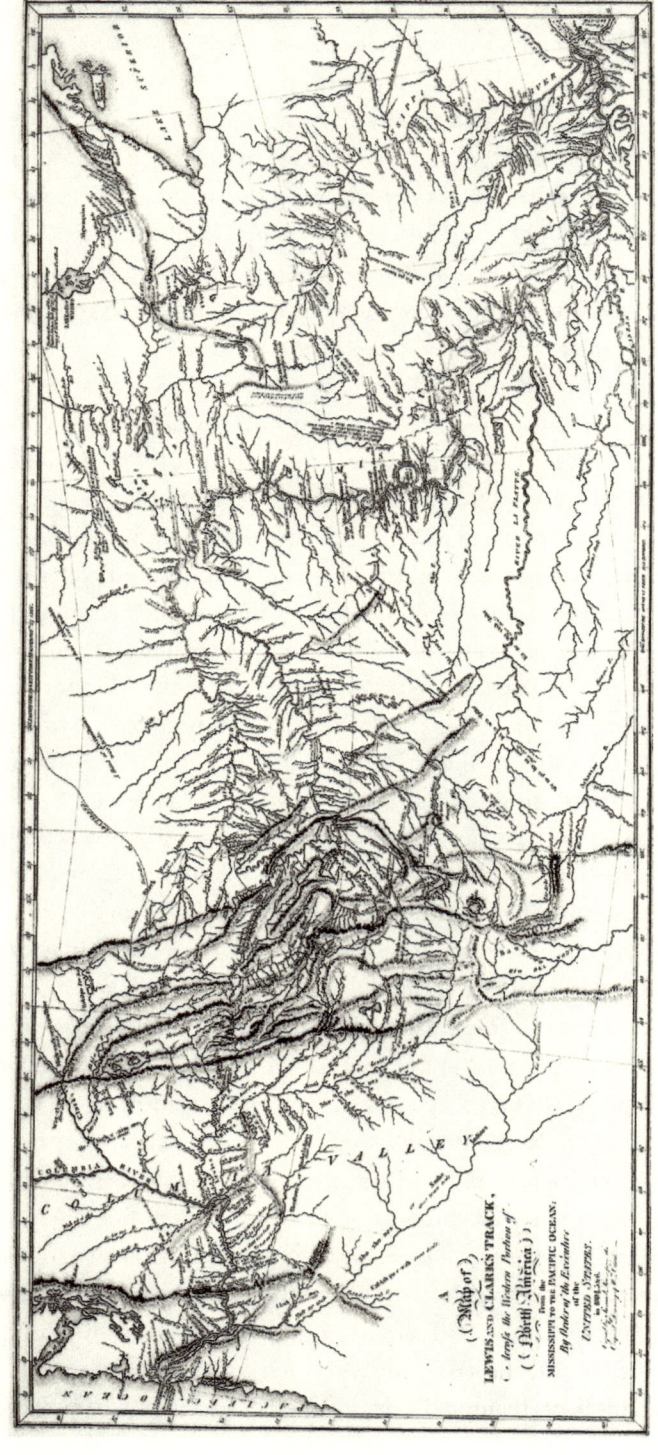

Figure 5.1. William Clark, "A Map of Lewis and Clark's Track, Across the Western Portion of North America" (1810). Courtesy American Philosophical Society.

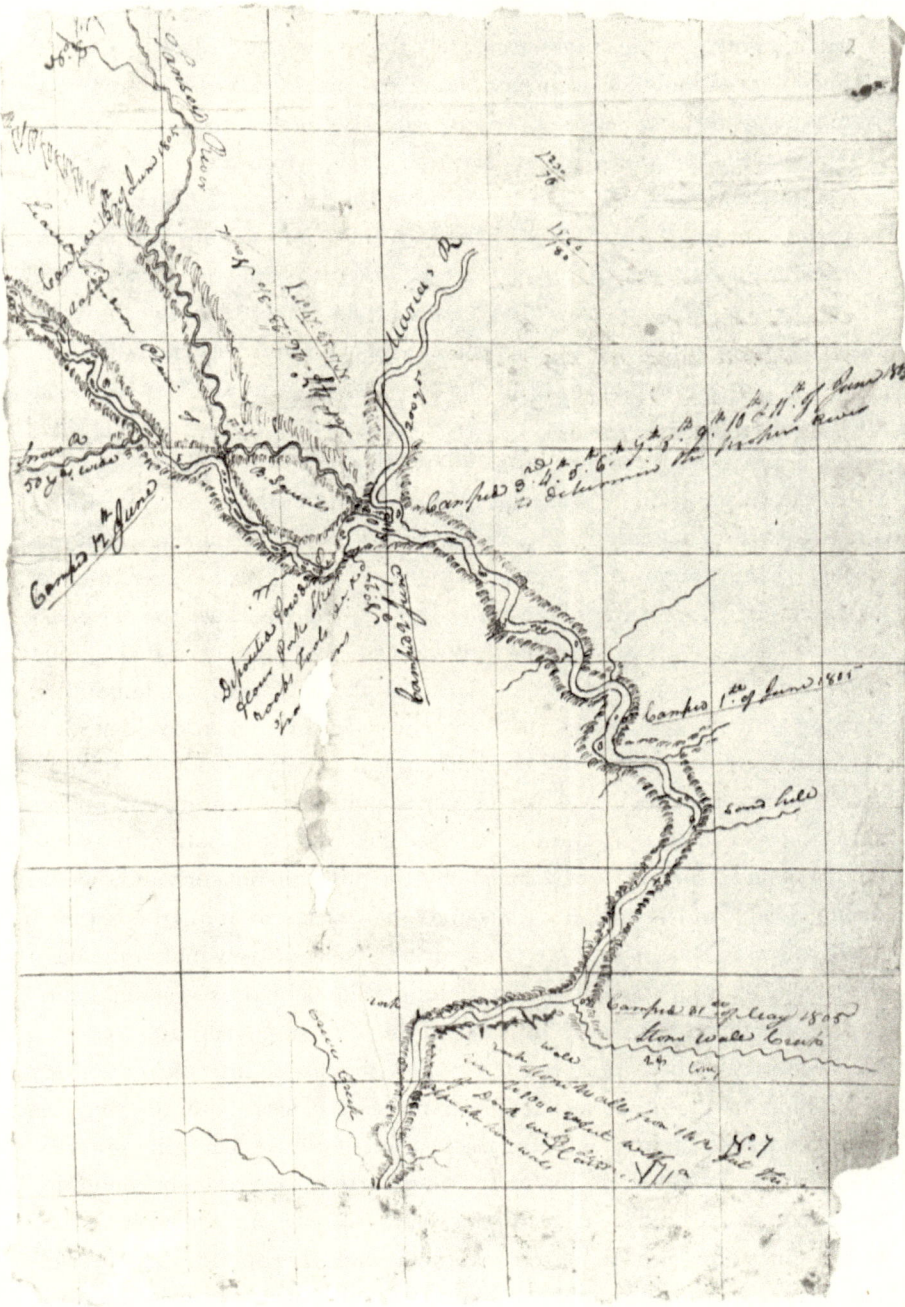

Figure 5.2. Route map of Lewis and Clark Expedition, May 31–June 13, 1805, depicting forks of the Missouri and Marias Rivers. Courtesy Beinecke Rare Book and Manuscript Library, Yale University.

Cruzatte was right. Unimpeded by Jefferson's instructions, the river pilot "read" his surroundings more accurately than Lewis and Clark.

Such moments of indecision show how experiences in the field were negotiated alongside—and scarcely eclipsed by—Jeffersonian preconceptions. They raise the obvious question, how did the Corps of Discovery make it across the continent? Read in its entirety, the Lewis and Clark *Journals* provides a record of the many, sometimes minute interactions between Enlightenment ideology, the western terrain, and the people they encountered along the way. The narrative unfolds in a kind of dialectic between expectations and the products/cultures of a local place. Once past the falls of the Missouri and a few months after the Marias, for example, Lewis experimented with one of his pet projects, a folding boat. With animal hides and wooden gunwales fitted around a collapsible iron frame, this vessel could theoretically carry eight thousand pounds of cargo to the head of the Missouri. Lewis mistakenly believed that the hull could be finished with materials "reaidily obtainable ... at all seasons of the year, and in every quarter of the country"; the design failed, however, precisely because the necessary materials were not then available.[19] By autumn 1805, the Corps of Discovery had crossed into a different ecological zone. The party could no longer find straight timber for gunwales; there were no pines for pitch; the vast herds of buffalo that were to supply the hull had migrated south. Changes in the land forced Lewis to improvise. The company patched together elk and buffalo skins to cover the frame, and they devised a composite sealant of beeswax, charcoal, and leftover tallow. Predictably, the pitch did not stick and the hull leaked. Had "I only singed my Elk skins," rather than scraping them, Lewis sadly reflected, "we could have reached the pine country which must be in advance of us from the pine which is brought down by the water and which is probably at no distance where we might have supplied ourselves with the necessary pich or gum. but it was now too late to introduce a remidy and I bid adieu to my boat, and her expected services" (July 9, 1805). He abandoned his "Experiment," and the bruised morale (one might argue) explains the deflated tone of his prose. Any "further experiments [would be] madness," he concluded. The company sank his boat into the river.

Two lines of critical thought converge around this episode. The first involves the fracturing republican plan. According to Lawson-Peebles, the "madness" over the boat "symbolizes the collapse of Enlightenment Order in an environment which it is not prepared to cope." Such an argument parallels Lewis's strategies for rendering western landscapes: He moves from the picturesque (the prairies of the upper Missouri), to the sublime (cliffs and mountains), to silence (in the Bitterroots). This interpretation certainly explains the role of aesthetic conventions in his prose, but it reads selectively from a voluminous record. As noted, Clark kept a log past the Bitterroots, and Lewis rejoined the account in January 1806. Their observations from the return journey were just the kind of material that Jefferson sought (a taxonomy of bears, for example). More to my point, the narrative of heroism-to-hubris understates the improvisation—the daily interactions upon local landscapes—that gives the *Journals* a shape. The boat failed because Lewis did not fully consider his surroundings, not because of the design. As with the decision at the Marias River, the expedition would weigh imperial projects of "improvement" against the environment. A second line of thinking is suggested by the postcolonial critic Terry Goldie. Goldie notes that canoes seek to limn a Eurocentric "art/nature dichotomy," providing a vessel through which whites gain entrance into "the symbolic power of nature." It suggests an intimacy with place; the association with "Indianness," in turn, naturalizes the indigene, and by rendering a culture outside history, suggests an entitlement for the colonizing group.[20] Lewis himself imagines a "canoe" for republican space: Euroamericans would limn the art-nature distinction in an effort to establish themselves as native to the continent. By grafting nature to an Enlightenment order, early national culture pursued an identification over and with appropriated environs.

The point returns me to my obvious question: How did the expedition cross the continent? An engine for moving the party upriver, and one that captures the play between incorporation and improvement, was caloric. Food was a principal point of exchange between culture and the environment. Lewis saw meals as an exercise of refinement, and he would triangulate his culinary preferences against how a republican Self and its Other consumed the land. The Corps of Discovery, which traveled light for an expedition of its size, relied mostly upon trading and hunting for food; not surprisingly, the calories that fueled them upriver—whether from buffalo, salmon, roots, dog, or horse—receive almost daily mention in the *Journals*.[21] A sated Lewis calls the high prairies of present-day South Dakota and Montana "a common and boundless pasture," where he kills for "amusement" whatever "the party can consum" (April 25, 1805). During these times, he casts a discriminating eye over the edible landscape. A May 8 description of the "white apple," or breadroot, notes, "I have no doubt but our epicures would admire this root very much . . . in their ragouts and gravies in stead of the truffles morella," and on May 9 he recalls a particularly memorable recipe for sausages. Toissant Charbonneau, the métis trader who purchased Sacagawea from slavery and fathered the baby she carried west, prepares "the *boudin blanc*," a treat unique to the plains. As "we all esteem [it to be] one of the greatest delacies of the forrest," Lewis writes, "it may not be amiss therefore to give" the recipe "a place" in the company's record. He renders the process in loving detail: "About 6 feet of the lower extremity of the large gut of the Buffaloe is the first mosel [morsel] that the cook makes love to, this he holds fast at one end with the right hand, while with the forefinger and thumb of the left he gently compresses it, and discharges what he says is *not good to eat*." As the ritual progresses, the language becomes even more high toned. The "skilfull opporater C-o seizes his recepticle," stuffs the casing with "what he says is *bon pour manger*," and repeats the process until he has "skilfully exchanged the outer for the inner." The sausage is then "baptised in the missouri with two dips and a flirt, and bobbed into the kettle; from whence, after it be well boiled it is taken and fryed with bears oil untill it becomes brown, when it is ready to esswage the pangs of a keen appetite or such as travelers in the wildernness are seldom at a loss for." With a smack of the lips, the recipe ends. The pleasure of this passage derives from its intoned communion between culture and the environment. The subject is cooking, but the nod to implied readers suggests a second craft: kneading out the daily grind through narrative, positioning the enlightened explorer between refined culture and the frontier. Like Charbonneau, Lewis processes the products of the country. With exchanges of the "outer for the inner," the author shapes and contains nature. The setting of this passage is both textual and topographical; using word choices that are peppered with allusion, the author provides a palatable account for polite tastes in the early republic.

Elsewhere Lewis triangulates his literary-culinary tastes directly against native Americans. On August 16, he describes a second organ-meat encounter that reflects his ambivalence toward the Shoshone Sioux in the Bitterroot Mountains. At this stage of the expedition, the Corps of Discovery depended upon the Shoshones, who were themselves in a bad state. Once able to harvest salmon from the west and buffalo to the east, the Shoshones were trapped between the nearby Atsinas and the better-armed Blackfeet Sioux. Deprived of their hunting and fishing grounds, they welcomed the Corps of Discovery. The village chief Cameahwait presented Lewis with a spectacular otter and ermine tippet, along with the still more generous gift of horses and a guide across Lolo Pass to west-flowing waters. Caught between dependency and authorial pretensions, Lewis portrays his hosts with a studied detachment—he shows an awareness of the Shoshone's plight, while straining upward in literary style.[22] The rhetorically framed ambivalence becomes especially visible in his descriptions of food. When a hunter from the Corps of Discovery shoots an antelope, the famished Shoshones tumble "over each other like a parcel of famished dogs" and devour the butchered remains raw. Lewis focuses on one Shoshone, who tears away "intestens which had been previously thrown out" and works a meal from the innards. The scene does little to settle the author's empty stomach:

> Some were eating the kidnies the melt [spleen] and liver and the blood runing from the corners of their mouths, others were in a similar situation with the paunch and guts but the exuding substance in this case from their lips was of a different discription. one of the last who attracted my attention particularly had been fortunate in his allotment or reather active in the division, he had provided himself with about nine feet of the small guts one end of which he was chewing on while with his hands he was squezzing the contents out at the other. (August 16, 1805)

A burlesque of the previous passage, where Charbonneau baptizes the *boudin blanc* and exchanges the "outer" for the "inner," the language again focuses upon refinement, but Lewis this time marks a distance between the observer and his immediate setting. "I really did not untill now think," Lewis muses, "that human nature ever presented itself in a shape so nearly allyed to the brute creation." The métis Charbonneau—for the moment, high priest of the camp meal—had civilized game through preparation; the lack of "regular order" among the Shoshones, however, reveals the depths to which humans could presumably fall. Blood (streaming "from the corners of their mouths") forms the subject of a sentence, not the cook. The passage closes on a note of condescension, with Lewis remarking that "I viewed these poor starved divils with pity and compassion." With its figurative turns of phrase, the "brute creation" and "poor starved divils," the narrative retains its decorum. It remains every bit as high toned as before, following the conventional use of food to distinguish civilized consumption from a savage Other.[23] Ten days later, Lewis would excuse himself from the narrative, beginning a four-month absence that critics attribute to dashed hopes for the Northwest Passage. Hunger in the Bitterroot Mountains indeed corresponds with the terrain's failure to nourish imperial ambitions. As this scene reflects little erosion to narrative pretensions, however, I would emphasize once again the element of incorporation—the attempted synthesis of "improvement" and experiences on a local landscape. The Shoshones here close the triangulation between an enlightened epic, cultures of the land, and contact with native peoples.

The fundamental issue nearly always remains how the narrative negotiates metropolitan audiences and frontier settings. In a portrait rendered after Lewis's return to Philadelphia, the painter Charles B. J. F. Saint-Mémin would recall the Lolo Pass (figure 5.3). The clean-shaven and (suspiciously) well-scrubbed Lewis poses before snow-capped peaks, wearing the tippet Cameahwait had presented him. He fronts the viewer directly, turned just slightly west, as his rifle points indirectly toward the wilderness beyond. The portrait misleadingly depicts exploration as a solitary venture. Even as he sports the costume of a Shoshone Sioux, the iconography suggests terms by which the white explorer initiated the new nation's story over a colonized realm. The tippet in this way effaces a human presence, much as Terry Goldie describes. Yet even this one image of the individual on a vast and vacated landscape cannot eclipse fully the pervasive contact between colonizers and native Americans. The subject of white-native relations remains outside my immediate concerns here; suffice to say that the record was vexed. Lewis would begin his journal only upon entering where the "foot of civilized man has never trodden," depopulating almost two-thirds of a continent with this slight rhetorical gesture. The expedition obviously resulted in untold encounters between different groups, leading to the usual human exchanges across racial, ethnic, tribal, or national boundaries. In 1877, an elderly Nez Perce man with blonde hair and blue eyes informed a photographer that William Clark was his father; in 1806, Clark himself offered to raise the son of Sacagawea and Toissant Charbonneau, Jean Baptiste, "as my own." (Elsewhere, Clark upbraids Charbonneau for "Strikeing his woman.") The kinship took metaphorical turns as well: Jefferson invited chiefs from the western nations to visit the United States under the pretense that all Americans were "united in one family"—assuming, of course, that native interests would intersect with those of the republic. The many opportunities for contact would lead to collaboration as Euroamericans mapped, measured, cataloged, and described western environs. I return to my initial anecdote. A forced delay among the Nez Perce yielded much-valued dis-

Figure 5.3. Engraving from a portrait of Meriwether Lewis by Charles B. J. F. Saint-Mémin (1807). Courtesy Library Company of Philadelphia.

coveries in natural history. Lewis and Clark had confused the distinction between western bears, but they found help through a village that befriended them for reasons of its own. In the *Journals*, Lewis would position himself as the final arbiter on taxonomy, however much he depended upon the Nez Perce classification. The "Indian distinction" between a "Hoh-host" and a "Yâck-kâh" was indeed correct.[24]

Jane Colden and the Charleston Network

The exploits of a scientist-as-action-hero may seem to draw a sharp contrast to the first woman reported to master the Linnaean method, Jane Colden. But Colden became famous, much like Meriwether Lewis, through her explorations of the natural world. And gender was always an issue. Peter Collinson explained to Carl von Linné, the Swedish professor who instituted the binomial system, that Jane Colden "deserves to be celebrated" as the first "lady" botanist. Historians of science draw increasing attention to the boundaries and confluences in men's and women's spheres of nature. Feminist scholarship by Evelyn Fox Keller, Londa Schiebinger, Patricia Philips, Ann B. Shteir, and others suggest how gender relations informed natural history and vice versa.[25] The widened view shows how colonial and then early national intellectual work was both inclusive and exclusive. Knowledge was drawn from the ranks of ordinary people, even as those ranks closed in the formal transactions between men. It was a paradox that traces at least back to Linnaeus. By reducing natural history to the naming of genus and species, Carl von Linné effectively opened his discipline to anyone who could read a handbook; even as he subsumed all taxonomies under a single system, moreover, Linnaeus and his disciples sought the existing names and uses of objects in nature. Gender came into particularly visible play in this trafficking from popular, or "vulgar," knowledge to institutional authority. Based upon its stepparent in London, the Royal Society, the American Philosophical Society in Philadelphia provided a forum for "Uniteing Ingenious Men." Meriwether Lewis defined a persona in the *Journals* against this homosocial community. The same culture of masculinity that defined Jane Colden as the exception, as the first of her gender, fueled the narrative of a hero-botanist in the Lewis and Clark *Journals*.

Certainly the conditions were right in the Colden household to support a woman with scientific interests. Jane's parents, Cadwallader and Alice Christie Colden, valued education for both sexes, and the eight children who reached maturity enjoyed that blessed combination of domestic security and intellectual challenge. Cadwallader studied medicine at the University of Edinburgh (then London) before settling permanently in the Hudson River valley in 1728. A fixture in New York government and more famous still as a colonial savant, Cadwallader Colden owned the first copy of Linnaeus's *Genera plantarum* in America and entertained a steady stream of prominent visitors from both sides of the Atlantic. In addition to a voluminous and varied correspondence, his publications include a *History of the Five Nations* (1727), which remains essential reading on the Iroquois to this day; "Plantae Coldenghamiae" (1749), a highly regarded botanic survey of his self-christened estate; and *An Explication of the First Causes of Action in Matter* (1745, repeatedly revised), his brain-numbing tract on gravity. Alice Christie Colden was the daughter of Scottish clergy. She wrote well (although not frequently, family and friends complained) and managed the Hudson Valley estate with particular competence and visibility when business took Cadwallader to the city. Familiar correspondence often finds Alice Christie Colden in the garden, where she undoubtedly passed on botanic knowledge to her daughter. Among the children, Jane was the one who knew where medicine was kept and how to administer herbal remedies. She brought the same scientific rigor to plant study that she brought to domestic occupations. One visitor remarked that her cheese was the best he had eaten in America. It was no idle compliment; she perfected the method through experiments in 1756 that were recorded in her "cheese book," a singular document that survives today in the family's papers.[26]

In contrast to the domestic setting, where science blurred into what was later called home economics, Linnaean science would cast Jane Colden as the remarkable exception. Cadwallader described his daughter's training in the binomial system as an experiment in itself. A 1755 letter to John Frederic Gronovius of Leiden explains with a condescending air that "[ladies] are often at a loss to fill up their time." The "variety of dress" in different species of plants, for that reason, would make botany a worthwhile pursuit. Jane Colden provides a case in point: "Tho' perhaps she could not have been persuaded to learn the terms at first," Cadwallader translated the Latin characters for her, and she "has already a pretty large volume in writing of the Description of Plants." That "volume" was the "Botanic Manuscript," a 341-page catalog filled with descriptions and sketches (figure 5.4). News of her work spread quickly. Alexander Garden of Charleston, who also was an Edinburgh-trained physician, visited Coldengham in 1754 and reported to

Figure 5.4. Drawings from Jane Colden's "Botanic Manuscript." The top left drawing shows the "gardenia" also described by Alexander Garden. Courtesy British Museum (Natural History).

John Ellis (famous for a book on coral) that the "lovely daughter is greatly master of the Linnaean method," and she "cultivates it with great assiduity." Ellis suggested to Linnaeus from London that she had described a new species—the *Fibraurea*, or gold thread—and noted that she "merits your esteem." Collinson likewise reported to John Bartram that "Our Friend Coldens Daughter Has in a Scientificall Manner Sent over Several sheets" with ink pressings, and he too recommended Jane Colden as an "example to the ladies of every country." The vogue in Europe for natural history suggests that Jane Colden marked institutional boundaries primarily. Despite claims that she might serve as a leading "example," genteel English women were already stocking their greenhouses and gardens with exotics; botany was fashionable enough by 1771 for William Smellie to blast its "alluring seductions" in the first *Encyclopedia Britannica*.[27] Linnaean science remained open, as well, to forms of knowledge that were, if not gynocentric, then gender neutral. Example after example finds colonial naturalists like Bartram and Cadwallader Colden consulting with local physicians, white settlers, native Americans, and slaves. The condescending report to Gronovius, which bases women's botanic interests in the "variety of dress," ignores altogether the practical botany in his own household. The praise for Jane Colden's "Scientificall Manner" marks, most of all, the circuits of a masculine network. This network, which fetishized individual achievement, vaulted the practitioners over more local landscapes of discovery.

In its very format, the "Botanic Manuscript" negotiates this tension between existing knowledge and scientific protocol. Most entries run between seven and ten paragraphs, with each paragraph defining the features of a given specimen: Colden identifies the cup (calyx), flower (corolla), chives (stamen), pestle (pistil), seedbox or cover (capsule), leaves, and roots. Below the categorized descriptions, however, may appear a *nota bene* that comments on a telltale feature (the petals of silk grass are "shaped like a Cats E'ar") or that notes practical uses and provenance. Red mint, Colden observes, grows "wild in the Mohawks Country." The "Country People" brew "Thee of the Leaves of" Rattle to treat fever, "ague" (or chills), and "sikness of the Stomak." Physicians on Long Island treat inflammation of the lungs ("the Pleurisy") as well as "Colick" and the "bloody Flux" (dysentery) with silk grass. That medicine was "learn'd from a Canada Indian." The two-part structure covers a paradox that literary critics should consider in early American botanic writing. Pamela Regis argues that the rhetoric of natural history located species on a static, taxonomic field that removed nature to a verbless tableau. Regis writes: "Narrative suspends. Description replaces action." The emphasis upon removal to a static system, however, downplays the pervasive contact and open-ended basis of Linnaean science. As the binomial method broadened the appeal of botany to others, it engaged naturalists in multiplying forms of intercultural exchange. Lisbet Koerner observes that even the most self-aggrandizing reports from the field might credit "Surinam field slaves, Arctic shamans, Yemenite Jews, Finish rune-singers, and Pennsylvania Amerindians."[28] The "Botanic Manuscript" fits within a project that was imperial in scope but dialogic in practice.

Recognition becomes a pressing issue for Jane Colden because gender left this otherwise central figure at the margins. As the daughter of Cadwallader Colden, she gained some access to an international network; still, her manuscript study would never acquire the weight of authority that came with print. Letters by and from Jane Colden are sadly few and far between, and the only publication in her lifetime has a fuzzy history, but enough clues survive to connect the two and draw some generalizations about gender and environmental discourse. Collinson acknowledges receipt from Colden of some "plants very Curiously Anatomized," and a tantalizing letter to Charles Alston (professor of medicine at Edinburgh) indicates that she pursued university connections. The 1756 letter to Alston remarks upon the "unexpected honour" of his "obliging favour," and she returns his courtesy with the taxonomy of a plant. A request that her description remain unpublished, however, shows a reticence not always found in her male peers. Colden closes the note to Alston with a request "that you will not make anything publick from me, till (at least) I have gained more knowledge of Plants, and then perhaps I shall be able to make some amendments to my Discriptions." The circumstances surrounding her one publication suggest that the reluctance was genuine. Alexander Garden submitted the "Description of a new Plant" to the Edinburgh *Essays and Observations*, and it appeared in 1756, two years after his visit to New York. The short article, submitted without her knowledge, claims simultaneous discovery of a "gardenia" (a *hypericum*, not to be confused with the African cape jasmine). Garden described the plant in Latin, and Colden's text was in English. Having committed a faux pas, Garden's once-familiar correspondence between the family ends, and he offers a cryptic apology. Women might participate in botanic study, this and other examples suggest, but not in the transactions of mostly male institutions.[29]

The policing of gender is even more visible in Colden's contemporaries from South Carolina. In one of John Bartram's many travels, he met the Charleston horticulturalist Martha Daniell Logan. The two shared common interests. Logan's nursery supplied a thriving botanic culture, her *Gardener's Kalendar* ran for years in almanacs and offered advice for kitchen gardens, and she stocked Bartram's greenhouse with much-coveted hyacinths and lilies. In Bartram's letters with longtime correspondent Peter Collinson, however, Logan would serve as the butt of an inside joke. Bartram taunts his friend about "my fascinated widow" who sends him flowers, and Collinson pines in response for a "Mistress as Thou hath got who is always treating thee with Dainties." The playful and often homoerotic exchanges between the two efface the existing network in which Logan served a crucial role and that preceded his first visit in the 1760s. Among the "fascinated" women who traded plants and visits with Bartram were Sarah Hopton, Susannah Holmes Bee, Mary Woods Wragg, and Elizabeth Lamboll—all from influential families. The correspondence with Lamboll, which survives through her husband, shows Elizabeth most clearly as a female peer. She takes Bartram through her garden in the hot South Carolina sun and later offers specimens with instructions for planting. His correspondence with Peter Collinson casts the same person as transfixed by a man's superior knowledge, or "fascinated."[30]

Eliza Lucas (later Pinckney) preserved a letterbook that reveals quite explicitly how one negotiated gender as she engaged in the typically masculine culture of "improvement." Born in Antigua and most famous for introducing indigo as a commercially viable crop to South Carolina, she resisted early marriage and embarked upon a remarkable program of cultivating both herself and her surroundings in nature. A 1742 letter to her brother follows the same protocol as Filson's *Kentucke* or Jefferson's *Notes on the State of Virginia*. She situates South Carolina geographically and describes the soil before moving into plants and animals. The next paragraph discusses population (the "better sort" are "hospitable and honest," the poor should "never be wretched in so plentiful a country"), which leads to a review of polite refinements (the "gay" dress, "Eligant" churches, and "charming" springs). This rare example of a woman's cartographic text fits within an overarching program that involved music and law; readings in Petrarch, Virgil, and Robert Boyle; experiments with crops; and horticulture for pleasure and profit. The disciplined work at the same time would find the author negotiating gender in her letters. As Lucas explained with characteristic self-effacement, "I have a fertile brain at scheming."[31]

The jokes, just superficially at her own expense, marked a calculated transgression of social boundaries. In a culture where Cadwallader Colden jested how his daughter "took the bait" and genteel horticulturalists were cast as "fascinated" women, Lucas would use wit to pad her ambitions. She resolved not to marry at a young age, indulged in her "schemes," and accordingly anticipated resistance from family and friends. Like the heroine of a Willa Cather novel, Lucas experimented with crops and served the less fortunate in her community; she planted live oaks for shipbuilding and a cedar grove for meditation. But these projects of improvement—for herself and the land—invariably prompted clarifications and humorous asides about the expectations for a woman her age. As she updates relatives about her reading in the law, for example, she asks them to "not laugh" at her seriousness; elsewhere she jests that the concern with "weighty affairs" threatened to make her "an old woman." Gentle mockery serves as the means to clear a path for herself. Coping with suggestions that she belonged in Charleston, Lucas imagines a conversation among her future in-laws. A letter to her cousin fancies them saying: "'She is [a] good girl,' says Mrs. Pinckney. 'She is never Idle and always means well.' 'Tell the little Visionary,' says your Uncle, 'come to town and partake of some of the amusements suitable to her term of life.' Pray tell him I think these so, and what he may now think whims and projects may turn out well by and by. Out of many surely one may hitt."[32] Occasionally Lucas confesses to an impatience with the city. Playing "Cards or going a suet [sweet] figure around the room" denies women the "pleasures of a superior and more exalted Nature," and she worries that too much polite society can "effaminate the mind."[33]

The use of "effaminate" as a verb suggests that managing an estate or introducing and following leads in Virgil's *Georgics* blurred conventional gender roles. These acts bring female identity under scrutiny, I suspect, because they involved commercial or imperial enterprises, for Lucas participated in forms of botanic exchanges elsewhere that did not warrant self-deprecation.[34] What seemed to trip concern were practices outside gardening for pleasure and domestic uses; otherwise she could expect criticism for undertaking activities "too burdensome to a girl." The self-effacing humor quite possibly internalizes the kind of banter found in scientific correspondence between men. Bartram quipped that Logan and Lamboll were "fascinated" women, and a similar patronizing quality ("she easily took the bait") colored the early assessments of Jane Colden. Cadwallader Colden hinted to his correspondent in Leiden that a "variety of dress" drew women to serious botanic research, despite the quick work that Jane Colden made of the Linnaean system and the other hints of an existing basis of knowledge. As the family papers reveal, Alice Christie Colden was an avid gardener, and Jane was trusted with herbal remedies at home. The example of the first "lady" botanist documents a recurring paradox in colonial science, for even as the discovery of a new plant might assure one's reputation in a hierarchical institution, the disciples of Linnaeus collected what field slaves, shamans, rune-singers, Yemenites, or native Americans knew already. Early American writings about place negotiated homosocial networks against collective acts of discovery in the field. This paradox shaped Jane Colden's career or became visible in writings such as the "Botanic Manuscript" because what constituted knowledge of the natural world was gendered and ideologically defined already.

Alexander Garden's Trip to the Cherokee Mountains

The traces of collaboration complicate the standard reading of colonial narratives as one-sided dramas of dispossession. Constructing "place," by and large, involves the appropriation of resources and transfers of possession; eighteenth-century science, however, would involve both consolidation and intercultural exchange. Cadwallader Colden represented a view from Edinburgh, where natural history was part of the medical curriculum, and his botanic work in America operated between theory and practice—making him a useful point for tracing information from intellectual centers back to the field.[35] Like her father, Jane Colden researched with "country people," physicians, and native Americans. The claim that she "deserves to be celebrated" misleadingly suggests individual achievement, exemplifying meanwhile how homosocial networks drew from existing bodies of knowledge. The transfer between these two poles of neoclassical science—from the center to the periphery—linked taxonomy to stories, and those stories crystallized the dynamics of a contact zone. If the "translation" from local sources to institutional authority sometimes vanishes, then it is only because environmental discourse created the occasions for self-canonization. Lewis and Clark inherited the role of agents for the Enlightenment (the metropolitan center simply moved from Europe to Philadelphia), and the *Journals* take shape from the meeting of expectation and experience. Narratives emerged from a naturalist positioning herself or himself across cultural and geographic divides. In the Far West, the Corps of Discovery negotiated an ideological geography against the advice of native Americans, hunters, and river pilots. The same negotiations became the stuff of national epic back in Philadelphia. Lewis and Clark were simply the later and more famous products of a dialogue that defined colonial articulations of place.

A final example may illustrate this tension through the Charleston network. Alexander Garden, who was Jane Colden's one-time collaborator, studied medicine at Edinburgh, but unlike Cadwallader Colden, he groused constantly about his position as a colonial naturalist. He settled in South Carolina, where he found himself at the periphery of an empire but close to an undescribed store of nature. Two related themes run throughout his correspondence: a hunger for recognition in Europe, and frustration that his busy medical practice and the intellectual torpor of Charleston impeded his progress in natural history. He explains in a typical letter what scientific friendship meant to him. Responding to John Ellis, Garden writes: "I awaken as out of a dream. I read your Letter over & over—I fancy myself in Company with you by Anticipation I enjoy your Conversation—I have long tete a tete with you—I resolve at your instigation to pursue natural history." The fancied tête à tête and suggestion of courtship were rhetorical commonplaces that had particular appeal to Garden. Elsewhere he describes a vision of the afterlife, where he joins his European friends at "the skirts of a meadow." No longer separated by the Atlantic, they would botanize with Linnaeus among "legions of white candid spirits," enlarging "their mental faculties" in an intellectual, quasierotic kinship. Not only did this imagined fraternity leave women in an ambivalent position (Logan becomes the "fascinated widow"), it would distance natural history from more immediate settings. Complaints about Charleston unsurprisingly string throughout his correspondence: Were it not "what they learn from the Negroes Strollers and Old Women," he writes, "I doubt much if they would know a Common Dock from a Cabbage Stock." The dismissal obviously overlooked the horticultural network of Elizabeth Lamboll and Martha Daniell Logan; equally important, it sought to absolve his debt to the people who brought him specimens. A series of examples found Garden using "Negroes," "Old Women," and others to gather samples of American nature.[36]

The tension between individual achievement and experience in the field would become palpable in Garden's musings about travel. He begrudged John Bartram's mobility and pined for an opportunity to explore the interior of Carolina himself. In 1755, Garden got his wish—the chance to join a state-sponsored envoy to the "Cherokee Mountains," where he would botanize while officials settled affairs in the backcountry. The circumstances resembled those of Bartram's journey to Onondaga. With the Seven Years' War approaching and South Carolina in danger of losing its diplomatic edge on the western frontier to Virginia, Governor James Glen requested a council with the Cherokees. The two parties met midway at the town of Saluda, a "social margin" described by one historian as the "shared geographical middle ground." The diplomatic exchanges produced botanic ones as well. Garden returned with his expected larder of plants, which he classified and shipped abroad over the next few years. One particular specimen (a flower "with which the Indians dye red") elicited an evocative confession on provenance. "A lady procured this for me," he explains to Ellis, but she feared that the plant would lose its qualities when crossing "the great water, as they say." Garden continues, detailing a reluctant collaboration: "They formed many excuses for not gathering it at all, and could not at last be persuaded to gather any, till the frost came, which destroyed its bright dyeing quality. This they knew well it seems before, but they think that when they communicate any of their knowledge to the white people, the plant or herb immediately loses its wonted virtue, and for this reason it is difficult to procure any thing from them." Both parties saw the sacred in this flower (identified by the Cherokees as *gigage unasti-tsi*, and in English as puccoon, or bloodroot). The disciplines of Linnaeus believed that the identification of each new specimen further revealed the workings of Providence. The Cherokees likewise saw the plant as a link to the supernatural but in a different way. "Vegetation was more than a resource," Sarah H. Hill observes, and useful plants were "gathered with ritual," not simply turned over to strangers. The women delayed with a flower whose properties happen to vanish in early fall as a measure of preserving divinely given applications. Garden positions himself both inside and above the encounter, remarking upon native custom before turning to physical properties. (He asks Ellis to "give his opinion of" the specimen.) The Cherokees, for their part, avoid intellectual colonization. They do not gather specimens until the frost — retaining control in the same way that council leaders directed where Carolina officials should meet them — in order to appease the white naturalist, while preserving in their view the "virtues" of a given plant. In such moments of cultural contact, as knowledge of the botanic world was traded in a parallel diplomatic setting, authors would define a narrative persona.[37]

The dialogic basis of natural history, and the struggle for voice especially, will become a major theme in the next work that I discuss, William Bartram's *Travels*. How did the son and protégé of a more established naturalist forge his own view of the environment against immediate experiences in the field? In what ways did Bartram negotiate scientific discourse against the early national frontier? Alexander Garden demarcated the opportunities and limits that came with colonial intellectual work. His letters overseas (contrasting sharply with his correspondence in other venues) privileged a community botanizing in Heaven with Linnaeus over Charlestonians who did not know a "Common Dock from a Cabbage Stock." A discourse that saw taxonomy itself as an exercise of masculine community would set authors into a vexed negotiation with an Other. Three decades later, Meriwether Lewis saw the Louisiana Territory in the same way that Garden viewed the Cherokee Mountains—as the field of discovery and self-fashioning for an enlightened explorer. The acquisition of one flower suggests a disturbing trend, one that would lead to the Louisiana Purchase and later violent expansion by the United States. But William Bartram marks a certain ambivalence as the nation moved west and expansion potentially undermined republican principle. He forged his ideas of nature against often strained white-native relations. *Travels* wrestles with that irreconcilable paradox, and in the negotiation between frontier politics and the environment, Bartram forged the first masterpiece of pastoral literature in the United States.

*It cannot be denied that Bartram's text operated within—
if on the extreme edge of—a discourse of domination....
Bartram's subtle subversions did not overturn that carefully
constructed discourse for his intellectual generation or their
descendants. But that would be expecting too broad a result;
it is on the margins rather than at the center that one must
look for his impact. Whatever the resonance, however, it is
clear for at least one prominent American intellectual in
the 1790s, a prolonged and transformative encounter
with the Other led to a new vision of cultural
complexity and diversity in America.*
—EVE KORNFIELD

ON THE BORDERS
OF A NEW WORLD

WILLIAM BARTRAM'S *Travels*

WILLIAM BARTRAM IS best known for penning one long book with a cumbersome title, *Travels through North & South Carolina, Georgia, East & West Florida, the Cherokee Country, the Extensive Territories of the Muscogulges, or Creek Confederacy, and the Country of the Chactaws.* Although he is usually described as a revolutionary author and his book was published in 1791 under a federal copyright, Bartram might be read more accurately as a link between colonial and early national science. He was born in 1739, which makes him Jane Colden's contemporary more than Meriwether Lewis's, and early reports on "Billy" appeared alongside updates about the first "lady" botanist. In a previously cited letter from 1756, Peter Collinson acknowledged receipt of some "plants very Curiously Anatomized" by "Our Friend Coldens Daughter," and in the next paragraph, he lauded "Billy's Drawing & painting of the Tupelo" tree. A note from the same pen to Cadwallader Colden would suggest collaboration: "I wish your fair Daug^t was Near Wm Bartram he would much assist her at first Setting out," for "Johns Son [is] a very Ingenious Ladd," and Jane surely "Will improve" as she practices more. Because Bartram wrote *Travels* late in life, his explorations of the

149

Southeast (and through some parts of the country still outside the United States in 1791) would be equated with the early republic. When Thomas Jefferson, acting then as president, was planning an expedition to the Red River valley, he suggested that Bartram should join it. Bartram declined. He was in his late sixties, suffering the "consequent infirmities" of "advanced Age"; his "Eyesight [was] declining dayly," and he rarely left the garden home that his father had built.[1] Whether Bartram accepted Jefferson's offer or not, the invitation hints at the expectations for a natural history of the West.

The product of colonial and early national scientific cultures, *Travels* would capture the paradoxes—between collaboration and self-canonization, frontier politics and an identification with the land—that I traced in Meriwether Lewis and Jane Colden. Pastoral (or eco-) critics also see the book as a watershed in American nature writing. Lawrence Buell maintains that an "aesthetics of relinquishment" defines a pastoral text; in an act of authorial self-removal, the land plays an active role in the work, what Michael P. Branch calls the "topographical imperative." Bartram offered a prototype for the imagined place and a departure from the usual rhetoric of environmental change. Revolutionary authors such as Crèvecoeur and Jefferson envisioned "improvement" over already inhabited country, and propagandists from the Ohio ordinances to the Louisiana Purchase described the interior as a "future field of happiness" for the United States. Contemporary geographers who suggest that the construction of place demanded changes in the land, however, note that colonization does not automatically yield *topophilia*—a love of place that is not the same as possession. Yi-Fu Tuan distinguishes patriotism in its imperial tones from more intimate and sensitive forms of knowledge; *Travels*, in this vein, negotiates between the "relinquishment" that may be interpreted as *topophilia* and a backdrop of colonial expansion.[2] More than any other author of his time, William Bartram would weave into a single plot anticipated changes in the land, a veneration for nature, and sympathetic interactions with native people. *Travels* fell somewhere between the collaborative culture of Jane Colden and the national mythmaking in the Lewis and Clark *Journals*. These paradoxes would yield a narrative persona for Bartram, one that sought to preserve the moral integrity of an expanding republic and to establish a vocabulary for occupation.

Four Ways of Looking at a Sinkhole:
The Construction of a Literary Natural History

Again, biography may explain the emerging "topographical imperative." Yi-Fu Tuan notes that people use stories to shape spaces around their own identities. "Words contain and intensify feeling," he maintains. Stories help individuals articulate their relationship to a setting; geographic meaning evolves from the formation of individual biographies over natural and built environments. Bartram's own life captures what Tuan describes: the intensification of a remembered place through the narration of repeated experiences over the same physical terrain. Two overlapping journeys, one in the 1760s and the second just prior to the Revolution, would foster a *topophilia* that was too genuine and contradictory for the usual cant of progress-across-space. William's first trip to the Southeast, the region described in *Travels*, was in 1765–66 (figure 6.1). John Bartram had recently been named botanist to George III, and the small stipend that came with the title allowed father and son to explore the territories that had been ceded to England after the Seven Years' War. The two ventured through the Carolinas, along coastal Georgia, and into Florida. No journal by William survives, but the elder Bartram kept a notebook, which was later excerpted for William Stork's *An Account of East Florida*. John's *Diary of a Journey* scarcely rises above the occasion of a promotional tract, and whatever enthusiasm he felt for southern flora (and his letters show that he could be passionate to friends) receives no vent in the record of his journey. Duty-bound prose describes the practical uses of a recently ceded territory. Outside Charleston, a typical passage reads, a planter has "made surpriseing improvements in draining salt marshes & converting them into excelent rice fields."[3]

This uninspiring account would provide a psychological template for the more memorable *Travels*. A second tour gave William the opportunity to recross the rich natural and emotive landscape that he visited with his father, and in John Seelye's words, "we have only to lay one journal next to the other to measure the generational gap."[4] Family dynamics created a situation that was ripe for narrative. Battling what is today recognizable as depression, William had struggled to find his own identity. He squandered opportunities that came with his connections, betrayed the early promise for his work, and showed few gains from the college education that his father never had. After turning away numerous jobs and failing most recently as a planter in Florida, William seemed interested only in work as a

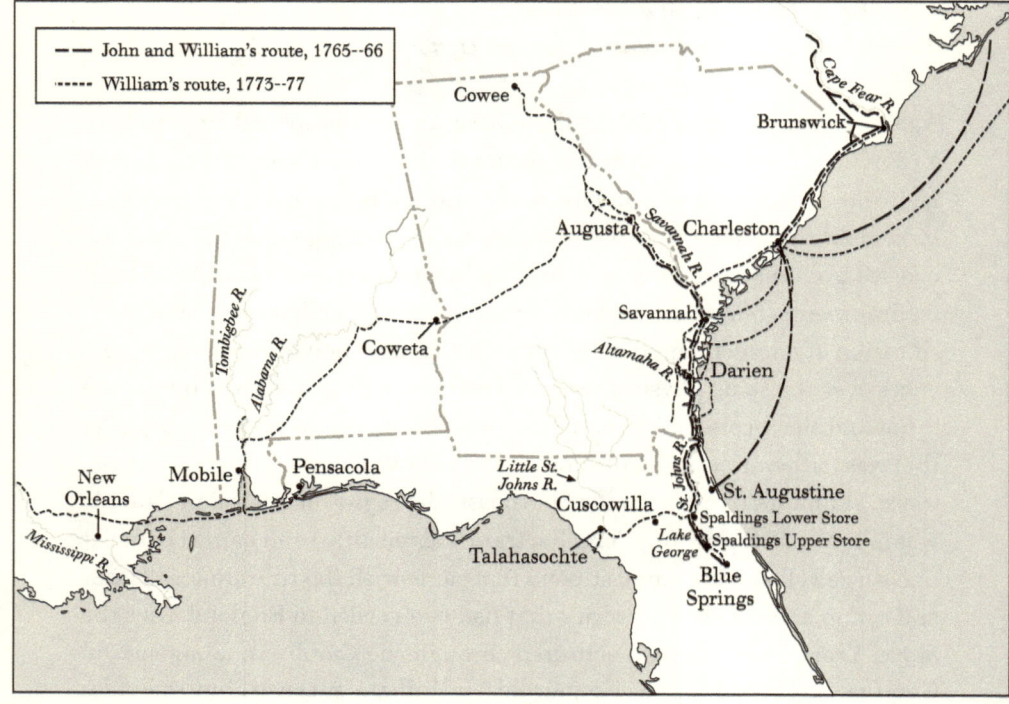

Figure 6.1. Routes of John and William Bartram's travels.

botanic artist. John Fothergill, a fellow of the Royal Society, finally came to the rescue and—whether out of sympathy for the family or in the interest of obtaining new seeds, sketches, and samples—gave "Billy" a fifty-pound commission to explore the southern colonies.[5] Fothergill's grant marked the beginning of *Travels*. William left from Charleston in 1773, traced routes he had taken eight years earlier, lost himself on new side paths and excursions, and remained in the wilderness much longer than anyone had expected or requested. By the time of his return in 1777, the younger Bartram had touched into present-day North and South Carolina, Georgia, Florida, Alabama, Mississippi, and Louisiana (figure 6.1).

Biographical tensions would yield a highly ambivalent work, one that evolved from an imperial culture of natural history, but as that culture was being re-formed on a national stage. Put differently, William established his American nature against John's more practical sense. "Men and manners undoubtedly hold the first rank" in nature, the second sentence of *Travels* declares, but "how far the writer of the following sheets has succeeded in furnishing information on these subjects, the reader will be capable of determining. From the advantages the journalist enjoyed under his father JOHN BARTRAM, botanist to the king of Great-Britain, and fellow of the Royal Society, it is hoped that his labours will present new as well as useful information to the botanist and zoologist." The prosaic then bursts into religious euphoria in the next paragraph: "This world, as a glorious apartment of the boundless palace of the sovereign Creator, is furnished with an infinite variety of animated scenes, inexpressibly beautiful and pleasing, equally free to the inspection and enjoyment of all his creatures." Abrupt and without explanation, the transition speaks to the differences between the two Bartrams, and the remainder of the introduction swims between the various pressures that contributed to the work's formation.[6] The narrator wanders from travelogue, to taxonomy, to spontaneous effusion. A short account of Florida is, in modern terms, ecologically based: William describes a flower and then a spider on a leaf of the described plant, then he moves from insects to bumblebees, then to a bird that presumably eats that bee, and then back to the flower via the species that the red thrush favors (lviii–lx). An apology on behalf of native Americans follows this short botanic excursion and turns the author's environmental sensitivity to people. The dizzying introduction distills into just a few paragraphs the various themes that would work themselves out over the next five hundred pages. (The first of the book's four parts explores the Piedmont and the coast of South Carolina and Georgia; part 2, the most famous section, unfolds over central Florida; part 3 takes the author across the Southeast to the Mississippi River; the book closes with an ethnography of the native groups he encountered.)

The layered quality to *Travels*, evident from the opening two paragraphs, expresses some vexed father-son relations, but that ambivalence also was allowed to find its shape through a long period of composition. The text has a complicated history. William Bartram wrote *Travels* in stages, and over this process of time, he fused otherwise incompatible discursive modes. His first known account of the southern tour, subtitled *A Report to Dr. John Fothergill*, combines the genres of itinerarium, field notebook, and botanic report. Largely the reward for a patron and surprisingly restrained in tone, the *Report* lacks the effusiveness and drama that characterizes the later book. Bartram balks before the very challenges that would give meaning and form to *Travels*. The description of Florida sinkholes is one example: "I thought [the 'natural Wells'] worth your notice, & for that end have indeavourd to give a true Idea of them by a description of their natural & simple appearance: altho the cause & design of them appear evident, yet I am not capable of entering into the various dark mazes in the progress of Nature, & will detain you no longer on my notions of this subject." Elsewhere, the author promises to provide only "the outward furniture of Nature," refusing to trouble the reader with "particular causes or design by Providence, such attempts I leave for the amusement of Men of Letters & Superior genius."[7] The earliest record of the journey, in short, reads like a prospectus that Bartram would complete himself.

A second and very different manuscript, written sometime before 1783, casts the same tour as a spiritual autobiography. Only recently transcribed by the scholar Nancy Hoffmann from three notebooks in the Pennsylvania Historical Society, this version recounts his years in the South with a more visibly defined persona, using Quaker theology to portray wilderness as the setting for a religious quest. Long meditations on the divine operations in nature, which are held against a corrupt civilization, give this text the purpose and tone that one finds in *Travels*. The pacing and enthusiasm contrast starkly with the *Report*. In Hoffmann's transcription:

> We next cross't over a [charming] levell green meadow or cove of the savana & a {r}rived at a remarkable high hilly Grove{,} here we alighted {in} a pleasant [green grassy] vista & turn'd our horses to graze{,} whilst we amus'd ourselves ranging about this singular & astonishing exhibition of the works of the Al{l}mighty{;} {A} [vast] {group} of rocky hills <almost> sorond **** a {large} [bason of waters] <which is> the genera{l} receptacles of the water draining from every part of the vast {S}avan{n}a by lateral conduits winding about {&} [join-<ing>] one after another {joining} the main creek or general {C}onductor{,} which at [last] {length} delivers them into this {S}ink{,} where they de{s}cend by slow degrees through Rocky {C}averns *into the bowels of the earth*{,} whence they are car{r}ied by secret subterraneous chan{n}e{l}s{,} and deliverd <in>to other receptacles & ba{sons} aris<ing> again to the surface <of the Earth> [by other] [fountains ponds] {forming other} Rivers {Ponds} & Lakes{,} where plung<ing> or decending again {and} again arising{,} & so on repeatedly{,} [before they reach] {they probably dichare themselves on} the sea Coast.

The language has a pulse, an aquatic quality that comes with Bartram's making the country his own. As figure 6.2 demonstrates, one can reconstruct the textual history of *Travels* from descriptions of Florida sinks and streams. John's deferential *Diary* almost removes the observer from the country he describes. Despite tactile descriptions (water "tasting sweet and loathsome"), lines like "What a surprizing fountain must it be" suggest that the subject is somewhere else — and discursively, it was. The network of correspondence in colonial natural history prevented stronger expressions of actually being there. William would initially share that restraint: "I am not capable of entering into the various dark mazes," the *Report* explains, and only the manuscript would allow the botanist to front the wonder of Florida's underground steams directly. Privately he would consider traversing a sink filled with alligators, crossing "any part of the {Bason}{,} & the River for a great distance in{to} the Savan{n}a upon their heads."[8] This action, running across alligator heads, provides a neat metaphor for the naturalist who adventures into his own psychic terrain.

But more than just personal pressures led to *Travels*, and the book found its success by transferring private anxieties to key issues then facing the United States. Critics commonly note that the work provides a parallel or "small scale model" of the Revolution, and Bartram shaped his narrative for publication in the late 1780s.[9] The Quaker influence (then taken for closet Toryism) was squelched, and the manuscript makes few nods to expansion, portraying wilderness as an inspiration rather than a commodity. The inclusion of stock taxonomic language, added perhaps by another hand, continues the equation of nature and nation that one finds in *Notes on the State of Virginia* and the Lewis and Clark *Journals*. The result is an example of Euroamericans defining their own botanic realm; at the same time, *Travels* would respond to important shifts in frontier policies. In 1789, relations between the United States and the Creek nation reached a crisis, leading to Henry Knox's federal Indian policy. Knowledgeable about the groups that would be affected, Bartram penned a manuscript (undated, but from the latter part of the decade) that pleads for decency in Creek treaties and that parallels Knox's lofty idealism. "Let us my Brethren convince the World," Bartram implores,

> that the Citizens of the United States are Men in every Sense. Let us support our dignity in all things. Let our actions, in this memorable *age of our establishment, as a Nation or People*, be as a Mirror to succeed-

From John Bartram, *Diary of a Journey*

We landed where a sandy bluff joined the river; it produced live and water-oak, palms and bay; coasting the east side, we soon came to a creek, up which we rowed a mile, in 4 and 6 foot water and 30 yards broad, of the colour of the sea, smelled like bilge water, tasting sweet and loathsome, warm and very clear, but a whitish matter adhered to the fallen trees near the bottom; the spring head is about 30 yards broad, and boils up from the bottom like a pot; plummed it, and found five fathom water; multitudes of fish resort to its head, as very large garr, cats, and several other sorts; the alligators very numerous either on the shore or swimming on the surface of the water, and some on the bottom, or rather bold as to allow us row very near to them. What a surprizing fountain must it be, to furnish such a stream, and what a great space of ground must be taken up in the pine-lands, ponds, savannahs, and swamps, to support and maintain so constant a fountain, continually boiling right up from under the deep rocks, which undoubtedly continue under the most part of the country at uncertain depths?

From William Bartram, *Report to Fothergill*

As These vast funnell shaped holes, natural Wells, or sinks as they are termed here, have a very singular apperance, & have not heard of any thing like to them in any other Country, I thought it worth your notice, & for that end have indeavourd to give a true Idea of them by a description of their natural and simple apperance: altho the cause & design of them appear evident, yet I am not capable of entering into the various dark mazes in the progress of Nature, & will detain you no longer on my notions of this subject. We pass't by a large round sink about 20 yards diameter, observed a prodigious large Alegator basking on the brink, he plunged in at my near approach, and disappeared[.] continued over a pleasant well timbered grassy Pine Forest. come to camp by the side of a wet Savanah near a pond; It being not yet sunset and observing a dark homock of Oaks at some distance, I went to it with one of our party in hopes of seeing some Bear & deer; This Grove was very extendsive, The Trees were Live Oak[,] Water Oak[,] chestnut leaved white Oak.

Figure 6.2. John and William Bartram's portrayals of sinkholes.

ing Generations. Let us leave to our Children, a monument inscribed with Lessons of Virtue, which may remain from age to age, as approved examples for their Posterity: that they, in similar cases may say to one another; see how benevolently, how gratefully[,] how nobly, our forefathers acted!

From William Bartram, manuscript for *Travels*

This bason or Grotto is what The Indian Traders call a sink hole, a singular kind of *vortex* or condu(i)t to the subterranious receptacles of the Waters. . . . There is always a menadering {C}reek, or {C}hannell w(i)nding & turning through the {S}avanas, which receives the waters spread over {them} by an un{n}umerable lateral smaller branches, which slowly convey<s> along & finally delivers them into the bas(o)n or Grotto{,} [& there] with bands & *** <Nations> of the numerous finny Tri(bes) performing their pilgrimage, to the [sacred] {grand} fountain <:> See, them, continually p(our)ing in ***** <And> when here arived, all qu<i>et & peaceble.[still & slow] * incircle the {little} caerulean Hemisphere{,} [ceremonious rite] perhaps <for a time> bid * adieu to all transmundane varieties & pleasures decend<ing> into the dark caverns of the earth{,} Where [perhaps] {probably} they are parted or seperated from each other by inumerable paths or secret r(o)cky avenues{,} bid farewell to each other, and after encountering various obstacles, and beholding New & unthought of scenes of pleasure and disgust, after many days absence from the surface of the world{,} emerge again from the dark {C}averns{,} & appear sporting, in the pellucid water of s{o}me far distant Lake.

(O) (G)od {!} I am incapable of speaking sufficiently of thy Majesty and excellence{,} for they glory is equally incomprehen*sible and u(n)utterable{,} I attemp{t} in Vain to Sing thy praise{!} for then am I as <if> anhilitated{,} or lost in astonishment & dread{,} Again <I> become sensible of my existence{,} but Yet <am> dumb & silent.

From William Bartram, *Travels*

Behold now at still evening, the sun yet streaking the embroidered savannas, armies of fish pursuing their pilgrimage to the grand pellucid fountain, and when here arrived, all quiet and peaceable, encircle the little cerulean hemisphere, descend into the dark caverns of the earth; where probably they are separated from each other, by innumerable paths, or secret rocky avenues; and after encountering various obstacles, and beholding new and unthought of scenes of pleasure and disgust, after many days absence from the surface of the world, emerge again from the dreary vaults, and appear exulting in gladness, and sporting in the transparent waters of some far distant lake.

The various kinds of fish and amphibious animals, that inhabit these inland lakes and waters, may be mentioned here, as many of them here assembled, pass and repass in the lucid grotto: first the crocodile alligator; great brown spotted garr, accoutred in an impenetrable coat of mail.

This document acutely marks the contradictions of an expanding "empire of liberty." Bartram predicts that fair treatment will lead to the acceptance of market-based systems of land use, insisting that the Creeks remain "strongly inclined to our modes of civilization"; as Gregory Waselkov and Kathryn E. Holland Braund note, however, the author overestimates "the desire of the Indians to adopt Euro-American agricultural practices."[10]

The argument builds from a concern with national legacies, in short, while it poignantly recognizes the moral questions that faced the United States. Those unresolved tensions lead the author to a literary mode, the pastoral, that is capable of sustaining such contradictions. With a sophistication not seen again in the United States until Thoreau, *Travels* negotiates private doubts alongside national ambitions through an engagement with the physical environment. The convergence of personal and public anxieties, nurtured through a long composition process, would result in a work that could bridge otherwise competing discourses. As the need for fair frontier policies collided with the politics of expansion, the manuscript persona of a "philosophical pilgrim" would metamorphose into the book's "Puc-Puggy"—his Seminole name, meaning "flower gatherer," and a socially benign figure that could straddle two worlds. This hybrid self might negotiate between the republic's Scylla and Charybdis of preserving principles and laying claim to place. Literature provided a fluidity that the framers of a government could not offer; accordingly, *Travels* swims within the paradoxes that were defined by the western ordinances. Bartram "didn't edit the *Travels* for false consistency," as Bartram's biographer Thomas P. Slaughter notes, and the pastoral would remain open to unreconcilable contrasts.[11] A careful review of the book suggests that this ambivalence was deliberately crafted and that Bartram shaped his mixed emotions into plot. Using the traces of prior manuscripts, I will establish how encounters from the middle ground would provide the fabric for a national idyll. The result would be the first classic of environmental literature written in the United States, an expression of Euroamerican wilderness that would limn the colonizing culture that William Bartram did not fully reject.

Transformations, Personal and Political

Anticipating the American Adam, that hypermasculine plot of empire that would become commonplace in the next century, William Bartram portrays an individual stepping outside society, confronting wilderness, and forging a new identity.[12] The plot of a hero-naturalist would allow the author to portray nature as neither the subject for veneration nor colonization but, as Slaughter reminds us, somehow in between. Part 1, a short tour of lower Carolina and Georgia, begins with a deliberate setting out: "At the request of Dr. Fothergill, of London ... I embarked for Charleston." Having received his instructions from the metropolitan center, the author goes through the usual steps of securing a route—checking political waters, making connections, and gathering letters of introduction. These early chapters emphasize hospitality, the meetings with wealthy or powerful men, and commerce. When Bartram crosses the line between "settled" and "wild" country, he reminds readers: "It may be proper to observe, that I had now passed the utmost frontier of the white settlements on that border" (14). The crossing of a frontier gets punctuated by an infamous encounter with a lone Seminole, a threatening figure with an "angry and fierce" demeanor. In a stylized fashion, Bartram relinquishes himself to the situation ("I resigned myself entirely to the will of the Almighty") and shakes hands with his potential enemy. A chief at a trading company later explains that the Seminole was "one of the greatest villains on earth, a noted murderer," who had promised to "kill the first white man he met" (15–16). The episode plays a fairly clear role in the plot. Bartram's editors note that the encounter occurred much later in real time; by folding a brush with death into the opening pages, the author establishes the theme of native-white relations against the botanic self.[13]

The rest of the Carolina tour chronicles one of the more controversial land deals of the revolutionary Southeast. Bartram reviews the New Purchase of 1773, which ceded some 2.5 million acres to alleviate a Creek debt. The proceedings set two nations against one another and exacerbated generational as well as geographic tensions *within* those nations. Bartram entered a milieu that was dangerous for its many differences of opinion; in a telling note, the governor of Georgia advised him to avoid the survey that followed the treaty. The New Purchase accordingly receives a contradictory treatment in *Travels*. Bartram, on first glance, writes that the Treaty of Augusta, which was connected to the purchase, "concluded in unanimity, peace, and good order" (22). His report from the field acknowledges tensions more openly, however, and recounts an argument over a faulty compass: The Creeks charge "that the little wicked instrument was a liar" (26). The ethnography that closes *Travels*, finally, lays bare intertribal tensions that had come to the surface with the Creek cession. "The Cherokees," Bartram confesses, "do homage to the Muscogulges with reluctance, and are impatient under that galling yoke. I was witness to a most humiliating lash, which they passively received from their red masters, at the great congress and treaty of Augusta, when these people acceded with the Creeks, to the cession of the New Purchase" (307). The varying shades of emphasis suggest how ideological fractures could be exposed by a figure from the margins, particularly one who incorporated several different modes of writing into one book. "Doubling back on itself," Eve Kornfield remarks, Bartram's text "opens more questions than it closes."[14] The mixed report of the New Purchase picks up a theme that had been established with the lone Seminole. *Travels* offers a literary space wherein native-white relations could be retold, where they could be scrutinized closely, where the misgivings from expansion could be "opened" (in Kornfield's term) and then explained away.

The Florida tour develops this thematic germ into a fully realized narrative. Like the short journey to the Piedmont in part 1, part 2 moves from society to wilderness; experiences in a liminal setting then suggest a new direction for the Euroamerican nation vis-à-vis native Americans. Some 250 pages or so take the author from St. Augustine, near the mouth of the St. John's, to the river's headwaters and from one side of Florida to the other. Along the way, Bartram has some of the more memorable episodes of the entire book: He meets alligators, survives a hurricane, and explores the crystalline "Basons," where every other sentence begins "Behold!" Textual evidence suggests that Bartram deliberately shaped this material. Notes from (at least) two trips up the St. John's are folded into one single journey, and the natural history at the close of part 2 includes observations that were not made until several years later. In light of this sometimes awkward reshuffling, the shift in modes begs the question, why disclose the information here? A conventional arrangement would have been to tuck the natural history into an appendix, creating an equivalent to the ethnography in part 4. Bartram instead stops the account midstream, emphasizing the "good story" behind his collection.[15] In keeping with an affective science, the tableau bridges personal experience and taxonomy, allowing in turn the intersection of scientific interests and the frontier.

The translation into taxonomy unfolds, not surprisingly then, from a scene that reveals diverging views of the nonhuman world. The scientific chapters open with Bartram's "drawing some curious flowers" while awaiting the schooner that would return him to Georgia, when a diamondback rattler (the first subject of the coming description) slithers into camp (164). In Bartram's telling, the Seminoles with him lack the "freedom or courage" to take care of the snake themselves, and they gather in "affright and trepidation, whilst the dread and revered serpent leisurely traversed their camp, visiting the fire places from one to another, picking up fragments of their provisions and licking their platters" (165). The naturalist tries to ignore the ruckus that follows, but the natives call his name — it being Bartram's "pleasure," they amusingly protest, "to collect all their animals and other natural productions of their land." Puc-Puggy should now "collect" the "natural production" of a coiled viper. He clocks the snake with one blow of a stick, cuts off its head, and carries the trophy home. The Seminoles' unlikely paralysis (and the uncharacteristic image of a snake licking up leftovers) suggests an absent or distorted perspective. The mythology of southeastern groups might supply that perspective. A standard source on the Creeks notes that "Indians would not willingly kill a rattlesnake" because they associated it with the underworld. The nineteenth-century ethnographer James Mooney notes that the same snake played a large role in Cherokee mythology. When the sun refused to move directly across the sky, stalling midway and scorching the earth, the rattlesnake intervened: "Since then," one does not kill the species "because he is kind and never tries to bite if we do not kill him." Still one more tale maintains that anyone who kills a rattler must offer atonement, lest a relative of the victim seek revenge. A fear of reprisal, or associations with powerful spirits, may explain why three Seminole men then try to scratch some blood from Bartram — to make him "more mild and tame." The gesture would "appease the manes" (or soul) of the naturalist's sample (166). The arrogance in Bartram's version, recalling Alexander Garden's episode with the red-dyeing flower, suggests where white and native understandings of the animal world differed. In the context of a literary natural history, the story renders possible the shift from the narrative-experiential to the descriptive-taxonomic mode; in textual logic — and therefore distancing itself from the native perspective — the anecdote begins the path from field to cabinet. The scientist draws the snake's head and sends the sketch to London. The zoological drawings eventually work their way into the British Museum, and the appearance of the snake provides the pretense for an overview of southern fauna (figure 6.3).[16] For the Seminoles, meanwhile, one simply did not kill a rattler without caution or without offering some form of atonement.

The episode expands upon a motif also found in Alexander Garden, Jane Colden, and Meriwether Lewis: As writers described nature, they would negotiate relations with an existing population. By translating anecdote to public science, in a shift from the autobiographical to the scientific, Bartram asks readers to consider how one *comes to acquire* a given collection. This question then forms the basis for a distinctly American science. The rattlesnake scene links the otherwise directionless travelogue to the taxonomic

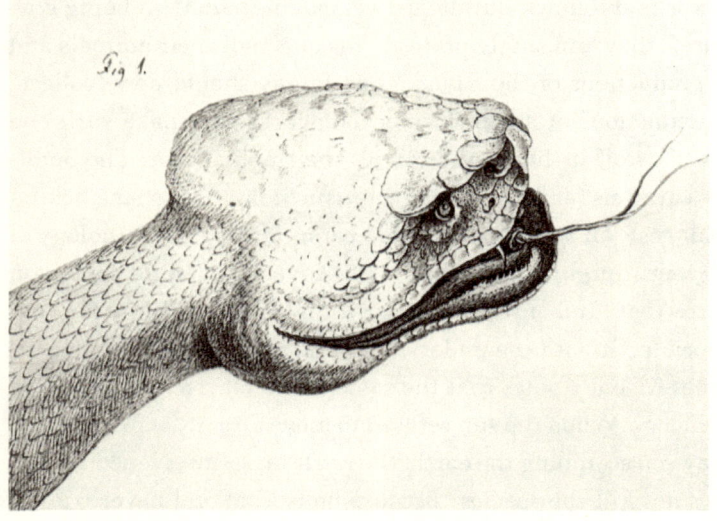

Figure 6.3. William Bartram's sketch of a diamondback rattlesnake, probably the sample described in *Travels*. Courtesy British Museum (Natural History).

tables, precisely because Bartram's basis of authority had been in the wandering. The discussion of snakes, in fact the entire chapter that effectively closes part 2, begins with the story of how he obtained a sample. The catalog that follows is accordingly both authoritative and anecdotal, scientific and poetic, experiential yet oddly fictive—from the middle ground but narratively poised. Herpetological notes come with an apology for the author's pacifism, his reluctance to kill a rattlesnake in other cases, and reflections on his father (168–69). The ornithological table in *Travels* corrects omissions by Catesby, the accepted (but British colonial) source on American birds, and offers a gentle apology for an American's method. By remaining in a single region through the course of seasons, one encounters a wider variety of species (180). Pastoral critics generally praise Bartram for depicting the world ecologically (and for that reason, the author is often held as the progenitor of a national tradition). Where Linnaeus divided and classified, Charles Adams notes, Bartram would recognize "the full diversity *and* complex unity of nature."[17] This recognition, in turn, demands that one abandon the standard narratives of territoriality and "improvement." The experiences speak for a way of habitation that is ecological, that is rooted in locale. The word for Bartram's four years in the South, "peregrinations," has a nonlinear prefix. This seemingly minor semantic distinction marks his tour from a path of *e*migration or *im*migration. A "peregrination" takes one around a circumference; knowledge comes from the *peri*phery or *peri*meter. The botanic pilgrim of *Travels* saunters without apparent direction, following what Thoreau would later call his internal compass and the "subtle magnetism in nature."[18] Yet these wanderings also provide new stories of place, albeit from the margins. The narrative suggests an alternative basis through which citizens of the republic might inhabit the continent; consequentially, stories like that of the rattlesnake leave the Seminoles in the background, acting with no rational motive of their own.

The pastoral opens a textual area where Bartram might situate himself advantageously between worlds. This literary realm allows one to renarrate the relations that passed between members of different social groups, and the book as a result addresses the sense of dislocation that accompanied colonization. Bartram marks a clear shift in authority from Alexander Garden or even from *Notes on the State of Virginia*. Jefferson would present the weights of mammals to refute the Comte de Buffon and establish how the continent could sustain European conceptions of progress; the very engagement in the *querelle d'Amerique*, however, locates the subject of his study on a discursive field whose center was somewhere else. Bartram, by contrast, charts a corridor of bird migration that paralleled the eastern seaboard of the United States. In a departure from comparable texts, the focal point remains in America. Bartram argues that ornithological work is best accomplished by "residing a whole year at least in the various climates from north to south to the full extent of their peregrinations." The wandering, or relinquishment to place, provides the foundation for his scientific report. What deserves note is how he couches these observations against his father's legacy. "There may perhaps be some persons who consider this enquiry not to be productive of any real benefit to mankind," William writes,

> and pronounce such attention to natural history merely speculative, and only fit to amuse and entertain the idle virtuoso; however, the ancients thought otherwise, for with them, the knowledge of the passage of birds was the study of their priests and philosophers, and was considered a matter of real and indispensible use to the state, next to astronomy, as we find their system and practice of agriculture was in a great degree regulated by the arrival and disappearance of birds of passage, and perhaps a calender under such a regulation at this time, might be useful to the husbandman and gardener. (178)

The insecurity dissolves into a pastoral moment, one where the author may orchestrate the tensions between usefulness and an attention to ecology, between neoclassical and romantic environmentalisms. As if to anticipate the doubts of his audience, the "idle virtuoso" suggests practical applications for his study; the "arrival and disappearance" of migratory birds are noted for agricultural purposes.

This peripheral identity, therefore, might limn the usual literature of improvement, but it suggests nonetheless a vocabulary for defining place. The passage above epitomizes the pastoral moment: The hybrid Puc-Puggy mediates between the usual expansionism and Pratt's "anti-conquest." A shuffling between narrative modes locates Bartram on the edges of the republican ideological geography; working between Euroamerican categories, the text liquefies the conventional classifications of environmental writing. Historian Donald Worster draws two lines from the eighteenth century: the imperial natural history of Linnaeus or Buffon, and the Acadian ecologies of Bartram or Gilbert White. But Bartram's apology for ornithological work suggests some permeability between the two, the chance for an "idle virtuoso" to benefit the "husbandman and gardener." The son-of-John-Bartram may serve imperial interests through a relinquishment to ecological processes (in this case, bird migration). Framed between a utilitarian view and the veneration that his father shared but did not publicly express, the pastoral allows William Bartram to sustain a paradox. *Travels* offers the classic machine in the garden. And as remains the case always with the American pastoral, elegy comes with a loss that one does not completely reject. The author of the eighteenth-century idyll, to follow Leo Marx, wanted to "reconcile his admiration for the primitive with what he knew of the needs of a truly civilized society."[19] One cannot say therefore that Bartram was completely "torn" (as Thomas Slaughter correctly observes) or that Puc-Puggy was ready to turn back the dump trucks of civilization. (As part 4 of this book suggests, we are decades away from Natty Bumppo.) The romanticism instead reflects an awareness of incipient change, articulated by a negotiation across modes of written expression and against the context of an expanding nation. The imagined wilderness of the text, however far its creator might wander, remains within the frame of a Euroamerican historical geography. Even while establishing himself on the borders of his own world, Bartram would articulate the (granted, problematic) interests of a federal republic.

A review of part 2 against the earlier versions of *Travels* suggests how events were plotted in order to support an inherently contradictory pastoral.

Following the same formula of the Piedmont journey, the Florida tour begins with a farewell to the city. William meets a local agent, collects letters of introduction, and cannot pass the barrier islands of Georgia without suggesting why they have remained undeveloped (37–43). As the narrator moves up the St. John's, touring the same river that the two Bartrams botanized the previous decade, the focus is on the relation of an individual to society. Settlements have a way of disappearing from the text (the *Report* puts more emphasis upon agriculture). When he passes near the old plantation he ran in the 1770s, nothing is said. Those being memories that Bartram would want to leave behind, the narrator describes a condition of increasing solitude in the wilderness. Any repressed doubts surface only in the forthrightness with which a new identity is defined: "Continually impelled by a restless spirit of curiosity," Bartram writes, "my chief happiness consisted in tracing and admiring the infinite power, majesty and perfection of the great Almighty Creator, and in the contemplation, that through divine aid and permission, I might be instrumental in discovering, and introducing into my native country, some original productions of nature, which might become useful to society" (48). The son of the botanist to George III, the failed planter, is on the verge of becoming Puc-Puggy, the peripheral self who also could serve the public good.[20]

The following chapters of *Travels* develop this paradox by pushing the traveler deeper into the wilderness and closer to an Adamic identity. The text spirals away from community in stages. At first, friends offer companionship outside a corrupt society. In a passage toned down from the spiritual autobiography, the philosophical wanderer joins a backwoods feast: "The simple and necessary calls of nature, being satisfied," he writes, "we were together as brethren of one family, strangers to envy, malice and rapine."[21] Those companions then peal themselves away from the narrative, until the hero finally is left bare before nature. The entrance into absolute solitude is portrayed with a suspiciously dramatic stroke. "At the upper end of this bluff is a fine Orange grove," Bartram writes, "here my Indian companion requested me to set him on shore, being already tired of rowing under a fervid sun, and having for some time intimated a dislike to his situation, I readily complied with his desire, knowing the impossibility of compelling an Indian against his own inclinations . . . when labour is in the question; before my vessel reached the shore, he sprang out of her and landed, when uttering a shrill and terrible whoop, he bounded off like a roebuck, and I lost sight of him" (74). In the earlier drafts, no natives are present, and a trader accompanies this "solitary traveler" to his destination.[22] What the account sacrifices in accuracy, however, it gains in effect, as the isolation in a wilderness serves as a cauldron for psychological change. Here the reader finds a hurricane (then out of season, probably folded in from a second tour) and the "crocodiles" that the poet James Dickey likens to images from William Blake. Without commenting upon these frequently anthologized scenes, I would emphasize that the stock sublime (where every other sentence begins with "Behold!") accompanies a relinquishment to the nonhuman world. A flood nearly carries away the naturalist's collections, and he battles alligators for his dinner. Raw nature casts the pilgrim into a tumult that he cannot order. Language, by contrast, reconnects him to the social world. As Bartram pulls his boat past witnesses at a nearby plantation, he recovers: "Indeed I saw plainly that they were greatly terrified" (91). The elegantly deployed "indeed" in this sentence finds the author once again rejoining human companions, the scenes as such vacillating between a social order and the sublime.

The chapters following the St. John's tour shift the emphasis from a man in the wilderness to the wilderness setting of a new nation. Following the trajectory of his own plot, Bartram directs his attention from isolation to the future of the land he describes and the relation of his botanic self to native Americans. A series of trips across Florida take him to the Alachua Savanna, a wet prairie draining a sandy ridge that was (and still is) a remarkable preserve for many forms of plant and animal life. This rich ecosystem provides Bartram with a geographic focal point, and here the environmental politics that frame his book come to a head. Early American naturalists, of course, would always couch their work against the prospects of future development, but what resonates in *Travels* is how the text positions expansion against an "anti-conquest." With the Seminole town of Cuscowilla, a village perched on the ridge of the prairie, Bartram identifies "a fine situation for a capital town" (115). Just a few pages later, however, the narrator would acquire his new name, an identity that reportedly came to him from a native American source. *Travels* explains how the chief known as Cowkeeper "received me with complaisance, giving me unlimited permission to travel over the country for the purpose of collecting flowers, medicinal plants, &c. saluting me by the name of PUC-PUGGY or the Flower hunter, recommending me to the friendship and protection of his people" (118). The rearrangement of the Florida tours, I have been suggesting, leads the published work to this moment. The earlier manuscripts had made no mention of a Puc-Puggy. But in light of national themes, the book constructs a welcoming for the naturalist—he botanizes with the Seminole's approval. The interest in "flowers" and "medicinal" plants apparently leads Cowkeeper to offer his protection to the narrator. Only three pages earlier, the text had mentioned putting a "capital town" on Cowkeeper's land.

Here, as much as at any point in the narrative, Bartram holds the paradoxes of his book in suspension. His descriptions of Alachua from the 1770s were probably written on site, and they entered the published *Travels* with almost no changes. The terrain clearly captured Bartram's imagination. A 1786 broadside used an account of the prairie to promote the book, and while the advertisement did not lead to publication, it nonetheless suggests what this region meant to the author.[23] Standing on the edge of the fields, contemplating "the unlimited, varied, and truly astonishing native wild scenes of landscape," he bursts out like Shakespeare's Miranda, "how is the mind agitated and bewildered, at being thus, as it were, placed on the borders of a new world!" (120). The appeal of this "native wild landscape" derives from an apparent civil order that had manifested itself over the physical terrain. Anthropomorphic descriptions graft human traits onto the natural realm. Hills and groves "re-echo" the "cheerful, social voices" of the "lordly bull" and cattle. "Herds of sprightly deer," "squadrons" of horses, and "civilized communities of the sonorous, watchful crane, mix together" (119–20). Dusk finds the cranes returning to their roost as one unit: "In well disciplined squadrons, now rising from the earth, [they] mount aloft in spiral circles, far above the dense atmosphere of the humid plain; they again view the glorious sun, and the light of day still gleaming on their polished feathers, they sing their evening hymn, then in a strait line, majestically descend, and alight on the towering Palms or lofty Pines, their secure and peaceful lodging places." The travelers follow suit: "All around being still and silent, we repair to rest" (121). This overlap between birds and people reads almost as poetry, the very rhythm of the language suggesting an epiphany over physical place.

What happened? When viewed today, the Alachua Savanna does not strike most Americans as immediately remarkable. The prairie lacks the jaw-dropping beauty of the Grand Canyon or Yosemite, biodiversity alone not being enough to qualify it for what David Mazel wittily calls the "environmental canon."[24] So one might reasonably ask, what about the Alachua

Savanna so inspired William Bartram? The very rhythm of his language, as noted, suggests an enthusiasm that few modern visitors share and therefore a distance between eighteenth-century and contemporary environmental aesthetics. As Bartram describes Cuscowilla, a Seminole village that bordered the wet prairie, the built environment harmonizes with its natural setting. This blending of the human onto a natural order would resonate especially for intellectuals who, in the 1780s, imagined similar plans for a territorial government. Much as settlement in the federally zoned Northwest Territory was meant to evolve *from the fallen tree*, *Travels* suggests an organic historical geography for Florida. Bartram exclaims, "such a natural landscape, such a rural scene, is not to be imitated by the united ingenuity and labour of man" (123). He collapses the Enlightenment stage theory (illustrated with Pownall's "Design" in chapter 1) onto a single continuum, moving from wilderness to farm to town on an implicitly temporal frame. The wetlands being too buggy for human habitation, much of the country remains undeveloped. The aloof deer is protected in open range, and he raises a "white flag" to escape the encroaching hunter. Communal farms border the prairie, suggesting an intimacy of culture and nature, and the town sits comfortably above on the sandy ridge nearby (122). The landscape that overwhelms Bartram is not a wilderness without people, therefore, but a harmonization of built and natural environments. His enthusiasm for the savanna recalls questions that emerge again and again in early national literature: What kind of civilization could the continent support? What were the relations between nature and a social order? Authors such as Bartram approached these questions with an antiquarian eye, and the same signs of past civilizations that struck Solomon Drowne and the founders of Marietta in 1788 would surface in *Travels*. Gordon M. Sayre observes that markers of antiquity cut to the nation's own sense of promise and potential ruin, and an equivalent historical sense shapes Bartram's response.[25] "Passing through a great extent of ancient Indian fields," he remarks upon "the ancient Alachua, the capital of that famous and powerful tribe." The "stately trees," abandoned orange groves, and "luxuriant herbage" are all that remain where thousands once gathered to play ball on these "happy fields and green plains" (126). What was there, and what would the future yield for this region? The savanna provides the uncanny mirror to Euroamerican conceptions of empire, and in this fusion of politics and ecology, and in this projection of time over place, *Travels* invokes the very hopes and concerns that circulated with the recently passed western ordinances.

It does so, to complicate matters, through a strategy that allows the author to embrace the spatial politics of a new nation, while casting himself as sympathetic to a region's indigenous population. The rhetorical graft negotiates a contradiction that was apparent to Euroamerican intellectuals. Bartram fails to endorse or castigate civilization as he knew it; instead, the text ambles within the scientific and ideological frame that his contemporaries defined. But veneration would invariably lead to some form of violence, to the "anti-conquest," as both the products of the land and native claims were consumed. On the return trip across Florida, the author again meets the "sonorous" sandhill crane. He describes the height and wingspan of the bird, the shape of its body, and its plumage, and he closes with a breathtaking analogy between the sound of quills in flight and the creek of an ocean vessel. Following that odd tradition of early American ornithology, however, the artist revels over what was just killed. The travelers dress his sample for soup, and while Puc-Puggy may prefer the crane's "seraphic music in the etherial skies" to the food in his dish, he still eats the soup (140). A more alarming paradox emerges with imagined property-relations. The people at Talahasochte open the territory to the botanist, equating his "flower gathering" to symbolic adoption. The "King" would compliment him for such peaceful pursuits. As Bartram explains the meeting, he was told that "I was as one of his own children or people, and should be protected accordingly, while I remained with them, adding, 'Our whole country is before you, where you may range about at pleasure, gather physic plants and flowers, and every other production'" (150). Just three pages before, Bartram had recommended the soil for "Corn, Rice, Indigo, Sugar-cane, Flax, Cotton, Silk, Cochineal and all the varieties of esculent vegetables" (148). The country "before him," once again, gets sited for future development. The account of his adoption helps palliate that paradox between botany and expansion that defines eighteenth-century environmental literature. While Bartram concedes that a cession would depend upon the Seminoles (they are the "sovereigns of these realms"), his notes toward a plantation economy suggest an underside to his imagined relations with them. Veneration or identification invariably accompanies some form of appropriation or anticipated loss. Puc-Puggy may love the sound of a sandhill crane in flight, but he can eat the bird in his soup. One also wonders what the "King" at Talahasochte meant by "Our whole country is before you"—or if he even said that at all.

Four Views of the Alachua Savanna: The Ideological Work of Travels

Earlier examples of scientific writing find colonial authors constantly weighing their own knowledge and understanding against native conceptions of the natural world. William Bartram's father noted Iroquois beliefs about animal spirits in his 1751 tour, and Alexander Garden collected a red-dye flower despite Cherokee fears that the plant would lose its "virtues." The clash with, and incorporation of, indigenous ecologies often followed efforts by Euroamericans to establish their own colonial culture as native to the place. The parallel negotiation between nature and natives explains why so many examples of environmental writing include episodes of an adoption. The Shawnees adopted Daniel Boone, a point that John Filson de-emphasizes, while the narrator of Crèvecoeur's *Journey into Northern Pennsylvania and the State of New York* claims symbolic kinship with the Oneida nation. In *Travels*, Bartram would suggest a friendship with the Seminoles, and his botanic interests happened to intersect with questions then fronting the government on Indian policies. The nickname Puc-Puggy locates the botanist between two worlds, and the text finds him among southeastern natives as he presents the bulk of his observations. His argument for scientific authority also suggests terms by which the republic might occupy the continent.

Travels emerges from the differences between imperial natural history and the quest for place. Nowhere does the ambivalence become clearer than in the portrayals of the Alachua Savanna. A series of visual and verbal descriptions suggest a wide range of approaches to one landscape. A 1775 sketch drawn for Fothergill includes roads and the cardinal points of a compass. A cartouche identifies Cuscowilla and a store (figure 6.4). A second and more personal image, however, empties the same country of human traces and portrays the savanna more as a memory space. Slaughter maintains that the latter drawing symbolizes an attempt "to escape the past through a back door." Certainly the landscape is an internal one, as the sketch folds in upon itself in a curious way. The eroticized palm suggests a horizontal perspective, one that breaks the usual equation between the bird's-eye view and possession, while the lake is set on a vertical axis (figure 6.5). This internal play between perspectives opens the text to an ambivalence that is latent in any pastoral. One finds a similar shifting of vantage points in Bartram's prose accounts of the savanna. The 1777 *Report* focuses upon economics and contends that "no country can well exceed the [extensive] Savannahs"

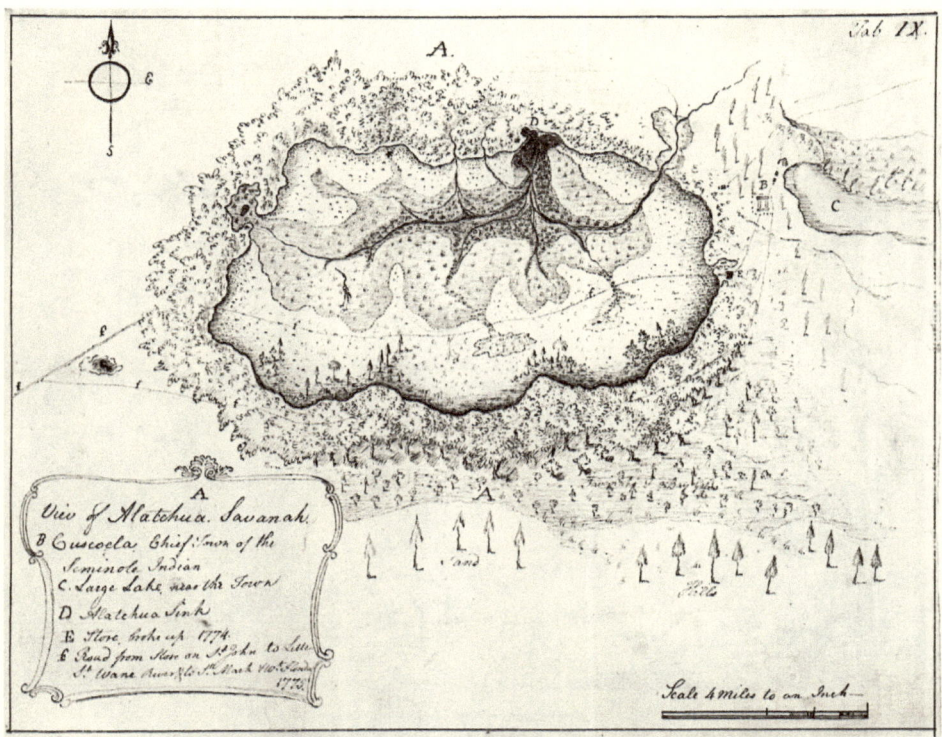

Figure 6.4. William Bartram's "View of Alatchua Savanah," drawn for his patron, John Fothergill. Courtesy British Museum (Natural History).

for future settlement. A tone of veneration prevails in *Travels*, where the "squadron" of cranes, their feathers gleaming against the "glorious sun," are reverently singing "their evening hymn." The return visit from Talahasochte, by contrast, emphasizes development. "Next day we passed over part of the great and beautiful Savanna," *Travels* explains, which "would if peopled and cultivated after the manner of the civilized countries of Europe, without crouding or incommoding families, at a moderate estimation, accommodate in the happiest manner, above one hundred thousand human inhabitants, besides millions of domestic animals; and I make no doubt this place will at some future day be one of the most populous and delightful seats on earth" (158). Bartram probably knew of the design by a Georgia planter named Joseph Bryan, whom he visited in 1776, to secure from the Seminoles a ninety-nine-year lease for the prairie. Even though this eccentric plot failed, knowledge of Bryan's attempts gives the more effusive de-

Figure 6.5. William Bartram's "The Great Alachua Savanna." Courtesy American Philosophical Society.

scription a distinct undercurrent. As Bartram scholars note, the author "is strangely silent on these schemes."²⁶

None of the four views of Alachua Savanna captures Bartram's America. Rather, the differing portrayals point to a process of establishing one's own perspective during a period of tremendous social flux—during a time when political legislation equated nationhood with the land, as the United States debated whether it had precedent over indigenous claims and as leaders in the new republic sought to extract property while maintaining Enlightenment principles. Bartram's aesthetics unfold, even as critique, against the same ideological geography that drove the northwest ordinances. The pastoral would allow him to portray wilderness as anterior to "civilization," as cause for elegy, but without directly confronting programs for expansion. Like almost every author discussed in this book, Bartram would couch his assessments of nature against the presence of native Americans. And while he provided a remarkably fair portrayal of southeastern people, and even as *Travels* urges decency in treaties, Bartram invariably would hold to the interests of the union. I return to the manuscript on the Creeks cited at the beginning of this chapter. This document concedes that frontier policies represented a moral test, but Bartram's insistence that the United States "support our dignity in all things" would leave him on one side of a social divide. The hope that natives would join in the march of progress allowed him to accept the name Puc-Puggy, while being aware of plans by speculators to capitalize upon resources that were already in use.

A transformation in character, from the son of John Bartram to a botanist in his own right, and the shift from an eighteenth-century ecology to a more romantic one, would permit him to hold ideological tensions in a pastoral aporia, to articulate a liminal space that was not native nor Euroamerican but between worlds. The classic plot of a machine in the garden, in other words, would maintain contradiction in dramatic solution: The book simultaneously acknowledges the spatial geography of the new republic, a culture's need for stories that were rooted in the land, and the desire to be indigenous — even if at the expense of native peoples. A literary natural history and arguably the first masterpiece of American environmental writing would develop from this vexed historical moment. Synthesized across several discursive modes, the text bridges the tensions between veneration and the demands of a more utilitarian framework, between both being a friend to the Seminoles and anticipating the development of their country. The preface to John Bartram's *Observations* of Iroquois country explained that "knowledge must precede a settlement."[27] William Bartram seems to remove himself from the conflicts that followed such pronouncements by immersing himself in the botanic realm. The play between discourse allows him to have it both ways. For it was the pressures of expansion that gave shape to a national pastoral. The next generation of authors would transfer this identification with wild nature into a rhetoric of dispossession.

PART IV

*Settlement &
Appropriation*

In any of its versions, imperialist nostalgia uses a pose of "innocent yearning" both to capture people's imaginations and to conceal its complicity with often brutal domination.
—RENATO ROSALDO

Nature, ambiguously regarded as a fact of direct experience and as the domain of the natural and inevitable, seems the ideal preserve for our cherished ideals.
—NEIL EVERNDEN

Reversing the Revolution through Nature

ANNE GRANT, TIMOTHY DWIGHT

IN A 1794 version of the cartographic text, the *Natural and Civil History of Vermont*, Samuel Williams observes that the rapid pace of immigration to northern New England had led to the neglect of existing place-names. He regrets that what "the original inhabitants assigned to our mountains, plains, and valleys, are mostly lost." The sentiment was an increasingly common one in the early national period, as nostalgia was used to define a distinctly American experience and identity. Critics of romantic literature tend to remark upon a willingness in the United States to eulogize vanishing nature and natives—although the semantic equation for people-of-the-forest has deeper roots. Historian Shepard Krech notes that "savage," a word used since the late sixteenth century to describe the indigenous populations of America, devolved from the Latin *silvaticus*. If romanticism marked a break from the revolutionary generation, then it was in a growing schism between past and present possibilities. Whereas later Indian policies were defined by removal, intellectuals such as Thomas Jefferson and Henry Knox imagined cultural transformations across changing environs. They saw "improvements" through agriculture and commerce that would alter indigenous economies, thereby allowing the cessions of tribal lands. Environmental literature treated "wilderness" as a verb, David Mazel notes, with leaders in the new nation seeking to *environ* the interests of an expanding republic.[1] At the risk of oversimplifying, it could be said that romanticism would shift the terms from verb to noun—nature and natives that once were the subjects of "improvement" would now be protected or removed. The mournful regret of writers like Samuel Williams, who seem penitent on the surface, reflects a tidal shift to sentimentality and fixed racial divides.

Any sea changes from the Enlightenment to romantic eras resist pat explanations, obviously, although I might suggest a few reasons for the permutations in *sylvan* ideology—for the rising identification with *what* or *whom* is native to the continent. First and foremost, the "benevolent plan" was doomed from the beginning. As noted, Henry Knox failed to consider varied indigenous interests on their own terms, and his plans for gradual improvement would not keep pace with the rapid expansion onto native territories. As the underfunded program unraveled, writers indulged a teary-eyed sentimentalism that cast Indians as either a defeated or endangered race. Alongside the imperial wishful thinking (where extinction seemed inevitable) came a burgeoning appreciation for the "forest primeval." Occurring at the same time were dire changes in the land: Geographic historian Michael Williams notes that 1810 to 1860 were "pivotal and crucial" years for American forests. And the economic costs of habitat disruption were increasingly apparent. Euroamericans on the eastern seaboard noted the effects of disappearing flora and fauna, climatic change, shifts in the water table, and exhausted soil. Authors predictably forged a national cult of wilderness—and what better symbol of the sylvan realm than the Indian? Still one more explanation lies in politics. The French Revolution found commentators on both sides of the Atlantic seeking the stability that wilderness presumes to offer. Reeling from the terror in Paris, the Duc de La Rochefoucauld-Liancourt came to America and sought out new prospects. His two-volume *Travels through the United States of North America* (1799), penned with a "peevish irritability of feeling," subsumed any personal losses beneath the romantic descriptions of impervious monuments such as Niagara Falls. J. Hector St. John de Crèvecoeur authored his *Voyage dans la Haute Pennsylvanie et dans l'Etat de New-York* (1801) under a similar state of mind, and he contrasted the recent upheavals in France with the "imprint of magnificence and time" in old-growth American forests. Conservatives in the United States likewise fretted that their experiment in democracy had gone too far. As Gordon S. Wood explains, the American Revolution created a society that its leaders had not "wanted or expected"; New England writers such as Samuel Williams and Jedidiah Morse freighted their descriptions of the continent with a concern for stability. So "fast do alterations and revolutions succeed each other," wrote the Congregationalist minister and geographer Morse, "that it is not an easy matter to keep pace with them."[2]

The final chapters of this book seek to recover the politics that were embedded within the attempts by genteel authors to make themselves *native* to the continent. The mournful rhetoric suggests an identification with "untouched" spaces, and the sylvan sentimentalism without question responded to exhausted Indian policies, yet the appreciation for *things disappeared* mitigated an anxiety about class as well. Since the mid-eighteenth century, Euroamerican elites had triangulated environmental ideology against native Americans and backcountry squatters; they commonly railed against white "savages," even as they benefited from the backbreaking work of pioneering. With this triangular logic just slightly revised, the nineteenth century would find genteel writers venerating threatened habitats and displaying their own refinement through an identification with the "nonhuman" realm. In 1824, the frontier clergyman Joseph Doddridge published a memoir in the Jeffersonian strain, *Notes on the Settlement and Indian Wars of the Western Parts of Virginia and Pennsylvania from 1763 to 1783*. He offers a typical performance: Even though Doddridge would welcome new crops to the trans-Appalachian West, he believes that "memorializing" could help to root society. He catalogs the extinct buffalo, elk, and panther; he notes the decline of blackberries, raspberries, gooseberries, cherries, and wild plums. The same concern with disappearance ties into a second theme: to chronicle his indoctrination into the "polish of civilized life." Like Crèvecoeur, who criticized the "do nothings" that failed to improve their estate, Doddridge would show contempt for Irish immigrants who squandered resources, or did not know the local history of the land, or killed a deer out of season.[3] In a wider view, Doddridge draws from the same nostalgia found in James Fenimore Cooper's 1823 novel, *The Pioneers*, a book that is commonly read both as pastoral fiction and as a template for Indian removal. Before turning to this better-known work, however, I will address the dynamics between nature and class that would come to ground the "Indianness" in early national green thought. An important question remains, one that ecocritics (as well as scholars attuned to the representation of native Americans) must address:

How did the identification with the *natural*, whether the "forest primeval" or native people, register the continuing effort to wrest order upon unstable frontiers? Images of nature take yet one more turn in early national writing, as an identification with wilderness suggests an order in backcountry settings that were not so easily controlled.

Anne Grant's Colonial Ecology

Few authors mark this reactionary trend more clearly than the Scottish antiquarian and poet Anne Grant. In an 1808 volume about her childhood outside colonial Albany, *Memoirs of an American Lady*, Grant sets an elegy for colonial British America against her love for the outdoors. Born Anne MacVicar in 1755, she emigrated from Glascow to New York when her father, Duncan MacVicar, served in the Seven Years' War. Duncan MacVicar later used his military bounty to speculate in what is now Vermont, which was then contested between New Hampshire and New York. Two different versions of the author's life survive: an autobiography that was posthumously published, and *Memoirs of an American Lady*. Differences in the latter suggest how Grant reworked the past around her own longing for a stable social station, particularly in the chapters about Vermont. Where the manuscript life explains how poor health drove Duncan MacVicar back to Scotland, forcing him to abandon his frontier claims, the published book blames the unruly settlers there. This case of selective memory may be explained partly through later financial woes. Grant wrote *Memoirs of an American Lady* many years after her return to Scotland, with one husband dead and eight children to support with her pen, so she channeled private worries into a larger elegy for a vanished colonial order. The "American Lady" of her book was Madame Margaretta Schuyler (not Grant), who was the descendant of a Dutch family and an embodiment of the Hudson Valley's old guard. "Madame," or "Aunt," as Margaretta Schuyler was known, would provide a foil for the Stamp Act repeal, the American Revolution, Mary Wollstonecraft's feminism — and for my purposes, economic upheaval in Vermont. With the stability symbolized by Schuyler, Grant would seek redress to the squabbling that ruined her father. One of the more fully realized pastorals of the early national period evolves from this search for entitlement on the New England frontier.[4]

The lives of Anne Grant and Margaretta Schuyler intertwine most readily through the category of place. The Dutch patroons represent a golden age. In the earlier chapters of the selectively shaped *Memoirs of an American Lady*, no inhabitant has too little or too much (1:161). Grant longs for a lost time: "Before increased wealth and extended territory these 'wassel days' quickly receded; yet it was pleasing to indulge the remembrance of a spot, where peace and felicity, the result of a moral excellence, dwelt undisturbed, for alas! hardly a century" (1:69). The anticipated end of these "wassal days" leads to the classic strategy of an English country house poem, with the account of Madame Schuyler's estate reading like a colonial cousin to Ben Jonson's "To Penshurst." Members of the family are "worthy patriarchs," "self-ennobled," "disinterested," and the center of a humane economy (1:179, 181). The Schuylers trade fairly with native Americans, little money passes "from one hand to another" in a "kindly commerce of presents," and even slavery is "softened into smile"—or checked by the "salutary terror" of being sold down South (1:80, 271, 273). Much of this does not hold up to close scrutiny.[5] On the Schuyler's barn: "Never did cheerful rural toils wear a more exhilarating aspect than while the domestics were loading the luxuriant harvest in this capacious repository" (1:175). The obvious alienation of labor in the country-house motif (the barn being a "capacious repository" that servants cheerfully fill) suggests a dislocation from history, and two key events frame this colonial idyll. The first was the Crown's eroding authority in America. The Stamp Act repeal of 1766, Grant writes, "occasioned great joy, but produced little gratitude" (2:147). Schuyler would remain above politics, of course, but the author explains this with the implausible recollection that "Madame" would dread the "future anarchy, the horror of civil war, and the dereliction of principle which generally results from tumultuary conflicts" (2:182). Grant times her own exit from America with the Stamp Act riots, identifying herself through some creative chronology with Lieutenant Governor Cadwallader Colden. In 1765 (three years before the MacVicars left New York), Colden in fact received death threats over the stamps, and a New York City mob burned his carriage. Grant claims that these riots occurred "the night before [our family] embarked for Europe." She blasts the protests, calling them "fits of excess and fury" (2:195). The book on America, and hence the friendship with Margaretta Schuyler, closes here.[6]

The second strand of plot recounts Duncan MacVicar's troubled claims in Vermont—a colony that Grant likened elsewhere to a "volcanic island in the tumult of civil commotion." Having acquired some six thousand acres in the territory disputed between two states, MacVicar entertained ambitions of becoming a colonial baron under New York jurisdiction (2:191). This paper fortune was made during an unparalleled era of property creation in British America, however, and the patent left him in a cross fire over who should benefit from pioneering. Speculators like MacVicar (usually associated with New York) grumbled about settlers who were "savages" and who needed direction; white pioneers (casting their lots with New Hampshire) maintained that property was worthless without people to "improve" it, and they believed that political authority should remain with the resident population.[7] Grant confesses that her father's interests were speculative, the family "did not mean to farm," and she predictably gripes about anyone that challenged his claims (2:134–35). The rivals from New England are "conceited, litigious, and selfish beyond measure." These "vulgar, insolent, and truly disagreeable people," Grant continues, "flocked indeed so fast, to every unoccupied spot, that their malignant and envious spirit, their hatred of subordination, and their indifference to the mother country, began to spread like a taint of infection" (2:137–38). The "vagabonds and banditti" persecute Duncan MacVicar and drive him to despondency, he returns to Scotland while his investments disappear, and there he dies (2:198). Anne Grant follows the New York–New Hampshire controversy through the Revolution and traces how the upheaval and then confiscation ruined her financially. Her dreams of landed status go the way of Albany's "wassal days." "Thus began the petty state of Vermont," she concludes, "and thus ends the *history of an heiress*" (2:199, emphasis hers).

The imagined ruin, in turn, prompts an identification with nature. Duncan MacVicar had found solace in the woods because "birds and fish did not talk of tyranny or taxes" (2:147). The same affinity with the "nonhuman" realm frames her descriptions of the Schuyler estate. During a hot summer of 1762, the eight-year-old Anne MacVicar notices how the birds "fatigued" themselves while trying to feed their young. "After all I had heard and seen of Aunt [Schuyler]," she explains, "I thought it incumbent on me to be good and kind to some being that needed my assistance." She devotes each morning (with the help of her slave Marian) to slaughtering "innumerable insects" and leaving the spoil in birds' nests (2:136). An identification with the natural order, seen here in the chance to fashion one's behavior after a landed family, fosters an appreciation for wild habitats. With an ecological conscience that might strike readers as contemporary, Grant notes that "impenetrable swamps" provide nesting grounds for geese and ducks (1:93). Wetlands are "sacred" from "the human foot," and the young author seeks

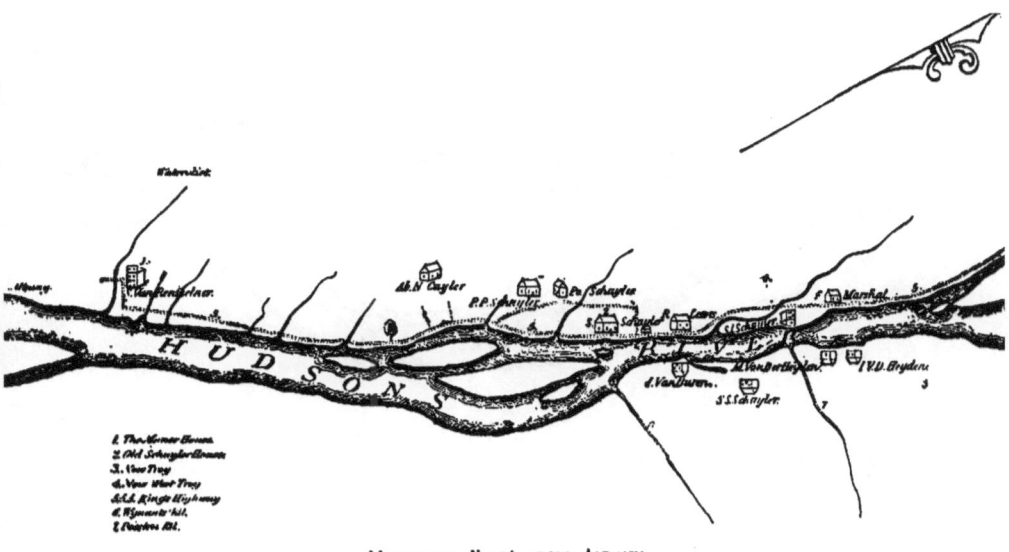

Figure 7.1. "Map of the Flats Above Albany," from Anne Grant's *Memoirs of an American Lady* (1808). Courtesy Odum Library, Valdosta State University.

similar "sanctuaries" where she might "herbalize" (2:173–74). But the concern for wild land (however exceptional for this place and time) serves the immediate purpose of justifying a precommercial economy.

A focal point in *Memoirs of an American Lady* is an island on the Hudson River, immediately opposite the Schuyler estate (figures 7.1, 7.2). It is "a remnant of wild magnificence of nature amidst the smiling scenes produced by varied and successful cultivation" and thus an appropriate site for memorializing Margaretta Schuyler (1:148). The island's story connects nature to Madame and to her marriage with Philip Schuyler; then to the first patroon of Rensselaerwyck; and therefore to an organic social order. Grant remarks that a "natural boundary" divides Philip's holdings from those of his brothers; she emphasizes the fertility of the river flats; yet once more effacing labor, she notes how impressive crop yields came "with a slight degree of culture" there. But the island's appeal lies in its resistance to development. A "broad belt" of mature sycamores and "wild fruit trees" form a barrier against ice, while in the summer, "numberless birds and small animals" dwell "in perfect safety" in areas that are "impossible to penetrate" (1:150). The low water around the shoals "furnished an amusing spectacle": bald eagles, "the ospray, the heron, and the curlew," standing "in great num-

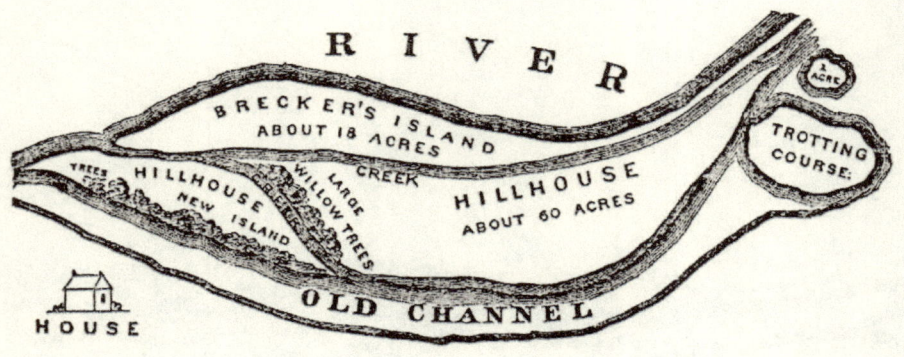

Figure 7.2. Map of Hudson River islands, from Anne Grant's *Memoirs of an American Lady* (1808). Courtesy Odum Library, Valdosta State University.

bers in a long row," while ducks, "teal and other acquatic birds, sported once on the calm waters" (1:150–51). Clearly fancied and metaphoric (one can scarcely imagine a bald eagle standing peacefully alongside the osprey), these birds enjoy a security that Grant's family did not. The island offers a refuge, an "enchanting" or "magic" spot, where the author becomes "bewildered"—where she finds sanctuary from the leveling forces that ruined her family. The Schuyler plot is distinguished from the usual Euroamerican farms. The family demonstrates its taste by preserving a few "primeval trees," which shelter cattle, and offers an alternative to more rapacious forms of development. This balance between developed land and wilderness recalls William Bartram's description of the Alachua Savanna, where the Seminoles maintained their farms on the borders of an open prairie. But while Bartram suggests a possible balance for the expanding republic, Grant uses a pastoral strategy to escape the realities of expansion altogether.

An ecological sense in *Memoirs of an American Lady* grows from the regret for a social hierarchy that the author perceived to be endangered. Grant suggests how the harmony of culture and place might lift one above politics. With Madame Schuyler established as an implicit ideal, the closing chapters review the prospects of America after the War of Independence. The Revolution opened the new nation to leveling forces with which its leaders could not cope; it was a hydra, yet even after the hydra had been slain, Grant maintains, "the deleterious dregs remain." She would come to fear a society "where no one has a right, and every one a claim," where property (like her father's six thousand acres) was confiscated, and she argues that "self-interest" and "party hatred" would continue to choke up "the paths of rectitude" (2:202–3). Grant laments that Americans lack "permanence" and "fixity," and she blasts settlers who do not know their place—in the literal and the metaphoric sense. The attention to natural processes in *Memoirs of an American Lady* convey a desire to reverse the excesses of democracy; nature offers a counterweight, by extension, to the leveling forces of a frontier. In regions like Vermont, Grant argues, one "becomes coarse, savage, and totally negligent of all the forms and decencies of life." The pioneer "grows wild and unsocial" and so on (2:217). She then couches such judgments against a pastoral sense that she sees lacking in others. "When listless indolence or lawless turbulence fly to shades the most tranquil," Grant writes, the less rooted settlers "degrade nature instead of improving or enjoying her charms. Active diligence, a sense of our duty to the source of all good, and kindly affections towards our fellow-creatures, with a degree of self-command and mental improvement, can alone produce the gentle manners that ensure rural peace, or enable us, with intelligence and gratitude, to 'rejoice in nature's joys'" (2:217).

The language recalls the usual sentiments of elites when addressing the frontier. Grant views the environment in terms of improvement; the border regions demand "self-command" and "diligence." The same contrast of "rural peace" with a "wild and unsocial" backwoods population surfaces again and again in descriptions of Ohio and Kentucky. Where poets and legislators in the United States looked to interior lands for transformation and change, however, Grant perceives a value in the existing habitats. Certainly she welcomes agriculture, but development must be sustainable and respectful, and this environmentalism serves as the basis for aristocratic pretensions. Green cultural critic Neil Evernden observes that "the domain of the natural and inevitable" provides an "ideal preserve" for cherished values. Grant portrays her own sensitivity to native flora and fauna, like the "preserve" of her island, against the upheaval that accompanied the Revolution. Literary historian Robert Pogue Harrison notes, in a remarkable book on literary forests, that romantic woods possess a quality of inaccessibility that makes them ideal for marking what is lost. A nostalgia for the woods "keeps open [a] vision of historical alternatives," and amid changes in the colonial scene, it may ground an older order in the physical terrain. Grant shows a special fondness for wetlands (rather than forests), but the upshot is the same. The areas where birds nest are "enchanting" and "magic"; she becomes "bewildered" in spaces untouched by development. This foil of the nonhuman parallels an idyll for a precommercial order where boundaries were "natural" and people of all classes recognized the Schuylers' social station.[8]

Marking Change, Registering Loss: Timothy Dwight's Travels

Like the island in the Hudson River owned by an old Dutch family, the past imagined by *Memoirs of an American Lady* would remain outside the currents of change on the northeastern frontier. The image of the Schuylers —sustainable farmers, generous patrons, landscapers who balance utility and beauty—contrasts starkly with the "indolent" and "lawless" banditti of Vermont. This desire to reverse the Revolution recalls a slightly better-known work, but one that describes the same region at about the same time, Timothy Dwight's *Travels in New England and New York* (1821–22). A Congregationalist minister, Federalist, president of Yale University, and patriotic poet in his early days, Dwight held the preservation of a moral order across geographic space as one of his guiding purposes. He sounded his authorial voice with *The Conquest of Canaan* (1785), a biblical epic written while Dwight's father was dying in a Crown-supported frontier colony. The 1794 prospect poem *Greenfield Hill* divines the future of America under New England leadership from a hilltop parish in Fairfield, Connecticut; critic Robert Lawson-Peebles calls this georgic a combination "of the geopolitics of Tom Paine" and "the Puritan typology of mission." *Travels* evolved from the later effort to cultivate a millennial-environmental vision beyond the campus walls of Yale. During university recesses, Dwight took to exploring the country, and by the time of his death in 1817, he had covered over twelve thousand miles in journeys that took him from Long Island to Canada and from Maine to western New York. The exhaustive notes from these tours provide a veritable encyclopedia for the region and performed the valuable service of capturing a country undergoing tremendous change—of seizing the "form and colors" of a country before they disappeared.[9]

The work continues the business of nudging the continent up the ladder of civilization, following the conventions of early national frontier writing but from a federalist rather than republican perspective.[10] It was probably never meant as "a book that required following from front to back" (as the novelist Charles Frazier says of Bartram's *Travels*), Dwight providing most of all an exemplum for how an educated elite should root a Christianized vision of progress-across-space. In the John Carter Brown Library is an edition of Dwight's *Travels* that belonged to Nicholas Brown. With some pages heavily annotated and others uncut, this invaluable copy suggests how Dwight was read — and when he was read at all. Brown came from an established Providence family: They were tied to the university, speculated in real estate ventures such as the Ohio Company, and were central figures in New England's commercial economy. Nicholas Brown's copy shows that he skipped quite a bit (where the pages remain uncut), but when the subject turns to his home state, he offered enthusiastic seconds. Where Dwight discusses the "low morals" in eastern Connecticut, for example, his reader added in the margins, "because it bounds on R. Id." A comment about the "plain ignorant" people near Brown's hometown was underlined, and an observation about "badly built, and decayed barns" was punctuated with three exclamation points. The close of the chapter drew this approving conclusion: "A most original account indeed of the genius of R Id." These annotations, such as the "indeed," suggest how elites used the cartographic text to identify and envision their ideas of "civilization." Martin Brückner has argued convincingly that "the discourse of geography" provided "material figures of national consent" in the federal republic. Writers such as Jedidiah Morse, Samuel Williams, and Dwight used geography as the "container" for a "socially unified but spatially divided citizenry."[11]

Yet the uncut pages also suggest that *Travels* would hold the attention of even the most supportive readers for only so long. It was Dwight's dying request to publish "these travels of mine." The book represents the last example of a cartographic text by a revolutionary author, in other words, and it is valuable if for no other reason than as a work that outlived its genre. The organization of chapters recalls the scarcely breathing conventions of a topographical description.[12] Book 1, a "Journey to Berwick," uses the pretense of a tour to Vermont to review New England's natural and civil history, with Dwight not leaving New Haven until the fifteenth letter. The journeys to New Hampshire, Vermont, and the Canada line explore the frontier, valuing the same civility found in Thomas Pownall, Eliza Lucas Pinckney, or Crèvecoeur. Turning a form usually associated with republican authors to conservative ends, Dwight describes northern New England as a Connecticut in the making, with the "*conversion of a wilderness*" continuing from carefully tended Puritan roots (1:7, emphasis his). The later volumes shift the emphasis from New England to the region's satellites in New York.

Travels then closes, after two short tours of the Connecticut valley, with standard fare: a review of the Iroquois, drawn from previous sources; the rebuttal of some earlier European travels in America; and observations on the history and prospects of the region and nation. The very concerns that lead Dwight to disputed territories, however, fuel a second function of the book, which is to memorialize local place. Specific sites in the country trigger a historical memory. He shares Anne Grant's concern about the absence of "fixity" and "permanence" in America, and the rich collections of regional lore would foster an attention to environmental change.

The pastoralism, once again, was rooted in conservative politics. In an 1806–7 session with Yale seniors, Dwight offered this remarkably undemocratic opinion: "It is said that man has a natural right to suffrage, but that is absurd." *Travels* fell within an overarching plan by the educator and minister to check rising influences from the south and west. Fiercely opposed to the Jefferson and Madison administrations (from 1800 to 1817, when most of *Travels* was written), Dwight branded the settlers of the Louisiana Territory "semi-savages"; he blasted the War of 1812, which Federalists took as a sign of rising power from the west, as "unnatural, impolitic on our part, causeless and unjust." He published a pamphlet anonymously in 1815 defending a movement to reunite England and the American states from New York to Maine. *Travels*, as a result, contains many cautionary tales about the dangers of expansion. Dwight labels anyone or anything that lacked local attachment, even tinkerers, as "wanderers, accustomed to no order, control, or worship."[13] Like other conservatives, he believed that Vermont epitomized the union's potential for anarchy, and he treated the state as a "front line" in the battle for a moral society. Although Vermont entered the union in 1791, it had a history of radicalism that dated to the colonial era. In 1749, Governor Benning Wentworth of New Hampshire began issuing patents in what was then the New Hampshire Grants, and a battle ensued with New York that also would set pioneers against proprietors. When the likes of Duncan MacVicar attempted to remove New England settlers from the Vermont "Grants," the inhabitants mounted a resistance under Ethan Allen and his famous Green Mountain Boys. Much like the Yankee-Pennamite fiasco on the Susquehanna, this controversy bled into the Revolution, and after the war Vermonters continued to follow their own interests by establishing an independent commonwealth. Eventually Vermont became the fourteenth state, but these events would lead the conservative author Samuel Williams to grumble that affairs had approached "a state of nature." The situation, in short, was perfect for Timothy Dwight. He traveled to Vermont several times, and the political contests would culminate in a composite tour he describes in a chapter entitled "Journey to Vergennes." The conservative cousin of "Susquehannah," "Journey to Vergennes" folds two trips (from 1798 and 1806) into one narrative, using the comparative travelogue to measure the region's potential for Christian civilization.[14]

I will refrain from discussing "Journey to Vergennes" at length, except to note that like Crèvecoeur, Dwight conflated nature and class, and he fretted that the citizens of Vermont were limited by their physical surroundings.[15] Even as he noted a dependence upon pioneer labor for economic expansion, Dwight would anticipate the day when the "foresters" (as they were known in New England) disappeared further into the woods. Their job was none other "than to cut down trees, build log houses, lay open forested grounds to cultivation, and prepare the way for those who come after them" (2:321). The Vermont frontier, in this view, required supervision; it required the same close attention that Governor Arthur St. Clair brought to Ohio and a restraint of the excesses that the War of Independence had unleashed. Where the Puritans of seventeenth-century New England enjoyed "the prevailing high sense of religion and morals" and "compelled the inhabitants into habits of regularity and good order," the Revolution had fostered a situation "less favorable to the existence . . . of internal peace" (2:323). Dwight welcomes immigration "in regular society," yet he regrets that Vermonters were always "censuring the weakness and wickedness of their superiors"—griping about "persons of such merit with public offices" around every "kitchen fire, in every blacksmith's shop, and in every corner of the streets" (2:321–22). Casting its lot with a governing and economic elite over the people who actually worked the land, *Travels* seeks to balance an expanding civilization against a backward-looking stability. Only through the continued attention of authors, educators, and clergymen like himself would the frontier be replaced with "good order, peace, and prosperity" (2:353).

This same desire to reverse the Revolution would lead Dwight to an affinity for local history and to the very pastoral strategy that Grant advances through the Schuyler family. *Travels* announces its concern with place in the preface, which explains how readers might share "the emotion experienced by" one "standing on the spot which was the scene of an interesting transaction" (1:4). Much as the Vermont journeys seek consolidation over historically unstable grounds, Dwight provides the kind of lore that would fix a culture to the physical terrain. Scarcely a chapter of *Travels* passes without an anecdote about the country he visits: "Permit me to detail to you exactly what thoughts which occurred to me on this spot," Dwight implores at Lake Champlain (2:312); he asks the same at Plymouth Rock, at the home of King Philip, at Ticonderoga and Concord (1:257, 280). Each site of the Puritan and Yankee past is linked to a teleological history that traces the redemption of a "savage" wilderness.[16] No detail is too arcane: A ghost saved Hadley, Massachusetts (1:257); a boxing match settled the boundary between New London and Lyme, Connecticut (2:366); Mount Cube was named for a lost dog named Cube (2:79). Visiting Portland prompts a long yarn about General Wadsworth's escape from a British prison (2:117–35); at Fort Stanwix in New York, an Indian used his teeth to scalp a British soldier (3:137); Williamstown, Massachusetts, provides the tale of a palmer worm that bore through a twenty-year-old plank, a legend adopted, of course, by Thoreau (2:276).

Environmental historians and the occasional ecocritic observe that *Travels* offers a starting point for understanding the changing landscape of early New England.[17] An attention to locale, born from a desire to preserve the region's past, makes Dwight far more receptive to his physical surroundings than earlier authors of a cartographic text. Sharing the fears of rootlessness found in Joseph Doddridge and Anne Grant, Dwight would register the toll that expansion had taken on area habitats, on flora and fauna. Alongside the stories of battle heroics, boxing matches, and lost dogs, he remarks upon the disappearance of rattlesnakes; the decline of moose, bears, and wolves; the vanishing oyster beds and dolphins (whose skins were harvested for gloves) on the Long Island Sound. Although mills had boosted industry in New England, Dwight observes, the damming of rivers had blocked the passages for spawning fish. New Haven green used to be covered with scrub oaks and was home to wild turkey and partridges. Such observations facilitate a *caring* about the country: How could one pass through downtown New Haven today and not feel a bit more attached to the place, knowing that wild turkeys once roosted there? The recognition of loss roots a society. In a previous discussion of Lewis Evans, I noted that the experience of crossing physical space triggers memories, and the stories born from those crossings were a means through which cultural boundaries were defined. Ethnographer Kent C. Ryden emphasizes the role of a sign in this process: The sign "slaps a date on a piece of geography, making it notable and giving it meaning"; it calls "our imagination to further layers of significance." The stories preserved in *Travels* do the same thing. The process of constructing place, as Dwight clearly realized, is both cumulative and retrospective. Academic geographers have explained how an individual biography develops from the repetition of specific paths across space. Not only does Dwight retrace the paths of New England's history, establishing the biography of a region through his own tours, he builds the geographic significance by setting the stories to paper. The land becomes a part of the people, and the people become a part of the land.[18]

The retrospective sense fosters an appreciation for wilderness, which in turn nudges this otherwise crusty work away from the usual calls for ecological imperialism. After the "Journey to Vergennes," for example, Dwight shifts the focus from New England's future frontier to the past. *Travels* looks backward with deliberate effect in a chapter entitled "Journey to Cape Cod." This excursion brings him to the tip of a land mass but also to the starting point of a region's history. Within the larger structure of the four volumes, the scene closes the exploration of New England and provides a bridge into the New York tours. The very setting and location of these descriptions in the narrative, as a result, free Dwight from earlier associations of wilderness — as land awaiting development — and allow him to pursue a more poetic path. While describing the beaches below Provincetown, Dwight muses over what ordinarily might have been dismissed as worthless scrub land. The dunes, he writes, are

> naked, round, and extremely elegant; and often rough, pointed, wild, and fantastical, with all the varied forms which are seen at times in drifts of snow. Some of them are covered with beach grass, some fringed with whortleberry bushes, and some tufted with a small and singular growth of oaks. The variety and wildness of the forms, the height of the loftier elevations, the immense length of the range, and the tempestuous tossing of the clouds of sand formed a group of objects, novel, sublime, and more interesting than can be imagined. It was a barrier against the ambition and fretfulness of the ocean, restlessly and always employed in assailing its strength and wearing away its mass. To my own fancy it appeared as the eternal boundary of a region, wild, dreary,

and inhospitable, where no human being could dwell, and into which every human foot was forbidden to enter. (3:59)

A rich description unfolds from this impasse between the New England and New York tours. Cape Cod exemplifies a liminal space, a bioregion that would resist development, where the "wild, dreary" waste is granted an aesthetic appeal. The usual emphasis upon progress fades as Dwight's "fancy" ranges over an area where the "human foot was forbidden to enter." He continues by describing how sea grass preserves the dunes. This check on erosion, providentially "exhibited in this place" by the Creator, should "claim the admiration and gratitude of man" (3:61). A different side emerges, in other words, from the usual narrative of improvement. In implicit argument against "ambition," Dwight appreciates the sublimity of a "desolate" and "tempestuous" scene.[19]

An unexpected tension thus emerges from a work that had outlived its time, giving *Travels* the resonance that makes it the minor classic it is. The very geographic history that shapes the four volumes (and that gives a theme to tedious sections like "Journey to Vergennes") creates the room for a chronicling function, and this play across time—and therefore discourses—richly counters the main current of progress and change. Literary critic John Sears notes that the descriptions of "enduring value" occur when Dwight negotiates "between what he wished to see in the landscape and what was actually there."[20] The landscape of Cape Cod serves as a fitting transition between thematic and literal routes—from New England to New York, from the Puritan past to its future. The "boundary" to a sublime that Dwight would ordinarily fear seems slightly more comfortable in light of the recognition of that past; such memorializing gives him license to recognize undeveloped environs. At nearby Plymouth Rock, he suggests the beginning for religion in America and therefore for his own narrative: "No New Englander," Dwight writes, "can stand upon the rock where our ancestors set the first foot without experiencing emotions entirely different from those which are excited by any common object of the same nature" (3:73). The local lore, as noted, awakens his appreciation for nature. He can equate "wildness" with elegance, and the dunes provide a barrier to "ambition." The concern for fixing a society to its past through memorial recalls the descriptions of an island in *Memoirs of an American Lady* and finds the author humbled before a providential ecology.

The Roots of a Pastoral

Exemplifying how a literary work can outlive its genre, *Travels* pushes the usual concerns of a cartographic text from prescriptions of environmental change to the veneration of "wildness." On one hand, much of Dwight follows the expected rhetoric of progress-across-space. He argues for an orderly settlement that was commensurate with the terrain, much as Crèvecoeur did in "Susquehannah," and the closing chapters observe conventions from *Notes on the State of Virginia*—debunking European descriptions of America, challenging the Comte de Buffon. Marking a departure from earlier examples of the cartographic text, on the other hand, Dwight exhibits an almost preromantic conservation ethic. This contradiction was not as stark as it might seem. Cultural critic Renato Rosaldo notes that imperial ideology is usually at "play with domination," leading to paradoxes where "people destroy their environment and worship nature."[21] Dwight consolidated his own position through a kind of *topophilia* among the dunes of Cape Cod. The aesthetic here yet once more finds the republican author injecting himself into decisions about the land. Although contemporary readers might see his environmental views as forward thinking, Dwight's narrative unfolded from a continued charge of republican writing: to establish the terms by which a society would occupy its physical place. The pastoralism followed the ongoing effort to provide roots in a colonized domain.

An attention to the political work of environmental writing may explain the apparent contradictions in *Travels*. Standard surveys of nature writing in the United States rely upon a continuum from domination to veneration, with authors such as Dwight mentioned perhaps as confused or transitional figures. "Dwight's political conservatism," historian Jane Kamensky notes, "translated into a nascent conservation ethic." But the focus upon a longer tradition (as indicated by the word "nascent") does little to explain the ambivalence. Kamensky argues that Dwight's outlook is "Janus-faced" and that scenes like the dunes of Provincetown "strained his appreciation of both romantic wilderness and progress." For while *Travels* might present what is now seen as far-sighted attitudes toward nature, the author elsewhere adopts an "antiecologist" position. Dwight celebrates the size of old-growth trees, while elsewhere dismissing undeveloped woods as "a mere forest" (2:336). He has nothing but praise for the estate of a man who invented the potash kettle, an invention that all but leveled New England, and he argues for draining Lake Erie (2:175, 3:238). Clogged roads through untimbered regions generate outright hostility toward the natural world. Because the topsoil in woodlands served the function of retaining water, the roads through these parts could become swampy. Several passages find Dwight slogging through these miry paths, grumbling about the thick canopy overhead, and anticipating the "civilizing influence" of denuded landscapes that would bring more passable routes (2:86, 3:124, 4:35). The recognition of disappearing flora and fauna does not mean that the author wishes to turn back a teleologically ordained history. Rather, the nostalgia remains fixed to a culturally bound conception of place and therefore an imagined political realm.

The calls for conservation represent a triumph of common sense, in conclusion, but they emerge from an overriding concern with preserving the leadership of an educated elite. The fixity seemingly found in nature, as demonstrated in Anne Grant, provides a rhetorical counterweight to the leveling forces that accompanied the Revolution. I have shown through previous examples how frontier writers triangulated their perceptions of nature against an Other. Literary critics who begin from the nineteenth century note how a nostalgia for *things disappeared* accompanied federal scripts for Indian removal.[22] But policy makers and authors in the early republic viewed the frontier primarily through economics and certainly not on a strict racial divide. Governor Arthur St. Clair in the Northwest Territory (like many of his scribbling contemporaries) derided backwoods whites as "savages." For both Dwight and Anne Grant, an appreciation of nature provided the foil against which these suspicions were aired. The "foresters" of New England, says Dwight, are "loose, lazy, shiftless and unprincipled people" (4:3) Besides being impossible to govern, these settlers lack taste in their landscaping. He chides the "bare, bleak and desolate" country where inhabitants "cut down their forests and groves" and leave little "to enliven the scene" (3:49). Stumps epitomize a dearth of leadership on the frontier (2:238). The failure to harbor a bit of nostalgia for old-growth forests would suggest the need for a hierarchical order. In a move that was pedagogical to the core, he positioned the authority of his own group on the continent by directing how resources should be managed and used.

How, then, did this environmental ethos unfold alongside calls for Indian dispossession? As the costs of changes in the land became increasingly evident, the rhetoric of entitlement would set Euroamerican authors into vexed and troubling relationships with indigenous peoples. Earlier and often violent acts of usurpation, on one hand, led republican authors to justify expansion through nature, while on the other hand, the fears of dissolution in a democratic society supported notions of a hierarchy grounded in the physical place. The histories of settlement such as *Memoirs of an American Lady* and *Travels* offset the instability of frontier life through strategically deployed appreciations for the "untouched" realm — for an island in the Hudson that escaped development, or for the dunes at Cape Cod that blocked "ambition." Writing in the same years that Dwight's last book was published, James Fenimore Cooper would shape those conservative anxieties into plot with his novel *The Pioneers, or the Sources of the Susquehanna; A Descriptive Tale*. The cartographic text finds a reinvigorated form, and through a fictive hybridity, Cooper establishes a leading family (much resembling his own) as the proper heir to Indian claims. The heiress of the novel, Elizabeth Temple, happens to mark the changes that followed new settlements. She gives voice to the vanishing flora and fauna, and without rejecting Euroamerican expansion altogether, suggests that — in nature — whites could play Indian themselves.

*To a person who has witnessed all the changes
in the western country, since its first settlement,
its former appearance is like a dream, or romance.*
—JOSEPH DODDRIDGE

Disappearance and Romance

COOPER'S *The Pioneers*

Nature, Nostalgia, and Native Americans

ONE TASK OF this book has been to trace out conflicts of the backcountry, showing how narratives took new turns from initial points of contact to their later circulation in print. In "Traits of Indian Character," Washington Irving lodged a protest against Andrew Jackson's involvement in the Creek War. This conflict, which merged into the War of 1812, had roots in native responses to the "benevolent plan," and it marks one of the fatal blows to that program. Creek politics are too complicated to explain here (rifts were widening from the "reforms" instigated by Indian agent Benjamin Hawkins and Tecumseh's revitalization movement); it is enough to say that, in 1814, the federal government and Andrew Jackson capitalized upon the political instability and joined assimilationist Creeks in an attack on the Red Stick Creeks at Horseshoe Bend, in present-day Alabama. After claiming victory, the wildly popular Jackson made his way to New Orleans to fight the British, leaving the Red Sticks to seek refuge among the Seminoles, a division of the Creek Confederacy. The United States meanwhile demanded a cession of some 23 million acres of Creek land. Irving's sketch first appeared in *Analectic Magazine*: In the periodical version, he blasted Jackson and General John Coffee, expressing sympathy for the "misguided tribes of Indians that have been drawn into the present war." The same essay appeared six years later in *The Sketch Book of Geoffrey Crayon*, but without the topical references. Stripping the content of its earlier context, the author vaguely waxes philosophical about Indians in a kind of melancholy romance. "There is something in the character and habits of the North American savage, taken in connection with the scenery over which he is accustomed to range," Irving muses, "that is, to my mind, wonderfully striking and sublime." He takes a fashionable British view that the United States should not "stigmatize the Indians," and he fears that they will "vanish like a vapour from the face of the earth, their very history will be lost in forgetfulness, and the places that now know them will know them no more." Following a convention of the time, Irving cites Logan's speech from *Notes on the State of Virginia*, and he clucks at the "miserable hordes" of settlers that corrupted the natives. The show of sympathy for Indian people, however, would eventually work against them. As federal policies took a new turn in the 1820s, "Traits of Indian Character" would be used to make the case for Jacksonian removal. Southern politicians argued, with echoes of Washington Irving, that native Americans could never "reclaim" their innate nobility, living so close to unruly pioneers. Tribal lands should therefore be surrendered to whites.[1]

The plea for a dying Indian recalls the sentimentality of a better-known but equally stylized piece, also from *The Sketch Book*, "Rip Van Winkle." As the story goes, the lazy but ultimately benign Rip leaves his peaceful Dutch village for a hunt, falls asleep in the Catskills, sports with the ghosts of a "wild mountain," and returns to a faction-ridden United States. Setting his tale just a short sail downriver from Anne Grant's Albany, Irving uses the pastoral mode in yet one more attempt to turn back the clock and escape the partisanship that characterized the early United States. The story imagines a country that "was yet a province of Great Britain," when the name Van Winkle summoned the "chivalrous days of Peter Stuyvesant." The bulk of Rip's time before his nap passed idly: hunting, fishing, or chatting by the village inn under an old tree and a portrait of King George III. When Rip returns to the same porch after his long nap, however, the tree has become a maypole, and he finds a different kind of character: "a lean, bilious-looking fellow, with his pockets full of handbills, [who] was haranguing vehemently about rights of citizens—elections—members of congress—liberty—Bunker's Hill—heroes of seventy-six." All of this was "perfect Babylonish jargon to the bewildered Van Winkle." His ties to the mountains, his "bewilderment" there, leaves little room for politics. Irving mockingly suggests that Rip escaped the "petticoat government" of a shrewish wife, but the docile descendant of an old Dutch family would scarcely know how to respond when asked, "Federal or Democrat?"[2]

The juxtaposition of these two sketches in one book should draw attention to the uneasy dialogue between frontier politics and the quest for place in early national culture. Critics of romantic literature note that elegies for the vanished race were a shorthand for dispossession—which explains why the sympathies expressed in "Traits of Indian Character" would serve the interests of living native peoples for only so long. Language that initially critiqued Jackson's exploitation of the Creek War would eventually find its way into arguments for dispossession and into the rhetoric of removal that critics such as Lucy Maddox, Renée Bergland, and Susan Scheckel ably chart.[3] Yet conflicts on the early national frontier elude scholarly readings that suggest a strict racial boundary. As the Creek Confederacy split over federal policies of trade and "improvement," genteel citizens blamed most of the problems in the relations with native peoples upon backcountry whites. "Rip Van Winkle" makes subtle play with class and regional anxieties in the early republic, longing for the colonial order that was associated with the old Hudson Valley. Rip's encounter with the spirits of a place leave him ill-suited to address the question "Federalist or Democrat?" Irving gently locates his own preferences (be those fleeting or sincere) in a peaceful landscape that preceded such partisan debate. Triangulating race and dispossession against region and class, *The Sketch Book* would cement a connection for what might vanish—nature, Dutch customs, or native Americans—through a romantic pastoral.

The same nostalgia would provide the fabric for a national myth in a second New York book, James Fenimore Cooper's *The Pioneers*. The plot of this 1823 novel recalls the intent of a geographic literature—to legitimate one's claim on a contested space—through an equation of landscape and entitlement. Like most border accounts, the story would begin from the vagaries of possession. Judge Marmaduke Temple had obtained an extensive patent on Lake Otsego during the upheaval of the American Revolution, and the changes that accompanied his development set him against the book's most memorable character, Natty Bumppo. Their rivalry unfolds through an ambiguous figure named Oliver Edwards, who turns out to be the estate's legitimate heir and who wins the affection of Temple's daughter, Elizabeth, but while living with Natty and the Delaware Chingachgook. Through the course of this "descriptive tale," Cooper recalls scenes of a bygone world — the turkey shoot and other sports, the bounty of nature and its waste, the verbal slapstick behind spurious political plots — but questions of identity and legitimacy bring the story together and foreground different uses of the physical environment. After Natty shoots a deer out of season and is forced to serve jail time, and once Chingachgook has died in a ritual purging of native lands, the landholding family is restored through the marriage of Oliver Edwards-Effingham and Elizabeth Temple. Security comes at last to the inherited patent, and (to continue the equation suggested by Irving, Dwight, or Grant) Oliver and Elizabeth symbolically wed an appreciation of nature with a more stable political order. Their union marks thus the ascendancy over what once was claimed by Chingachgook.

Given the charge of dispossession in a cartographic text, where else could the novel end but by an Indian's grave? The closing chapter to *The Pioneers* finds Natty Bumppo about to disappear but anxious about how the people of Templeton will remember the past. He stands with Oliver and Elizabeth before Chingachgook's final resting place. "But before I go," the hunter asks, "I should like to know what 'tis you tell these people... of the old Delaware, and of the bravest white man that ever trod these hills." Oliver reads the markings, while Natty offers some parting corrections:

> "This stone is raised to the memory of an Indian Chief, of the Delaware tribe, who was known by the several names of John Mohagan; Mohican"—
>
> "Mo-hee-can, lad; they call theirselves! 'hee-can."
>
> "Mohican; and Chingagook"—
>
> "'Gach, boy;—'gach-gook; Chingachgook; which, intarpreted, means Big-sarpent. The name should be set down right, for an Indian's name has always some meaning in it."[4]

Dramatizing the penchant for memorials by his contemporaries, Cooper pronounces a chapter of the middle ground closed, while initiating a new era of mythology. The transitional figure, Natty, addresses the errors before vanishing from the scene, before heading "toward the setting sun" (like the close of a John Ford Western), having opened "the way for the march of the nation across the continent" (456). Literary critic Eric Cheyfitz notes in a defining essay that the metaphoric in *The Pioneers* dispossesses the native object through translation. With the figurative severed from the literal, Cheyfitz maintains, the named Indian is "carried across" the divide that distinguishes myth from the past. Misspelled, the word on the stone displaces the significance of Chingachgook's actual name. The "Indian is translated out of the world of 'man' to become in the logic of this passage, another species altogether." All that remains is a "fantastic frontier," Cheyfitz argues; in this elegized West, racial lines remain strictly upheld, natives die heroically, and figures of the middle ground vanish into the sunset.[5]

Building upon Cheyfitz's suggestion that the figurative becomes normative through an act of translation, and drawing from the studies on literary dispossession by other scholars, I argue that Cooper lends a transparency to ideology through a rhetoric of nature. This rhetoric serves the crucial role in *The Pioneers* of grounding story to place; an ecological sense in the novel, as with works like *Memoirs of an American Lady*, distances the author from factions "unsettling" a frontier. In a world where patriot agitators spoke "Babylonish jargon," Cooper seeks a language of "Indianness," a semantic concreteness that grounds a social hierarchy in the physical terrain. Events in the author's personal life drove this plot for legitimacy. The model for Judge Marmaduke Temple was William Cooper, a wheelwright who became rich through speculation in present-day Cooperstown. Having made a fortune from hard work and shadowy beginnings, William Cooper later tried to present himself as landed gentry, and in the transition from developer to political leader, identified himself with the party of Timothy Dwight. Biographies paint an unflattering portrait of a local operator with new money, national aspirations, and few scruples: doing the Federalist's dirty work by bullying settlers into the party line, palming election tickets into their hands, or stuffing ballot boxes himself.[6] The pretensions and embarrassing legacy of the father, in turn, fueled the son's literary ambitions. During the period in which *The Pioneers* was written, a series of lawsuits devoured William Cooper's claims. James, as the sole heir, did nothing to fight the litigation, channeling his energies instead into the imagined territory of literary romance. The novel's plot for legitimacy mirrors the family's crumbling financial estate and disturbing political legacy in compelling ways. By revisiting the past, the author sought to excise an unseemly history and suggest new bases for entitlement on the American interior.[7]

These psychic pressures, not to mention a growing romanticism, would lead the novelist to the more stable field of nature. Fueled by personal anxieties that paralleled the dynamics between John and William Bartram, *The Pioneers* might claim the title of the first ecological novel written in the United States. Roderick Nash argues in a widely cited survey that Cooper marks a turning point in American environmental values by presenting wilderness as "a moral influence, a source of beauty and a place of exciting adventure"; in a conclusion that makes the classic error of confusing the teller and the tale, Nash holds that both "Natty and Cooper believed in 'the honesty of the woods!'"[8] But the context of authors such as Dwight, Irving, and Grant suggests that the "honest" woods had an ideological spin, and Cooper relies upon the pastoral to distinguish his more romantic environmental persona from the abrasive land ethic and politics of his father. In 1810, William Cooper wrote a pamphlet that outlined his success as a developer, *A Guide to the Wilderness*. Following the usual formula of tracing progress across space, it describes the transformation of a forest into farmland and suggests arrogant links between ecological change and military conquest. "Leave to Cæsar the boast of having destroyed two million men," marvels New York attorney William Sampson in a preface to the *Guide*; "let yours be that of having cut down two millions of trees." From an empty (or *emptied*) wilderness, William Cooper builds a village of "8,000 souls, with schools, academies, churches, meeting houses, turnpike roads and a market town."[9] The legacy that the father left for the son, articulated through competing views of land use, might explain why *The Pioneers* would cast forests as a "moral influence." The novel's pastoralism recalls the conservative implications of place that were advanced at this time. In terms of party loyalties, James Fenimore Cooper held to a strange hybrid of Federalist stability and Jacksonian democracy; he shared the aristocratic pretensions of his father yet believed that laws should come from the people and that a political order should have local roots. *The Pioneers* accordingly makes light of pretenders who extend their reach, contrasting upstarts with a natural aristocracy that can recognize the "honesty of the woods." With the need for an organic claim driving the plot, the novel suggests a hierarchy through an attentiveness to one's physical surroundings. Cooper in this way would imagine a republican subject over the land as he revised his father's shadowy legacy. The advancement of civilization on the frontier, the novel implies, depended upon the class of inhabitants that recognized proper relations between the human and the natural worlds.

Romancing the Contact Zone

This construction of border identity occurs through the agency of a cartographic text. As the critic Wayne Franklin notes of *The Pioneers*, Cooper "found an opportunity and left a tradition," and the novel begins like many of the works discussed already—with a survey of physical space. The first sentence explains, "Near the centre of the State of New-York lies an extensive district of country, whose surface is a succession of hills and dales, or, to speak with greater deference to geographical definitions, of mountains and valleys" (15). A beginning from geography recalls Lewis Evans and Thomas Pownall, who used topographical descriptions as the basis of historical narrative; Crèvecoeur and Jefferson, who structured their accounts through the agency of a map; Eliza Lucas Pinckney, who drew the borders of Carolina to outline a culture's pursuit of refinement; or Timothy Dwight, whose visits to physical landmarks trigger a historical memory. The critic James D. Wallace notes that *The Pioneers* addresses a fundamental question—"Who owns America?"—that is the premise of any cartographic text. Yet the language also opens the usual rhetoric of possession to complication. As the phrase "with greater deference to geographical definitions" hints, the plot works outside the expected boundaries of a utilitarian account, blurring the borders between fancy and reportage in expedient ways. The allowance for fiction offers a West in revision—outside the more baldly imperialistic grammar of Cooper's predecessors. Such mythmaking, as noted in my introduction, might frustrate western historians. Patricia Nelson Limerick grumbles that the "process of invasion, conquest, and colonization" often "provoked shiftiness in verbal activity."[10] Indeed, the need for some "shiftiness" to explain away a legacy of conquest would provide the occasion for plot. Whatever his faults as an author, Cooper realized that nations were narrated, that those narratives were inherently unstable because challenges to authority were endemic to border society, and finally, that dubious claims to nature called for a certain amount of dissembling.

The Pioneers accordingly works from geographic foundations into a romance of the contact zone. The novel sifts through tensions that other authors sought to explain away and incorporates them into plot, bringing the various contests for natural resources and legal authority into dramatic play. The story begins with the performance of a typical backcountry conflict. It is Christmas Eve, 1793 (thirty years before the novel was published), and Judge Marmaduke Temple is returning to Lake Otsego with his daughter

Elizabeth, who had been away at school. Some hounds in the woods sense a buck, fast becoming a rarity in those parts. The Judge stops to load a double-barreled rifle and then fires twice at a dear crossing his path. They hear a third shot from an "unseen marksman," and the deer falls. Natty Bumppo and an unnamed youth in native dress step into the scene and claim a disputed prize. The debate that follows presents three frontier types—the speculator, the hunter, and the Indian—on an atemporal scale. Natty leads the argument, holding that "game is becoming hard to find," with the Judge's "clearings and betterments," and he contends that a backwoodsman's "right to shoot on these hills, is of older date than Marmaduke Temple's right to forbid" it. The Judge counters in legalese, and he argues that the later shots were what the courts call "an act of supererogation," a redundancy to his first and mortal wound (22–25). Natty is not convinced. Clearly at a disadvantage, Temple offers to buy the buck, split the venison, vote, even flip a coin. But Natty holds to the law of the woods and explains that the decision was not his anyway; the young man had fired the killing shot. Finally, they inspect the deer and count bullets in a nearby pine. With one shot unexplained, the Indian youth lifts his coat to reveal a bloody wound. Natty gets the deer, the young man goes with the Judge for treatment (only after Elizabeth's pleading and another lengthy debate), and the stranger's entrance into the Temple home sets the plot in motion.[11]

Few novels written in the United States open this cleanly, and while *The Pioneers* drags elsewhere, its first chapter neatly crystallizes key environmental and social issues from the 1820s and the previous thirty years. As the toll of expansion upon local ecologies became evident and the nation appeared to outgrow its boundaries, Americans who divided over resource use would not only question the bases of entitlement on the border regions but also the future of a democratic society. In the Northeast, changes in the land were prompting legal battles. Historian Arthur F. McEvoy cites an 1805 ruling by the New York Supreme Court, *Pierson vs. Post*, in which two parties vie for their rights to game. The situation resembles what Cooper describes: Post flushed out a fox, but Pierson shot it, raising the question over "when a wild animal became somebody's property." McEvoy (who brilliantly applies this dilemma to California fisheries) concludes that any explanation of "environmental change should account for the interembeddedness and reciprocal constitution of production and cognition." Commonly celebrated as an early ecological novel, *The Pioneers* may indeed be read as attempt to shape "cognition" during a period when both habitats and social demographics were changing. The opening chapter shows how vanishing game prompted a question of propriety—*who decided how the land should be used?*—which in turn exposed the fractures of authority on the frontier. What were the bases of a social order in a border republic? The "relations between man and man or between man and nature must be governed by some kind of law," critic George Decker suggests of *The Pioneers*, and the novel captures a "transitional phase," when an inscrutable source of justice was lacking. Critics invariably note that the opening scene presents figures who represent successive historical eras. Because the characters come from different epochs, no reconciliation is possible.[12] The novel stages the relations that passed between people as they struggled for control of a particular environment.

In these performances of contested nature, unfolding in a setting that is more allegorical than realistic, the individual most often weighing out the law is Elizabeth Temple. She appears as the mediator, surveying the rules in highly formalized scenes where the perspective invariably returns to her.[13] A holiday turkey shoot, for example, provides the "sport" or display of backwoods abilities. The contest serves as "an exhibition of the far-famed skill of Leather-stocking," Cooper writes; with Elizabeth serving the role of the Lady, she appoints Natty Bumppo her "knight" (199, 187). Before stumbling onto the shoot, the steward of the Temple house, Richard, had been showing Elizabeth the "improvements" to their estate (182–83); on the other side of the coin, the scarcity of turkey in the wild prompts a rare outburst by "Indian John" about changes in the land (185). By pairing the town's two best marksmen, Natty and the woodchopper Billy Kirby, Cooper creates an "open collision" between a hunter and the forces of expansion. Natty represents the "honesty of the woods," while Kirby is likened to "the conqueror of some great city" (191). As with the opening chapter, the turkey shoot sparks a disagreement over laws. When Natty takes a turn, his rifle snaps and he loses his shot. Billy argues that another chance should require a second schilling, because "it's the law of the game in this part of the country"; Natty volleys back sarcastically, "It's likely you know the laws of the woods better than I do, Billy Kirby!" Even after Elizabeth sponsors her "knight" for a second try (with Natty hitting his mark, of course) the overzealous Richard offers to lead a committee that would draft written "regulations" (195–99). This excess of language contrasts with the transparent authority of an elite. It is Elizabeth's grace, plus the appearance of Marmaduke Temple, that brings the dispute to a close.

In nearly every encounter of human order and nature, Elizabeth appears as the intermediary figure around whom environmental values are defined. Chapter 1 finds her "unconsciously rejoicing in the escape of the buck" that Oliver shot (20). The next morning, back in Templeton, she gazes "in mute wonder, at the alterations that a few short years had made in the aspect of the country" (40). These reservations about expansion set the proprietor's daughter in a liminal position. She exclaims, "the enterprise of Judge Temple is taming the very forests," referring to her father formally as "Judge Temple" and objectifying the forests with "very" (212). The concern for changing environs, unsurprisingly then, never overtakes economics, and as with most pastorals, her recognition of loss is set against material advantages that she does not fully reject. The strongest arguments for preservation, usually from Natty, seem unrealistic in comparison. He constantly complains, "You've driven God's creaters from the wilderness" (356), and his failure to heed Judge Temple's game laws lands him in the town's makeshift jail. When Oliver challenges Elizabeth about Natty's violations, she makes her loyalties clear. "What can my father do?" she asks. "Should we offer the old man a home and a maintenance, his habits would compel him to refuse us. Neither, were we so silly as to wish such a thing, could we convert these clearings and farms, again, into hunting-grounds, as the Leatherstocking would wish to see them" (280). Elizabeth's objections here should offer a corrective to critics who seek to locate *The Pioneers* in a historical continuum and to take one character's perspective as the statement of a land ethic. As Roderick Nash maintained, Natty (presumably speaking for Cooper) views the woods as "a moral influence, a source of beauty and a place of exciting adventure."

But this anticipation of a later romanticism overlooks the centrality of Elizabeth and the role that nature plays in a plot of possession. Natty serves only a transitional function (as several critics have argued). A celibate hybrid, he can survive only in Cooper's literary imagination, and when the book ends, he must disappear.[14] Certainly Natty offers lessons in appreciating the natural world, but those teachings advance allegories for how a member of the landholding family should possess the land; the stories of ecological waste in *The Pioneers* invariably reify class boundaries. In a scene where Richard dredges Lake Otsego, one of the novel's more memorable episodes, Natty and Chingachgook refuse to take their meal from a massive pile of dying fish. "I eat of no man's wasty ways," the Leatherstocking protests (265). They paddle Elizabeth and Oliver away from the spoilage and toward a symbolic baptism that models how humans should interact with their surroundings.[15] The case for sustainability overlaps with the legitimacy plot in the language. As Natty begins to fish, Elizabeth stares into the "secrets of the lake," looking over the gunwale of her canoe and into the liquid genius of place. A "fish of unusual size" rises to her sight, and Cooper suggests a mutual curiosity "between the heiress of the land and the lord of these waters" (269). As the fish offers its blessing to Elizabeth, Natty acts in a way that contrasts with the noisy townspeople:

> "That will do, John," said Natty, raising his prize by one of his fingers, and exhibiting it before the torch; "I shall not strike another blow to-night."
> The Indian again waved his hand, and replied with the simple and energetic monosyllable of—
> "Good."
> Elizabeth was awakened from the trance, created by this scene, and by gazing in that unusual manner at the bottom of the lake, by the hoarse sounds of Benjamin's voice, and the dashing of oars, as the heavier boat of the seine-drawers approached the spot where the canoe lay, dragging after it the folds of the net. (270)

Silent, chaste, balanced, and dreamlike, the episode suggests how nature plays into a drama of imperial translation. One fish is enough, and that one fish comes without effort or speech. The scene has a symbolic logic only, where the lead characters are pure figure. (If Natty wanted to minimize human impact on the lake, he would have grabbed a fish from the net.) The cacophony nearby frames this silent communion with nature; amid "hoarse sounds," language is reduced to the wave of a hand and a "simple" monosyllable—"Good."

The self-consciousness toward a language of nature suggests that this passage is a likely reflection of Cooper's own ambitions as a novelist. The scene engages the author's anxieties about legitimacy and sets those anxieties against the physical environment. In an earlier chapter, I discussed Terry Goldie's observation that canoes provided an intermediary between Europeans and the indigene. Obviously a religious metaphor, the fish serves a similar role: It naturalizes a claim to place, and "the lord of these waters" distinguishes the heiress from the noisier townspeople. As the hoi polloi dredge more bass than they can eat from Lake Otsego, Elizabeth gains a lesson in sustainability that is relayed, as Cheyfitz might suggest, in a transparent language. What she learns in the translation comes from an "Indian" who needs only monosyllables and the wave of a hand; Chingachgook and Natty model an inherently noble form of harvesting resources. Such implications establish a lead character as indigenous to her locale, even as they gloss more immediate struggles that the author wished to forget. Clearly James Fenimore Cooper regretted the waste that drove a border economy, even though he was a beneficiary. As environmental historians have noted, frontier speculation (which *The Pioneers* dramatizes) capitalized upon a backwoods population that was often portrayed as unruly and inefficient. While Elizabeth may exclaim that "Judge Temple is taming the very forests," the girdling and clear-cutting and burning of trees nonetheless raised property values. Most writers accepted the leveling of wilderness as a regrettable and ugly but necessary process; the abuse was lamentable, in other words, even as it generated wealth.[16] Investors would depend upon this displaced labor while pretending to stand above the fray. William Cooper benefited from the people holding the seine (if I may link the family and fiction), not from the silent Chingachgook. The symbolic confluence between "heiress of the land and the lord of these waters" exercises a conservation sense in order to privilege a natural aristocracy—Oliver and Elizabeth—over the rest of Templeton, when in fact the material debts were elsewhere. The novel at its most vivid moments uses an environmental ethos not only to reconcile a culture and its place but to position a national subject as the proper beneficiary of contested resources and to revise the forces that built the novelist's estate.

"This, Then, Is Thy Indian Blood?":
Becoming Native to Place

This fictional case for an organic aristocracy presents the lead characters as close to their physical surroundings, to what is native of the place, so that the conservation-minded Elizabeth Temple may find herself in the same boat (literally and figuratively) as Chingachgook. But how does that environmental imperative fit into the dispossession plot? I have suggested the ways in which authors in the early nineteenth century could turn the pastoral against unwelcome political changes on the frontier. Increasingly, the calls for an innate nobility (in a democratic society) found authors adopting native Americans as a metaphor of landedness. This conservative appropriation paralleled a disintegration in federal programs. While Indian policies in the United States had failed from the beginning to recognize non-European cultures on their own terms, Enlightenment discourse did at least start from a belief in common humanity, and revolutionaries believed that they could change people as they changed the land. A combined effort by religious and public groups sought to "civilize" native nations by introducing Euroamerican systems of agriculture, education, and property, as well as Christian moral values and domestic gender roles. Many native Americans engaged with these programs, rejecting some tenets while incorporating others, even as critics expressed their reservations about the slow rate of "progress." The ideas of improvement codified by Henry Knox would eventually fuel arguments for usurpation. The "noble" character of Indians became something to protect, and land-hungry whites argued that a proximity to frontier settlements reversed the good intentions of a "benevolent plan." The concern for the natives' "improvement," ironically, became grounds for dispossession; by 1825, President James Monroe would argue that only removal could "make them a civilized people."[17]

And in a rather predictable paradox, the pressing demand for interior land accompanied a rising use of native Americans in literature and art. The symbolic and "safely dead Indian" would provide an ideal vehicle for grounding a culture in its place, for justifying possession where little justification existed, and for screening out class anxieties in the United States. Authors before Cooper, as I have shown, had already established a tradition of adopting an indigenous voice in respect to the environment. Native Americans offered a kind of passport or intellectual currency when describing the continental interior. Thomas Jefferson appropriated a speech by the Mingo Logan, or Tahgahjute, in the name of patriot science; William Bartram adopted the name Puc-Puggy, given to him by a Seminole chief, to legitimate his botanic self; the author of Crèvecoeur's *Voyage* would describe himself as an adopted member of the Oneida nation. So when James Fenimore Cooper sets the daughter of an heiress and the last surviving "Mohegan" in the same boat, he continues the long process of defining a national landscape in part through the agency of race. Ethnohistorian Philip J. Deloria notes that such instances of "playing Indian" assuaged insecurities about entitlement in the once colonial (but now colonizing) state. As authors in the early republic imagined a dying race, Deloria observes, they sought to legitimate the United States as an ascending empire: Anyone who participated in the mourning, in turn, would be a "member of a special extra-American elite."[18]

Oliver Edwards-Effingham baffles Templeton's white inhabitants by "playing Indian," but he serves as the ideal figure of "translation" because he represents both a colonial hierarchy and what was native to the place. He is the legitimate heir to the Temple patent (we learn near the story's end), and as the opening chapter establishes, the inhabitant of two worlds. The vague history of Temple's patent works itself out through the physical body of the youth. It is the Judge's poorly aimed shot in chapter 1 that brings Oliver into the manor house, and from the beginning, Cooper uses Oliver's wound to set pretensions against a natural order of things. The injury is first subjected to a foundationless "display of professional skill" by the inept town doctor, Elnathan Todd. As Todd talks around the solution, however, Oliver moves the bullet to the surface of his skin through a chance motion. Internal force expels the foreign object. Then, to complete the allegory, Mohegan John, or Chingachgook, finishes the case. The steward Richard recommends such cooperation as the perfect solution in a romance of the middle ground: "Give me a regular physician, like Doctor Todd, to cut into flesh, and a native to heal the wound" (88). The rest of the story would turn on the competing allegiances of the mysterious Oliver, as he vacillates between the hunters' hut and the Judge's office. The plot cannot resolve itself until Oliver comes forward with the secret that was inside him. In Cooper's sovereignty plot, it takes a (pretend) native "to heal the wound." Oliver marries Elizabeth (but only after Chingachgook has died) and secures the line of an ascendant family.

At ease in the drawing room or with Natty and Chingachgook, Edwards-Effingham exemplifies the pastoral figure who brings wilderness indoors — and legitimacy to the usurping home. Cheyfitz argues that Oliver serves as a "figure of translation," and Cooper hints at the young man's ambiguous allegiances throughout the novel. During his Christmas Eve visit, Oliver's hand rests on a "little ivory-mounted piano," touching the "instrument, as if accustomed to dwell on such places" (68); the inability of lesser characters to recognize his innate character marks *their* lack of refinement (110); Elizabeth sees him as "a genteel savage," the "descendant of King Philip, if not a grandson of Pocahontas" (214). As the embodiment of the colonial stage theory, Oliver even protests to Elizabeth that "your society has tamed the lion in me" (412). This transformation occurs with a kind of inevitability that suggests it was meant to happen all along—and on the Judge's terms. As a pastoral can voice regret without sacrificing power, Oliver's role sometimes appears to be little more than settling Temple's (and Cooper's) uneasy conscience. He has surprisingly little agency for such an important character. Even the treatment of Oliver's wound was for the Judge's benefit. When Oliver declines to spend the night in the hall on Christmas Eve, Elizabeth protests, "the knowledge, that you decline our assistance, would give my father great pain" (92); Temple later insists that it is "in my power to compensate you for what I have done" (201). What Oliver actually wants, and in a manner typical for a one-sided plot, seldom matters or alters the story.

The "figure of translation" instead serves a narrowly imperial function: Even Oliver's performance of hybridity, it turns out by the end, has been to facilitate a transfer of possession. Facing the task of asserting a family line, Cooper reinvents the "contact zone" to acknowledge conflicts, but he also must explain away the prior traces of a more permeable culture. The fact of a living native—in a point upon which Americanist and postcolonial critics agree—gets replaced by a purely figurative one.[19] Near the close of *The Pioneers*, as the legitimacy plot comes to an easy resolution, Oliver finally reveals his identity. The elder Effingham (a dying claimant) explains the past, and the heir allows that he is only symbolically Delaware, that he was just "playing Indian." Judge Temple questions Edwards-Effingham and begins this disturbing exchange:

> "This, then, is thy Indian blood?"
>
> "I have no other," said Edwards smiling;—"Major Effingham was adopted as the son of Mohegan, who at that time was the greatest man in his nation; and my father, who visited those people when a boy, received the name of the Eagle from them, on account of the shape of his face, as I understand. They have extended his title to me. I have no other Indian blood or breeding; though I have seen the hour, Judge Temple, when I could wish that such had been my lineage and education."
>
> "Proceed with thy tale," said Marmaduke. (441)

Having served the function of bridging a past and a future, the transitional figure may disallow a hybrid stage. Oliver's whiteness makes him a suitable spouse for Elizabeth. His links to the colonial past neatly excise Temple's ignoble origins, and his "Indianness"—which is not the same as Indian blood—establishes him as landed aristocracy in a democratic republic. This transfer of possession (imagined while the author's own estate was disappearing) occurs through an act of narration that *even the characters* allow is mere narration. As Marmaduke Temple insists, "Proceed with thy tale."

When and how does a story become grounded in the physical terrain? In *The Pioneers*, nature provides the means through which an untenable narrative is normalized, for without the ecological conscience, the novel would falter upon its own gymnastic turns of plot. Like Grant, Crèvecoeur, or Dwight, Cooper offers a series of clues that links a romantic land ethic to the capacity to lead a frontier society. A refraction against class grounds both aristocratic pretensions and the imagined self onto the land.[20] Chingachgook embodies the "safely dead Indian": He is "the last of his family, and his particular tribe, the Delawares," is known by the "mournful appellation of Mohegan" (85). Natty's regret for "things disappeared" lumps vanishing people and habitats into a single category. In a constant refrain, he grumbles about expanding settlements, diminished game, and a lost way of life. "I have known the Otsego water for five-and-forty years now," he cries,

> and I will say that for it, which is, that a cleaner spring or better fishing is not to be found in the land. Yes, yes—I had the place to myself once; and a cheerful time I had of it. The game was plenty as heart could wish, and there was none to meddle with the ground, unless there might have been a hunting party of the Delawares crossing the hills, or maybe, a rifling scout of them thieves, the Iroquois. There was one or two Frenchmen that squatted in the flats, further west, and married squaws; and some of the Scotch-Irishers, from the Cherry Valley, would come on to the lake, and borrow my canoe, to take a mess of parch, or drop a line for salmon-trout; but in the main, it was a cheerful place, and I had but little to disturb me in it. John would come, and John knows. (291)

The outburst begins an exchange that allows Cooper to encompass several perspectives, and those shifts epitomize the colonial pastoral. Chingachgook responds to Natty in the native language: "The land was owned by my people." Oliver joins the mourning, adding that it "must have been a sight of melancholy pleasure, indeed," even as he paradoxically scans "the clearings, groaning with corn [that] were cheering the forests with the signs of life." His view suggests how one might bracket the past without disavowing a legacy. Chingachgook represents the dispossessed, but he will die; Natty gives voice to loss, and he disappears as well. Only Oliver, the ascendant, may indulge melancholia, while simultaneously scanning the fields that "were cheering the forests." This play between environmental personae allows Cooper to indulge regrets without sacrificing power. A veneration for the wild begins once the country appears to have changed hands.

Elegy serves this bracketing function, closing the frontier while leaving open the romantic wilderness. With *The Pioneers*, authors might safely consider a fully realized counternarrative of conquest. Natty might summon a "cleaner" place, one that is untouched or that precedes despoilment ("there was none to meddle with the ground"). As with all idylls, however, the vantage point is the time of writing. "The pastoral moment in Cooper's fiction," critic H. Daniel Peck notes, "occurs when the eye takes possession of its rightful holdings."[21] And with the spoils would come a lingering feeling of culpability. As Cooper establishes an imaginative claim to the interior, he would cast earlier contests in dramatic oppositions, with clear racial boundaries and a compelling sense of responsibility to whites. The terms under which natives disappear are nothing short of self-indulgent.

Mount Vision is awash in flame. The story is almost complete, and Chingachgook appears ready to disappear with the smoke. He addresses a canister of gunpowder, blaming it for the loss of his land: "This is the great enemy of my nation. Without this, when could the white men drive the Delawares! Daughter, the Great Spirit gave your fathers to know how to make guns and powder, that they might sweep the Indians from the land. There will soon be no red-skin in the country. When John has gone, the last will leave these hills, and his family will be dead" (403). The dying native takes "a parting look at the objects of the vale," the forest fire nearly surrounds him, and perhaps conscious of the conflagration that approaches, he bids farewell. His decline represents the imagined end of one civilization and the rise of an ascending republic.

Nostalgia, Guilt, and Nation Building

Chingachgook actually escapes the fire, but the point gets made anyway. He dies soon enough. A final image of him — on the burning Mount Vision, about to explode — is too dramatic to be believed (yet too powerful to dismiss). Death by demolition (from the exploding can of powder) suggests a neatly causal relationship between military strength and Indian removal, and it also attempts to rhetorically close a middle ground. The drama between "white men" and the "red-skin" sets two races in opposition; any sympathies or lasting signs of being in between cultures get sanitized with the clear division between enemies or by a condescending sympathy for a vanishing race. Distancing a culture from its shared past, this explanation of ecological and social change mostly indulges Euroamerican guilt. Cooper tellingly places the burden of responsibility on gunpowder, attributing blame for Indian losses to force and leaving little room for morally neutral causes, such as disease. But the easy symmetry and the timing of his regret warrant scrutiny. Just as the treatment of Oliver Edward's shoulder was to assuage the guilt of the Judge, Chingachgook's farewell speaks first and foremost to cultural anxieties about possession. The elegy more likely reveals Euroamerican concerns about the land, not its former inhabitants, and reflects the ongoing concern in early national literature with identifying place. Historian Timothy Silver notes that, during the colonial period, settlers who altered the physical terrain commonly felt a "guilt associated with conquest and an emerging nostalgia for 'noble savages' and precontact America."[22] This feeling would only intensify as the United States increasingly equated itself with the continent and as federal policies shifted during the 1820s from "benevolent improvement" to removal.

Americans to this day talk about the injustices done to native Americans almost as readily as they venerate the wilderness, which should say something. Environmental historians, on the other hand, trace less immediate causes for changes in the land (and thus changes in possession). While the ecological impact of colonization on the continent is almost too profound to fathom, it altered ecosystems in ways that its colonial and revolutionary writers never fully explained and certainly could not control. The most significant invaders were, by all accounts, microbial. The wilderness was not virgin country; in Francis Jennings's memorable phrase, "it was widowed."[23] And yet disease rarely factors into romantic stories of native decline (or if it does, then only to present conquest as an inevitability). Anne Grant, for example, imagines a dialogue between an Indian and a white trader. She observes that native Americans suffered under the diminishment of land and game, and she writes powerfully—and accurately—about the effect of rum. Only a short paragraph at the end of this long dialogue alludes to disease, however; she notes briefly that "small-pox was also fatal to them." The syntax suggests that even authors who understood the impact of microbes did not have the narrative license to explore this explanation more fully. The transitional word "also" becomes necessary because smallpox did not fit within the logic of her account. Disease fails to enter Grant's *Memoirs of an American Lady*, or Cooper's plot, for that matter, because germs do not implicate whites. Disease was a crushing but morally neutral conqueror; death by infection lacks the poetic punch of an Indian holding gunpowder on a burning mountainside. The image of a lone "Mohegan" (or Delaware, or whatever he is—Cooper does not care) lends a poignant culpability that the more accurate explanations lack. Chingachgook instead fulfills the stereotype of the Indian as the "original conservationist," and he provides the human link to a wilderness that was fast becoming myth.[24] *The Pioneers* looks forward to a national future with this partial amnesia, indulging a narcissistic counternarrative to progress at the expense of the past.

Figurative history in *The Pioneers* severs romance from the country that William Cooper settled and exploited and that native Americans occupied before him. Chingachgook serves a strictly symbolic role in this transfer, providing the human figure through which a change of possession is imagined. He is already old in the novel. He fittingly dies once the Temple patent has been restored and a land ethic for the new generation has been established. Even the celebratory scenes of the Indian's former power emasculate him. "I have fought in as many battles as any warrior in your tribe," he cries over his drink in the town tavern, "but cannot boast of my deeds at such a time as this" (165).[25] Once "master of these noble hills," he would be supplanted by the youthful Temple-Effingham marriage (206). As Chingachgook exemplifies the figurative claimant (not the real one), the new patentee is only a symbolic "Indian." As noted in a previously cited passage, the patriarch asks: "This, then, is thy Indian blood?" Edwards returns with a smile, "I have no other." The game of "playing Indian" ends, and through fiction—only fiction—the acclimation between a culture and a place occurs. Frontier authors since the 1750s had sought to establish a narration that would colonize space but at least acknowledge the presence of native Americans. Lewis Evans portrayed the border regions as a vast domain that the Six Nations held in check. His fiction of suzerainty provided a grammar for Anglo-American expansion, relying upon a native empire that was more narrated than real. Jefferson adopted an indigenous voice as the republic's own and conveniently overwrote the vagaries of a middle ground in the process. William Bartram defined an environmental persona through an Indian nickname. Cooper continues this imagining of the frontier and stages hybridity through a novel that has the same cartographic frame. His opening to *The Pioneers* shows "deference" to a geographic literature but quickly moves into the more malleable space of romance. Even his characters, at times, acknowledge that the narrative exists only as narrative. And what anchors the transfer of sovereignty is a language of nature.

Pastoralism gives moral weight to an otherwise untenable plot. Cooper's task being the *naturalization* of culture, he acknowledges the social permeability found on the border regions, but once the process of making one's self native has been completed, the transitional (or "translating") character asserts his European identity. Oliver's disavowal of "Indian blood" comes with a smile; the admission is made retrospectively, safely after the fact. The "tale" offered to Marmaduke Temple (and that the cartographic text invariably provides) imagines the interdependence between Euroamericans and native Americans, even while anticipating the dismissal of a middle ground. "By the end of the novel Oliver is not only the legal heir to the state which Judge Temple has held in trust for Edwards Effingham," Thomas Philbrick notes, "but symbolically he is the inheritor of the Indian's moral claim to the land."[26] One culture dies, the other is ascendant, and an environmental imperative secures the equation. The image of a "last" Delaware allows the author not only to acknowledge (an emasculated) past but to position a local aristocracy as the rightful heirs of the place. The parting figure, Chingachgook, provides the beginning of a counternarrative and helps instill a pastoral sense that will provide further justification in the heiress's claims to a previously contested domain.

Continuing from where an eighteenth-century cartographic text began, in short, the novel accomplishes what its more utilitarian predecessors could not. Cooper leaves the legacy of a romanticized wilderness and a closed frontier, and like Lewis Evans's "Map of the Middle Colonies," this fiction would ground property relations that were themselves imagined. A preservationist sentiment, moreover, smoothes the class anxieties that would rumble throughout earlier accounts of similar border regions. Elizabeth Temple's environmental sense—reflected in her capacity to weigh preservation versus development—establishes her as the proper claimant to the land. And while Cooper may reverse the usual sentiments of progress-across-space, countering the calls for improvement with a veneration for wilderness, his use of the disappearing Delaware continues an old trick that dates back at least to Lewis Evans. The semifictional Lake Otsego, at the source of the Susquehanna River, falls within Iroquoia. Yet Natty and Chingachgook, the characters who represent the novel's moral conscience, call the Iroquois "thieves." An identification with the Delawares thus displaces the region's legitimate claimant. One should scarcely expect accuracy from Cooper, but he was stretching the past by any standard. Susan Cooper (author of *Rural Hours* and the model for Elizabeth) wrote in 1850 that "this ground lies within the former bounds of the Six Nations and a remnant of the great tribes of the Iroquois still linger about their old haunts, and occasionally cross our path."[27] In a shell game that alienates one group's claims by privileging a second, Evans exaggerated the Iroquois's hegemony in order to minimize the Delawares' sovereignty elsewhere; the novel reverses the names of these two tribes but uses the same strategy. Cooper uses a dying Delaware in order to imagine a transfer of land that (as his daughter notes) "lies within the former bounds of the Six Nations." Once again, as authors defined a national self over the land, they invented relations with native Americans. Following an earlier literature, here through a sentimentalized design, *The Pioneers* suggests terms for occupation and legitimized usurpation. The uncertainty of any claim on the border region leads a novelist in 1823 back to where Lewis Evans began in 1755 — to a narrative of the frontier that was, at best, a fiction.

Now tell your people they will become lost when they follow the ways of the white man.
—JESUS CHRIST *(in a vision to Handsome Lake)*

You are our brethren of the same land: we wish to see your prosperity, as brethren should do. Farewell.
—THOMAS JEFFERSON *(in a response to Handsome Lake)*

CODA

Parallel Republics

IN 1799, THE Seneca prophet Handsome Lake received the first of three visions that provided the foundation for an Iroquois religion. The slow cultural recovery that followed may stand in vital contrast to the dying Chingachgook, for it shows how the indigenous peoples from upstate New York adjusted to and evolved in a colonized state. More than most native groups, the Six Nations suffered setbacks with the American Revolution—which is not to say that they faced extinction or defeat. The formidable Iroquois Confederacy divided during the war. The nations that remained loyal to England, such as the Mohawks, uprooted to Canada, while others like the Senecas remained in the United States. Those that stayed worked in partial and problematic terms through a program that was closer to the modern-day reservation system than to Henry Knox's lofty idealism. From "slums in the wilderness," as ethnographer Anthony F. C. Wallace termed the impoverished setting, Handsome Lake received his visions for social reform. His first message focused on sin and damnation, cataloging the ills that accompanied poverty. In the second vision, the "Sky Journey," Handsome Lake met George Washington and Jesus Christ, who informed the seer (in

217

a remarkable exchange from the middle ground) that "your people . . . will become lost when they follow the ways of the white man."[1] The third vision rounded out a code that provided steps for moral reform—and that was forged against that ever-pressing concern, land.

Two years later, in 1801, the Seneca prophet traveled to Washington, D.C., to outline his beliefs for Thomas Jefferson. No written transcript of the message survives, although Jefferson responded with a letter that supports the call for temperance, while predictably ignoring territorial grievances. He informs "Brother Handsome Lake" that "we are always ready to buy land" and uses the exchange as an occasion to endorse republican principles, insisting that the union will "never ask" for cessions until "you wish to sell." The interests of the republic once again subsume more fluid and immediate negotiations on a middle ground. Insistent that native Americans would be better served by adopting white "civilization," Jefferson continues:

> Nor do I think, brother, that the sale of lands is, under all circumstances, injurious to your people. While they depended on hunting, the more extensive the forests around them, the more game they would yield. But, going into a state of agriculture, it may be advantageous to a society, as it is to an individual, who has more land than he can improve, to sell a part, and lay the money in stocks and implements of agriculture for the better improvement of the residue. A little land, well stocked and improved, will yield more than a great deal without stock or improvement.

The advice turns conversation into a monologue. Jefferson takes on a patriarchal role, and while assuming that native Americans and Euroamericans shared the continent, he presumes to dictate the proper use of natural resources. His letter closes: "You are our brethren of the same land: we wish to see your prosperity, as brethren should do. Farewell."[2]

For native Americans whose lives were overturned by Euroamerican expansion, however, invasion could not end with a curt, simple "farewell." They adapted, resisted, changed, sometimes thrived, and often suffered in a colonized world. From 1789 through the Monroe and Adams administrations (1817–29), intellectuals and leaders in the republic saw Indians much as they regarded nature—as subjects for "improvement"—but this perspective faded with the rising influence of the southern and western states. By the end of his presidency, the Virginian James Monroe reversed his position to favor removal, and Andrew Jackson's election in 1828 stood as a referendum against republican policies. Even if one allows for the profound effect of imperialism upon native lives, however, their interests were never singly determined by the United States. Nor would romantic elegies script real questions of identity; as the critic Cheryl Walker reminds us, "textuality itself" was not "the death knell of indigenous cultures." Expansionist policies affected indigenous societies in complex ways—indeed, in ways that conventional "literary" works from the period do not adequately explain. In the mid–eighteenth century, the Delaware Neolin's vision of the afterlife fueled forms of resistance such as Pontiac's pan-Indian "rebellion" in the West. Little Turtle and the Ohio nations fought settlements in the Northwest Territory through 1794, and Tecumseh united a western and southern military front against the United States a generation later. Still others explored peaceful paths of survival that engaged the republican plan in a selective manner. Divided into "assimilationist" and "preservationist" camps, the Senecas weighed federal- and church-sponsored overtures against the traditional paths of regeneration. The Cherokees were typically defined "as a model" of the "Christian Indian republic," Mary Young notes, yet acculturation set "competitive, contentious, and exploitative relationships" into play, with different parties vying for influence.³ At the individual and group levels, native Americans evolved alongside alterations in their cultures, economies, and physical surroundings.

One writer who exemplified this difficulty of living between worlds was the Cherokee journalist Elias Boudinot. In 1821, visitors to an Indian mission school in Cornwall, Connecticut, witnessed an exhibition of student "progress." Several groups were represented—Choctaws, Osages, Hawaiians—but the individual who most impressed observers was the young Boudinot, whose very "appearance" refuted the idea that "savages are not capable of being civilized and polished." Born Buck Watie in 1804, from parents who had partially assimilated already, Boudinot entered the school in 1817 and converted to Christianity three years later. The missionaries attempted to instill in him a faith in shared humanity, but that faith proved to be short-lived. In 1824, he married the white daughter of a Connecticut physician, and their engagement incited a riot on the village green of Cornwall—the couple was burned in effigy, and the trauma disabused Boudinot of any hopes that the United States would ever become fully integrated. He went back south during a time when the Cherokee nation was experiencing profound changes of its own. Tribal leaders passed a constitution in 1827, and in a revolution for native philology, the Cherokee Sequoyah developed a syllabary (like an alphabet but based on syllables) that made it possible to read and write in his own language. Boudinot founded a bilingual newspaper in 1828, the *Cherokee Phoenix*, that used the new syllabary alongside columns in English (which used Latin type fonts). He ran the newspaper for another four years, until his forced retirement.[4]

The fate of both the *Cherokee Phoenix* and its first editor would attest to the difficulty of straddling worlds. In print, Boudinot would seek to establish that natives (like the land) could be improved, yet his refrain of progress-across-space homogenized factions within the Cherokee nation. Many natives could not read the *Cherokee Phoenix*, and its editorial content suggests they were not necessarily the sole audience. The split identity symbolized by the two type fonts — one Latin, the other Sequoyah's — was more often a demonstration of "Indianness" than an honest effort to reach a wider range of people. Boudinot offered arguments, presumably from inside, that addressed policy debates between citizens of the United States. To combat dangerous assertions that native Americans were "declining" and that they could "never be reclaimed where they are," he maintained repeatedly that the Cherokees had embraced "civilization" — that they were "redeemed [from] a savage state" (116, 130, 94). The tallies of "STATISTICAL and ACCURATE information" (emphasis his) detail changes in the land. Like Timothy Dwight, Boudinot would count the mills, shops, orchards, crop yields, livestock, and redeemed souls to provide a kind of balance sheet for "civilization" on Indian soil (117, 99–101). At the same time, he would underestimate the influence of the more traditional majority. Even as the *Cherokee Phoenix* presumed to speak "the whole truth" (164), its editor in fact was alienated by his own assimilation. That assimilation led to tragedy. In 1832, Boudinot reversed his position from a defense of native "civilization" to one favoring removal to the West. Political changes in the United States suggested that usurpation was inevitable: Despite a ruling by the Supreme Court that upheld Cherokee claims over the state of Georgia, Andrew Jackson had sided with Georgia and sanctioned the appropriation of tribal claims there. When Boudinot changed his editorial stand on the issue, taking the side of removal, he was relieved of his services as editor. In 1835, he joined the small party that signed the Treaty of New Echota, the agreement that led to the Trail of Tears. Tribesmen later stabbed and tomahawked Boudinot to death, exercising a traditional law of retribution that, ironically, the *Cherokee Phoenix* claimed no longer existed.[5]

Poised at the end of one period and marking the painful beginning of another, Boudinot thus provides a compelling record of how early national writers negotiated issues of environmental change, political identity, and frontier relations. He worked from the compromised yet politically expedient position that a Jeffersonian model seemed to provide. In doing so, he offers a point for identifying the attenuating and easily reversed principles of the early republic, particularly as they related to land. John Carlos Rowe suggests, in a magisterial survey, that Americanist literary scholarship should turn to "a common historical subject"—to texts that may be read for "a more nuanced cultural and political history" and that expose the "particularly complex intersection of literary culture and U.S. imperialism."[6] Boudinot found himself at one such "intersection." On one hand, he signed the treaty that led to the Trail of Tears—thereby setting into motion the script that had been provided by Cooper, Irving, and Philip Freneau. On the other hand, he sought to advance an indigenous state by working from *within* the spatial politics of the revolutionary generation. His status as a harbinger of removal, his position in "history," does not then explain the complexities of his prose. Boudinot's writing takes its most complicated turns in the attempt to narrate a story of the land upon Enlightenment terms—put differently, he attempts to *environ* the Cherokee republic over a still open and fractious frontier.

In 1826, Boudinot published his signature essay, "An Address to the Whites." Taken from a lecture tour that was to fund a Cherokee school and provide type for the *Cherokee Phoenix*, it incorporates the usual ideological geography into a defense of tribal territories. Boudinot begins by presenting his own speakerly presence as evidence of the nation's refinement: "You here behold an *Indian*," he intones (69). The next step is to situate his homeland on a map of the continent. "The Cherokee nation lies within the charted limits of the states of Georgia, Tennessee, and Alabama," Boudinot explains. "Its extent as defined by treaties is about 200 miles in length from East to West, and about 120 in breadth. This country which is supposed to contain about 10,000,000 of acres exhibits great varieties of surface, the most part being hilly and mountaneous, affording soil of no value. The vallies, however, are well watered and afford excellent land, in many parts particularly on the large streams, that of the first quality" (71). The remainder of this paragraph follows the conventions of the cartographic text. In the manner of Eliza Lucas Pinckney or Thomas Jefferson, the statement of boundaries leads to an appraisal of climate ("temperate and healthy"), agriculture, and the promise of civil society. Boudinot outlines a commercial future that appears to be grounded in the terrain: "There can be no doubt that the Cherokee Nation, however obscure and trifling it may now appear" will become "one of the Garden spots of America" (71). Census numbers (which refute the myth of a disappearing Indian) lead to reflections upon trade and an insistence that his people have "forsaken their ancient employment" of hunting to commence "a life of agricultural labour" (72).

The rehearsal of this progress-across-space theme provides the unlikely example of a native incorporating the republican grammar of dispossession. Facing increasing dismissals from federal leaders, Boudinot would construct his nation through the rhetoric of an Other. He refutes stereotypes by inhabiting them, adopting the standard terms of "improvement" in order to direct the interests of an indigenous state. The occasional sentimentality of "An Address to the Whites" shows that Boudinot knew exactly what he was doing. Philip J. Deloria argues that whites who were "playing Indian" during the early national period "were metaphors come to life"; they often used a graveyard mentality that "foreordained [how] less advanced societies should disappear in the presence of those more advanced." The conventional reading suggests that the colonizing culture would be haunted by, and therefore compelled to elegize, a displaced race. Boudinot accordingly translates this translation. He inverts conventional power relations, and in doing so, reasserts the interests of the potentially dispossessed. Eric Cheyfitz notes that the "figurative" Chingachgook of *The Pioneers* gets imagined out of existence. Read as metaphor, as a figure whose significance had become dislocated from its meaning, the Delaware gets "carried across" the threshold from the real world into myth. Boudinot, by this reasoning, carries the myth back into reality.[7] He offers an instance of self-mistranslation: The native speaker embodies a persona that had been imposed upon him in order to stake his claim in a hybrid world.

The "ghosting" of his own narrative returns Boudinot to the topic of land. By "carrying *back* across" an imperial rhetoric (to amend Cheyfitz's phrase), the Cherokee resituates the terrain as narrative. And as with any cartographic text, the fictional state presumes to displace the real one. Tellingly then, the text slips at precisely the same point that *Notes on the State of Virginia* did—with boundaries. Theda Perdue observes that Boudinot would leave out a sliver of country in western North Carolina, an area occupied by conservative Cherokees that the author probably wished to ignore. Like

Jefferson before him, Boudinot sets the figurative upon an empirical footing. He relies upon conventional markers of Enlightenment history and catalogs heads of cattle and stock, looms and spinning wheels, mills, plows, blacksmiths, schools, public roads, volumes of "good books," and redeemed souls (72–73). A strict duality between "civilized" and "savage" leaves little room for native agricultural practices or beliefs. Boudinot suggests that hunting was an "ancient employment," despite the fact that Cherokees had farmed for centuries; he distorts key theological points as well. The point is not that Boudinot was wrong; read as a literary artifact, "An Address to the Whites" captures the process of self-invention and rhetorical boundary-crossing that was necessary for survival on a middle ground.[8] The language reveals how a "translating" figure worked between worlds. The sentences regularly pause with qualifying phrases, halting suggestively as if to adjust for one's audience. From the opening paragraph, Boudinot allows that "the term *Indian* is pregnant with ideas the most repelling and degrading" (65). He continues with almost torturous grammatical turns: "But such impressions, originating as they frequently do, from infant prejudices, although they hold too true when applied to some, do great injustice to many of this race of beings" (68). The highly embedded syntax disrupts the flow of thoughts, and appearing as it does again and again, marks a gap between the speaker and his audience. As Cheyfitz suggests, rhetorical divides were topographical ones as well.[9] Neither was easily crossed.

Still, native Americans might occasionally regain the control of metaphors that "carried across" terms of possession. As he uses stock tropes to span a cultural divide, Boudinot makes an argument for a Cherokee republic, complicating the usual space-time plot that always seemed to end with a "vanished" race. The fiction of a "disappearing" Indian, as noted previously, would surface repeatedly in arguments both for and against dispossession. Native Americans were cast as a noble people that had declined because of their proximity to white settlement; for their own protection, leaders in the United States maintained, they should be removed. Boudinot might then suggest that evidence of a Cherokee civilization "needs not the display of language," but he offers precisely that. The narrator demonstrates his own humanity through allusions to *The Merchant of Venice*, the Bible, and in a particularly ironic reversal, Washington Irving. The Cherokees risk a "melancholy" or "mournful" extinction. "They will vanish like a vapour from the face of the earth," Boudinot says with reference to "Traits of Indian Character." Must they "perish" and "go down in sorrow to their grave?" With a liberal use of Irving, Boudinot then seeks to transfer rhetoric into action. The fate of a nation, Boudinot offers, must "hang upon your mercy as to a garment. Will you push them from you, or will you save them? Let humanity answer" (79). Humanity, of course, did not answer; the state of Georgia did. Boudinot's rhetorical question was answered by the Trail of Tears, with the forced removal leading to his murder. The Cherokee literally became the "dead Indian" that so many poets describe, although not for the reasons they typically imagine. Read in the context of an earlier literature, Boudinot can be seen to negotiate a dangerous "intersection" with fatal but unquestioned subtlety. He does so by reframing one of the fundamental questions of the cartographic text: namely, how were native-white relations narrated alongside prescriptions of environmental change? This very act of self-mistranslation refuted the cult of the "dying Indian." It would demonstrate that (whatever might spring from Cooper's mind) a middle ground still existed in the 1820s. Boudinot was able to invert republican notions of environment and race because that discourse—if in uneven ways—had engaged him in the first place.

A different phase of native-white relations—and as a result, environmental writing—would begin with the removal era. A novel like *The Pioneers* casts the wilderness as closed and intercultural relations on the frontier as fixed along strict racial divides. Just three years later, however, Elias Boudinot could still draw from the earlier literature—from a literature in which relations between humans and the land were less stable and ideas of nature and the social relations there had not yet fixed themselves into a national mythology. In Enlightenment writings about place, the fractures that followed attempted usurpations would show in even the most imperial of texts.

Authors could never quite explain away existing property-histories, any more than they could subsume existing understandings of the natural world. In an important study that defines American literature as the quest for place, D. H. Lawrence hints that a wilderness must always remain open: "As yet, there is too much menace in the landscape."[10] This "menace" took many forms—my purpose having been to register textual presences—for as Euroamerican authors sought to make themselves indigenous to the continent, they entered into complicated engagement with its existing populations. Boudinot exposes the pretensions and lacunae in a literature that conventionally served the purposes of entitlement, showing how the Cherokees struggled to define an identity against changing environs. As he set a story of this parallel republic to paper, he would continue the process by which both American nature and the human relations there were imagined. It is a valuable lesson in the history of the United States. For there are few fictions more persistent than the equation between nationhood and the land.

NOTES

Preface
1. Crèvecoeur, *Letters from an American Farmer*, 227; Davies, *Documents of the American Revolution*, 3:43.

Introduction
1. Drown[e], *Oration Delivered at Marietta*, 9–10, 15. Drowne actually misquotes *The Fairie Queene*, which reads "And made a sunshine in the shadie place." See MacLean, *Edmund Spenser's Poetry*, 30.

2. On the mounds, see Cayton's survey of Ohio political culture, *Frontier Republic*, 28–29; an eighteenth-century scientific assessment is Sargent and Barton, *Papers Relative to Certain American Antiquities*, 6; Sayre discusses mounds in a literary and historical context in "The Mound Builders," 229–30. On frontier hardship, see Dwight Smith, *Western Journals of John May*, 49–52; Perkins explores settler psychology through oral histories in *Border Life*, 78.

3. Drown[e], *Oration Delivered at Marietta*, 10, 16; Drowne to Booth, May 15, 1787; Drowne to Drowne, November 22, March 4, 1788, Solomon Drowne Collection, John Hay Library, Providence, Rhode Island; Varnum, *Oration Delivered at Marietta*, 12.

4. Dwight Smith, *Western Journals of John May*, 94, 125, 148; Cayton, "Marietta and the Ohio Company," 197; Carmony, "Spencer Records' Memoir," 359.

5. Crèvecoeur, "TRANSLATION of the Extracts," 36, 39. The Ohio Company produced these *Articles of an Association* for promotional purposes, and included treaties and political acts as well as promotional essays.

6. Crèvecoeur's "Extracts" were reprinted in Cutler, *Explanation of the Map*, 24, 41, 43–44.

7. Crèvecoeur, *Journey into Northern Pennsylvania*, 33. Philbrick wrote in 1970 (and little has changed) that "few good books have suffered the misfortune to which the *Voyage* has been subjected" (*St. John de Crèvecoeur*, 60).

8. Work by geographers in the past two decades examines how social structures define, and are defined by, space. Tuan offers a humanist approach in *Space and Place*, 56. More influenced by Marxism, Pred discusses the connections between individual biography and institutional work in the construction of place in "Of Paths and Projects," 245, and

"Social Becomes the Spatial," 337. Focusing upon narrative, Ryden describes place as "that complex of meaning that gives a landscape significance in the eyes of the people who inhabit it, marking it off from the surrounding terra incognita" (*Mapping the Invisible Landscape*, xiv).

9. Crèvecoeur, *Journey into Northern Pennsylvania*, 34–37.

10. Tichi, *New World, New Earth*, 70; Jehlen, *American Incarnation*, 3; Kolodny, *Lay of the Land*, 7; Seelye, *Beautiful Machine*, 5–12; Lawson-Peebles, *Landscape and Written Expression*, 7.

11. Smith-Rosenberg does not focus on the frontier per se, although scholars of the early republic have used the argument to interpret cohesion and dissent in different venues. See "Dis-Covering the Subject," 844. Countryman and Deloria are quoted from a roundtable that offers an excellent introduction to current Indian history. See Countryman, "Indians, the Colonial Order, and the Social Significance," 362; Deloria, "Revolution, Region, and Culture," 364. Hinderaker, who traces Ohio culture from the colonial period through the Revolution, discusses the implicit violence in an "empire of liberty" in *Elusive Empires*, 263.

12. Semonin offers a general discussion of nature and nationalism in "'Nature's Nation,'" 6; Branch provides an excellent model in the "history of ideas" sense in "Early Romantic Natural History Literature," 1063; Looby links politics and descriptions of the natural world in "Constitution of Nature," 252; Regis argues that Linnaean language informs literary natural histories in *Describing Early America*, 4–5. On romantic and patriotic forests, see Harrison, *Forests*, 108, and Michael Williams, *Americans and Their Forests*, 125.

13. For the bored delegate, see Burnett, *Letters of Members*, 8:740. A central study of hybrid culture in the Ohio Valley and a starting point for frontier history in the past decade is White, *Middle Ground*, x–xv. See also the valuable but less frequently cited study by McConnell, *A Country Between*, 211.

14. Burnett, *Letters of Members*, 8:106; Cayton, *Frontier Republic*, x; Onuf, *Statehood and Union*, xiii; Hinderaker, *Elusive Empires*, 226. Burnett provides an essential resource on the Ohio debates; Cayton and Onuf summarize the scholarship in *Midwest and Nation*, 1–12. See also Aron, "Lessons in Conquest," 138.

15. The history of this poem illustrates the close ties between literary and political culture. When Humphreys asked his former commander to write a memoir, Washington declined, citing a lack of the necessary skills, but not without encouraging Humphreys to take on the task himself. Five years later, the poem appeared in the *American Museum*. See Humphreys, "Address to the Armies," 238, 240, and Worthington Ford, *Writings of George Washington*, 10:472–73.

16. Nathan Dane and Charles Pinckney probably designed the seal; for the story of this unlikely collaboration, see Reinke, "*Meliorem Lapsa Locavit*," 68–74.

17. For representative thinking from the literature connecting radicalism and the West, see Paine, *Public Good*, 5. See also the documentary history edited by Hulbert and Matthews, *Ohio in the Time of the Confederation*, 1:14. White, *Middle Ground*, 418. On "lawless banditti," see Cayton, "Marietta and the Ohio Company," 187. Sosin includes petitions from settlers who threaten to leave the United States for rival empires in a documentary history that largely supports the Turner hypothesis, *Opening of the American West*, 87. For lively discussions of treasons and plays for empire, see Seelye, *Beautiful Machine*, and Slaughter, *Whiskey Rebellion*, 29–45. Jurisdictional crises are discussed

in Onuf, *Origins of the Federal Republic*, 76–77, 93–100; a standard reference on the old land companies is Abernethy, *Western Lands and the American Revolution*, 270–73; a useful cartographic overview is Cappon, *Atlas of American History*, 60–62.

18. On America "redeeming" Europe, see Volney, *View of the Soil and Climate*, vi; on the "public good," see Paine, *Public Good*, 35–37; similar arguments are made in Mirabeau, *Reflections on the Observations*, 1; Todd, *Wollstonecraft Anthology*, 65.

19. Berkhofer, "Jefferson, the Ordinance of 1784," 124; Barnhart, *Valley of Democracy*, 136; Boyd et al., *Papers of Thomas Jefferson*, 6:608; Hulbert and Matthews, *Ohio in the Time of the Confederation*, 1:69. Boelhower makes groundbreaking use of semiotics to interpret Jeffersonian policy in "Stories of Foundation," 403; more detailed discussions of the document's origins, however, are provided by Berkhofer and in the explanatory essays in Boyd et al. Complaints about loose governance come from Worthington Ford, *Writings of George Washington*, 10:303–4, 446–47, and Cutler and Cutler, *Life, Journals and Correspondence*, 128. On the "hard names," see Burnett, *Letters of Members*, 7:511.

20. On surveyors' fears in the region, see Hinderaker, *Elusive Empires*, 136, and Gipson, *Lewis Evans*, 34–35. Nobles uses Hutchins to make a convincing case for the use of maps by historians in "Straight Lines and Stability," 25. On the Hutchins survey, see also Barnhart, *Valley of Democracy*, 40, and Rowena Buell, *Memoirs of Rufus Putnam*, 102. A useful review of the survey is Pattison, *Beginnings of Land Survey System*, 105–43. Reports of Armstrong and Hutchins are in Hulbert and Matthews, *Ohio in the Time of the Confederation*, 2:107, 160, 152. See also William H. Smith, *St. Clair Papers*, 2:14. Many members of Congress displayed particular arrogance in the survey, noting that the "Geographer is now in Ohio," and "Measures have been taken" to "Extinguish" existing claims (Burnett, *Letters of Members*, 8:809, 7:402, 327).

21. Burnett, *Letters of Members*, 8:620, 662; Onuf, *Statehood and Union*, 56–59. Finkelman argues that "the constitution for an 'empire of liberty' actually fostered a colonial mentality on the part of some of the residents" ("Northwest Ordinance," 8). See also Rackove, "Ambiguous Achievement," 18, and Pattison, *Beginnings of Land Survey System*, 16.

22. Cutler and Cutler, *Life, Journals, and Correspondence*, 393–97, 401–5; Seelye, *Beautiful Machine*, 82.

23. On market relations in Ohio, see Onuf, "Settlers, Settlements, and New States," 181–85. On infrastructure development and expansion, see Larson, "'Wisdom Enough to Improve Them,'" 230. An indicator of how trade would alter habitats comes from Christopher Colles, who reported to Congress that "a source of wealth and greatness must speedily be open'd to this fertile country, if the natural defects were removed by art, and the water carriage improved by Inland Navigation" (Hulbert and Matthews, *Ohio in the Time of the Confederation*, 2:92).

24. On Marietta as a rowdy frontier town, see Cayton, "Marietta and the Ohio Company," 190. The generally exaggerated boosterism about Ohio was defined against Kentucky, even though Lexington in the 1790s offered lessons in French and in ballroom dancing, a subscription library, a Masonic Lodge, and Transylvania Academy. See Rohrbough's cultural history, *Trans-Appalachian Frontier*, 63. On the Kentucky and Ohio antagonism, Thaddeus Harris writes that "*Here*, in Ohio, they are intelligent, industrious and thriving; *there*, on the backskirts of Virginia, ignorant, lazy, and poor. *Here* the buildings are neat, though small, and furnished in many instances with brick chimneys and glass windows; *there* the habitations are miserable cabins. *Here* the grounds are laid out

in a regular manner, and inclosed by strong posts and rails; *there* the fields are surrounded by a rough zigzag log fence" (Thwaites, *Travels to the West*, 357–58).

25. Schwaab, *Travels in the Old South*, 60. For discussions of the frontier that illustrate the documents reprinted in Schwaab, see Faragher, *Daniel Boone*, 89, and Jordan and Kaups, *American Backwoods Frontier*, 3, 64.

26. St. Clair is quoted in Varnum, *Oration Delivered at Marietta*, 10; Dwight Smith, *Western Journals of John May*, 55–67; the British observer is Jones, *Journal of Two Visits*, 82–83; on "civilizing" natives, see Hulbert and Matthews, *Ohio in the Time of the Confederation*, 1:2.

27. On republican progress and prejudice against native Americans, see Merrell, "Declarations of Independence," 210. West provides a short synthesis of the Northwest Territory in the longer history of the American West in "American Frontier," 126; on republican politics and racial discourse, see Horsman, *Race and Manifest Destiny*, 92, 106. Prucha is strong on federal Indian policy in *Great Father*, 106; for a summary of republican policy, see Sheehan, "Indian Problem in the Northwest." A concise discussion of Manifest Destiny is Stephanson, *Manifest Destiny*.

28. Freneau, "On the emigration to America," 230.

29. Merchant, *Ecological Revolutions*, 50. For an argument that distills the lessons of environmental history (bringing together nature, law, and culture), see McEvoy, "Toward an Interactive Theory," 214. Worster argues in a similar vein that environmental history "deals with the role and place of nature in human life," in *Wealth of Nations*, 47–48. Burnett's *Letters of Members* indicates that the union thought about surveys first and native treaties second. Nathan Dane writes, "The Indians express a general uneasiness at our progress Westward [but] the hostile Indians must be brought to terms, or the disposition of those federal lands suspended" (8:508).

30. Rohrbough, *Trans-Appalachian Frontier*, 83–84; Rowena Buell, *Memoirs of Rufus Putnam*, 109–18, 343; Downes, *Council Fires on the Upper Ohio*, 318–28; West, "American Frontier," 127–28; Calloway, *American Revolution in Indian Country*, 285–91; White, *Middle Ground*, 454–68.

31. Dwight Smith, *Western Journals of John May*, 61; Cayton and Onuf, *Midwest and Nation*, 34. Cayton notes that Indians and white frontiersmen fought over "control of a certain kind of environment" ("Northwest Ordinance from the Perspective of the Frontier," 15). On the aesthetics of dispossession, see note 43; Freneau as the precursor of removal is discussed in Bergland, *National Uncanny*, 40–41. Bellin uses Philip Freneau's Tomo-Cheechi essays to argue that Freneau portrayed "Indians [as] *homo naturalis*, not *homo œcinomicus*" in *Demon of the Continent*, 56.

32. Little Turtle is quoted in Volney, *View of the Soil and Climate*, 384.

33. Krech maintains that the Indian is often perceived as "ecologist and conservationist" and then shows how natives transformed their environment (in often wasteful ways) in *Ecological Indian*, 16. Although Fisher does not address wilderness specifically, he outlines how cultural constructs (like "wilderness") become a given in *Hard Facts*, 6. Raymond Williams, whose reflections on nature have surprisingly shaped environmental history more than ecocriticism, is quoted from *Problems in Materialism and Culture*, 67. Nash's standard history is *Wilderness and the American Mind*, 41; a one-sentence summary of Nash's "story line" appears in Ian Marshall's highly readable combination of ecocriticism and backpacking, *Story Line*, 3.

34. Two central works, one primary and the other scholarly, illustrate the reluctance

of pastoral writing to link itself with populated landscapes. Abbey's *Desert Solitaire*, a tribute to the predeveloped Arches National Monument, calls the park (before it has been filled with people) a "tombstone"; Lawrence Buell bypasses imperialism altogether in his pathbreaking study, classing ecocriticism as "the work of decolonization." See Abbey, *Desert Solitaire*, xi, and Lawrence Buell, *Environmental Imagination*, 55. I take Elliott West slightly out of context by arguing that a concern for depopulated landscapes misses what could be a more interesting survey of American environmental writing; see his "Longer, Grimmer," from the landmark collection, *Trails toward a New Western History*.

35. Sosin, *Opening of the American West*, 86; Burnett, *Letters of Members*, 8:610. Leopold, who remains a touchstone for the contemporary pastoral tradition, is cited from *Sand County Almanac*, 262. Glotfelty and Fromm, "Literary Studies," xxiii. Branch concludes one of few surveys of the period with the disclaimer that a "pre-Thoreauvian literature of nature" engendered the "justly famous accomplishments" of Thoreau, John Muir, Mary Austin, Annie Dillard, and Barry Lopez ("Indexing American Possibilities," 297). Lyon includes only two pre-1800 authors in "Taxonomy of Nature Writing," 278. Although I take issue with the studies cited above, I must note that *The Ecocriticism Reader* (from which these essays came) gave my own study a critical vocabulary.

36. Joni Adamson Clarke, "Toward an Ecology of Justice," 16; Mazel, *American Literary Environmentalism*, 35–36. Sweet offers an avenue for green early American studies in his use of sustainable economic theory, which weighs economics against environmental capacity. An ecological sense is evident, Sweet notes, in the earliest British promotional literature. See his "Economy, Ecology, and *Utopia*," 400.

37. Bayet, "Overturning the Doctrine," 314; Goméz-Pompa and Kraus, "Taming the Wilderness Myth," 297. The volume edited by Callicott and Nelson, *Great New Wilderness Debate*, provides a particularly useful multinational guide and suggests an (often unattributed) influence upon American environmental historians such as Cronon and White. Lawrence Buell makes a thin case for exporting American environmental ideology. "If as, John Locke once wrote, in the beginning all the world is America, as the twentieth century nears its close the world has become sufficiently westernized to ensure for American culture . . . a disproportionately large share in determining world environmental attitudes during the next century" (*Environmental Imagination*, 22).

38. Cronon, *Changes in the Land*, 11; Richard White distills arguments made elsewhere in his short but eloquent *Organic Machine*, ix; Standing Bear, "Indian Wisdom," 201; Merrell, *Indians' New World*, 171, 182. On wilderness as "an escape from history," see Cronon's influential challenge to accepted doctrine, "Trouble with Wilderness," 80. On the human role in shaping the environment, see a useful review essay by Sherow, "Evening on the Konza Prairie," 12; Silver makes a similar case in *New Face on the Countryside*, 42.

39. The term "melancholy fact" borrows from Carr, who takes the term from Henry Knox, in *Inventing the American Primitive*, 51.

40. White, *"It's Your Misfortune,"* 613–21; Limerick, *Legacy of Conquest*, 324; White, "Trashing the Trails," 33; Robinson, "Clio Bereft of Calliope," 73; Limerick, "Making the Most of Words," 169, 184. On hard distinctions between history and myth, see Henderson, "Dispelling the Myth," 25.

41. Pratt, *Imperial Eyes*, 4; Kolodny, "Letting Go Our Grand Obsessions," 3; Shuffelton, introduction to *Mixed Race*, 8. As Spengemann notes, early Americanists should pay attention to linguistic evolution, to "mutations . . . in a coherent, temporally continuous

system" (*New World of Words*, 37). The concerns of literary critics and frontier historians are compared and contrasted in Cayton and Teute, "On the Connection of Frontiers," 1–15.

42. Hulme, *Colonial Encounters*, 12. A revealing critique of *Colonial Encounters* is Jehlen, "History before the Fact," which was followed by Hulme's "Making No Bones," which was in turn followed by Jehlen's "Response to Peter Hulme." Disturbed by the discourse and fact, Jehlen suggests that Hulme's "critical readings co-opt the universe of explanation." The impulse in Hulme "to produce an *authentic* counternarrative" is, in Jehlen's opinion, "admirable and ultimately self-defeating," and alternatively, she suggests that lapses in European chronicles (what Hulme terms narrative cruces) "represent the limits of discourse, the moments in which discourse does not know what to say"—the record of a moment "when alternatives coexist" ("History before the Fact," 680, 692). In defense, Hulme writes that "colonial discourse is not adjunct or accessory to Western colonialism" but "part and parcel of it" ("Making No Bones," 183–84). Unconvinced, Jehlen notes in a short response that "treating an interpretation independently of its object seems to me a dubious enterprise" ("Response to Peter Hulme," 188).

43. Goldie, *Fear and Temptation*, 4–6; the centrality of Goldie's argument here is demonstrated by the inclusion of this chapter as "The Representation of the Indigene" in *The Post-Colonial Studies Reader*. Maddox notes that in nineteenth-century American culture, "*civilization* and *extinction* are themselves rhetorically oppositional" (*Removals*, 8). On nations imagined through natives, see Carr, *Inventing the American Primitive*, 9; on ghosts, see Bergland, *National Uncanny*, 4; Scheckel argues that Indian policy "called into question the very principles on which the idea of America was founded" (*Insistence of the Indian*, 4). Maddox, Carr, Bergland, and Scheckel focus upon removal probably because their studies deal mostly with nineteenth-century authors; Enlightenment authors, as a result, are read as the precursors of what came later. The temptation to reduce the history of white-native relations to a morality play becomes almost unavoidable when one adopts a long view of American literary culture. Rowe, for example, provides a model for scholarly engagement in his *Literary Culture and U.S. Imperialism* but uses "Indians" to prick the American conscience. A misleading but telling side comment on Lewis and Clark illustrates his intentions: "To their credit, many leaders and warriors rejected [their] presents," he writes, "although several leaders did pledge allegiance to their 'Great Father'" (9). Rowe continues the dig in a footnote that cites Stephen Ambrose, who was his undergraduate adviser for a time, and argues that the Lewis and Clark expedition is "vastly overrated" for its "patriotic value" (301n). Although accurate about Ambrose's flag waving, Rowe falls into the same trap—reading history as a moral axiom, with righteous natives "rejecting" presents from the colonizing invaders. The native response to Lewis and Clark in fact varied according to what specific individuals and groups could gain or lose from the new arrivals. It was not to anyone's "credit" (or shame) to reject (or accept) gifts; natives acted as humans and followed their own personal and local interests. Rowe's moral imperative causes him to lose sight of how real people acted in specific historical contexts.

44. Bellin, *Demon of the Continent*, 5.

Chapter One

1. Morton, *Beacon Hill*, 53; Brückner maps out the role of geography in popular and public literature in "Lessons in Geography," 314.

2. Cappon offers a useful introduction to colonial geography, with an emphasis on genre, in "Geographers and Map-Makers," 244; Wroth discusses the Evans map as a representative text in *American Bookshelf*, 49. For reviews of British maps of eighteenth-century America, see Ristow, *American Maps and Mapmakers*, 25, and Cumming, *British Maps of Colonial America*, 59. On expansion and national identity, see Jack Greene, *Pursuits of Happiness*, 181–85, 197. On narrative and space, I draw from Ryden, *Mapping the Invisible Landscape*, 17.

3. On natural history as "global consciousness," see Pratt, *Imperial Eyes*, 15. Regis provides a useful introduction to natural history but makes the misleading argument that early national literature was shaped by a single (Linnaean) rhetoric in *Describing Early America*. Irmscher's thematic approach (focusing upon the narration of a self through one's collection) more ably allows for the fluidity in natural history writing. See *Poetics of Natural History*. Examples of natural history and geography intersecting can be found in Benjamin Smith Barton's proposal for a *Geographic View of the Trees and Shrubs of North America* (the book never materialized) and Morton's *Beacon Hill*, which footnotes passages from William Bartram's *Travels*. See Benjamin Smith Barton, *Fragments of the Natural History of Pennsylvania*, vii, and Morton, *Beacon Hill*, 54.

4. For explanations by academic geographers of how humans construct "place" and how place involves the appropriation of space and nature, see Sack, *Human Territoriality*, 32–34; Pred, "Social Becomes the Spatial," 337; and Giddens, "Time, Space and Regionalisation," 277–78. On social conflicts embedded within conceptions of space, see Peter Jackson, *Maps of Meaning*, 2.

5. Donald Greene, *Political Writings*, 202; Kennedy wrote likewise that with "Pen and Ink," geographers take "forceful possession" (*Serious Considerations on the Present State*, 4). Nobles notes that mapping marked "an attempt . . . to impose a human and political order over" over the land ("Straight Lines and Stability," 10); Harley remarks that mapping was "a medium in a wider colonial discourse for redescribing topography in the language of the dominant society" ("New England Cartography," 297); Boelhower observes that surveys "desemanticized local place" ("Stories of Foundation," 403).

6. Benedict Anderson, *Imagined Communities*, 174–75; Cheyfitz, *Poetics of Imperialism*, 67. Cheyfitz's influential book may be read to mean that translation goes one way, and the emphasis upon appropriation through language has fed a tendency by literary critics to fret over the recovery of native voices—while declaring such recovery impossible. This concern becomes less pressing as one moves away from sources like belletristic poetry and the novel. The frontier described by Lewis Evans can be reconstructed partially from William Johnson's voluminous correspondence, and from collections of state papers such as the *New York Colonial Documents* and the *Colonial Records of Pennsylvania*, which contain extensive minutes on frontier diplomacy.

7. Fenton, "Northern Iroquois Cultural Patterns," 297; Tooker, "League of the Iroquois," 418. Sturtevant et al.'s *Handbook of North American Indians*, which is organized largely by tribe, provides a useful starting point. Jennings reconstructs Iroquois diplomatic culture and is particularly strong on political dealings (see especially *The Ambiguous Iroquois Empire*, *Empire of Fortune*, and *The History and Culture of Iroquois Diplomacy*), although historians maintain that a moral imperative sometimes reduces his arguments to victimization. Richter provides a more comprehensive view of the Iroquois in *Ordeal of the Longhouse*, while work by Merrell (*Into the American Woods*), White (*The Middle Ground*), and others focuses less on single empires like the Iroquois

and more on shared (and diverging) cultures on the frontier—particularly those groups "beyond" the Covenant Chain that governed native-white relations on the northeastern frontier.

8. Jennings, *Empire of Fortune*, 75. Richter notes that by the 1720s, the Iroquois were "among the colonized" (*Ordeal of the Longhouse*, 256). Jennings argues similarly: "No matter how cleverly the Iroquois devised strategy and dedicated themselves to carrying it out, no matter how they maneuvered and twisted about, no matter how much they blustered and threatened, they were in the last analysis prisoners of systems of empire that were not of their own making" (*Ambiguous Iroquois Empire*, 372).

9. A dearth of concrete data, the result of Evans's having not ventured beyond the Susquehanna River, would render the backcountry and its inhabitants to culturally bound misconceptions, to the "Us-Themism" that Gould and White describe in "mental maps"; on how the lack of geographic knowledge can feed stereotypes and invention, see their *Mental Maps*, 22–23.

10. Merrell, *Into the American Woods*, 157; Merrell, "Shickellamy," 228, 241–42; John Bartram, *Observations*, iii, 18; Berkeley and Berkeley, *Correspondence of John Bartram*, 201–5; Hazard, *Minutes of the Provincial Council*, 4:654; Paul Wallace, *Conrad Weiser*, 147.

11. John Bartram, *Observations*, viii, 11, 14, 16, 19, 32, 41. Mancall discusses indigenous land use in *Valley of Opportunity*, 39. Haunted sites for native Americans are discussed in Merrell, *Into the American Woods*, 146–47; an intriguing eighteenth-century record is Weiser's "Notes on the Iroquois and Delaware Indians," 319–20.

12. John Bartram, *Observations*, 37. "Pompions" is probably a misprint of pumpkins. For overlapping descriptions, see ibid., 19, and Evans, "Extract from Mr. Lewis Evans's Journal," 169. Just outside Onondaga, Bartram describes a hill that "when cleared will have an extensive prospect of fertile vales on all sides" (*Observations*, 35).

13. Gipson, *Lewis Evans*, 56, 81–83; Labaree et al., *Papers of Benjamin Franklin*, 5:448; Klinefelter, *Lewis Evans and His Maps*, 40–43. The traces of native influence (which include straight lines for rivers and simplified shapes for larger bodies of water) are discussed in Malcolm Lewis, "Indicators of Unacknowledged Assimilations," 14–16.

14. Jennings, "Indian's Revolution," 325; Richter, *Ordeal of the Longhouse*, 272; Jennings, *Empire of Fortune*, 81. On Mohawk conflicts over land, see Nammack, *Fraud, Politics and the Dispossession*, 22–38. Hendrick's speech is reprinted in O'Callaghan, *Documents Relative to the Colonial History*, 6:783, 788.

15. Jennings, *Empire of Fortune*, 82; O'Callaghan, *Documents Relative to the Colonial History*, 6:794–95, 800, 854–55; Shannon, *Indians and Colonists*, 48–50.

16. On native grievances, see Nammack, *Fraud, Politics, and the Dispossession*, 41–43, and Jennings, *Empire of Fortune*, 101–8. The Mohawk Canadaraga explained, "We understand that there are writings for all our lands, so that we shall have none left but the very spot we live upon and hardly that" (O'Callaghan, *Documents Relative to the Colonial History*, 6:865). On land deals, see Shannon, *Indians and Colonists*, 130–34. Franklin provided a draft that argued strength through unity, proposing a parliament, president, central land offices, and a common forum for negotiating treaties. For a discussion of the Albany Plan, see Labaree et al., *Papers of Benjamin Franklin*, 6:387–92; Shannon, *Indians and Colonists*, 184–97; and Gipson, *British Empire before the American Revolution*, 5:123–42. On the fate of the plan, see O'Callaghan, *Documents Relative*

to the Colonial History, 6:919; Jennings, *Empire of Fortune*, 115–16; and Alden, "Albany Congress," 200–203.

17. Labaree et al., *Papers of Benjamin Franklin*, 3:193, 5:457, 9:78, 62; William Clarke, *Observations*, 38; Kennedy, *Importance of Gaining and Preserving*, 7; Sullivan et al., *Papers of Sir William Johnson*, 11:786; Berkeley and Berkeley, *Correspondence of John Bartram*, 163. Shannon reviews the imperial and colonial context in *Indians and Colonists*, 56–76. An insightful reading of Franklin's pamphlets in an economic context is Stourzh, *Benjamin Franklin and American Foreign Policy*, 40, 49. For literary readings of Franklin and the Conestoga massacre, see Mulford, "*Caritas* and Capital," 355. Bellin claims that Franklin's *Narrative* "[catches] history in the act" (*Demon of the Continent*, 120). A personal memo by William Johnson written after the war reads, "Such Indians as are yet our Friends to be kindly used and make it their Interest to continue so, untill we are better able to do without them" (Sullivan et al., *Papers of Sir William Johnson*, 4:325).

18. Gipson, *Lewis Evans*, 146.

19. Ibid., 151–58; Sullivan et al., *Papers of Sir William Johnson*, 9:310; White, *Middle Ground*, 240. The Mohawk Little Abraham reports on communication between the eastern and western nations of the Iroquois Confederacy. See Sullivan et al., *Papers of Sir William Johnson*, 9:747. In 1755, Robert Hunter Morris reported that both "the Delawares, & the Shawanese, have taken up the Hatchet against us," and William Johnson wrote in 1754 on "the present Shattered State of ye Six Nations and their Allies" (ibid., 2:368). See also ibid., 1:429, 9:477.

20. Gipson, *Lewis Evans*, 175. Samuel Johnson expressed his misgivings in a London review of Evans, which concluded that two European nations "are now disputing their boundaries, and each is endeavouring the destruction of the other by the help of the Indians, whose interest is that both should be destroyed" (Donald Greene, *Political Writings*, 188; thanks to Professor Dustin Griffin for pointing out this source). Klinefelter notes that Evans was "one of the most vocal of colonial advocates" for expansion to Ohio (*Lewis Evans and His Maps*, 27). Wroth discusses the attacks on Evans in the colonial press in *American Bookshelf*, 52–54.

21. Evans allows that "Nations on the further Side of the Lakes are subdued by the Confederates; but I am not enabled to relate the Particulars with any Certainty," and he writes elsewhere that the Shawnees have lost their "Property" while noting that they "bear [the Confederates] with great Reluctance" (Gipson, *Lewis Evans*, 156–57, 159).

22. Neolin is quoted in Anthony Wallace, *Death and Rebirth of the Seneca*, 118–19. The map is reconstructed in G. Malcolm Lewis, "Indigenous Maps and Mapping," 26. My thanks to Professor Lewis for providing a source for the map. See also Dowd, *Spirited Resistance*, 36.

23. Cappon, "Geographers and Map-Makers," 253; Wroth, *American Bookshelf*, 52, 159; Hutchins, *Topographical Description*, 71–72.

24. Pownall, *Topographical Description*, 9–10. A short biography is Labaree, "Thomas Pownall," 161–63. Pownall's land speculation is discussed in Abernethy, *Western Lands and the American Revolution*, 15. My thanks to Viki Soady, who translates Pownall "through which the birds alone had flown, paths never worn by wheels" and "what was only a little path made into a road."

25. Pownall, *Topographical Description*, 97, 24, 119. Seelye uses this passage as a touch-

stone for progress across space in *Beautiful Machine*, 48–55. What makes Pownall's ideological geography exceptional is that he provided a rare, clear-eyed assessment of white-native relations. A confidential report to the Board of Trade on the Albany Congress observes that there "was a matter which does not appear on the face of it." The Iroquois Confederacy lacked its former cohesion; as Pownall notes, when the "Covenant Belt was deliver'd to & receiv'd by the Indians," the participating Iroquois failed to give a "Yo heigh-igh," their form of assent. Instead they sounded "but one great Indiscriminate Yo heigh-eigh, till being reminded that the other was expected of them, they afterward give the Yo-hieh-eigh according to the usual Custom" (McAnear, "Personal Accounts of the Albany Congress," 741). See also Nammack, *Fraud, Politics, and the Dispossession*, 31.

26. O'Callaghan, *Documents Relative to the Colonial History*, 10:243, 6:897, 997. See also Jennings, *Empire of Fortune*, 261. Anne Grant, whom I discuss in part 4 of this book, called Johnson's office "difficult both to execute and define" (*Memoirs of an American Lady*, 2:14). The Shawnees and Delawares attacked frontier settlements despite British demands that the Iroquois keep their "dependents" in submission. See Sullivan et al., *Papers of Sir William Johnson*, 2:413–15. On the sum required to maintain the hierarchy and the growing fear of western confederacies, see ibid., 1:505, 10:461.

27. John Jordan, "Journal of James Kenney," 192, 131. Sosin discusses land companies in his helpful study of colonial policy, *Whitehall and the Wilderness*, 27–28, 40–46, 155–57. See also Gipson, *British Empire before the American Revolution*, 11:430–33, 456–57. George Washington is quoted in Abernethy, *Western Lands and the American Revolution*, 12, 116–18, but Pynchon catches the gist of things in his caricature of Washington, who sneers "Proclamation-Schmocklamation," in *Mason and Dixon*, 277. Johnson argues that "fixed Boundaries between our Settlements & their Hunting Grounds" would secure peace and Indian alliances (Sullivan et al., *Papers of Sir William Johnson*, 2:879); on hints of his ties to the Suffering Traders, see ibid., 5:37–39, 6:473, 563.

28. On Johnson's predispositions, see Sullivan et al., *Papers of Sir William Johnson*, 5:16, 6:407; on his instructions, see ibid., 6:147; for the report of the treaty, see ibid., 6:454. On the Fort Stanwix treaty, see Anthony Wallace, *Death and Rebirth of the Seneca*, 122; White, *Middle Ground*, 351–53; McConnell, *A Country Between*, 248–54; Gipson, *British Empire before the American Revolution*, 11:443–47; Downes, *Council Fires on the Upper Ohio*, 44; Sosin, *Whitehall and the Wilderness*, 194; Abernethy, *Western Lands and the American Revolution*, 86; and Billington, "Fort Stanwix Treaty of 1768," 182–94. Johnson maintained of the Shawnees, "I cannot think their presence very necessary" (Sullivan et al., *Papers of Sir William Johnson*, 6:335).

29. Pownall, *Topographical Description*, 41, 23–26, 36, 31.

30. Ibid., 100.

31. John Bartram, *Observations*, 24; Merrell, *Into the American Woods*, 156; Rountree, "Powhatans and Other Woodland Indians," 27–29; Weiser, "Notes on the Iroquois and Delaware Indians," 166.

32. Klinefelter, *Lewis Evans and His Maps*, 26; Wroth, *American Bookshelf*, 50.

Chapter Two

1. Stork, *Account of East Florida*, iv, 26; Stork, *Description of East-Florida*, ii; Hutchins, *Topographical Description*, 74–76. Wayne Franklin discusses use in his essential guide to an often utilitarian literature, *Discoverers, Explorers, Settlers*, 28.

2. Cronon discusses native conceptions of property in *Changes in the Land*, 62; Henderson makes a similar case with direct reference to the Ohio Valley in "Dispelling the Myth," 5. On the Fort Stanwix treaty, see Sullivan et al., *Papers of Sir William Johnson*, 7:29. Correspondence between Crown officials suggests that they understood the difference in conceptions of property. Thomas Gage wrote to Johnson that the "Ohio Indians . . . could not without Jealousy and disgust see their hunting Grounds ceded," meaning that he recognized the seasonal usage that defined this country (ibid., 7:160).

3. Whereas the history of the Iroquois has been explored in depth (and as one group), the colonial Shawnees do not provide a stable (or clearly documented) field of study. White discusses fragmentation in *Middle Ground*, 2. See also Henderson, "Dispelling the Myth," 13, and McConnell, *A Country Between*, 207–32. Callender discusses the Shawnees' social structure in "Shawnee," 622–27; on collective governance, see Howard, *Shawnee!*, 24–42.

4. On Shawnee war efforts, see Sullivan et al., *Papers of Sir William Johnson*, 7:160, 184, 316. Population numbers are from Barnhart, *Valley of Democracy*, 35–37; Rohrbough, *Trans-Appalachian Frontier*, 25; Aron, *How the West Was Lost*, 198. West discusses "ebbing and surging" in the Ohio Valley in his useful article, "American Frontier," 115–16. Native responses to white settlement can be drawn from John Jordan, "Journal of James Kenney," 152. Official records note the same concerns. See Sullivan et al., *Papers of Sir William Johnson*, 6:335; Sosin, *Opening of the American West*, 11; and Davies, *Documents of the American Revolution*, 12:189. Dragging Canoe is quoted in the documentary history, Ranck, *Boonesborough*, 159. On migration, see Abernethy, *Western Lands and the American Revolution*, 82–83; Aron provides a more recent discussion in *How the West Was Lost*, 25. On frontiersmen, see Faragher, *Daniel Boone*, 89. See also Jordan and Kaups, who establish the links between environment and settlement in *American Backwoods Frontier*, 3, 64. Accounts of overhunting appear in Ranck, *Boonesborough*, 176, and Schwaab, *Travels in the Old South*, 60.

5. James Robertson, *Petitions of the Early Inhabitants*, 67. On class tensions, see John Jordan, "Journal of James Kenney," 182. On land claims, see Abernethy, *Western Lands and the American Revolution*, 228, 249–63; Aron, *How the West Was Lost*, 72; Faragher, *Daniel Boone*, 128–29, 238–40; and Rohrbough, *Trans-Appalachian Frontier*, 144. François André Michaux wrote, "I did not stop at the house of one inhabitant who was persuaded of the validity of his own right but that seemed dubious of his neighbors" (Thwaites, *Travels to the West*, 227). Toulmin wrote that the "civil divisions of the state are perpetually varying with the increase of population" (quoted in Tinling and Davies, *Western Country in 1793*, 68).

6. Abernethy, *Western Lands and the American Revolution*, 338–41; Rohrbough, *Trans-Appalachian Frontier*, 26; Horsman, *Race and Manifest Destiny*, 112.

7. North Carolina's governor, Josiah Martin, called Transylvania "an Asylum to the most abandoned," George Washington blasted the state as "inimical to American freedom," and John Adams grumbled that "they are charged with republican notions and Utopian schemes." See Ranck, *Boonesborough*, 149, 245; James Robertson, *Petitions of the Early Inhabitants*, 48–49; and Burnett, *Letters of Members*, 8:440. Camden-Yorke is discussed in several classic studies of the West, including Abernethy, *Western Lands and the American Revolution*, 116; Sosin, *Whitehall and the Wilderness*, 159–61; and Rohrbough, *Trans-Appalachian Frontier*, 48. Sheidly reconstructs the Henderson Purchase from a native perspective, emphasizing divisions within the Cherokees, in "Hunting and

the Politics of Masculinity." On Henderson and Transylvania, see Aron, *How the West Was Lost*, 62-63, and Faragher, *Daniel Boone*, 127-30.

8. Filson, *Kentucke*, 107-8. All references to Filson, unless otherwise noted, will be cited internally and are from this text. On the iconography of the plow (and agriculture as a masculinist enterprise), see Knobloch, *Culture of Wilderness*, 70-74.

9. William Carlos Williams, *In the American Grain*, 138; Slotkin, *Regeneration through Violence*, 269.

10. Mazel, *American Literary Environmentalism*, 3, 46; Daniel Defoe uses "environ" as a verb, as the sea "environs" the narrator, in *Robinson Crusoe*, 46.

11. James Robertson, *Petitions of the Early Inhabitants*, 55-56.

12. Pratt, *Imperial Eyes*, 39; Irmscher, *Poetics of Natural History*, 9. "In Boone's narrative," Regis argues, "Kentucky's civil history is completed and its natural history sanctioned" (*Describing Early America*, 138).

13. Regis, *Describing Early America*, 142. Lofaro compares the Trumbull and Filson texts in "Eighteenth Century 'Autobiographies,'" 88, 92-93. Boone is used as fodder for poets in McGann, *Byron*, 656, and William Carlos Williams, *In the American Grain*, 137-38. For the issue of whether one can recover the "real" Daniel Boone (and by extension his relations with the Shawnees), I return to the cautions expressed by Joshua David Bellin. Bellin maintains that the "'text' and the 'real' are not opposed but interrelated." The narrative emerges from the continued attempt to interpret an encounter (*Demon of the Continent*, 9). His point has repercussions here, as the photograph of the rifle stock was reprinted in a journal article that, for the life of me, I cannot find. The reference must be real because I diligently copied down the upper- and lowercase letters on a sheet of paper. By citing my own faulty memory, I continue the tradition of inventing Daniel Boone in the absence of a physical presence. Whether one finds this explanation acceptable could be what divides academic disciplines; see my discussion of the new western history in my introduction.

14. Callender, "Shawnee," 627-28. See also Henderson, "Dispelling the Myth," 3; Clark, *Shawnees*, 55-58; and Howard, *Shawnee!*, 188.

15. My discussion of Boone's life draws from Faragher, *Daniel Boone*, 19, 73-76, 108-9, and Aron, *How the West Was Lost*, 77, 84. On the permeability between native Americans and pioneers, see Jordan and Kaups, *American Backwoods Frontier*, 77-78. Spencer Records notes that his hunting party was once attacked because whites and natives were indistinguishable in Carmony, "Spencer Records' Memoir," 365-67. For the gloss of the Shawnees intervention, see Filson, *Kentucke*, 52-54.

16. Lofaro notes that the beginning "sounds like a political eulogy of the present and future glory of Kentucky" ("Eighteenth Century 'Autobiographies,'" 89); Slotkin emphasizes the religious tone in *Regeneration through Violence*, 279.

17. I borrow this pun on plot from Brückner, "Surveyed Self as William Byrd."

18. Namias focuses on the gendering of captivity narratives and is one of few critics to discuss masculinity (*White Captives*, 83). Soper discusses the role of nature "in policing social and sexual divisions" in her philosophical examination, *What Is Nature?*, 7. The paradox between Boone and domestic life is obvious, for if he cherished family, why would he excuse himself for years on end? The stories that negotiated this tension are often funny. When Boone returned from the Shawnees, his wife Rebecca had a baby. According to the legend, he says, "You need not distress yourself so much about it, I do not blame you one bit.... It will be a Boone any how, and besides I have been obliged to

be married in Indian fashion a couple of time. Pho'pho! Dry your tears and welcome me home. And that was the last of it." The legend is quoted in an article by Faragher that crosses historical and narrative interests, "'They May Say What They Please,'" 386.

19. Sewell, "'So Unstable,'" 40; Burnham, *Captivity and Sentiment*, 3. Castiglia emphasizes captivity as a site of gender transgression in *Bound and Determined*, 2–5.

20. For equivalents to Boone's captivity, see Darlington and Barsotti, *Scoouwa*, 61, and Derounian-Stodola, *Women's Indian Captivity Narratives*, 144. Contemporary interpretations are in Faragher, *Daniel Boone*, 164–66, and Aron, *How the West Was Lost*, 42–45. Governor Henry Harrison writes specifically on Boone's capture and notes that the Shawnees "have shown . . . much humanity to their prisoners" (Davies, *Documents of the American Revolution*, 15:107). See also Chester Young, *Westward into Kentucky*, 58.

21. Faragher, *Daniel Boone*, 199–200; Aron, *How the West Was Lost*, 53. A possible motive for the court-martial had been preferential treatment to Boone by the British at Detroit. See Chester Young, *Westward into Kentucky*, 63, 172n.

22. Carmony, "Spencer Records' Memoir," 336. Mazel argues that wilderness resists narrative closure in *American Literary Environmentalism*, 56; Perkins reconstructs settlers' interior lives in *Border Life*, 78.

23. Hinderaker, *Elusive Empires*, 226; Cayton and Teute, "On the Connection of Frontiers," 8.

24. Burnett, *Letters of Members*, 1:210; William H. Smith, *St. Clair Papers*, 2:103. On the threat of settlers leaving federal territories, see Sosin, *Opening of the American West*, 98, and Burnett, *Letters of Members*, 8:102.

Chapter Three

1. On western history, see West, "Longer, Grimmer," 103–11. A current biography of Crèvecoeur remains to be written. I draw from Stone's introduction to Crèvecoeur, *Letters from an American Farmer*, and from Julia Post Mitchell, who provides a more detailed discussion of the war years, especially, in *St. Jean de Crèvecoeur*, 53–55. A particularly acute assessment of Crèvecoeur's politics is Jehlen, "J. Hector St. John Crèvecoeur," 204–22. A transcription of the "Susquehannah" manuscript is in Dennis Moore, *More Letters from the American Farmer*, 163–204. All references to "Susquehannah," are from the Moore edition and will be cited internally, unless otherwise noted. The piece was published in a more readable but less scholarly form as "On the Susquehanna" and "The Wyoming Massacre" in Crèvecoeur, *Letters from an American Farmer*, 353–90. Moore's edition is recommended for classroom and scholarly use because it captures the authorial missteps that make the manuscript so interesting. In this chapter, I distill reading from several sources. Mancall reviews the economic history of the Susquehanna Valley in *Valley of Opportunity*; Stefon situates the region in the context of the Revolution in "Wyoming Valley"; Dennis Moore discusses Crèvecoeur and the Yankee-Pennamite war in the introduction and notes to *More Letters from the American Farmer*; Harvey's voluminous study *History of Wilkes-Barré* (available in microfilm) cites a wealth of primary material; each volume of Boyd and Taylor's *Susquehannah Company Papers* begins with helpful introductory essays; Calloway discusses the native communities that Crèvecoeur reportedly would have visited in *American Revolution in Indian Country*.

2. Hales discusses the "spatial contrast" in one of the few essays on "Susquehannah," "Landscape of Tragedy," 41. Brückner argues that geography provided figures of consent in "Lessons in Geography," 314. On Crèvecoeur as a mapmaker, see Philbrick, *St. John*

de Crèvecoeur, 17–19, and Julia Post Mitchell, *St. Jean de Crèvecoeur*, 17. Even if Crèvecoeur did not literally intend to supply a map for "Susquehannah," overlapping errors suggest that he might have relied upon Lewis Evans. Evans's "Map of Pensilvania, New-Jersey, New-York, and the Three Delaware Counties" was criticized for its placement of Lackawaxen Creek (a tributary of the Delaware River), which also is where Crèvecoeur's route becomes impossible to trace. See Klinefelter, *Lewis Evans and His Maps*, 34. My thanks to Julie Armstrong for accompanying me on a futile mission to reconstruct Crèvecoeur's route; over a minor league ballgame in Scranton, we concluded that the route was a fiction or, at best, weakly reconstructed from memory.

3. Jennings, *Invasion of America*, 15. The complaint about Lydius is quoted in Mancall, *Valley of Opportunity*, 78; other warnings appear in Sullivan et al., *Papers of Sir William Johnson*, 1:441, 3:851, 4:20, 38. Twenty years later, an Onondaga council party objected that Lydius only "pretended to make a purchase" (Boyd and Taylor, *Susquehannah Company Papers*, 6:348).

4. The circuit-riding minister Philip Vickers Fithian notes "elders higher than my Head as I sat on my Horse" (Albion and Dodson, *Philip Vickers Fithian's Journal*, 50). John Ettwein remarks upon "the noblest timber I ever saw in America" (John Jordan, "Rev. John Ettwein's Notes," 209). See also the reports from John Sullivan's 1779 raid, where one member remarks that "I never saw an equal" to the Susquehanna Valley, in Cook and Conover, *Journals of the Military Expedition*, 103. On beaver lands, see Mancall, *Valley of Opportunity*, 68, and Cronon, *Changes in the Land*, 106. Crèvecoeur, who had a keen eye for property, explains elsewhere why the valley was so fertile in *Journey into Northern Pennsylvania*, 44.

5. Sullivan et al., *Papers of Sir William Johnson*, 2:877; Merrell discusses Shickellamy's role in "Shickellamy," 232.

6. Harvey, *History of Wilkes-Barré*, 917. The assumption that Crèvecoeur witnessed the Battle of Wyoming rests upon superficial readings of "Susquehannah" and a secondhand report by Thomas Jefferson. See Boyd et al., *Papers of Thomas Jefferson*, 11:110. Newspapers carried stories of the "massacre" with a strong political slant, arguing, "Thus while our defenceless wives and children [were] cut off by merciless savages, and our country laid waste and destroyed, is the humane King of Great Britain offering his idle and delusive propositions of peace!"(*Pennsylvania Packet*, July 16, 1778). In a similar critique, Edmund Burke suggested that "diabolical modes of war" jeopardized ties between the colonies and the mother country ("Speech on the Use of Indians," in Langford and Todd, *Writings and Speeches of Edmund Burke*, 3:355–61). See also Burke's account from *Dodsley's Annual Register* for 1779, reprinted in Harvey, *History of Wilkes-Barré*, 1061–64. On the Wyoming massacre as propaganda, see Williamson and Fossler, *Zebulon Butler*, 64, and Graymont, *Iroquois in the American Revolution*, 173–74. Useful comparisons might be made to the scalping of Jane McCrea, which is discussed in Namias, *White Captives*, 117–44.

7. Sullivan et al., *Papers of Sir William Johnson*, 9:144; Burnett, *Letters of Members*, 1:230, 421, 186. Onuf argues that a collapse of imperial authority fostered schemes of land grabbing and divisions over state boundaries that were symptomatic of the revolution in *Origins of the Federal Republic*, 52.

8. On Job Chillaway, see Stefon, "Wyoming Valley," 144, and Harvey, *History of Wilkes-Barré*, 422, 456, 650, 701. Merrell discusses how the Catawbas in Carolina adopted native forms of property exchange and tenancy in *Indians' New World*, 188.

9. Limerick, *Legacy of Conquest*, 27; Paine, *Public Good*.

10. Hales, "Landscape of Tragedy," 56. See also Dennis Moore, *More Letters from the American Farmer*, lii.

11. On Teedyuscung, see Stefon, "Wyoming Valley," 138–39.

12. For the sake of brevity, I skip over the middle section of "Susquehannah," which is important to the sketch's overall structure. In the comparative tour of the two rivers, the Wyoming Valley appears to graft agricultural potential onto a New England civil order. Wilderness welcomes civilization, as the river "contains the most usefull Richesses & affords conveniences for future Ease & Improv^{t}" (Dennis Moore, *More Letters from the American Farmer*, 175). Water yields commerce (the river "*affords* conveniences"), and the environs suggest a sound foundation; the more remote settlements on the East Branch of the same river, by contrast, present shakier beginnings. Crèvecoeur announces his decision to investigate the Pennsylvanians with a primitive verbal bridge, "least you might think me unfaithfull & careless," and this trip made in fairness brings mostly hardship. Where a cabin sheltered the author during a previous passage through the wilderness, his mixed-race party instead spends a night on the East Branch in "perfect chaos." The travelers find no game. They fend wolves from their camp by tossing out their moccasins (180–81). The proximity to savage nature anticipates (what is to be) a tragic alienation from "civilized" life.

13. Boyd and Taylor, *Papers of the Susquehannah Company*, 3:xiii, 4:xix–xxi; Stefon, "Wyoming Valley," 137. Dennis Moore notes the confused chronology in *More Letters from the American Farmer*, 372n. A record of rising tempers, which appeared to peak in 1775, is captured in Burnett, *Letters of Members*, 1:229.

14. An example of illegibility is evident in a passage that Crèvecoeur's 1925 editors omit. The genetic text reads: "Chicannery, contention the Love of Party & Tumults had follow'd them from Connecticut & in short is the growth of all countries, but hitherto they had lain Ineffcatious & dormant; [4] these [5] Passions were [2] soon [3] Kindled by [1] the new scituation of these People [2] & they flourished very Rapidly" (184). Earlier editors of "Susquehannah" glossed this jumbled clause (in which even the numerical insertions are confused) with an ellipsis. See Crèvecoeur, *Letters from an American Farmer*, 374.

15. Burnett, *Letters of Members*, 1:421, 186; Harvey, *History of Wilkes-Barré*, 933; Calloway, *American Revolution in Indian Country*, 31; Hinderaker makes a similar point in his discussion of the "alchemy of property" in *Elusive Empires*, 134.

16. Brant is quoted in Calloway, *American Revolution in Indian Country*, 122. A source of controversy was a road cleared from the Delaware River to the Wyoming Valley (funded by the Connecticut investors). This led to death threats, and William Johnson noted in 1769 that "at every village on my way to Seneca," the natives "spoke a great deal [of] the intrusions of the New England people in Pennsylv[ania]" (Sullivan et al., *Papers of Sir William Johnson*, 7:93, 10:537–38, 541). See also Harvey, *History of Wilkes-Barré*, 830.

17. My purpose is not to review the history of the battle, although a relevant controversy involves the destruction of property—namely, who directed the destruction and why. Historian Barbara Graymont observes that British officers after the battle granted the Wyoming settlers the right to continue farming, but the Iroquois ignored this stipulation (*Iroquois in the American Revolution*, 171–72). Stefon indicates that Butler ordered the destruction in "Wyoming Valley," 136. Butler's report, however, does not mention

that he gave orders to destroy the town, but it does emphasize property damage and adds that "not a single person has been hurt [except those who] were in arms" (Davies, *Documents of the American Revolution*, 2:166). The terms of capitulation, which argued that the Wyoming settlers should keep their farms and that private property be respected, are reprinted in Harvey, *History of Wilkes-Barré*, 1034. "Susquehannah" offers evidence enough to suggest that Crèvecoeur himself recognized that the Iroquois were concerned with changes in the land. Before the so-called massacre, Crèvecoeur notes, a "few Indians came down" to protest that they had been had been "much disturbed in their Huntings" by the increase of cows and horses (Moore, *More Letters from the American Farmer*, 195). He curiously weighs the loss of property against human loss. That the damage stops with soldiers and possessions seems to be a surprise in Crèvecoeur's portrayal of the battle. "Happily these fierce people" were satisfied, he writes, "with the death of those who had opposed him in arms," the narrator explains (199). The transitional word, "happily," suggests no plausible motive. The "fierce people" spare women and children only by a fortunate (or "happy") coincidence. These slips suggest an awareness on the part of the author of what motivated the attack but a desire to cast the attack as lacking a rational motive.

18. Literary critics have commented over the past century whether treaty transcripts represent a valid form of indigenous literature. Van Doren maintained that the "Indian treaty was a form of literature which had no author," contending that "for once life seems to have made itself almost unaided into literature" (Boyd, *Indian Treaties*, xvii–xviii). Wroth argued in 1928 (and little has changed) that the literature has "been neglected by readers and teachers of early American literature" ("Indian Treaty as Literature," 749). Contemporary scholars hold a lower estimation than these earlier appraisals. For almost dismissive discussions in standard references, see Wiget, *Native American Literature*, 22–25, and Ruoff, *American Indian Literatures*, 47–52. Kroeber sees the treaties as an occasion for moral censure, noting that they "were ceremoniously signed and then consciously violated" (*American Indian Persistence and Resurgence*, 3). Certainly the early history of white-native relations is one of "violation," yet this view also obscures the complicated local rivalries that came into play in treaty council and the way in which an indigenous form crossed into print culture. In an exemplary crossover study that combines legal history and narrative, Robert Williams Jr. argues that in the "time when the West had to listen seriously" to native groups, stories provided "channels of communication and dialogue" (*Linking Arms Together*, 5, 87). Although Williams makes the valuable point that whites had to adopt native protocol, I question whether his vision of the "multicultural frontier" (which he sees as the message of treaty visions) is not itself a contemporary ideal rather than an accurate reflection of political realities. Gustafson examines the eighteenth-century market for native oratory and provides a nuanced reading of treaties in *Eloquence Is Power*, 112–14.

19. Boyd, *Indian Treaties*, 35–36; the treaty is reviewed briefly in the "Descriptive Treaty Calendar," in an invaluable guide edited by Jennings, *History and Culture of Iroquois Diplomacy*, 180; see also Brandão, *"Your Fyre Shall Burn No More,"* 22–25. Druke discusses wampum in treaties in "Iroquois Treaties," 88–90. Mann discusses the councils of clan women, or Gantowisas, in *Iroquoian Women*, 105–7. My reading of the 1742 treaty intends to introduce the element of native agency into literary studies. For a point of comparison, see Rowe's discussion of Charles Brockden Brown, which uses the 1737 Walking Purchase as a point of reference. The Walking Purchase is one of the more flagrant abuses

by Euroamericans in a long history of such abuses. Reading Brown's *Edgar Huntly*, Rowe maintains that "the modern reader" must "recognize the secret complicity between the mystifying, but apparently innocent, game of Brown's early American novels and the deceptive and finally genocidal discourses of the treaties, laws, and political policies adopted by Europeans in regard to native peoples" (*Literary Culture and U.S. Imperialism*, 39); in the suggestion that the Lenni-Lenape became "a shadowy reflection of the settlers' own savagery," however, he continues a tradition that keeps native peoples at the margins by privileging the novel over other mediums. My reading of the Walking Purchase (upheld through the 1742 treaty) suggests that the Iroquois advanced their position by upholding an empty bargain, and in treaty literature (rather than novels) they became more than a "shadowy reflection." As treaties displaced native groups, others sought their own advantage through council. One cannot discount the injustice done to the Delawares in 1737, but I would argue that Rowe misleadingly suggests that all native Americans met imperial violence in the same way.

20. Boyd, *Indian Treaties*, 17, 37; Gustafson, *Eloquence Is Power*, 121; Cheyfitz, *Poetics of Imperialism*, 37; Rowe, *Literary Culture and U.S. Imperialism*, 303n. The study of colonial translation would be enriched by collaboration with ethnohistorians, who have discussed the role of "go between" as both interpreter and cultural intermediary. See Merrell, *Into the American Woods*; Hagedorn, "Brokers of Understanding"; and Hagedorn, "'A Friend to Go between Them.'" The public rhetoric, Hagedorn and Merrell suggest, belies the considerable degree of decision making that occurred off the record. William Johnson acknowledges as much in a letter to Thomas Penn, noting that in "private meetgs. with the Chiefs . . . most points are discussed" (Sullivan et al., *Papers of Sir William Johnson*, 6:472).

21. Boyd, *Indian Treaties*, 18, 25; Sullivan et al., *Papers of Sir William Johnson*, 6:466. Fenton offers an archetype of the condolence ceremony in "Structure, Continuity and Change," 18–19; Merrell situates the "woods edge" ceremony in treaty culture in *Into the American Woods*, 20–27. White explores the shared fictions reached on a middle ground in "Fictions of Patriarchy," 66. On the importance of "method," see colonial historian William Smith Jr., who noted that natives are "displeased with an irregular harangue" (*History of the Province of New York*, 51). An instance where Pennsylvania ignored protocol was in an 1753 treaty at Carlisle, where the commissioners learned that "the *Indians* could not proceed to Business while the Blood remained on their Garments, and that the Condolences could not be accepted unless the Goods, intended to cover the Graves, were actually spread on the Ground before them" (Boyd, *Indian Treaties*, 125).

22. Canasatego's strategy recalls a point made by Robert Williams Jr., that stories "educate a derelict treaty partner about appropriate behaviors in a treaty relationship" (*Linking Arms Together*, 88).

23. Boyd, *Indian Treaties*, 26–28.

24. Gustafson argues that Canasatego employs "metaphors of gender to imagine a masculine public domain in which legitimate land sales could take place" (*Eloquence Is Power*, 115). I agree with Gustafson, although I believe that her argument continues a focus upon dispossession and puts less emphasis upon the ways in which native speakers pursued more local interests. The gendering of tribal hierarchies was common enough in eastern woodland culture to suggest that speakers could work a *mis*translation to their own advantage. The Delaware Teedyuscung likens his ascendancy to removing his "petticoats" and notes elsewhere that the Six Nations "have made men of us, and as such we are

now come to this treaty." See Jennings, *History and Culture of Iroquois Diplomacy*, 24, and Boyd, *Indian Treaties*, 144. For the use of "women" in a similar context, see Sullivan et al., *Papers of Sir William Johnson*, 4:361.

Chapter Four

1. Boyd et al., *Papers of Thomas Jefferson*, 6:478, 498–99, 506; Burnett, *Letters of Members*, 1:231, 7:421. Robert Taylor reviews the outcome of the Yankee-Pennamite War in "Trial at Trenton," 545.

2. Boyd et al., *Papers of Thomas Jefferson*, 7:603–7; Berkhofer, "Jefferson, the Ordinance of 1784," 241, 243. Boyd (who edited the *Susquehannah Company Papers* before they became Jefferson's *Papers*) argues for the links between the court of commissioners' decision and the Ordinance of 1784 (Boyd et al., *Papers of Thomas Jefferson*, 7:571, 574). See also Burnett, *Letters of Members*, 7:327, 462. Benjamin Lincoln would write in 1792 that as the lands were subject to "improvement," so natives "in consequence of their stubbornness [shall] dwindle and moulder away" (quoted in Roy Pearce, *Savages of America*, 69).

3. Sheehan observes that *Notes on the State of Virginia* served as a model for policy in *Seeds of Extinction*, 5. Freneau is quoted from "On the emigration to America," 230; see my discussion of this poem in the introduction. As I have been arguing, literary critics discuss the diminishing native agency in federal policy. "In order to create the future," Carr argues, "the nation had to argue that the *present* (the living Indian) was already in the *past*" (*Inventing the American Primitive*, 33, 9). Enlightenment policy prefigures the "ghosting" noted by scholars such as Bergland and Scheckel and discussed in my introduction. The negotiation of republican space and native voices also provides an occasion for "intercultural" criticism, as Jefferson imagined his literary ambitions against native Americans. This chapter focuses accordingly on how interactions with native peoples led to republican self; on "intercultural" criticism, see Bellin, *Demon of the Continent*, 5.

4. Literary readings of *Notes on the State of Virginia* usually note the tension between chaos and order and a movement between speculation and fact. Scheick maintains that "artistic or imaginative order" provided a *via media* against unlimited freedom ("Chaos and Imaginative Order," 222). Ferguson describes a drama for "intellectual control" (*Law and Letters in American Culture*, 41). Davy observes that the subject "moves generally from factual statements about nature in Virginia . . . to proposals about Virginia and ultimately the United States as a whole" ("Argumentation and Unified Structure," 586). Daufenbach argues that in the quest for control, civilization, and landscape blend, channeling "natural energy . . . into social or economic energy, implying that productivity is a natural event" ("'The Eye Composes Itself,'" 108). With reference to Jefferson's attitudes toward nature, Hellenbrand cites a "geologic" and moral aesthetic, which allows nature to lead the author "out of tumult and into harmony" ("Roads to Happiness," 7). Clayton Lewis argues that a "sense of open possibility" gives Jefferson's language an agility and freshness that qualifies *Notes on the State of Virginia* as a literary masterpiece ("Style in Jefferson's *Notes*," 672). Wayne Franklin makes a similar point, if on a broader canvas, remarking that an "accelerating movement of comprehension, the embracing of emptiness by lines which are first outlines," is the plot of mapmaking in the New World (and presumably, the plot of *Notes on the State of Virginia*) (*Discoverers, Explorers, Settlers*, 29). Breitwieser sees a productive "disjunction" between experience and theory in observation, thereby suggesting an active pragmatism in Jefferson's thought ("Jefferson's

Prospect," 324). Douglas Anderson reframes the book around caverns, nothing that a "strangely indeterminate interior" is left unexplained, and "Jefferson is careful to deprive his reader of a secure interpretative footing" ("Subterraneous Virginia," 238, 243).

5. Peden's introduction to Jefferson's *Notes on the State of Virginia*, xiv–xvi; Ferguson, *Law and Letters in American Culture*, 39, 44–46.

6. Jefferson, *Notes on the State of Virginia*, 3–4; Jehlen, *American Incarnation*, 57, 19. Hereafter, references to *Notes on the State of Virginia* will be cited internally.

7. Sullivan et al., *Papers of Sir William Johnson*, 7:218.

8. Breitwieser, "Jefferson's Prospect," 319.

9. Franklin, *Discoverers, Explorers, Settlers*, 30. The recourse to nature serves what ecofeminist Soper calls a "policing function," as the terrain seems inherently bound to commerce (*What Is Nature?* 74). Miller notes that Jeffersonian discussions of "raw nature" commonly moved from "facts to values" (*Jefferson and Nature*, 252, 255).

10. Boyd et al., *Papers of Thomas Jefferson*, 6:139. Making overt the connection between frontier travel and scientific discovery, George Rogers Clark writes in response, "You scarcely ride a day through many parts of the Western Cuntry but you meet with Some Curious work of Antiquity, the Cituation of the Cuntries whare they are found Respecting Each other fully Evince the uses they ware fore, and the powerfull nations that Inhabited those Regions" (ibid., 6:159–60).

11. Buffon, *Barr's Buffon*, 1:162, 7:30, 39–40, 47–48. Useful discussions of race in the *Histoire naturelle* appear in Popkin, "Philosophical Basis"; Sloan, "Idea of Racial Degeneracy"; and Berkhofer, *White Man's Indian*, 38–44.

12. On the influence of De Pauw, see Echeverria, *Mirage in the West*, 13. De Pauw is quoted in Gerbi, *Dispute of the New World*, 53; see also Raynal, *Philosophical and Political History*, 7:150–51. William Robertson would argue after Buffon that the "principle of life seems to have been less active and vigorous" in North America (*History of America*, 17–18). Beaujour states that "not a single species is there more beautiful or perfect than in the old continent" (*Sketch of the United States*, 82). Dwight refutes Buffon in *Travels*, 4:223.

13. Echeverria, *Mirage in the West*, 41–44; Price, *Observations*, 19; Condorcet, "Influence of the American Revolution," 91.

14. For claims that Buffon did not answer critics, see the memorial, Condorcet, "Life of George Louis LeClerc," xiii. Bernard Lacepedé noted that Buffon died without using the gift of the moose from Jefferson. See Donald Jackson, *Letters of Lewis and Clark*, 47.

15. Solomon Drowne quoted from his journal, February 11, 1789, Solomon Drowne Collection, 78, John Hay Library, Providence, Rhode Island. *Notes on the State of Virginia* attracted a number of attacks for its discussions of slavery. See Imlay, *Topographical Description*, 221–36, and Clement Clarke Moore, *Observations upon Certain Passages*. A well-known review of Jefferson's place in the intellectual justifications of slavery is Winthrop Jordan, *White over Black*, 429–81.

16. Hagedorn, "'A Friend to Go between Them,'" 61; Hagedorn, "Brokers of Understanding," 396; Merrell, *Into the American Woods*, 57–58; Gustafson, *Eloquence Is Power*, 121; Krupat, "Approach to Native American Texts," 120. Ruoff argues that an oral text "often derives from versions taken down or remembered," and the tendency to generalize makes the genre "problematic at best" (*American Indian Literatures*, 51). On language and power in council discourse, see Merritt, "Metaphor, Meaning and Misunderstanding."

17. On the Shawnees' resentment, see Davies, *Documents of the American Revolution*, 2:224–25, 254, 3:385, 6:225; Sosin, *Opening of the American West*, 11; and Sullivan et al., *Papers of Sir William Johnson*, 7:184, 316. The southern Indian agent John Stuart provides a clear-eyed assessment, noting that "incessant acquisition for land . . . affords discontent and jealousy to all the Indian tribes [who] cannot see our advances into the heart of their most valuable hunting grounds with pleasure" (Davies, *Documents of the American Revolution*, 8:36). On war chiefs, see Sullivan et al., *Papers of Sir William Johnson*, 7:182, 332, 8:58. As a Shawnee council leader explained, "Our wisest Chiefs have had great trouble in preventing some our rash unthinking young Men" from declaring war (ibid., 7:408).

18. Logan's parents were Oneida and French, according to Anthony Wallace, *Death and Rebirth of the Seneca*, 123. White explains why Logan's village was a middle ground. On Yellow Creek, the Mingos traded quite frequently with a white settlement across the river, and John Gibson, who translated the famous address, had a child by Logan's sister. The first victims of Cresap's rampage were a pair of travelers (one a Shawnee, the other a Delaware) returning from the colonial markets at Fort Pitt. Cresap himself vested these murders with the common symbol of taking scalps. See White, *Middle Ground*, 358. On the integration of white material culture into the daily life of the Ohio nations, see McConnell, *A Country Between*, 217.

19. Anthony Wallace, *Death and Rebirth of the Seneca*, 101; Davies, *Documents of the American Revolution*, 8:114, 134, 144, 195; White, *Middle Ground*, 357–59; McConnell, *A Country Between*, 274–79; Abernethy, *Western Lands and the American Revolution*, 105–15; Thwaites and Kellogg, *Documentary History of Dunmore's War*, 9–19, 376–78, xxii; Downes, *Council Fires on the Upper Ohio*, 155–57; Faragher, *Daniel Boone*, 98–99; Burnett, *Letters of Members*, 1:172.

20. Gustafson, *Eloquence Is Power*, 117–18; Hutchinson, Rachal, and Rutland, *Papers of James Madison*, 1:138, 120–22, 136–38, 186; Jefferson, *Notes on the State of Virginia*, 298–300; Brant, *Virginia Revolutionist*, 281–84.

21. Boyd et al., *Papers of Thomas Jefferson*, 1:234. Observing that Jefferson had little personal contact with Dunmore, Malone argues that Jefferson's earliest differences with Dunmore were tied primarily to the Revolution (not necessarily Kentucky) (*Jefferson the Virginian*, 169–73).

22. Davies, *Documents of the American Revolution*, 5:135; Prucha, *Great Father*, 29.

23. Sheehan, *Seeds of Extinction*, 44; Isaac, "First Monticello," 98. Horsman notes that white leaders "could see no reason why the advance of white settlers across the continent could not be compatible with the presence of Indians who had been transformed from 'savages' to 'civilized beings'" (*Race and Manifest Destiny*, 106).

24. Krupat, "Post-Structuralism and Oral Tradition," 115; Paul Ford, *Works of Thomas Jefferson*, 7:137, 249, 381–83. Jefferson possibly omitted a report from George Rogers Clark that would have contradicted his conclusions in the Greathouse-Cresap controversy. See James, *George Rogers Clark Papers*, 1:3–9.

25. Sheehan, *Seeds of Extinction*, 12.

Chapter Five

1. Ronda discusses the Nez Perce in *Lewis and Clark*, 159–60, 228. Because several editions of the *Journals* exist, I refer to entries by date (unless otherwise noted) from Moulton, *Journals of Lewis and Clark*. The bears are described on May 14 and May 31,

1806; the woodpecker, May 16, 1805; *cous*, May 4, 1806; the "horned toad," May 29, 1805. On bears, see Moulton's editorial note, 7:315; see also Cutright, *Lewis and Clark*, 297.

2. Pratt defines the "anti-conquest" in *Imperial Eyes*, 38–68. Jehlen situates the *Journals* within a legacy of imperial expansion in "Literature of Colonization," 157. Brückner maintains that the readings of heroism and hubris "engender historico-fictional accounts of their own, celebrating the fitful and uneven narrative of the *Journals* as a tale of both masculine and narrative endurance" ("Contested Sources of the Self," 37). The link between nationalism and the Lewis and Clark expedition became clear to me as I polished up this chapter, when the *Time* magazine for July 8, 2002, crossed my desk. The cover read: "Lewis and Clark: How an amazing adventure 200 years ago continues to shape how America sees itself. PLUS: A fold-out map of the journey." The issue includes a scorching essay by Sherman Alexie, "What Sacagawea Means to Me (and Perhaps to You)," which the editors distinguish from "factual" reporting with the sidebar, VIEWPOINT.

3. On rhetorical collapse, see Seelye, *Beautiful Machine*, 197–201, and Lawson-Peebles, *Landscape and Written Expression*, 3, 196–230. See also Hallock, "Literary Recipes." White suggests a useful point of departure, emphasizing work as a form of learning the land, in "'Are You an Environmentalist,'" 176–77. Natives pelted the expedition with rocks on April 11, 1806.

4. Mazel, *American Literary Environmentalism*, xxi.

5. Henry Knox is quoted in Berkhofer, *White Man's Indian*, 144. The principles and paradoxes of "expansion with honor" have received ample commentary. A standard source is Horsman, *Expansion and American Indian Policy*, 54–59; he offers a useful distillation in "Indian Policy." Prucha notes the role of *Notes on the State of Virginia* in his magisterial survey, *Great Father*, 137. Sheehan discusses the connections between intellectual culture and public policy in *Seeds of Extinction*, 8–12; Carr uses Knox to contextualize literary responses to Indian policy in *Inventing the American Primitive*, 22–51.

6. Ramsey claims the "whole field" in *Oration on the Cession of Louisiana*, 8, 14. For context on the debates, see Tucker and Henderson, *Empire of Liberty*, 142–63; DeConde, *This Affair of Louisiana*, 21–55; Furtwangler, *Acts of Discovery*, 70–90; and Donald Jackson, *Letters of Lewis and Clark*, 11–12. For the range of responses in this rich literature, see Tucker, *Reflections, on the Cession of Louisiana*; Magruder, *Political, Commercial, and Moral Reflections*; *Debates in the House of Representatives*; Leonard, *Oration Delivered at Raynham*; and W. M. P., *Poem on the Acquisition of Louisiana*. One of the more extreme arguments comes from Charles Brockden Brown, who argues for an immediate "STRIKE!" on New Orleans after Spain ceded the territory to France in *Address to the Government*, 56.

7. For letters of introduction (which catalog Lewis's education), see Donald Jackson, *Letters of Lewis and Clark*, 23–25, 44–46, 52, 54–55.

8. On Jefferson's instructions, see ibid., 61–66. On symmetrical geography, see Allen, *Passage through the Garden*, 125; Ronda discusses how Jefferson simplified native politics and trade relations in *Lewis and Clark*, 254.

9. Self-fashioning is the best explanation for the first gap by Lewis. The only account published in his lifetime, by Patrick Gass, also begins on April 7, 1805. The preface to Gass's journal makes allusion to Columbus, and offers free embellishment about the "powerful and warlike" Indians, who were "of gigantic stature, fierce, tremendous and cruel" (Moulton, *Journals of Lewis and Clark*, 10:1–5).

10. In this leg of the tour, birds become the "numerous progeny of the creation" (June 4, 1805); a grizzly bear is either a "monster" or a "gentleman"; buffalo are "attended by their shepperds the wolves" (June 3, 1805); mosquitoes, gnats, and prickly pears become "the trio of pests... equal to any three curses that ever poor Egypt laiboured under, except the *Mahometant yoke*" (July 24, 1805). Lewis helps navigate one of the boats and quaintly allows that he "learned to push *a tolerable good pole* in their fraize" (July 24, 1805).

11. Ronda comments on the lack of narrative form in the Fort Clatsop sections in *Lewis and Clark*, 169–72.

12. On the distance covered, see Donald Jackson, *Letters of Lewis and Clark*, 331; on botanic discoveries, see Cutright, *Lewis and Clark*, 196–306. The ornithological observations provide clues to the migratory paths that are confirmed in contemporary guidebooks, while twentieth-century ethnographers have used the *Journals* to reconstruct cycles of trade. Lewis writes that the "white brant," or snow goose, is found "below tidewater where they remain in vast quantities during the winter" (March 8, 1806), while the winter wren "has lately returned and dose not remain all winter" (March 4, 1806). The March 5 entry notes the arrival of the osprey and blue-winged teal, which according to contemporary guidebooks, would have just arrived from Mexico; a similar note remarks upon the canvasback duck, which probably had begun its journey from the coast to the interior. See Terres, *National Audubon Society Field Guide*, and Roger Peterson, *Field Guide to Western Birds*. For a contemporary ethnographic study that uses the *Journals* to piece together human trade patterns further upriver, see Sappington, "Lewis and Clark Expedition."

13. Success as journalists depended upon a sensitivity to seasonal variations in local ecologies, an ability to record human interactions with biotic cycles, and an attention to the relations that social groups formed with one another on the land. Sometimes the explorers got lucky in this regard—on April 17, 1806, Lewis describes a chive that had not been identified in America—while elsewhere markers of seasonal flow escaped them. The Corps of Discovery missed high season at the Dalles, for example, a trading mart on the eastern slope of the Cascade Mountains that peaked between October and November. Arriving too late in 1805 and too early in 1806, they would find only the remains of dried fish, fleas, and rotten skins. For an ecological history of the Douglas Fir Bioregion, where Lewis and Clark camped for the winter, see Bunting, *Pacific Raincoast*. W. Raymond Wood notes that the Columbia plateau can be seen as a "single social and economic system with a constant recycling of elements, which was encouraged by local ecological diversity" ("Contrastive Features," 165).

14. Bergon maintains that the "details cannot be disentangled from the literary" in one of few literary assessments to deal with the quotidian, although he too reverts to categories of the epic. He argues that the massive accumulation of data is epic in "Wilderness Aesthetics," 142; he makes a similar case in "*Journals* of Lewis and Clark," 135.

15. Several indicators suggest that it was the static taxonomic tables that would distinguish Lewis's edition. When the enlisted men began advertising proposals for rival editions, he peevishly attacked "spurious" accounts on the grounds that the authors could not provide a proper "natural history of the country." The split between the tour and the scientific material complicated later efforts to shepherd the *Journals* into print. On plans for the *Journals*, which valued in particular tables of native languages, see Donald Jackson, *Letters of Lewis and Clark*, 386, 394, 396, 483. An 1810 letter to Clark suggests

how Nicholas Biddle worked. Biddle writes, "To day I have sent you & ten men up into a bottom to look for wood to make canoes after the unhappy failure of your iron boat" (ibid., 551). The transported reader joins the explorers in the path of discovery.

16. Ibid., 592. The preparation of the *Journals* was treated as a patriotic project from the outset, and the failure to generate subscribers drew criticism. See "An Editorial Comment" from the April 1819 *Monthly Anthology and Boston Review*, reprinted in Thwaites, *Original Journals*, 7:391. The linking of personal tragedy and national ascendancy persists in the title of Ambrose's best-selling biography, which was from Jefferson's memorial: *Undaunted Courage: Meriwether Lewis, Thomas Jefferson, and the Opening of the American West*. Moulton continues in this vein with the expressed hope that his edition "will help to keep this incredible story of courage and endurance alive for another two hundred years" (Moulton, *Journals of Lewis and Clark*, 13:9).

17. Allen reviews the history of the Samuel Lewis map in *Passage through the Garden*, 375. Brückner argues that Lewis and Clark were "bad students" who rejected the Jeffersonian master narrative for native geographies, and he maintains that this disjunction reveals the instability of republican identity ("Contested Sources of the Self," 32–33). I suggest that the Biddle map returns to script, however, and that the play between a "master narrative" and an Other was ongoing.

18. Allen reconstructs the Marias-Missouri crisis in "Lewis and Clark," 15; see also his *Passage through the Garden*, 61, 277n. Brückner draws out the Mandan and Hidatsa geographies that are embedded in the Lewis and Clark maps in "Contested Sources of the Self," 37–41. Jefferson is quoted in Donald Jackson, *Letters of Lewis and Clark*, 61. The episode at the river provides a rare moment of dissent in the enlisted men's accounts. Patrick Gass wrote, "The left Fork which is the largest we are doubtful of" (Moulton, *Journals of Lewis and Clark*, 9:161). Lewis's stock response to the falls has received more than its share of commentary, and besides Lawson-Peebles and Seelye, one might consult Jehlen, "Literature of Colonization," 157; Brückner, "Contested Sources of the Self," 42; and Furtwangler, *Acts of Discovery*, 31. I would add to Furtwangler's point that cascades offered a well-traveled corollary between aesthetics, nature, and nationalism. On patriotism and waterfalls, see La Rochefoucauld-Liancourt's account of Niagara in *Travels through the United States*, 1:220–22.

19. The story of the folding boat is chronicled in Donald Jackson, *Letters of Lewis and Clark*, 40, 233. The boat was an ongoing headache and delayed Lewis in joining the company at its base camp. Furtwangler sees the boat as an example of "serendipity" (*Acts of Discovery*, 17).

20. Lawson-Peebles, *Landscape and Written Expression*, 213; Goldie, *Fear and Temptation*, 21–22.

21. On food, Furtwangler wittily observes that the travelers "passed through America as America passed through them" (*Acts of Discovery*, 108). White discusses work, and by extension calories, in "'Are You an Environmentalist,'" 176–77. The company's staples are discussed in the *Journals* on April 14, 1804, April 16, May 15, May 26, 1805.

22. An excellent discussion of the Shoshones is Ronda, *Lewis and Clark*, 144; Jehlen notes that Lewis's account is "curiously uncharged" in "Literature of Colonization," 154.

23. For an example of the rhetorical distancing from cannibalism that Lewis might have known, see Ledyard, *Journals of Captain Cook's Last Voyage*, 75; in this reading, I draw from Greenfield, *Narrating Discovery*, 65.

24. Jefferson's suggestion of kinship is from Donald Jackson, *Letters of Lewis and Clark*, 281; Charbonneau is scolded for beating Sacagawea on August 14, 1805; on semiotic displacement, see Goldie, *Fear and Temptation*, 4–5. Ronda makes mention of Clark's parentage in *Lewis and Clark*, 233.

25. Terrall coins the term "scientist-as-action-hero" in "Gendered Space, Gendered Audiences," 216; the article is from a useful cluster of essays, "Gender and Early Modern-Science," in the same issue. Collinson is quoted from the essential collection edited by James Smith, *Correspondence of Linnaeus*, 1:94. Keller traces gender constructions in the early years of the Royal Society in *Reflections on Gender and Science*, 43; Schiebinger provides an account of gender ideology and Linnaean practice in *Nature's Body*, 11–39; Philips provides an excellent review of women scientists in *Scientific Lady*; Shteir's invaluable guide to early women's botany is *Cultivating Women, Cultivating Science*.

26. Hindle's composite biography provides a useful context on the Colden family ("Colonial Governor's Family," 234); I review Jane's life and work in Hallock, "Jane Colden." Hindle discusses Cadwallader's scientific work in the essential *Pursuit of Science in Revolutionary America*, 49. The Colden family papers (an excellent and underutilized source) cover most aspects of the family's life; for Alice Christie Colden's not writing and for the cheese book, see Colden et al., *Letters and Papers*, 2:8, 5:55–63. The compliment on her cheese is reprinted in Rickett, "Jane Colden as Botanist," 23. Evidence of Jane Colden's competency in herbal medicine is suggested by a letter to Alice Christie Colden that prescribes for "Emetick wine in sage." Cadwallader writes, "I believe Jenny knows it & I think it is marked Vinum Benedictum" (Colden et al., *Letters and Papers*, 8:306). Three relevant articles came to my attention after this chapter was written: Parrish, "Women's Nature"; Mulford, "New Science and the Question of Identity"; and Shuffelton, "Continental Poetics."

27. Colden et al., *Letters and Papers*, 5:29–30; James Smith, *Correspondence of Linnaeus*, 1:343; Berkeley and Berkeley, *Correspondence of John Bartram*, 393; James Smith, *Correspondence of Linnaeus*, 1:39, 45. Wilson notes the condescending air in descriptions of Jane Colden in "Dancing Dogs of the Colonial Period," 227. Smellie is quoted in Schiebinger, *Nature's Body*, 173.

28. Rickett, *Botanic Manuscript of Jane Colden*, 30, 46, 80; Regis, *Describing Early America*, 25; Koerner, "Women and Utility in Enlightenment Science," 250.

29. Colden to Alston, May 1, 1756, Edinburgh University Library (La.III.375/48), Edinburgh; [Colden and Garden], "Description of a new Plant"; Berkeley and Berkeley recount the episode in their useful biography, *Dr. Alexander Garden of Charles Town*, 48. Stephanie Volmer's ongoing research maps the fluidity between manuscript and print culture, and she argues that letters served as a fluid medium through which knowledge entered published transactions; I draw from her paper, "Viewing Nature with a Purpose." Shteir notes that a young Elisabeth Linné published a piece in the *Transactions of the Royal Swedish Academy of Sciences* in 1762 but that Linné was not encouraged in botany after marrying (*Cultivating Women, Cultivating Science*, 54).

30. Logan, "Gardener's Calendar," 44–48. On "fascinated" women and a ramble under the "Intense Heat of a Mid Day Sun," see Berkeley and Berkeley, *Correspondence of John Bartram*, 559, 629, 654. Irmscher uses the Bartram-Collinson friendship as a centerpiece for male botanic friendship in *Poetics of Natural History*, 12–32. Pinckney assembles the Bartram-Lamboll correspondence and provides useful commentary in *Thomas and Elizabeth Lamboll*, 12–27.

31. Pinckney, *Letterbook of Eliza Lucas Pinckney*, 35, 39–40. Scott offers a short biographical sketch in "Self-Portraits," 63–71.

32. For the imagined conversations and the cartographic text, see Pinckney, *Letterbook of Eliza Lucas Pinckney*, 38–39, 41. Burges discusses Pinckney's sensitivity to gender roles in eighteenth-century South Carolina, demonstrating how the letters vary in tone according to audience, in "Audience Awareness." A conflict remains in Burges's argument in the suggestion that Lucas accepted the limits of a woman's sphere yet negotiated her voice according to the recipient of a letter; by making such calculations for her audience, I maintain, carefully measured acts of transgression are revealed.

33. Pinckney, *Letterbook of Eliza Lucas Pinckney*, 48. The *Oxford English Dictionary* traces the use of "effeminate" in a verb form from the sixteenth to the eighteenth century.

34. An affectionate letter to Lucas's future husband's first wife covers a gift of wine, offering witty puns on Bacchus and "Xtian temperance." Later in life, Pinckney stocked the ponds and gardens of her English friends with turtles, ducks, oaks, and magnolias. See Pinckney, *Letterbook of Eliza Lucas Pinckney*, 64, 113, 119, 155.

35. The *Botanic Manuscript of Jane Colden* explains how pokeweed or "Phytolacca decandra" was used to treat "cancirs," although Jane Colden was not the first to make this point. Cadwallader investigated the plant in 1745, after receiving a clinical study on Hannah Murray of Connecticut. Suffering from a tumor or cyst, Murray learned about pokeweed from a neighbor "whose Breast had been eat off to her bare ribbs"; in a second case, Isaac Dickerman treated cancerous spots on his face with plaster (then ointment) drawn from the "Leaves, Stalk and Berries" of the *phytolacca*. Reports of pokeweed circulated in print, and Cadwallader Colden concluded to others that it would "make a perfect cure," excepting the painful application. See Rickett, *Botanic Manuscript of Jane Colden*, 82, and Colden et al., *Letters and Papers*, 3:121, 124, 4:317. Cadwallader Colden also discussed *phytolacca* in an unpublished copybook for his children and in a short commentary on names points to the paradox in Linnaean science between folk practice and institutional knowledge. "Tho the Phytolacca be known to allmost every one in America by the name of Pokeweed," he explains, "I think it proper on this occasion to add a description of it to preserve the knowledge of this plant, for vulgar names are observed frequently to change and thereby many useful discoveries of the ancients are lost to the moderns" (Cadwallader Colden's Copybook, Rosenbach Library, Philadelphia, Pennsylvania).

36. Berkeley and Berkeley, *Dr. Alexander Garden of Charles Town*, 29, 33, 233; Pinckney, *Thomas and Elizabeth Lamboll*, 19; James Smith, *Correspondence of Linnaeus*, 1:331. A November 26, 1764, letter by Garden to Richard Bohun Baker reveals the former's debts to his patients for botanic specimens. The medical correspondence, which provides a useful contrast to Garden's scientific persona, are in the Baker-Grimke Papers (folder 24), South Carolina Historical Society, Charleston. For examples of eroticism and the rhetoric of courtship in natural history writing, see Colden et al., *Letters and Papers*, 2:276–77, and Berkeley and Berkeley, *Correspondence of John Bartram*, 614. Situating Garden's pursuit of intellectual kinship against the context of his loyalism, Reid argues that his "act of contemplating nature provided an opportunity to participate in the love of God" ("Loyalism and the 'Philosophic Spirit,'" 8). Denny argues similarly that letters enabled Garden "to perform his duty toward mankind" ("Linnaeus and His Disciple in Carolina," 165). The erotics of male intellectual friendship, Keller shows, can be traced to Platonic communities where "desire begets love" and "love begets knowledge" (*Reflections on Gender and Science*, 23). Exploring an example from early modern Europe, the

Accademia dei Lincei, Biagioli argues that a "chaste" and "brotherly homosocial bond" allowed members of the academy to seek "knowledge itself" ("Knowledge, Freedom, and Brotherly Love," 141, 156).

37. James Smith, *Correspondence of Linnaeus*, 1:436. Hatley provides a diplomatic context for the Saluda conference in *Dividing Paths*, 80. Hill discusses the supernatural in plant collection in *Weaving New Worlds*, 13. Densmore reviews the Chippewas' use of puccoon in several methods of dyeing in *How Indians use Wild Plants*, 369–73. See also Waselkov and Braund, *William Bartram on the Southeastern Indians*, 270–71. My thanks to Kathryn Holland Braund and Ina Warren, who responded to my query about puccoon on the lively Bartram Trail Conference listserve.

Chapter Six

1. Berkeley and Berkeley, *Correspondence of John Bartram*, 393; Colden et al., *Letters and Papers*, 5:190. William Bartram's response to Jefferson is quoted in Waselkov and Braund, *William Bartram on the Southeastern Indians*, 23, 277n.

2. Lawrence Buell, *Environmental Imagination*, 144; Branch, "Early Romantic Natural History Literature," 1074. Particularly relevant to early Americanists is Tuan's distinction between *topophilia* and patriotism, which he describes as a surrogate for genuine love of place (*Topophilia*, 101).

3. Tuan, *Space and Place*, 107; Harper, *Diary of a Journey*, 13; Berkeley and Berkeley, *Life and Travels of John Bartram*, 221–71. On John's rise, see especially Slaughter, *Natures of John and William Bartram*, 46–51.

4. Seelye, "Beauty Bare," 41. Harper suggests that the later journey to west Florida and the Mississippi was a "way of carrying out his father's unrealized hopes" (*Diary of a Journey*, 62). The two Bartrams are usually treated in a single biography. See Ernest, *John and William Bartram*, and Slaughter, *Natures of John and William Bartram*.

5. Slaughter poignantly discusses the psychological pressure in *Natures of John and William Bartram*, 117–31. The fame of *Travels* has overshadowed Bartram's botanic art, which explains why few scholars recognize the drawings as the basis for the expedition. See Ewan, *William Bartram*, 5–6.

6. Harper, *Travels of William Bartram*, li. All further references to the *Travels*, unless otherwise noted, are from this essential edition. Critics commonly note that the polyphonic work brings together several genres into a single narrative line. See Larry Clarke, "Quaker Background," 435; Adams, "William Bartram's *Travels*," 119; Dickey's introduction to William Bartram, *Travels*, ix; and Fagin, *William Bartram*, 145–47.

7. Harper, *Travels in Georgia and Florida*, 156, 138.

8. Hoffmann (to whom I owe a great deal on Bartram's manuscripts) transcribes the earlier version of *Travels* in "Construction of William Bartram's Narrative," 254–56. The manuscript is a complicated one. The sign <> marks text inserted by Bartram; [] marks deletions by the 1791 editors; {} marks text inserted by editors; ** marks heavy cross-out.

9. Douglas Anderson, "Bartram's *Travels*," 13; Looby, "Constitution of Nature," 252–73; Adams, "William Bartram's *Travels*," 114. Cashin explores the absence of a political context in "'Philosophical Pilgrim.'"

10. Bartram is quoted in Waselkov and Braund, *William Bartram on the Southeastern Indians*, 198, 197, 285n. See also Horsman, *Expansion and American Indian Policy*, 49–52.

11. Hoffmann, "Construction of William Bartram's Narrative," 157, 51–68; Slaughter,

Natures of John and William Bartram, 185. See also Slaughter's discussion of politics and the Quaker voice in ibid., 195–96.

12. On Bartram and the plot of an individual in isolation, see Arner, "Pastoral Patterns in William Bartram's *Travels*," 133. See also Terrall (discussed in the previous chapter), "Gendered Space, Gendered Audiences," 216.

13. Waselkov and Braund, *William Bartram on the Southeastern Indians*, 35, 231. The reshuffling of scenes reveals the break between literary critics and a prior generation of more literal-minded historians. Harper, who reconstructed the Bartram trail, complains about the author's reshuffling. Bartram's indifference to accurate dates, distances, and dimensions "constitute[s] a virtual 'blind spot' in his mental vision" (*Travels in Georgia and Florida*, 130).

14. For reviews of the New Purchase, see Braund, *Deerskins and Duffels*, 150–52; Cashin, *William Bartram and the American Revolution*, 53–75; and Kornfield "Encountering 'the Other,'" 300. Bellin points to this episode to suggest how "Bartram's text registers doubts about the absoluteness of Euro-American conceptions of, and claims to, the continent" ("Wicked Instruments," 3).

15. Bartram remarks that "I have never travelled the continent south of New Orleans," when to this point he had not been west of Florida (Harper, *Travels of William Bartram*, 179). Irmscher, who does not see a shape to *Travels*, maintains that this is "not a tidy narrative" (*Poetics of Natural History*, 37). But I argue that Bartram narrates the story of his own collection.

16. Ewan, *William Bartram*, 79; Mooney, *Myths of the Cherokee*, 253, 295–96; Swanton, *Creek Religion and Medicine*, 490. Slaughter argues that the snake passage illustrates a conflict of personae between William (reverential of native cultures) and Puc-Puggy (the arrogant son) in *Natures of John and William Bartram*, 144–49. Bartram probably understood native beliefs about rattlesnakes, as he remarked elsewhere that "they hold this animal in a degree of veneration & regard" (Waselkov and Braund, *William Bartram on the Southeastern Indians*, 250). Gary E. Cooper pointed out the uncharacteristic behavior of Bartram's rattlesnake to me.

17. Adams, "Reading Ecologically," 70.

18. Thoreau, *Natural History Essays*, 104.

19. See Worster, "Two Roads Diverged: Ecology in the Eighteenth Century," in *Nature's Economy*, 5–53; Oelschlaeger makes a similar case in his influential *Idea of Wilderness*, 103–5; on pastoral ideology, see Marx's landmark study, *Machine in the Garden*, 86.

20. Bartram writes of Mount Royal, "About fifteen years ago I visited this place, at which there were no settlements of white people but all appeared wild and savage" (Harper, *Travels of William Bartram*, 64). He writes earlier: "Mo^ت. Royal gives name to a large Plantation belonging to L^d. Egmont, was formerly an Indigo Plantation but now given up . . . there is about 150 Acres of Land cleared here & has been planted with Indigo" (Harper, *Travels in Georgia and Florida*, 150). Bartram's participation in plantation economy does not receive mention in discussions of green multiculturalism. For an interpretation different from my own, see Ian Marshall, *Story Line*, 35–36, 45–46. In a renarration of Bartram's route, Cashin traces repeated interests where Bartram downplayed human involvement and emphasized his immersion in nature (*William Bartram and the American Revolution*, 76–124).

21. Harper, *Travels of William Bartram*, 71. For revisions, see Hoffmann, "Construction of William Bartram's Narrative," which reads: "We contemplated no other pleasure

than what naturally arises from the rational and moderate gratification of the Passions & appetites given to us by the Great and bountiful Deity" (153).

22. Harper, *Travels of William Bartram*, 354; Harper, *Travels in Georgia and Florida*, 151–54.

23. Slaughter, *Natures of John and William Bartram*, 188.

24. Mazel, *American Literary Environmentalism*, 2.

25. Sayre, "Mound Builders," 239–42. See also Adams, "William Bartram's *Travels*," 115, and Anderson, "Bartram's *Travels*," 14. A self-consciousness about empire pervades Bartram's descriptions. The "magnificent" Mount Royal, made from shells, he wrote, "all appeared wild and savage" in the 1760s in an "uncultivated state" but possessing an "almost inexpressible air of grandeur" (Harper, *Travels of William Bartram*, 64). A planter had cleared the "venerable grove" of oranges and live oaks there, but he had shown some taste and "preserved the mount." The indigo, cotton, and corn went to seed. This layering of several uses over a single landscape captures Bartram's historical poetics: "The prospect from this station is so happily situated by nature, as to comprise at one view, the whole of the sublime and pleasing" (ibid., 65). It is not "nature," of course, that supplies this prospect, as the author stands atop an artificially constructed mountain of shells, and it is the various traces of past work that so often informs Bartram's landscapes; it is a stylized response to the environmental politics that followed the Revolution.

26. Harper, *Travels in Georgia and Florida*, 161; Gallay, *Formation of a Planter Elite*, 94, 145–46; Waselkov and Braund, *William Bartram on the Southeastern Indians*, 202, 243.

27. The "Preface" was probably penned by John Fothergill. See John Bartram, *Observations*, iii.

Chapter Seven

1. Samuel Williams, *Natural and Civil History of Vermont*, 33; Mazel, *American Literary Environmentalism*, 35; Krech, *Ecological Indian*, 17–19.

2. Michael Williams, *Americans and Their Forests*, 110, 225; La Rochefoucauld-Liancourt, *Travels through the United States*, 1:xi; Crèvecoeur, *Journey into Northern Pennsylvania*, xvi; Morse, *American Universal Geography*, vi; Gordon S. Wood, *Radicalism of the American Revolution*, 365. Branch ably reviews the factors leading to early national pastoral writing in "Early Romantic Natural History Literature." On the iconography of forests, see Silver, *New Face on the Countryside*, 191, and Daniels, "Political Iconography in Later Georgian England," 43.

3. Doddridge, *Notes on the Settlement*, 60, 74, 82, 99, 102; Crèvecoeur, *Journey into Northern Pennsylvania*, 37, 45, 102.

4. Grant, *Memoirs of an American Lady*, 1:59. All further references will be cited internally, unless otherwise noted. To establish how *Memoirs of an American Lady* is crafted retrospectively, readers should consult J. P. Grant, *Memoir and Correspondence*, 9–10. Gallagher, in one of few articles on this surprisingly neglected author, argues that Mary Wollstonecraft was an implicit counterpoint to Margaretta Schuyler ("Anne MacVicar Grant," 158).

5. Cadwallader Colden recounts some choice episodes of Schuyler corruption in a 1751 letter to the geographer and naturalist John Mitchell. Nicholas Schuyler, of the "noted & principal family at Albany," sold several kegs of rum at Fort Oswego. Thinking that the natives would not open the kegs until they returned home, he filled the casks with water

and closed the bungs with liquor-drenched rags. Schuyler was ordered to be prosecuted, but in Colden's words, the "Govr thought proper to wink" at the episode. A second instance found David Schuyler "fram[ing] boundaries" on a deed with the Mohawks "so as to take in ten times the quantity of land that the Indians intended to give him." It fell upon Colden later to keep the Mohawks from murdering Schuyler. See Colden et al., *Letters and Papers*, 9:104–6.

6. Gallagher notes that Grant left America in 1768 (which was two years after the Stamp Act repeal) ("Anne MacVicar Grant," 155). The hate mail to Colden is worth noting. An anonymous letter threatens, "You'll die Martyr to your own Villainy, & be Hang'd like Porteis [John Porteous] as a Memento to all wicked Governors, and that every Man, that assists you, Shall be surely put to Death" (Colden et al., *Letters and Papers*, 7:65, 85, 105).

7. Bellesiles, *Revolutionary Outlaw*, 25, 50; Alan Taylor, *Liberty Men and Great Proprietors*, 8, 29.

8. Evernden, *Social Creation of Nature*, 25; Harrison, *Forests*, 156.

9. Kafer, "Making of Timothy Dwight," 193–94; Lawson-Peebles, *Landscape and Written Expression*, 145; Elliott, *Revolutionary Writers*, 69; Dwight, *Travels*, 4:128. All further references to *Travels*, unless otherwise indicated, are cited internally and are from the Solomon edition. *Travels* suffers in coherence (and from sheer bulk) because Dwight was at the end of his life; for the deathbed orders that outline his publication plans, see Dwight Family Papers (series 1, box 1, folder 3), Sterling Library, Yale University, New Haven, Connecticut.

10. Dwight famously branded anything associated with republican or Jeffersonian politics as "infidelity," although his politics often have been caricatured. On Dwight's elitism, see Volkomer, "Timothy Dwight and New England Federalism," 76. For more balanced arguments, see Snyder, "Foundations of Liberty," 382–83, and Harris, "Revelation and the American Republic," 455.

11. Brückner, "Lessons in Geography," 313–14; Frazier, *Cold Mountain*, 15. For Nicholas Brown's annotations to Dwight's *Travels*, see the copy in the John Carter Brown Library, Providence, Rhode Island, 3:35. On the Brown family's economic base, see Hedges, *Browns of Providence Plantation*; on the Brown family's speculation in Ohio, see Brown Family Papers (P-L20C 198), John Carter Brown Library, Providence, Rhode Island. I suspect that Nicholas Brown's response was typical. A Vermont reader of Jedidiah Morse objects to the statement that, in Vermont, public representatives "must profess the protestant religion." The reader writes, "doubted," and adds that "Zenas Allen, an Atheist, was chosen to represent the town of Tinmouth for 1802" (John Carter Brown Library copy of Morse's *American Universal Geography*).

12. My suggestion that Dwight's *Travels* adheres to the conventions of a cartographic text differs from Silverman, who argues in the only book-length study on the author that "Dwight makes no formal effort to unify this melange" (*Timothy Dwight*, 115).

13. On suffrage and "semi-savages," see "Notes taken from observations made by Dr. Dwight," Dwight Family Papers, Sterling Library, Yale University, New Haven, Connecticut; Dwight, *Remarks on Inchiquin's Letters*, 15; and Silverman, *Timothy Dwight*, 132. See also Dwight's remarks on the notorious Yazoo Purchase in Georgia and the disastrous Lyman expedition that ended his father's life in *Travels*, 1:160, 226.

14. Alan Taylor, *Liberty Men and Great Proprietors*, 49; Williams, *Natural and Civil History of Vermont*, 227. Morse shared that fear of excess liberty and argued that the

Revolution had brought an excess of freedom and a "litigious temper [which] is the genuine fruit of republicanism" (*American Geography*, 147). Lawson-Peebles notes that the political condition of Vermont is symbolized by the textual fracturing of "Vergennes" (*Landscape and Written Expression*, 143).

15. The road to Vergennes follows a "narrow defile" through "shaggy mountains" that "forbid every excursion of the eyes." Dwight observes that "savages" used the same route to invade English communities, and the country was "suited to the[ir] gloomy purposes." (The scenery draws the same conclusions that Crèvecoeur offers on the East Branch of the Susquehanna.) Dwight observes that the houses in "this desert region were few and solitary," and he worries that the lack of connection will degrade humanity (*Travels*, 2:285). He asks rhetorically: "Without learning, what would their country be? A wilderness. What their state of society? That of savages" (2:276). The terrain also serves as the basis for assessing Vermont's politics. Dwight dismisses the capital city of Montpelier, arguing that nothing "could possible be raised upon this spot," and suggests that the location would hold public discourse to "a limited scale" (2:293, 304). He rails against the atheism of its early leader, "this freak of Colonel [Ethan] Allen," and blasts a government that would "not lift a finger" to build a church (2:293, 402). By contrast, the plans for a seminary in Middlebury (later Middlebury College) represent the equivalent to Crèvecoeur's predictions for Wilkes-Barre on the east Susquehanna. Dwight dislikes the clay soil in Vermont, and he argues that it will impede commerce, but he takes consolation that "the seeds of future respectability [have been] sown" (2:289). The 1798 report closes positively and maintains that "the local situation" as well as "the sober and religious character of the inhabitants" promise to render this "a very desirable seat" for learning (2:290). And by 1810, Dwight already had begun to memorialize: "When it is remembered that, twenty-five years ago, this spot was a wilderness, it must be admitted that these efforts have done the authors of them the highest honor" (2:292).

16. Silverman calls the strategy of siting stories geographically "observation plus a memory" (*Timothy Dwight*, 118).

17. Cronon remarks that dutiful students of "New England ecology could do no better than to read Dwight from cover to cover" (*Changes in the Land*, 210). Kamensky speculates that "Dwight's political conservatism . . . translated into a nascent conservation ethic" ("'In These Contrasted Climes,'" 108). "As a traditionalist," Lawrence Buell maintains, the Federalist traveler "regards an assimilation of its past as part of one's total rapport with the landscape" (*New England Literary Culture*, 328).

18. Cronon, *Changes in the Land*, 106–7; Dwight, *Travels*, 2:24, 213, 235; Ryden, *Mapping the Invisible Landscape*, 6. On paths, time, memory, and the construction of place, I draw from Pred, "Of Paths and Projects," 236–37, and Tuan, *Space and Place*, 149.

19. Certainly Dwight offers his share of conventional landscapes, and he woodenly relies upon stock aesthetic responses to convey a political order. Dwight was almost blind anyway, and that should affect how heavily we lean upon his visual appreciation, but much like Meriwether Lewis, Dwight would suggest a social harmony through the picturesque. For example, Dwight captures his feelings about the parish of his grandfather, Jonathan Edwards, through the Connecticut Valley. "When the eye traces this majestic stream," Dwight writes, one sees "delightful fields" and "sprightly towns" that "gem the whole landscape in its neighborhood." The pitch gradually builds, moving from farmland, into rolling hills, to the noble Green Mountains, which presides over the farms and

villages. Through a single, long sentence that rises toward the sublime, Dwight explains how the "eye last of all fastens upon the Monadnock in the northeast, and in the northwest upon Saddle Mountain, ascending each at the distance of fifty miles in dim and misty grandeur, far above all the other objects in view; it will be difficult not to say that with these exquisite varieties of beauty and grandeur the relish for landscape is filled, neither a wish for higher perfection, nor an idea of what it is remaining in the mind" (*Travels*, 1:259). On the correlation of aesthetics and a moral vision, see Spears, "Common Observations," 47; Sears, "Timothy Dwight and the American Landscape," 312; and Lawson-Peebles, *Landscape and Written Expression*, 138.

20. Sears, "Timothy Dwight and the American Landscape," 313. Kamensky sees less flexibility in cases like these and argues that "settings that juxtaposed rugged landscape and white community strained Dwight's appreciation of both romantic wilderness and progress" ("'In These Contrasted Climes,'" 93).

21. The assertion that American climes were underproducing, which Jefferson refutes through the recourse to progress, leads Dwight to the example of old-growth forests. See *Travels*, 1:72–75, and Rosaldo, "Imperial Nostalgia," 108–20.

22. Looking just twenty years down the trail, to George Catlin, Mazel notes that the discourses of "savage" and "wilderness" were "functionally aligned within an overarching discourse of 'civilization'" ("'Beautiful and Thrilling Specimen,'" 131). I discuss the poetics of Indian removal in the next chapter.

Chapter Eight

1. *The Sketch Book* is cited from Kelly, *Selected Writings of Washington Irving*, 299–301, 306, 311; on topical jabs, see Irving, "Traits of Indian Character," 145; for a brief review of the Creek (or Red Sticks) War, see Heidler and Heidler, *Encyclopedia of the War of 1812*, 133–36; Dowd notes Tecumseh's role in the Creek War and argues that it was a "culmination" of the pan-Indian movement in *Spirited Resistance*, 170. Kathryn Holland Braund helped me with background on the Creek War (any mistakes are my own). Boudinot mocks the justifications for removal in Perdue, *Cherokee Editor*, 130–31. Laura Murray argues that Irving emphasizes American colonialism in "Traits" in order to displace the republic's colonization of native Americans in "Aesthetics of Dispossession," 206–7.

2. Kelly, *Selected Writings of Washington Irving*, 32–35, 44–45, 49; on New York as a metaphor for social stability, see Ringe, "New York and New England," 458–59; Daigrepont, "'Rip VanWinkle,'" 47–48. Colin Pearce writes that "Rip is a reminder that all communities, no matter how free and enlightened they become, need to be attentive to their past, and need, no matter what their prosperity and success, some sense of the mysterious and awe-inspiring" ("Changing Regimes," 127).

3. Bergland makes a direct connection between "Rip Van Winkle" and the ghosting of native peoples in *National Uncanny*, 57. For similar arguments, see Maddox, *Removals*, 24, and Scheckel, *Insistence of the Indian*, 19.

4. James Fenimore Cooper, *The Pioneers*, 452. This and all further citations, unless otherwise noted, are from the Penguin edition and hereafter will be cited internally. The Penguin volume is based upon the standard edition, with the original title *The Pioneers, or the Sources of the Susquehanna*, edited by James Franklin Beard.

5. Cheyfitz, "Literally White, Figuratively Red," 56. For current discussions of Cooper

and frontier myth (and one can easily get lost in a vast critical terrain), see Arac, "Nationalism, Hypercanonization, and Huckleberry Finn," 28–32; Lee Clark Mitchell, *Westerns*, 30–52; and Fisher, *Hard Facts*, 22–86.

6. Alan Taylor, *William Cooper's Town*, 169; Spiller, *Fenimore Cooper*, 12–25; Grossman, *James Fenimore Cooper*, 11–13.

7. Beard's introduction to James Fenimore Cooper's *The Pioneers* (SUNY Press edition), xix; Raillton, *Fenimore Cooper*, 112; Alan Taylor, *William Cooper's Town*, 407.

8. Nash, *Wilderness and the American Mind*, 76. This concern with "firstness" in the continuum of American environmental writing, and the measure of an author by whether she or he understood and cared about nature, continues to define the field of ecocriticism. The editors of Susan Cooper's *Rural Hours*, Johnson and Patterson, write in the introduction that "long before the state of environmental crisis we face at the end of the twentieth century," James Fenimore Cooper "undertook the work of educating a readership about the value and the necessity of human culture that was sustainable in the natural world" (xxi).

9. William Cooper, *Guide to the Wilderness*, 2, 10. Alan Taylor argues that "James Fenimore Cooper recomplicated his father's simpler and briefer narrative to press their own claims to the Otsego wilderness" (*William Cooper's Town*, 54).

10. Franklin, *New World of James Fenimore Cooper*, 3; James D. Wallace, *Early Cooper and His Audience*, 136; Limerick, "Making the Most of Words," 184.

11. Scheckel notes that the opening scene "prefigures the competing claims to the land that drive the plot of *The Pioneers*" (*Insistence of the Indian*, 20). I agree, but as the contexts of Anne Grant, Washington Irving, and Timothy Dwight suggest, the competing claims were not limited to racial lines but also involved class.

12. McEvoy, "Toward an Interactive Theory," 221, 228; Dekker, *James Fenimore Cooper*, 43. On historical changes, see McWilliams, *Political Justice in a Republic*, 102; Adams, '*Guardian of the Law*,' 55–57; and Philbrick, "Cooper's *The Pioneers*," 592. On law and nature, see Swann, "Guns Mean Democracy," 100, and Thomas, "*The Pioneers*." The second major plotline of the novel begins when Natty shoots a dear out of season, and the decision over when to hunt ties the question of racial identity to law. Oliver says to Natty, "You must remember the law," which leads Natty to question the youth's race and ask Chingachgook if the youth is "of the right blood" (*The Pioneers*, 290).

13. H. Daniel Peck remarks on this formality in a clever discussion of "scenery," a term that suggests both the theater and the outdoors, in *World by Itself*, 57. The interactions between men and nature often have a symbolic hue. When Natty and Chingachgook chase a buck, for instance, they pursue sentiment ("The old man enjoyed the chase more as a memorial of his youthful sports and deeds, than with any expectation of profiting by the success" [*The Pioneers*, 299]).

14. James Wallace, *Early Cooper and His Audience*, vii; Fiedler, *Love and Death in the American Novel*, 187–88.

15. On the canoe, see Goldie, *Fear and Temptation*, 21. (See also my discussion of Lewis and Clark in part 3.) Person notes that this episode equals a symbolic baptism, one that anticipates the close of the novel by connecting the future of the patent with the past ("Cooper's *The Pioneers*," 3).

16. Alan Taylor remarks that speculators needed the settlers (more than the settlers needed them), and proprietors "went along for a profitable ride" (*William Cooper's Town*, 329). See also Jordan and Kaups, *American Backwoods Frontier*.

17. Anthony Wallace, *Death and Rebirth of the Seneca*, 160–226; Monroe is quoted in Berkhofer, *White Man's Indian*, 159. Few were more sympathetic to native Americans than Mary Jemison, who spent most of her life among the Seneca, and she would claim in 1823 that "Indians must and will be Indians, in spite of all the means that can be used for their cultivation in the sciences and the arts" (Derounian-Stodola, *Women's Indian Captivity Narratives*, 150).

18. Deloria, *Playing Indian*, 36; Carr, *Inventing the American Primitive*, 32–33. Bergland notes that "Indian ghosts shaped the nation and the national literature, constructing America as a haunted community rather than a simple one" (*National Uncanny*, 59).

19. Goldie discusses how the figurative Indian leads back to other figures, noting that "each representation of the indigene is a signifier for which the signified is the image" (*Fear and Temptation*, 4).

20. In a memorable scene where a flock of half-dead birds suffer on the ground before him, Temple offers "sixpence a hundred for the pigeons' heads," and he blasts the poor practices of the townspeople. These displays of stewardship contrast with the lesser Richard, who badgers 'Duke for his obsession, sugar maples. Richard also "misreads" Oliver. In one of the early and persisting arguments about Oliver's identity, Richard maintains that "the lad never slept in any thing better than a bark shanty in his life" (*The Pioneers*, 250, 105, 222, 111).

21. Peck, *World by Itself*, 179.

22. Silver, *New Face on the Countryside*, 191.

23. Ibid., 70; Jennings, *Invasion of America*, 15.

24. Cronon and White discuss the Indian as "original conservationist" in "Ecological Change and Indian-White Relations," 417. Krech provides a fuller work of demystification in *Ecological Indian*.

25. Alan Taylor identifies Chingachgook as "the author's (and the reader's) sentimental indulgence rather than a viable claimant to Otsego" (*William Cooper's Town*, 54).

26. Philbrick, "Cooper's *The Pioneers*," 590.

27. Susan Cooper, *Rural Hours*, 108.

Coda

1. Anthony F. C. Wallace, *Death and Rebirth of the Seneca*, 244, 268.

2. Merrill Peterson, *Portable Thomas Jefferson*, 306–7.

3. On nativist movements, see Dowd, *Spirited Resistance*, 123–28. The plans for improvement brought intense political divisions. On the Senecas, see Anthony Wallace, *Death and Rebirth of the Seneca*, 202; on the Cherokees, see Mary Young, "Cherokee Nation," 524. McLoughlin discusses the political and cultural rivalries in *Cherokee Renascence in the New Republic*, 366–87. Cheryl Marshall is quoted from *Indian Nation*, 14, 38. Marshall directs her polemic against Berkhofer, Roy Harvey Pearce, and others who focus upon the "imagined" or "vanishing" Indians. Her point was instrumental in my own thinking through the aesthetics of removal. But her premise (that critics are complicit to a legacy of conquest if they focus only upon policy) assumes that the readers of such studies are blind to any reality beyond the rhetoric that is being bracketed.

4. Perdue, *Cherokee Editor*, 7–26, 51–54. All further references to the writings of Boudinot, unless otherwise noted, will be internally cited and are from this edition. Perdue provides a short, compelling review of Boudinot's life in the introduction to this volume. McLoughlin notes that the Cornwall episode "confirmed the worst fears of those

suspicious of white benevolence" (*Cherokee Renascence in the New Republic*, 368). For a model of Boudinot's experiences, see Bellin's observations on conversion in *Demon of the Continent*, 26. I am indebted to William Nesbitt for introducing me to Boudinot's work.

5. Perdue suggests that Boudinot was murdered ultimately because the nation he imagined "simply did not exist" (*Cherokee Editor*, 32). Mary Young discusses Boudinot's murder and Cherokee codes of justice in "Cherokee Nation," 520–21.

6. Rowe, *Literary Culture and U.S. Imperialism*, 23. Rowe is less interested in "the best that has been thought and said" than in such historical "intersections." Scheckel observes that the Removal Act of 1830 led to scrutiny about native roles in the United States (*Insistence of the Indian*, 102–7). My reading of Boudinot locates the Cherokees at the end of the republican period, during a time, as McLoughlin notes, that "Americans were shucking off the last vestiges of the Enlightenment" (*Cherokee Renascence in the New Republic*, 368).

7. Deloria, *Playing Indian*, 34, 64. Boudinot's rhetorical strategies resemble what Bergland convincingly traces in William Apess, noting that "Apess engages with the discourse of spectralization, and uses his own, *Indian* mirror to construct a phantom identity that serves to dispel the shades of doom that have been projected around the Indian, and to expose the racism that shadows Indian identity" (*National Uncanny*, 130).

8. Perdue suggests that Boudinot was misinformed about traditional forms of agriculture and that on theological issues he "was so thoroughly Christianized that he did not understand the religion of his own people" (*Cherokee Editor*, 80–81). The concern with what Boudinot actually knew, however, does not allow for the degree of performance that was endemic to a hybrid setting. I would not doubt Boudinot's religious faith but suggest instead that "An Address to the Whites" negotiates Indian identity on Eurocentric terms, and what Boudinot actually believed was secondary to his rhetorical intent. Perdue reviews Boudinot's reliability as an ethnographic source in "Rising from the Ashes." In a survey of native American journalism, Murphy and Murphy present the *Cherokee Phoenix* as a transparent source, one that was "read by the eager population" of Cherokees (*Let My People Know*, 25).

9. David Murray makes an important point about the Mohegan Samsom Occum that may applied to Boudinot, noting that "we need to be aware of the extent to which Occum may be using the complex situation of Indians talking to each other, but being overheard and stage-managed by whites, and turning it, if only marginally, to his own purposes" (*Forked Tongues*, 47). Boudinot's syntax "hiccoughs" on several occasions: "Some there are, perhaps even in this enlightened assembly, who at the bare sight of an Indian"; "It is a matter of surprise to me, and must be to all those who are property acquainted with the condition of the Aborigines of this country" (Perdue, *Cherokee Editor*, 68–69, 72). The language also pulses in a similar manner when Euroamericans address natives. As previously cited, Jefferson writes to Handsome Lake, "Nor do I think, brother, that the sale of lands is, under all circumstances, injurious to your people." The qualifications here— "brother" and "under all circumstances"—point to similar instances of cultural stress, as Jefferson presents cessions as mutually beneficial.

10. Lawrence, *Studies in Classic American Literature*, 56.

Bibliography

Manuscript Collections
Charleston, S.C.
   South Carolina Historical Society
      Baker-Grimke Papers
Edinburgh, Scotland
   Edinburgh University Library, Special Collections
New Haven, Conn.
   Sterling Memorial Library, Yale University
      Dwight Family Papers
Philadelphia, Pa.
   Rosenbach Library
Providence, R.I.
   John Carter Brown Library
      Brown Family Papers
   John Hay Library
      Solomon Drowne Collection

Books, Articles, and Dissertations
Abbey, Edward. *Desert Solitaire: A Season in the Wilderness*. New York: Ballantine, 1968.
Abernethy, Thomas P. *Western Lands and the American Revolution*. New York: Russell and Russell, 1937.
Adams, Charles H. *"The Guardian of the Law": Authority and Identity in James Fenimore Cooper*. University Park: Pennsylvania State University Press, 1990.
———. "Reading Ecologically: Language and Play in Bartram's *Travels*." *Southern Quarterly* 32, no. 4 (1994): 65–74.
———. "William Bartram's *Travels*: A Natural History of the South." In *Rewriting the South: History and Fiction*, edited by Lothar Hönnighausen and Valeria Gennaro Lerda, 112–20. Tübingen: Francke, 1993.
Albion, Robert Greenhalgh, and Leonidas Dodson, eds. *Philip Vickers Fithian's Journal, 1775–1776: Written on the Virginia-Pennsylvania Frontier and in the Army around New York*. Princeton: Princeton University Press, 1934.

Alden, John R. "The Albany Congress and the Creation of the Indian Superintendencies." *Mississippi Valley Historical Review* 27, no. 2 (1940): 193–210.

Alexie, Sherman. "What Sacagawea Means to Me (and Perhaps to You)." *Time*, July 8, 2002, n.p.

Allen, John Logan. "Lewis and Clark on the Upper Missouri: Decision at the Marias." *Montana: The Magazine of Western History* 21 (1971): 2–17.

———. *Passage through the Garden: Lewis and Clark and the Image of the American Northwest*. New York: Dover, 1991.

Ambrose, Stephen E. *Undaunted Courage: Meriwether Lewis, Thomas Jefferson, and the Opening of the American West*. New York: Simon & Schuster, 1996.

Anderson, Benedict. *Imagined Communities: Reflections on the Origin and Spread of Nationalism*. Rev. ed. London: Verso, 1991.

Anderson, Douglas. "Bartram's *Travels* and the Politics of Nature." *Early American Literature* 25, no. 1 (1990): 3–17.

———. "Subterraneous Virginia: The Ethical Poetics of Thomas Jefferson." *Eighteenth-Century Studies* 33, no. 2 (2000): 233–49.

Arac, Jonathan. "Nationalism, Hypercanonization, and Huckleberry Finn." *Boundary 2* 19, no. 1 (1992): 14–43.

Arner, Robert D. "Pastoral Patterns in William Bartram's *Travels*." *Tennessee Studies in Literature* 18 (1973): 133–45.

Aron, Stephen. *How the West Was Lost: The Transformation of Kentucky*. Baltimore: Johns Hopkins University Press, 1996.

———. "Lessons in Conquest: Towards a Greater Western History." *Pacific Historical Review* 63, no. 2 (1994): 125–47.

Barnhart, John D. *Valley of Democracy: The Frontier versus the Plantation in the Ohio Valley, 1775–1818*. Bloomington: Indiana University Press, 1953.

Barton, Benjamin Smith. *Fragments of the Natural History of Pennsylvania*. Philadelphia: Way and Groff, 1799.

Bartram, John. *Observations on the Inhabitants, Climate, Soil, Rivers, Productions, Animals, and other matters worthy of Notice. [Travels in Pensilvania and Canada]*. Ann Arbor: University Microfilms, Inc., 1966.

Bartram, William. *Travels through North & South Carolina, Georgia, East & West Florida, the Cherokee Country, the Extensive Territories of the Muscogulges, or Creek Confederacy, and the Country of the Chactaws*. Introduction by James Dickey. New York: Penguin, 1988.

Bayet, Fabienne. "Overturning the Doctrine: Indigenous People and Wilderness—Being Aboriginal in the Environmental Movement." In *The Great New Wilderness Debate: An Expansive Collection of Writings Defining Wilderness from John Muir to Gary Snyder*, edited by J. Baird Callicott and Michael P. Nelson, 314–24. Athens: University of Georgia Press, 1998.

Beard, James Franklin. Introduction to *The Pioneers, or the Sources of the Susquehanna; A Descriptive Tale*, by James Fenimore Cooper. Albany: State University of New York Press, 1980.

Beaujour, Louis-Auguste Félix, Baron de. *Sketch of the United States of North America*. Translated by William Walton. London: J. Booth, 1814.

Bellesiles, Michael A. *Revolutionary Outlaw: Ethan Allen and the Struggle for Indepen-

dence on the Early American Frontier. Charlottesville: University of Virginia Press, 1993.

Bellin, Joshua David. *The Demon of the Continent: Indians and the Shaping of American Literature*. Philadelphia: University of Pennsylvania Press, 2001.

———. "Wicked Instruments: William Bartram and the Dispossession of the Southern Indians." *Arizona Quarterly* 51, no. 3 (1995): 1–23.

Bergland, Renée L. *The National Uncanny: Indian Ghosts and American Subjects*. Hanover: University Press of New England, 2000.

Bergon, Frank. "The *Journals* of Lewis and Clark: An American Epic." In *Old West—New West: Centennial Essays*, edited by Barbara Howard Meldrum, 133–45. Moscow: University of Idaho Press, 1993.

———. "Wilderness Aesthetics." *American Literary History* 9, no. 1 (1997): 128–61.

Berkeley, Dorothy Smith, and Edmund Berkeley. *Dr. Alexander Garden of Charles Town*. Chapel Hill: University of North Carolina Press, 1969.

———. *The Life and Travels of John Bartram: From Lake Ontario to the River St. John*. Tallahassee: University Presses of Florida, 1982.

———, eds. *Correspondence of John Bartram*. Tallahassee: University Presses of Florida, 1992.

Berkhofer, Robert F., Jr. "Jefferson, the Ordinance of 1784, and the Origins of the American Territorial System." *William and Mary Quarterly*, 3rd ser., 29, no. 2 (1972): 231–62.

———. *The White Man's Indian: Images of the American Indian from Columbus to the Present*. New York: Knopf, 1978.

Biagioli, Mario. "Knowledge, Freedom, and Brotherly Love: Homosociability and the Accademia dei Lincei." *Configurations* 3, no. 2 (1995): 139–56.

Billington, Ray A. "The Fort Stanwix Treaty of 1768." *New York History* 25, no. 2 (1944): 182–94.

Boelhower, William. "Stories of Foundation, Scenes of Origin." *American Literary History* 5, no. 3 (1993): 391–428.

Boyd, Julian P., ed. *Indian Treaties Printed by Benjamin Franklin*. Introduction by Carl Van Doren. Philadelphia: Historical Society of Pennsylvania, 1938.

Boyd, Julian P., and Robert J. Taylor. *The Susquehannah Company Papers*. 11 vols. Wilkes Barré and Ithaca: Wyoming Historical and Geological Society and Cornell University Press, 1962–71.

Boyd, Julian P., et al., eds. *Papers of Thomas Jefferson*. 28 vols. Princeton: Princeton University Press, 1950–.

Branch, Michael P. "Early Romantic Natural History Literature." In *American Nature Writers*, edited by John Elder, 1059–75. New York: Scribner's, 1996.

———. "Indexing American Possibilities: The Natural History Writing of Bartram, Wilson, and Audubon." In *The Ecocriticism Reader: Landmarks in Literary Ecology*, edited by Cheryll Glotfelty and Harold Fromm, 282–302. Athens: University of Georgia Press, 1996.

Branch, Michael P., Rochelle Johnson, Daniel Patterson, and Scott Slovic, eds. *Reading the Earth: New Directions in the Study of Literature and Environment*. Moscow: University of Idaho Press, 1998.

Brandão, José António. *"Your Fyre Shall Burn No More": Iroquois Policy toward New France and Its Native Allies to 1701*. Lincoln: University of Nebraska Press, 1997.

Brant, Irving. *The Virginia Revolutionist*. Vol. 1 of *James Madison*. Indianapolis: Bobbs-Merrill, 1941.

Braund, Kathryn E. Holland. *Deerskins and Duffels: The Creek Indian Trade with Anglo-America, 1685–1815*. Lincoln: University of Nebraska Press, 1993.

Breitwieser, Mitchell Robert. "Jefferson's Prospect." *Prospects: An Annual Journal of American Cultural Studies* 10 (1985): 315–52.

Brown, Charles Brockden. *An Address to the Government of the United States, on the Cession of Louisiana to the French*. Philadelphia: J. Conrad, 1803.

Brückner, Martin. "Contested Sources of the Self: Native American Geographies and the Journals of Lewis and Clark." In *The Construction and Contestation of American Cultures and Identities in the Early National Period*, edited by Udo J. Hebel, 25–46. Heidelberg: Universitätsverlag C. Winter, 1999.

———. "Lessons in Geography: Maps, Spellers, and Other Grammars of Nationalism in the Early Republic." *American Quarterly* 51, no. 2 (1999): 311–42.

———. "The Surveyed Self as William Byrd: Plotting Land, Language and Identity in the Early Eighteenth Century." Paper presented at the biennial meeting of the Society of Early Americanists, Norfolk, Va., March 8, 2001.

Buell, Lawrence. *The Environmental Imagination: Thoreau, Nature Writing, and the Formation of American Culture*. Cambridge: Harvard University Press, 1995.

———. *New England Literary Culture from Revolution through Renaissance*. New York: Cambridge University Press, 1986.

Buell, Rowena, ed. *Memoirs of Rufus Putnam*. Boston: Houghton Mifflin, 1903.

Buffon, Georges Louis Leclerc, Comte de. *Barr's Buffon: Buffon's Natural History*. 10 vols. London: H. D. Symonds, 1797.

Bunting, Robert. *The Pacific Raincoast: Environment and Culture in an American Eden, 1778–1900*. Topeka: University Press of Kansas, 1997.

Burges, Judith C. "Audience Awareness in the Early Letters of Eliza Lucas Pinckney." *Postscript: Publication of the Philological Association of the Carolinas* 16 (1999): 69–77.

Burnett, Edmund C., ed. *Letters of Members of the Continental Congress*. 8 vols. Washington: Carnegie Institute, 1921–36.

Burnham, Michelle. *Captivity and Sentiment: Cultural Exchange in American Literature, 1682–1861*. Hanover: University Press of New England, 1997.

Callender, Charles. "Shawnee." In *Northeast*, vol. 15 of *Handbook of North American Indians*, edited by Bruce G. Trigger, 622–35. Washington: Smithsonian, 1978.

Callicott, J. Baird, and Michael P. Nelson, eds. *The Great New Wilderness Debate: An Expansive Collection of Writings Defining Wilderness from John Muir to Gary Snyder*. Athens: University of Georgia Press, 1998.

Calloway, Colin G. *The American Revolution in Indian Country: Crisis and Diversity in Native American Communities*. New York: Cambridge University Press, 1985.

Cappon, Lester J. *Atlas of American History: The Revolutionary Era, 1760–1790*. Princeton: Princeton University Press, 1976.

———. "Geographers and Map-Makers, British and American, from about 1750 to 1789." *Proceedings of the American Antiquarian Society* 81 (1971): 243–72.

Carmony, Donald F., ed. "Spencer Records' Memoir of the Ohio Valley Frontier, 1766–1795." *Indiana Magazine of History* 55, no. 4 (1959): 323–73.

Carr, Helen. *Inventing the American Primitive: Politics, Gender and the Representation of Native American Literary Traditions, 1789–1936*. New York: New York University Press, 1996.

Cashin, Edward J. "A 'Philosophical Pilgrim' on the Southern Frontier: New Approaches to William Bartram." *Georgia Historical Quarterly* 81, no. 3 (1997): 663–72.

———. *William Bartram and the American Revolution on the Southern Frontier*. Columbia: University of South Carolina Press, 2000.

Castiglia, Christopher. *Bound and Determined: Captivity, Culture-Crossing, and White Womanhood from Mary Rowlandson to Patty Hearst*. Chicago: University of Chicago Press, 1996.

Cayton, Andrew R. L. *The Frontier Republic: Ideology and Politics in the Ohio Country, 1780–1825*. Kent: Kent State University Press, 1986.

———. "Marietta and the Ohio Company." In *Appalachian Frontiers: Settlement, Society, and Development in the Preindustrial Era*, edited by Robert D. Mitchell, 187–200. Lexington: University Press of Kentucky, 1991.

———. "The Northwest Ordinance from the Perspective of the Frontier." In *The Northwest Ordinance, 1787: A Bicentennial Handbook*, edited by Robert M. Taylor Jr., 1–23. Indianapolis: Indiana Historical Society, 1987.

Cayton, Andrew R. L., and Peter S. Onuf. *The Midwest and Nation: Rethinking the History of an American Region*. Bloomington: Indiana University Press, 1990.

Cayton, Andrew R. L., and Fredrika J. Teute. "On the Connection of Frontiers." In *Contact Points: American Frontiers from the Mohawk Valley to the Mississippi, 1750–1830*, edited by Cayton and Teute, 1–15. Chapel Hill: University of North Carolina Press, 1998.

———, eds. *Contact Points: American Frontiers from the Mohawk Valley to the Mississippi, 1750–1830*. Chapel Hill: University of North Carolina Press, 1998.

Cheyfitz, Eric. "Literally White, Figuratively Red: The Frontier of Translation in *The Pioneers*." In *James Fenimore Cooper: New Critical Essays*, edited by Robert Clark, 55–95. London: Vision, 1985.

———. *The Poetics of Imperialism: Translation and Colonization from The Tempest to Tarzan*. Expanded ed. Philadelphia: University of Pennsylvania Press, 1997.

Clark, Jerry E. *The Shawnees*. Lexington: University Press of Kentucky, 1977.

Clarke, Joni Adamson. "Toward an Ecology of Justice: Transformative Ecological Criticism and Practice." In *Reading the Earth: New Directions in the Study of Literature and Environment*, edited by Michael P. Branch, Rochelle Johnson, Daniel Patterson, and Scott Slovic, 9–17. Moscow: University of Idaho Press, 1998.

Clarke, Larry R. "The Quaker Background of William Bartram's View of Nature." *Journal of the History of Ideas* 46, no. 3 (1985): 435–48.

Clarke, William. *Observations on the late and Present Conduct of the French, with Regard to their Encroachments upon the British Colonies in North America*. Boston: S. Kneeland, 1755.

Colden, Cadwallader. *Letters and Papers of Cadwallader Colden*. 9 vols. [Collections of the New-York Historical Society for the Years 1917–1936.] New York: A.M.S., 1973.

[Colden, Jane, and Alexander Garden]. "Description of a new Plant." In *Essays and Observations, Physical and Literary*, 2:1–7. Edinburgh: G. Hamilton and J. Balfour, 1796.

Condorcet, Marie Jean Antoine Caritat, Marquis de. "The Influence of the American Revolution on Europe." Translated by Durand Echeverria. *William and Mary Quarterly*, 3rd ser., 15, no. 4 (1968): 85–108.

———. "Life of George Louis LeClerc, Count of Buffon." Preface to *Barr's Buffon: Buffon's Natural History*, by Georges Louis Leclerc, Comte de Buffon, 1:i–xv. London: H. D. Symonds, 1810.

Cook, Frederick, and George S. Conover, eds. *Journals of the Military Expedition of Major General John Sullivan against the Six Nations of Indians in 1779*. Auburn, N.Y.: Knapp, Peck and Thomson, 1887.

Cooper, James Fenimore. *The Pioneers*. Introduction by Donald A. Ringe. New York: Penguin, 1988.

Cooper, Susan Fenimore. *Rural Hours*. Edited by Rochelle Johnson and Daniel Patterson. Athens: University of Georgia Press, 1998.

Cooper, William. *A Guide to the Wilderness*. Rochester, N.Y.: Gennessee, 1897.

Countryman, Edward. "Indians, the Colonial Order, and the Social Significance of the American Revolution." *William and Mary Quarterly*, 3rd ser., 53, no. 2 (1996): 342–62.

Crèvecoeur, J. Hector St. John de [Michel-Guillaume St. Jean de Crèvecoeur]. *Journey into Northern Pennsylvania and the State of New York*. Translated by Clarissa Spencer Bostelmann. Ann Arbor: University of Michigan Press, 1964.

———. *Letters from an American Farmer and Sketches of Eighteenth-Century America*. Edited and with introduction by Albert E. Stone. New York: Penguin, 1981.

———. "TRANSLATION of the Extracts from the Letters of the justly celebrated. . . ." In *Articles of an Association by the Name of the Ohio Company*, 36–44. New York: Samuel & John Loudon, 1787.

Cronon, William. *Changes in the Land: Indians, Colonists and the Ecology of New England*. New York: Hill and Wang, 1983.

———. "The Trouble with Wilderness; or, Getting Back to the Wrong Nature." In *Uncommon Ground: Toward Reinventing Nature*, edited by Cronon, 69–90. New York: Norton, 1995.

———, ed. *Uncommon Ground: Toward Reinventing Nature*. New York: Norton, 1995.

Cronon, William, and Richard White. "Ecological Change and Indian-White Relations." In *History of Indian-White Relations*, vol. 4 of *Handbook of North American Indians*, edited by Wilcomb E. Washburn, 417–29. Washington: Smithsonian, 1988.

Cumming, William P. *British Maps of Colonial America*. Chicago: University of Chicago Press, 1977.

Cutler, Manasseh. *An Explanation of the Map which Delineates that Part of the Federal Lands*. Salem: Dabney and Cushing, 1787.

Cutler, William Perkins, and Julia Perkins Cutler, eds. *Life, Journals and Correspondence of Manasseh Cutler*. 2 vols. Cincinnatti: Clarke, 1888.

Cutright, Paul Russell. *Lewis and Clark: Pioneering Naturalists*. Urbana: University of Illinois Press, 1969.

Daigrepont, Lloyd M. "'Rip Van Winkle' and the Gnostic Vision of History." *CLIO: A Journal of Literature, History, and the Philosophy of History* 15, no. 1 (1985): 47–59.

Daniels, Stephen. "The Political Iconography of Woodland in Later Georgian England." In *The Iconography of Landscape: Essays on the Symbolic Representation, Past Design and Use of Past Environments*, edited by Denis Cosgrove and Stephen Daniels, 43–82. Cambridge: Cambridge University Press, 1988.

Darlington, William M., and John J. Barsotti, eds. *Scoouwa: James Smith's Indian Captivity Narrative*. Columbus: Ohio Historical Society, 1978.

Daufenbach, Claus. "'The Eye Composes Itself': Text and Terrain in Jefferson's Virginia." In *Rewriting the South: History and Fiction*, edited by Lothar Hönnighausen and Valeria Gennaro Lerda, 99–111. Tübingen: Francke, 1993.

Davies, K. G., ed. *Documents of the American Revolution*. 21 vols. Shannon: Irish University Press, 1972–81.

Davy, George Alan. "Argumentation and Unified Structure in *Notes on the State of Virginia*." *Eighteenth-Century Studies* 26, no. 4 (1993): 581–93.

Debates in the House of Representatives, on the Bills for Carrying into Effect the Louisiana Treaty. Philadelphia: J. Conrad, 1804.

DeConde, Alexander. *This Affair of Louisiana*. New York: Scribner's, 1976.

Defoe, Daniel. *Robinson Crusoe*. New York: Bantam, 1981.

Dekker, George. *James Fenimore Cooper: The Novelist*. London: Routledge and Kegan Paul, 1967.

Deloria, Philip J. *Playing Indian*. New Haven: Yale University Press, 1998.

———. "Revolution, Region, and Culture in Multicultural History." *William and Mary Quarterly*, 3rd ser., 53, no. 2 (1996): 363–66.

Denny, Margaret. "Linnaeus and His Disciple in Carolina: Alexander Garden." *Isis* 38, nos. 113, 114 (1948): 161–77.

Densmore, Frances. *How Indians Use Wild Plants for Food, Medicine and Crafts*. New York: Dover, 1974.

Derounian-Stodola, Katherine Zabelle, ed. *Women's Indian Captivity Narratives*. New York: Penguin, 1988.

Doddridge, Joseph. *Notes on the Settlement and Indian Wars of the Western Parts of Virginia and Pennsylvania from 1763 to 1783*. New York: Burt Franklin, 1973.

Dowd, Gregory Evans. *A Spirited Resistance: The North American Indian Struggle for Unity, 1745–1815*. Baltimore: Johns Hopkins University Press, 1992.

Downes, Randolph C. *Council Fires on the Upper Ohio*. Pittsburgh: University of Pittsburgh Press, 1940.

Drown[e], Solomon. *An Oration Delivered at Marietta, April 7, 1789, In Commemoration of the Settlement formed by the Ohio Company*. Worcester: Isaiah Thomas, 1789.

Druke, Mary A. "Iroquois Treaties: Common Forms, Varying Interpretations." In *The History and Culture of Iroquois Diplomacy*, edited by Francis Jennings, 85–98. Syracuse: Syracuse University Press, 1985.

Dwight, Timothy. *Remarks on the Review of Inchiquin's Letters*. Boston: Samuel T. Armstrong, 1815.

———. *Travels; in New England and New-York*. 4 vols. New Haven: S. Converse, 1821–22.

———. *Travels in New England and New York*. 4 vols. Edited by Barbara Miller Solomon. Cambridge: Harvard University Press, 1969.

Echeverria, Durand. *Mirage in the West: A History of the French Image of American Society to 1815*. Princeton: Princeton University Press, 1957.

Elliott, Emory. *Revolutionary Writers: Literature and Authority in the New Republic*. New York: Oxford University Press, 1982.

Ernest, Earnest. *John and William Bartram*. Philadelphia: University of Pennsylvania Press, 1940.

Evans, Lewis. "Extract from Mr. Lewis Evan[s]'s Journal, 1743." In *A Topographical De-*

scription of the Dominions of the United States of America, by Thomas Pownall, 167–70. Edited by Lois Mulkhearn. Pittsburgh: University of Pittsburgh Press, 1949.

Evernden, Neil. *The Social Creation of Nature*. Baltimore: Johns Hopkins University Press, 1992.

Ewan, Joseph, ed. *William Bartram: Botanical and Zoological Drawings, 1765–1788*. Memoirs of the American Philosophical Society 74 (1968).

Fagin, N. Bryllion. *William Bartram: Interpreter of the American Landscape*. Baltimore: Johns Hopkins University Press, 1933.

Faragher, John Mack. *Daniel Boone: The Life and Legend of an American Pioneer*. New York: Holt, 1992.

———. "'They May Say What They Please': Daniel Boone and the Evidence." *Register of the Kentucky Historical Society* 88, no. 4 (1990): 373–93.

Fenton, William N. "Northern Iroquois Cultural Patterns." In *Northeast*, vol. 15 of *Handbook of North American Indians*, edited by Bruce G. Trigger, 296–321. Washington: Smithsonian, 1978.

———. "Structure, Continuity and Change in the Process of Iroquois Treaty Making." In *The History and Culture of Iroquois Diplomacy*, edited by Francis Jennings, 3–37. Syracuse: Syracuse University Press, 1985.

Ferguson, Robert. *Law and Letters in American Culture*. Cambridge: Harvard University Press, 1984.

Fiedler, Leslie. *Love and Death in the American Novel*. Rev. ed. New York: Stein and Day, 1966.

Filson, John. *The Discovery, Settlement And present State of Kentucke*. Wilmington: James Adams, 1784.

Finkelman, Paul. "The Northwest Ordinance: The Constitution for an Empire of Liberty." In *Pathways to the Old Northwest: An Observance of the Bicentennial of the Northwest Ordinance*, 1–18. Indianapolis: Indiana Historical Society, 1988.

Fisher, Philip. *Hard Facts: Setting and Form in the American Novel*. New York: Oxford University Press, 1985.

Ford, Paul Leicester, ed. *Works of Thomas Jefferson*. 12 vols. New York: Putnam's, 1904–5.

Ford, Worthington Chauncy, ed. *Writings of George Washington*. 14 vols. New York: Putnam's, 1891.

Franklin, Wayne. *Discoverers, Explorers, Settlers: The Diligent Writers of Early America*. Chicago: University of Chicago Press, 1979.

———. *The New World of James Fenimore Cooper*. Chicago: University of Chicago Press, 1982.

Frazier, Charles. *Cold Mountain*. New York: Vintage, 1997.

Freneau, Philip. "On the emigration to America, and peopling the western country." *American Museum* 1 (1787): 230.

Furtwangler, Albert. *Acts of Discovery: Visions of America in the Lewis and Clark Journals*. Urbana: University of Illinois Press, 1993.

Gallagher, Edward J. "Anne MacVicar Grant." In *American Women Prose Writers to 1820*, edited by Carla Mulford, Angela Vietto, and Amy E. Winans, 154–62. Volume 200 of *Dictionary of Literary Biography*. Detroit: Bruccoli, Clark, Layman, 1999.

Gallay, Allan. *The Formation of a Planter Elite: Jonathan Bryan and the Colonial Southern Frontier*. Athens: University of Georgia Press, 1989.

Gerbi, Antonello. *The Dispute of the New World: The History of a Polemic, 1750–1900*. Translated by Jeremy Moyle. Pittsburgh: University of Pittsburgh Press, 1973.

Giddens, Anthony. "Time, Space and Regionalisation." In *Social Relations and Social Structures*, edited by Derek Gregory and John Urry, 265–95. New York: St. Martin's, 1985.

Gipson, Henry Lawrence. *The British Empire before the American Revolution*. 15 vols. Caldwell, Ind., and New York: Caxton and Knopf, 1936–70.

———. *Lewis Evans*. Philadelphia: Historical Society of Pennsylvania, 1939.

Glotfelty, Cheryll, and Harold Fromm. "Literary Studies in an Age of Environmental Crisis." In *The Ecocriticism Reader: Landmarks in Literary Ecology*, edited by Glotfelty and Fromm, xv–xxxvii. Athens: University of Georgia Press, 1996.

———, eds. *The Ecocriticism Reader: Landmarks in Literary Ecology*. Athens: University of Georgia Press, 1996.

Goldie, Terry. *Fear and Temptation: The Image of the Indigene in Canadian, Australian, and New Zealand Literatures*. Kingston: McGill-Queen's University Press, 1989.

———. "The Representation of the Indigene." In *The Post-Colonial Studies Reader*, edited by Bill Ashcroft, Gareth Griffiths, and Helen Tiffin, 232–36. New York: Routledge, 1995.

Goméz-Pompa, Arturo, and Andrea Kraus. "Taming the Wilderness Myth." In *The Great New Wilderness Debate: An Expansive Collection of Writings Defining Wilderness from John Muir to Gary Snyder*, edited by J. Baird Callicott and Michael P. Nelson, 293–313. Athens: University of Georgia Press, 1998.

Gould, Peter, and Rodney White. *Mental Maps*. 2nd ed. Boston: Allen & Unwin, 1986.

Grant, Anne. *Memoirs of an American Lady with sketches of manners and scenes in America as they existed previous to the revolution*. Freeport, N.Y.: Books for Libraries, 1972.

Grant, J. P., ed. *Memoir and Correspondence of Mrs. Grant of Laggan*. London: Longman, Brown, Green, and Longman, 1845.

Graymont, Barbara. *The Iroquois in the American Revolution*. Syracuse: Syracuse University Press, 1972.

Greene, Donald J., ed. *Political Writings: Samuel Johnson*. New Haven: Yale University Press, 1977.

Greene, Jack P. *Pursuits of Happiness: The Social Development of Early Modern British Colonies and the Formation of American Culture*. Chapel Hill: University of North Carolina Press, 1988.

———, ed. *The American Revolution: Its Character and Limits*. New York: New York University Press, 1987.

Greenfield, Bruce. *Narrating Discovery: The Romantic Explorer in American Literature, 1790–1855*. New York: Columbia University Press, 1992.

Gregory, Derek, and John Urry, eds. *Social Relations and Spatial Structures*. New York: St. Martin's, 1985.

Grossman, James. *James Fenimore Cooper*. New York: Sloane, 1949.

Gustafson, Sandra N. *Eloquence Is Power: Oratory and Performance in Early America*. Chapel Hill: University of North Carolina Press, 2000.

Hagedorn, Nancy L. "Brokers of Understanding: Interpreters as Agents of Cultural Exchange in Colonial New York." *New York History* 76, no. 4 (1995): 378–407.

———. "'A Friend to Go between Them': The Interpreter as Cultural Broker during Anglo-Iroquois Council, 1740–1770." *Ethnohistory* 35, no. 1 (1988): 60–80.

Hales, John. "The Landscape of Tragedy: Crèvecoeur's 'Susquehannah.'" *Early American Literature* 20, no. 1 (1985): 39–63.

Hallock, Thomas. "Jane Colden." In *American Women Writers to 1820*, edited by Carla Mulford, Angela Vietto, and Amy E. Winans, 78–84. Volume 200 of *Dictionary of Literary Biography*. Detroit: Bruccoli, Clark, Layman, 1999.

———. "Literary Recipes from the Lewis and Clark *Journals*: The Epic Design and Wilderness Tastes of Early National Nature Writing." *American Studies* 38, no. 3 (1997): 43–67.

Harley, J. B. "New England Cartography and the Native Americans." In *American Beginnings: Exploration, Culture, and Cartography in the Land of Norumbega*, edited by Emerson W. Baker, 290–313. Lincoln: University of Nebraska Press, 1994.

Harper, Francis, ed. *Diary of a Journey through the Carolinas, Georgia, and Florida: From July 1, 1765, to April 10, 1766*. By John Bartram. Transactions of the American Philosophical Society, n.s., 33, no. 1 (1942).

———. *Travels in Georgia and Florida, 1773–1774: A Report to Dr. John Fothergill*. By William Bartram. Transactions of the American Philosophical Society, n.s., 33, no. 2 (1943).

———. *The Travels of William Bartram: Naturalist's Edition*. Athens: University of Georgia Press, 1998.

Harris, Marc L. "Revelation and the American Republic: Timothy Dwight's Civic Participation." *Journal of the History of Ideas* 54, no. 3 (1993): 449–68.

Harrison, Robert Pogue. *Forests: The Shadow of Civilization*. Chicago: University of Chicago Press, 1998.

Harvey, Oscar Jewell. *A History of Wilkes-Barré, Luzerne County, Pennsylvania*. Wilkes-Barré: n.p., 1909.

Hatley, Thomas M. *The Dividing Paths: Cherokees and South Carolinians through the Era of Revolution*. New York: Oxford University Press, 1993.

Hazard, Samuel, ed. *Minutes of the Provincial Council of Pennsylvania*. 16 vols. Harrisburg: Theophilus Fenn, 1851–53.

Hedges, James B. *The Browns of Providence Plantation: Colonial Years*. Cambridge: Harvard University Press, 1952.

Heidler, Jeanne T., and David S. Heidler, eds. *Encyclopedia of the War of 1812*. Santa Barbara: ABC-CLIO, 1997.

Hellenbrand, Harold. "Roads to Happiness: Rhetorical and Philosophical Design in Jefferson's *Notes on the State of Virginia*." *Early American Literature* 20, no. 1 (1985): 3–23.

Henderson, A. Gwynn. "Dispelling the Myth: Seventeenth- and Eighteenth-Century Indian Life in Kentucky." *Register of the Kentucky Historical Society* 90, no. 1 (1992): 1–25.

Hill, Sarah H. *Weaving New Worlds: Southeastern Cherokee Women and Their Basketry*. Chapel Hill: University of North Carolina Press, 1997.

Hinderaker, Eric. *Elusive Empires: Constructing Colonialism in the Ohio Valley, 1673–1800*. New York: Cambridge University Press, 1997.

Hindle, Brooke. "A Colonial Governor's Family: The Coldens of Coldengham." *New-York Historical Society Quarterly* 45, no. 3 (1961): 233–50.

———. *The Pursuit of Science in Revolutionary America*. Chapel Hill: University of North Carolina Press, 1956.
Hoffman, Ronald, and Peter J. Albert, eds. *Launching the "Extended Republic": The Federalist Era*. Charlottesville: University of Virginia Press, 1996.
Hoffmann, Nancy E. "The Construction of William Bartram's Narrative Natural History: A Genetic Text of the Draft Manuscript for 'Travels through North and South Carolina, Georgia, East and West Florida.'" Ph.D. diss., University of Pennsylvania, 1996.
Hönnighausen, Lothar, and Valeria Gennaro Lerda, eds. *Rewriting the South: History and Fiction*. Tübingen: Francke, 1993.
Horsman, Reginald. *Expansion and American Indian Policy, 1783–1812*. East Lansing: Michigan State University Press, 1967.
———. "The Indian Policy of an 'Empire for Liberty.'" In *Native Americans and the Early Republic*, edited by Frederick E. Hoxie, Ronald Hoffman, and Peter J. Albert, 37–61. Charlottesville: University of Virginia Press, 1999.
———. *Race and Manifest Destiny*. Cambridge: Harvard University Press, 1981.
Howard, James H. *Shawnee! The Ceremonialism of a Native Indian Tribe and Its Cultural Background*. Athens: Ohio University Press, 1981.
Hoxie, Frederick E., Ronald Hoffman, and Peter J. Albert, eds. *Native Americans and the Early Republic*. Charlottesville: University of Virginia Press, 1999.
Hulbert, Archer Butler, and John Matthews, eds. *Ohio in the Time of the Confederation*. Vol. 3 of Marietta College Historical Collections. Marietta: Marietta Historical Commission, 1918.
Hulme, Peter. *Colonial Encounters: Europe and the Native Caribbean, 1492–1797*. New York: Routledge, 1992.
———. "Making No Bones: A Response to Myra Jehlen." *Critical Inquiry* 20, no. 1 (1993): 179–86.
Humphreys, David. "Address to the Armies of the united states of America," *American Museum* 1 (1787): 230–40.
Hutchins, Thomas. *A Topographical Description of Virginia, Pennsylvania, Maryland, and North Carolina*. Edited by Frederick Charles Hicks. Cleveland: Burrows, 1904.
Hutchinson, William T., William M. E. Rachal, and Robert Allen Rutland, eds. *Papers of James Madison*. 17 vols. Chicago: University of Chicago Press, 1962–91.
Imlay, Gilbert. *Topographical Description of the Western Territory*. New York: Kelley, 1969.
Irmscher, Christoph. *The Poetics of Natural History: From John Bartram to William James*. New Brunswick: Rutgers University Press, 1999.
Irving, Washington. "Traits of Indian Character." *Analectic Magazine*, n.s., 3 (1814): 145–56.
Isaac, Rhys. "The First Monticello." In *Jeffersonian Legacies*, edited by Peter S. Onuf, 77–108. Charlottesville: University of Virginia Press, 1993.
Jackson, Donald Dean, ed. *Letters of the Lewis and Clark Expedition with Related Documents, 1783–1853*. Urbana: University of Illinois Press, 1962.
Jackson, Peter. *Maps of Meaning: An Introduction to Cultural Geography*. London: Unwin Hyman, 1989.
James, James Alton, ed. *George Rogers Clark Papers*. 8 vols. Springfield: Illinois State Historical Library, 1912–26.

Jefferson, Thomas. *Notes on the State of Virginia*. Edited and with an introduction by William Peden. Chapel Hill: University of North Carolina Press, 1954.

Jehlen, Myra. *American Incarnation: The Individual, the Nation and the Continent*. Cambridge: Harvard University Press, 1986.

———. "History before the Fact; or Captain John Smith's Unfinished Symphony." *Critical Inquiry* 19, no. 4 (1993): 677–92.

———. "J. Hector St. John Crèvecoeur: A Monarcho-Anarchist in Revolutionary America." *American Quarterly* 31, no. 2 (1979): 204–22.

———. "The Literature of Colonization." In *The Cambridge History of American Literature*. Vol. 1, *1590–1820*, edited by Sacvan Bercovitch, 13–168. New York: Cambridge University Press, 1994.

———. "Response to Peter Hulme." *Critical Inquiry* 20, no. 1 (1993): 187–91.

Jennings, Francis. *The Ambiguous Iroquois Empire: The Covenant Chain Confederation of Indian Tribes with English Colonies from Its Beginnings to the Lancaster Treaty of 1744*. New York: Norton, 1984.

———. *Empire of Fortune: Crowns, Colonies, and Tribes in the Seven Years War in America*. New York: Norton, 1988.

———. "The Indians' Revolution." In *The American Revolution: Explorations in the History of American Radicalism*, edited by Alfred F. Young, 319–48. DeKalb: Northern Illinois University Press, 1976.

———. *The Invasion of America: Indians, Colonialism, and the Cant of Conquest*. New York: Norton, 1976.

Jennings, Francis, ed. *The History and Culture of Iroquois Diplomacy*. Syracuse: Syracuse University Press, 1985.

Jones, David. *A Journal of Two Visits Made to Some Nations of Indians on the West Side of the River Ohio in the Years 1772 and 1773*. Fairfield, Wash.: Galleon, 1973.

Jordan, John W., ed. "Journal of James Kenney, 1761–1763." *Pennsylvania Magazine of History and Biography* 37, nos. 1–2 (1913): 1–47, 152–201.

———. "Rev. John Ettwein's Notes of Travel from the North Branch of the Susquehanna to the Beaver River, Pennsylvania, 1772." *Pennsylvania Magazine of History and Biography* 25 (1901): 208–19.

Jordan, Terry G., and Matti Kaups. *The American Backwoods Frontier: An Ethnic and Ecological Interpretation*. Baltimore: Johns Hopkins University Press, 1989.

Jordan, Winthrop. *White over Black: American Attitudes toward the Negro*. Chapel Hill: University of North Carolina Press, 1968.

Kafer, Peter K. "The Making of Timothy Dwight: A Connecticut Morality Tale." *William and Mary Quarterly*, 3rd ser., 47, no. 2 (1990): 189–209.

Kamensky, Jane. "'In These Contrasted Climes, How Chang'd the Scene': Progress, Declension, and Balance in the Landscapes of Timothy Dwight." *New England Quarterly* 63, no. 1 (1990): 80–108.

Keller, Evelyn Fox. *Reflections on Gender and Science*. New Haven: Yale University Press, 1985.

Kelly, William P., ed. *Selected Writings of Washington Irving*. New York: Modern Library, 1984.

Kennedy, Archibald. *The Importance of Gaining and Preserving the Friendship of the Indians to the British Interest*. New York: James Parker, 1751.

———. *Serious Considerations on the Present State of the Affairs of the Northern Colonies*. New York: n.p. 1754.

Klinefelter, Walter. *Lewis Evans and His Maps*. Transactions of the American Philosophical Society, n.s., 61, no. 7 (1971).

Knobloch, Frieda. *The Culture of Wilderness: Agriculture as Colonization in the American West*. Chapel Hill: University of North Carolina Press, 1996.

Koerner, Lisbet. "Women and Utility in Enlightenment Science." *Configurations* 3, no. 2 (1995): 233–55.

Kolodny, Annette. *The Lay of the Land: Metaphor as Experience in American Life and Letters*. Chapel Hill: University of North Carolina Press, 1975.

———. "Letting Go Our Grand Obsessions: Notes toward a New Literary History of the American Frontiers." *American Literature* 64, no. 1 (1992):1–18.

Kornfield, Eve. "Encountering 'the Other': American Intellectuals and Indians in the 1790s." *William and Mary Quarterly*, 3rd ser., 52, no. 2 (1995): 286–314.

Krech, Shepard. *The Ecological Indian: Myth and History*. New York: Norton, 1999.

Kroeber, Karl. *American Indian Persistence and Resurgence*. Durham: Duke University Press, 1995.

Krupat, Arnold. "An Approach to Native American Texts." In *Critical Essays on Native American Literature*, edited by Andrew Wiget, 116–32. Boston: Hall, 1988.

———. "Post-Structuralism and Oral Literature." In *Recovering the Word: Essays on Native American Literature*, edited by Brian Swann and Arnold Krupat, 113–26. Berkeley: University of California Press, 1987.

Labaree, Leonard Woods. "Thomas Pownall." In vol. 6 of *Dictionary of American Biography*, edited by John Arthur Garraty and Edward T. Jones, 161–63. New York: Scribners, 1935.

Labaree, Leonard Woods, et al., eds. *Papers of Benjamin Franklin*. 36 vols. New Haven: Yale University Press, 1959–.

Langford, Paul, and William B. Todd, eds. *The Writings and Speeches of Edmund Burke*. Vol. 3. New York: Oxford University Press, 1996.

La Rochefoucauld-Liancourt, François-Alexandre Frédéric, Duc de. *Travels through the United States of North America, the Country of the Iroquois and Upper Canada, in the years 1795, 1796, and 1797*. Translated by Henry Neuman. 2 vols. London: R. Phillips, 1799.

Larson, John Lauritz. "'Wisdom Enough to Improve Them': Government, Liberty and Inland Waterways in the Rising American Empire." In *Launching the "Extended Republic": The Federalist Era*, edited by Ronald Hoffman and Peter J. Albert, 223–48. Charlottesville: University of Virginia Press, 1996.

Lawrence, D. H. *Studies in Classic American Literature*. New York: Penguin, 1977.

Lawson-Peebles, Robert. *Landscape and Written Expression in Revolutionary America: The World Turned Upside Down*. New York: Cambridge University Press, 1988.

Ledyard, John. *Journals of Captain Cook's Last Voyage*. Chicago: Quadrangle, 1963.

Leonard, David A. *An Oration Delivered at Raynham*. Newport: Oliver Farnsworth, 1804.

Leopold, Aldo. *A Sand County Almanac with Essays on Conservation from Round River*. New York: Ballantine, 1970.

Lewis, Clayton. "Style in Jefferson's *Notes on the State of Virginia*." *Southern Review* 14, no. 4 (1978): 668–78.

Lewis, G. Malcolm. "Indicators of Unacknowledged Assimilations from Amerindian

Maps on Euro-American *Maps* of North America: Some General Principles Arising from a Study of La Vérendrye's Composite Maps, 1728–29." *Imago Mundi* 38 (1986): 9–34.

———. "The Indigenous Maps and Mapping of North American Indians." *Map Collector* 9, no. 1 (1979): 25–32.

———. "Maps, Mapmaking, and Map Use by Native North Americans." In *Cartography in the Traditional African, American, Arctic, Australian, and Pacific Societies*, edited by David Woodward and G. Malcolm Lewis, 151–82. The History of Cartography, vol. 2, bk. 3. Chicago: University of Chicago Press, 1998.

Limerick, Patricia Nelson. *The Legacy of Conquest: The Unbroken Past of the American West.* New York: Norton, 1987.

———. "Making the Most of Words: Verbal Activity and Western America." In *Under an Open Sky: Rethinking America's Western Past*, edited by William Cronon, George Miles, and Jay Gitlin, 167–84. New York: Norton, 1992.

Limerick, Patricia Nelson, Clyde A. Milner II, and Charles E. Rankin, eds. *Trails toward a New Western History.* Lawrence: University Press of Kansas, 1991.

Lofaro, Michael A. "The Eighteenth Century 'Autobiographies' of Daniel Boone." *Register of the Kentucky Historical Society* 76, no. 2 (1978): 85–97.

Logan, Martha Daniell. "Gardener's Calendar." In *The Palladium: or the Carolina and Georgia Almanac for the Year of Our Lord, 1796*, 44–48. Charleston: W. P. Young, 1795.

Looby, Christopher. "The Constitution of Nature: Taxonomy as Politics in Jefferson, Peale, and Bartram." *Early American Literature* 22, no. 3 (1987): 252–73.

Lyon, Thomas J. "A Taxonomy of Nature Writing." In *The Ecocriticism Reader: Landmarks in Literary Ecology*, edited by Cheryll Glotfelty and Harold Fromm, 276–81. Athens: University of Georgia Press, 1996.

MacLean, Hugh, ed. *Edmund Spenser's Poetry.* New York: Norton, 1982.

Maddox, Lucy. *Removals: Nineteenth-Century American Literature and the Politics of Indian Affairs.* New York: Oxford University Press, 1991.

Magruder, Allan B. *Political, Commercial, and Moral Reflections on the Late Cession of Louisiana to the United States.* Lexington: D. Bradford, 1803.

Malone, Dumas. *Jefferson the Virginian.* Vol. 1 of *Jefferson and His Time.* New York: Little, Brown, 1948.

Mancall, Peter. *Valley of Opportunity: Economic Culture along the Upper Susquehanna, 1700–1800.* Ithaca: Cornell University Press, 1991.

Mann, Barbara Alice. *Iroquoian Women: The Gantowisas.* New York: Peter Lang, 2000.

Marshall, Cheryl. *Indian Nation: Native American Literature and Nineteenth-Century Nationalism.* Durham: Duke University Press, 1997.

Marshall, Ian. *Story Line: Exploring the Literature of the Appalachian Trail.* Charlottesville: University Press of Virginia, 1998.

Marx, Leo. *The Machine in the Garden: Technology and the Pastoral Idea in America.* New York: Oxford University Press, 1964.

Mazel, David. *American Literary Environmentalism.* Athens: University of Georgia Press, 2000.

———. "'A Beautiful and Thrilling Specimen': George Catlin, the Death of Wilderness, and the Birth of the National Subject." In *Reading the Earth: New Directions in the Study of Literature and Environment*, edited by Michael P. Branch, Rochelle Johnson, Daniel Patterson, and Scott Slovic, 129–43. Moscow: University of Idaho Press, 1998.

McAnear, Beverly. "Personal Accounts of the Albany Congress of 1754." *Mississippi Valley Historical Review* 39, no. 4 (1953): 724–46.
McConnell, Michael N. *A Country Between: The Upper Ohio Valley and Its Peoples, 1724–1774*. Lincoln: University of Nebraska Press, 1992.
McEvoy, Arthur F. "Toward an Interactive Theory of Nature and Culture: Ecology, Production, and Cognition in the California Fishing Industry." In *The Ends of the Earth: Perspectives on Modern Environmental History*, ed. Donald Worster, 211–29. New York: Cambridge University Press, 1988.
McGann, Jerome J., ed. *Byron: The Oxford Authors*. New York: Oxford University Press, 1986.
McLoughlin, William G. *Cherokee Renascence in the New Republic*. Princeton: Princeton University Press, 1986.
McWilliams, John P., Jr. *Political Justice in a Republic: James Fenimore Cooper's America*. Berkeley: University of California Press, 1972.
Merchant, Carolyn. *Ecological Revolutions: Nature, Gender, and Science in New England*. Chapel Hill: University of North Carolina Press, 1989.
Merrell, James H. "Declarations of Independence: Indian-White Relations in the New Nation." In *The American Revolution: Its Character and Limits*, edited by Jack P. Greene, 197–223. New York: New York University Press, 1987.
———. *The Indians' New World: Catawbas and Their Neighbors from European Contact through the Era of Removal*. Chapel Hill: University of North Carolina Press, 1989.
———. *Into the American Woods: Negotiators on the Pennsylvania Frontier*. New York: Norton, 1999.
———. "Shickellamy, 'A Person of Consequence.'" In *Northeastern Indian Lives, 1632–1816*, edited by Robert S. Grumet, 227–57. Amherst: University of Massachusetts Press, 1996.
Merritt, Jane T. "Metaphor, Meaning and Misunderstanding: Language and Power on the Pennsylvania Frontier." In *Contact Points: American Frontiers from the Mohawk Valley to the Mississippi, 1750–1830*, edited by Andrew R. L. Cayton and Frederika J. Teute, 60–87. Chapel Hill: University of North Carolina Press, 1998.
Miller, Charles A. *Jefferson and Nature: An Interpretation*. Baltimore: Johns Hopkins University Press, 1988.
Mirabeau, Honoré-Gabriel Riqueti, Comte de. *Reflections on the Observations on the Importance of the American Revolution, and the Means of Making it a Benefit to the World*. Philadelphia: T. Seddon, 1786.
Mitchell, Julia Post. *St. Jean de Crèvecoeur*. New York: Columbia University Press, 1916.
Mitchell, Lee Clark. *Westerns: Making the Man in Fiction and Film*. Chicago: University of Chicago Press, 1996.
Mooney, James, ed. *Myths of the Cherokee*. New York: Dover, 1915.
Moore, Clement Clarke. *Observations upon Certain Passages in Mr. Jefferson's "Notes on Virginia," Which Appear to Have a Tendency to Subvert Religion, and Establish a False Philosophy*. New York: n.p., 1804.
Moore, Dennis D., ed. *More Letters from the American Farmer: An Edition of the Essays in English Left Unpublished by Crèvecoeur*. Athens: University of Georgia Press, 1995.
Morse, Jedidiah. *The American Geography; or A View of the Present Situation of the United States*. Elizabeth Town: Shepard Kollock, 1789.
———. *The American Universal Geography, or a View of the Present State of all the Em-

pires, Kingdoms, States, and Republics in the Known World, and of the United States of America in Particular. Boston: Isaiah Thomas and Ebenezer T. Andrews, 1796.

Morton, Sarah Wentworth. *Beacon Hill: A Local Poem, Historic and Descriptive.* Boston: Manning & Loring, 1797.

Moulton, Gary E., ed. *Journals of the Lewis and Clark Expedition.* 13 vols. Lincoln: University of Nebraska Press, 1978–83.

Mulford, Carla. "*Caritas* and Capital: Franklin's Narrative of the Late Massacres." In *Reappraising Benjamin Franklin: A Bicentennial Perspective*, edited by J. A. Leo Lemay, 347–61. Newark: University of Delaware Press, 1993.

———. "New Science and the Question of Identity in Eighteenth-Century British America." In *Finding Colonial Americas: Essays Honoring J. A. Leo Lemay*, edited by Carla Mulford and David S. Shields, 79–103. Newark: University of Delaware Press, 2001.

Mulford, Carla, and David S. Shields, eds. *Finding Colonial Americas: Essays Honoring J. A. Leo Lemay.* Newark: University of Delaware Press, 2001.

Mulford, Carla, Angela Vietto, and Amy E. Winans, eds. *American Women Prose Writers to 1820.* Volume 200 of *Dictionary of Literary Biography*. Detroit: Bruccoli, Clark, Layman, 1999.

Murphy, James E., and Sharon M. Murphy. *Let My People Know: American Indian Journalism, 1828–1978.* Norman: University of Oklahoma Press, 1981.

Murray, David. *Forked Tongues: Speech, Writing and Representation in North American Indian Texts.* Bloomington: Indiana University Press, 1991.

Murray, Laura J. "The Aesthetics of Dispossession: Washington Irving and Ideologies of (De)Colonization in the Early Republic." *American Literary History* 8, no. 2 (1996): 205–31.

Namias, June. *White Captives: Gender and Ethnicity on the American Frontier.* Chapel Hill: University of North Carolina Press, 1993.

Nammack, Georgiana C. *Fraud, Politics and the Dispossession of the Indians.* Norman: University of Oklahoma Press, 1969.

Nash, Roderick. *Wilderness and the American Mind.* New Haven: Yale University Press, 1982.

Nobles, Gregory H. "Straight Lines and Stability: Mapping the Political Order of the Anglo-American Frontier." *Journal of American History* 80, no. 1 (1993): 9–35.

O'Callaghan, E. B., ed. *Documents Relative to the Colonial History of the State of New York.* 15 vols. New York: Weed, Parsons, 1853–87.

Oelschlaeger, Max. *The Idea of Wilderness: From Prehistory to the Age of Ecology.* New Haven: Yale University Press, 1991.

Onuf, Peter S. *The Origins of the Federal Republic: Jurisdictional Controversies in the United States, 1775–1787.* Philadelphia: University of Pennsylvania Press, 1983.

———. "Settlers, Settlements, and New States." In *The American Revolution: Its Character and Limits*, edited by Jack P. Greene, 171–96. New York: New York University Press, 1987.

———. *Statehood and Union: A History of the Northwest Ordinance.* Bloomington: University of Indiana Press, 1987.

Paine, Thomas. *Public Good: Being an Examination into the Claim of Virginia to the Vacant Western Territory, and of the Right of the United States to the Same.* Philadelphia: John Dunlap, 1780.

Parrish, Susan Scott. "Women's Nature: Curiosity, Pastoral, and the New Science in British America." *Early American Literature* 37, no. 2 (2002): 195-238.
Pattison, William D. *Beginnings of the American Rectangular Land Survey System, 1784-1800.* University of Chicago Dept. of Geography Research Paper, no. 50. Chicago: University of Chicago Press, 1964.
Pearce, Colin D. "Changing Regimes: The Case of Rip Van Winkle." *CLIO: A Journal of Literature, History, and the Philosophy of History* 22, no. 2 (1993): 115-28.
Pearce, Roy Harvey. *The Savages of America: A Study of the Indian and the Idea of Civilization.* Rev. ed. Baltimore: Johns Hopkins University Press, 1965.
Peck, H. Daniel. *A World by Itself: The Pastoral Moment in Cooper's Fiction.* New Haven: Yale University Press, 1977.
Perdue, Theda. "Rising from the Ashes: *The Cherokee Phoenix* as an Ethnohistorical Source." *Ethnohistory* 24, no. 3 (1977): 207-18.
———, ed. *Cherokee Editor: The Writings of Elias Boudinot.* Rev. ed. Athens: University of Georgia Press, 1996.
Perkins, Elizabeth A. *Border Life: Experience and Memory in the Revolutionary Ohio Valley.* Chapel Hill: University of North Carolina Press, 1998.
Person, Leland S., Jr. "Cooper's *The Pioneers* and Leatherstocking's Historical Function." *ESQ* 25, no. 1 (1979): 1-10.
Peterson, Merrill D., ed. *The Portable Thomas Jefferson.* New York: Penguin, 1977.
Peterson, Roger Tory. *A Field Guide to Western Birds.* Boston: Houghton Mifflin, 1990.
Philbrick, Thomas. "Cooper's *The Pioneers*: Origins and Structure." *PMLA* 79 (1964): 579-93.
———. *St. John de Crèvecoeur.* New York: Twayne, 1970.
Philips, Patricia. *The Scientific Lady: A Social History of Women's Scientific Interests, 1520-1918.* New York: St. Martin's, 1990.
Pinckney, Elise. *Thomas and Elizabeth Lamboll: Early Charleston Gardeners.* Charleston Museum Leaflet, no. 28 (1969).
———, ed. *The Letterbook of Eliza Lucas Pinckney.* Chapel Hill: University of North Carolina Press, 1972.
Popkin, Richard H. "The Philosophical Basis of Eighteenth-Century Racism." *Studies in Eighteenth-Century Culture* 3 (1973): 245-62.
Pownall, Thomas. *A Topographical Description of the Dominions of the United States of America.* Edited by Lois Mulkhearn. Pittsburgh: University of Pittsburgh Press, 1949.
Pratt, Mary Louise. *Imperial Eyes: Travel Writing and Transculturation.* New York: Routledge, 1992.
Pred, Alan. "Of Paths and Projects: Individual Behavior and Its Societal Context." In *Behavioral Problems in Geography Revisited*, edited by Kenneth R. Cox and Reginald G. Golledge, 231-55. London: Methuen, 1981.
———. "The Social Becomes the Spatial, the Spatial Becomes the Social: Enclosures, Social Change and the Becoming of Places in Skåne." In *Social Relations and Spatial Structures*, edited by Derek Gregory and John Urry, 337-65. New York: St. Martin's, 1985.
Price, Richard. *Observations on the Importance of the American Revolution, and the Means of Making It a Benefit to the World.* Philadelphia: T. Seddon, 1786.
Prucha, Francis Paul. *The Great Father: The United States Government and the American Indians.* Lincoln: University of Nebraska Press, 1984.

Pynchon, Thomas. *Mason and Dixon*. New York: Holt, 1998.
Rackove, Jack. "Ambiguous Achievement: The Northwest Ordinance." In *The Northwest Ordinance: Essays on Its Formulation Provisions, and Legacy*, edited by Frederick D. Williams, 1–19. East Lansing: Michigan State University Press, 1989.
Raillton, Stephen. *Fenimore Cooper: A Study of His Life and Imagination*. Princeton: Princeton University Press, 1978.
Ramsey, David. *An Oration on the Cession of Louisiana to the United States*. Charleston: W. P. Young, 1804.
Ranck, George W., ed. *Boonesborough: Its Founding, Pioneer Struggles, Indian Experiences, Transylvania Days, and Revolutionary Annals*. Filson Club Publications, vol. 16. Louisville: Morton, 1901.
Raynal, Guillaume Thomas François, the Abbé. *A Philosophical and Political History of the Settlements and Trade of the Europeans in the East and West Indies*. 8 vols. Translated by J. O. Justamond. London: W. Strahan and T. Cadell, 1783.
Regis, Pamela. *Describing Early America: Bartram, Jefferson, Crèvecoeur, and the Rhetoric of Natural History*. DeKalb: Northern Illinois University Press, 1992.
Reid, Nina. "Loyalism and the 'Philosophic Spirit' in Scientific Correspondence of Dr. Alexander Garden." *South Carolina Historical Magazine* 92, no. 1 (1991): 5–14.
Reinke, Edgar C. "*Meliorem Lapsa Locavit*: An Intriguing Puzzle Solved." *Ohio History* 94, no. 1 (1985): 68–74.
Richter, Daniel K. *Ordeal of the Longhouse: The Peoples of the Iroquois League in the Era of European Colonization*. Chapel Hill: University of North Carolina Press, 1992.
Rickett, H. W. "Jane Colden as Botanist in Contemporary Opinion." In *Botanic Manuscript of Jane Colden, 1724–1766*, edited by Rickett, 22–24. New York: Garden Club of Orange and Dutchess Counties, 1963.
———, ed. *Botanic Manuscript of Jane Colden, 1724–1766*. New York: Garden Club of Orange and Dutchess Counties, 1963.
Ringe, Donald A. "New York and New England: Irving's Criticism of American Society." *American Literature* 38, no. 4 (1967): 455–67.
Ristow, Walter. *American Maps and Mapmakers: Commercial Cartography in the Nineteenth Century*. Detroit: Wayne State University Press, 1985.
Robertson, James Rood, ed. *Petitions of the Early Inhabitants of Kentucky to the General Assembly of Virginia*. New York: Arno, 1971.
Robertson, William. *The History of America*. Edinburgh: A. Strahan, 1803.
Robinson, Forrest G. "Clio Bereft of Calliope: Literature and the New Western History." In *The New Western History: The Territory Ahead*, edited by Forrest G. Robinson, 61–98. Tucson: University of Arizona Press, 1997.
Rohrbough, Malcolm J. *The Trans-Appalachian Frontier: People, Societies, and Institutions, 1775–1850*. New York: Oxford University Press, 1978.
Ronda, James P. *Lewis and Clark among the Indians*. Lincoln: University of Nebraska Press, 1984.
Rosaldo, Renato. "Imperialist Nostalgia." *Representations* 26, no. 1 (1989): 107–22.
Rountree, Helen C. "The Powhatans and Other Woodland Indians as Travelers." In *Powhatan Foreign Relations, 1500–1722*, edited by Helen C. Rountree, 21–44. Charlottesville: University of Virginia Press, 1993.
Rowe, John Carlos. *Literary Culture and U.S. Imperialism: From the Revolution to World War II*. New York: Oxford University Press, 2000.

Ruoff, A. LaVonne Brown. *American Indian Literatures: An Introduction, Bibliographic Review, and Selected Bibliography*. New York: Modern Language Association, 1990.

Ryden, Kent C. *Mapping the Invisible Landscape: Folklore, Writing, and the Sense of Place*. Iowa City: University of Iowa Press, 1993.

Sack, Robert David. *Human Territoriality: Its Theory and History*. New York: Cambridge University Press, 1986.

Sappington, Roy Lee. "The Lewis and Clark Expedition among the Nez Perce Indians: 'The First Ethnographic Study in the Columbia River.'" *Northwest Anthropological Research Notes* 23, no. 1 (1989): 1–34.

Sargent, Winthrop, and Benjamin Smith Barton. *Papers Relative to Certain American Antiquities*. Philadelphia: Thomas Dobson, 1796.

Sayre, Gordon M. "The Mound Builders and the Imagination of American Antiquity in Jefferson, Bartram, and Chateaubriand." *Early American Literature* 33, no. 3 (1998): 225–49.

Scheckel, Susan. *The Insistence of the Indian: Race and Nationalism in Nineteenth-Century American Culture*. Princeton: Princeton University Press, 1998.

Scheick, William J. "Chaos and Imaginative Order in Thomas Jefferson's *Notes on the State of Virginia*." In *Essays in Early Virginia Literature Honoring Richard Beale Davis*, edited by J. A. Leo Lemay, 221–34. New York: Burt Franklin, 1977.

Schiebinger, Londa. *Nature's Body: Gender in the Making of Science*. Boston: Beacon, 1993.

Schwaab, Eugene L., ed. *Travels in the Old South: Selected from Periodicals of the Times*. 2 vols. Lexington: University Press of Kentucky, 1973.

Scott, Anne Firor. "Self-Portraits: Three Women." In *Uprooted Americans: Essays to Honor Oscar Handlin*, edited by Richard L. Bushman, Neil Harris, David Rothman, Barbara Miller Solomon, and Stephen Thernstrom, 43–76. Boston: Little, Brown, 1979.

Sears, John F. "Timothy Dwight and the American Landscape: The Composing Eye in Dwight's *Travels in New England and New York*." *Early American Literature* 30, no. 1 (1989): 311–21.

Seelye, John. *Beautiful Machine: Rivers and the Republican Plan*. New York: Oxford University Press, 1993.

———. "Beauty Bare: William Bartram and His Triangulated Wilderness." *Prospects: An Annual Journal of American Cultural Studies* 6 (1981): 37–54.

Semonin, Paul. "'Nature's Nation': Natural History as Nationalism in the New Republic." *Northwest Review* 30, no. 2 (1992): 6–41.

Sewell, David R. "'So Unstable and Like Mad Men They Were': Language and Interpretation in Early American Captivity Narratives." In *A Mixed Race: Ethnicity in Early America*, edited by Frank Shuffelton, 39–55. New York: Oxford University Press, 1993.

Shannon, Timothy J. *Indians and Colonists at the Crossroads of Empire: The Albany Congress of 1754*. Ithaca: Cornell University Press, 2000.

Sheehan, Bernard W. "The Indian Problem in the Northwest: From Conquest to Philanthropy." In *Launching the "Extended Republic": The Federalist Era*, edited by Ronald Hoffman and Peter J. Albert, 190–222. Charlottesville: University of Virginia Press, 1996.

———. *Seeds of Extinction: Jeffersonian Philanthropy and the American Indian*. Chapel Hill: University of North Carolina Press, 1973.

Sheidly, Nathaniel. "Hunting and the Politics of Masculinity in Cherokee Treaty-Making, 1763–75." In *Empire and Others: British Encounters with Indigenous Peoples, 1600–1850*, edited by Martin Daunton and Rick Halpern, 167–85. Philadelphia: University of Pennsylvania Press, 1999.

Sherow, James E. "An Evening on the Konza Prairie." In *A Sense of the American West: An Anthology of Environmental History*, edited by James E. Sherow, 1–29. Albuquerque: University of New Mexico Press, 1998.

Shteir, Ann B. *Cultivating Women, Cultivating Science: Flora's Daughters and Botany in England*. Baltimore: Johns Hopkins University Press, 1996.

Shuffelton, Frank. "A Continental Poetics: Scientific Publishing and Scientific Society in Eighteenth-Century America." In *Finding Colonial Americas: Essays Honoring J. A. Leo Lemay*, edited by Carla Mulford and David S. Shields, 277–91. Newark: University of Delaware Press, 2001.

———. Introduction. In *A Mixed Race: Ethnicity in Early America*, edited by Frank Shuffelton, 1–14. New York: Oxford University Press, 1993.

———, ed. *A Mixed Race: Ethnicity in Early America*. New York: Oxford University Press 1993.

Silver, Timothy. *A New Face on the Countryside: Indians, Colonists, and Slaves in South Atlantic Forests, 1500–1800*. New York: Cambridge University Press, 1990.

Silverman, Kenneth. *Timothy Dwight*. New York: Twayne, 1969.

Slaughter, Thomas P. *The Natures of John and William Bartram*. New York: Knopf, 1996.

———. *The Whiskey Rebellion: Frontier Epilogue of the American Revolution*. New York: Oxford University Press, 1986.

Sloan, Richard. "The Idea of Racial Degeneracy in Buffon's *Histoire Naturelle*." *Studies in Eighteenth-Century Culture* 3 (1973): 303–10.

Slotkin, Richard. *Regeneration through Violence: The Mythology of the American Frontier, 1600–1800*. Middletown: Wesleyan University Press, 1973.

Smith, Dwight L., ed. *The Western Journals of John May, Ohio Company Agent and Business Adventurer*. Cincinnati: Historical and Philosophical Society of Ohio, 1961.

Smith, James Edward, ed. *A Selection of the Correspondence of Linnaeus and Other Naturalists*. 2 vols. New York: Arno, 1978.

Smith, William, Jr. *The History of the Province of New York*. Edited by Michael Kammen. Cambridge: Harvard University Press, 1972.

Smith, William Henry. *The St. Clair Papers*. 2 vols. Cincinnati: R. Clarke, 1882.

Smith-Rosenberg, Carroll. "Dis-Covering the Subject of the 'Great Constitutional Discussion,' 1786–1789." *Journal of American History* 79, no. 3 (1992): 941–73.

Snyder, K. Alan. "Foundations of Liberty: The Christian Republicanism of Timothy Dwight and Jedidiah Morse." *New England Quarterly* 56, no. 3 (1983): 382–97.

Soper, Kate. *What Is Nature? Culture, Politics and the Non-Human*. Oxford: Blackwell, 1995.

Sosin, Jack. *The Opening of the American West*. New York: Harper & Row, 1969.

———. *Whitehall and the Wilderness: The Middle West in British Colonial Policy*. Lincoln: University of Nebraska Press, 1961.

Spears, Timothy B. "Common Observations: Timothy Dwight's *Travels in New England and New York*." *American Studies* 30, no. 1 (1985): 35–52.

Spengemann, William. *A New World of Words: Redefining Early American Literature*. New Haven: Yale University Press, 1994.

Spiller, Robert E. *Fenimore Cooper: Critic of His Times*. New York: Russell & Russell, 1963.
Standing Bear, Chief Luther. "Indian Wisdom." In *The Great New Wilderness Debate: An Expansive Collection of Writings Defining Wilderness from John Muir to Gary Snyder*, edited by J. Baird Callicott and Michael P. Nelson, 201–6. Athens: University of Georgia Press, 1998.
Stefon, Frederick J. "The Wyoming Valley." In *Beyond Philadelphia: The American Revolution in the Pennsylvania Hinterland*, edited by John B. Frantz and William Pencak, 133–52. University Park: Pennsylvania University Press, 1998.
Stephanson, Anders. *Manifest Destiny: American Expansionism and the Empire of Right*. New York: Hill & Wang, 1995.
Stork, William. *An Account of East Florida, with a Journal kept by John Bartram of Philadelphia, Botanist to His Majesty for the Floridas; upon A Journey from St. Augustine up the River St. John's*. London: W. Nicoll, 1766.
———. *A Description of East-Florida: With a Journal. . . .* London: W. Nicoll, 1769.
Stourzh, Gerald. *Benjamin Franklin and American Foreign Policy*. Chicago: University of Chicago Press, 1969.
Sturtevant, William C., et al., eds. *Handbook of North American Indians*. 17 vols. Washington: Smithsonian, 1978–.
Sullivan, James, Alexander C. Flick, Almon W. Lauber, and Milton W. Hamilton, eds. *Papers of Sir William Johnson*. 14 vols. Albany: State University of New York Press, 1921–65.
Swann, Charles. "Guns Mean Democracy: *The Pioneers* and the Game Laws." In *Fenimore Cooper: The Critical Heritage*, edited by George Dekker and John P. McWilliams, 96–120. London: Routledge and Kegan Paul, 1973.
Swanton, John R. *Creek Religion and Medicine*. Lincoln: University of Nebraska Press, 2000.
Sweet, Timothy. "Economy, Ecology, and *Utopia* in Early Colonial Promotional Literature." *American Literature* 71, no. 3 (1999): 399–427.
Taylor, Alan. *Liberty Men and Great Proprietors: The Revolutionary Settlement on the Maine Frontier, 1760–1820*. Chapel Hill: University of North Carolina Press, 1990.
———. *William Cooper's Town: Power and Persuasion on the Frontier of the Early American Republic*. New York: Knopf, 1995.
Taylor, Robert J. "Trial at Trenton." *William and Mary Quarterly*, 3rd ser., 26, no. 4 (1969): 521–47.
Taylor, Robert M., Jr., ed. *The Northwest Ordinance, 1787: A Bicentennial Handbook*. Indianapolis: Indiana Historical Society, 1987.
Terrall, Mary. "Gendered Space, Gendered Audiences: Inside and Outside the Paris Academy of Sciences." *Configurations* 3, no. 2 (1995): 207–32.
Terres, John K. *The National Audubon Society Field Guide of North American Birds*. New York: Knopf, 1980.
Thomas, Brook. "*The Pioneers*; or the Sources of American Legal History: A Critical Tale." *American Quarterly* 36, no. 1 (1984): 86–111.
Thomson, James. *The Seasons and the Castle of Indolence*. Edited by James Sambrook. New York: Oxford University Press, 1972.
Thoreau, Henry David. *The Natural History Essays*. Edited by Robert Sattelmeyer. Salt Lake City: Pergerine Smith, 1980.

Thwaites, Ruben Gold, ed. *Original Journals of the Lewis and Clark Expedition, 1804–1806.* 8 vols. New York: Arno, 1969.

———. *Travels to the West of the Alleghanies: Made in 1793–96 by André Michaux, in 1806 by F. A. Michaux, and in 1803 by Thaddeus Mason Harris.* Vol. 3 of *Early Western Travels.* Cleveland: Clarke, 1904.

Thwaites, Ruben Gold, and Louise Phelps Kellogg, eds. *Documentary History of Dunmore's War 1774.* Madison: Wisconsin Historical Society, 1905.

Tichi, Cecelia. *New World, New Earth: Environmental Reform in American Literature from the Puritans through Whitman.* New Haven: Yale University Press, 1979.

Tinling, Marion, and Godfrey Davies. *The Western Country in 1793: Reports on Kentucky and Virginia by Harry Toulmin.* San Marino: Huntington Library, 1948.

Todd, Janet M., ed. *A Wollstonecraft Anthology.* Bloomington: University of Indiana Press, 1977.

Tooker, Elisabeth. "The League of the Iroquois: Its History, Politics, and Ritual." In *Northeast*, vol. 15 of *Handbook of North American Indians*, edited by Bruce G. Trigger, 418–41. Washington: Smithsonian, 1978.

Tuan, Yi-Fu. *Space and Place: The Perspective of Experience.* Minneapolis: University of Minnesota Press, 1977.

———. *Topophilia: A Study in Environmental Perception, Altitudes and Values.* Englewood Cliffs: Prentice-Hall, 1974.

Tucker, Robert W., and David C. Henderson. *Empire of Liberty: The Statecraft of Thomas Jefferson.* New York: Oxford University Press, 1990.

Tucker, St. George [Sylvestrus]. *Reflections, on the Cession of Louisiana to the United States.* Washington: Samuel Harrison Smith, 1803.

Varnum, James M. *An Oration Delivered at Marietta, July 4, 1788.* Newport: Peter Edes, 1788.

Volkomer, Walter E. "Timothy Dwight and New England Federalism." *Connecticut Review* 3, no. 2 (1970): 72–88.

Volmer, Stephanie. "Viewing Nature with a Purpose: Transatlantic Epistolary Exchange and the Problem of Scientific Authority." Paper presented at meeting of the Omohundro Institute of Early American History and Culture, Glasgow, Scotland, July 2001.

Volney, Constantin-François Chasseboeuf, Comte de. *A View of the Soil and Climate of the United States of America.* Translated by Charles Brockden Brown. New York: Hafner, 1968.

Wallace, Anthony F. C. *The Death and Rebirth of the Seneca.* New York: Knopf, 1970.

Wallace, James D. *Early Cooper and His Audience.* New York: Columbia University Press, 1986.

Wallace, Paul A. W. *Conrad Weiser, 1696–1760: Friend of Colonist and Mohawk.* Philadelphia: University of Pennsylvania Press, 1945.

Waselkov, Gregory, and Kathryn E. Holland Braund. *William Bartram on the Southeastern Indians.* Lincoln: University of Nebraska Press, 1995.

Weiser, Conrad. "Notes on the Iroquois and Delaware Indians." *Pennsylvania Magazine of History and Biography* 1 (1877): 163–67, 319–21, 2 (1878): 407–11.

West, Elliott. "American Frontier." In *The Oxford History of the American West*, edited by Clyde A. Milner II, Carol A. O'Connor, and Martha A. Sandweiss, 115–49. New York: Oxford University Press, 1994.

———. "A Longer, Grimmer, but More Interesting Story." In *Trails toward a New Western History*, edited by Patricia Nelson Limerick, Clyde A. Milner II, and Charles E. Rankin, 103–11. Lawrence: University Press of Kansas, 1991.
White, Richard. "'Are You an Environmentalist or Do You Work for a Living?': Work and Nature." In *Uncommon Ground: Toward Reinventing Nature*, edited by William Cronon, 171–86. New York: Norton, 1995.
———. "The Fictions of Patriarchy: Indians and Whites in the Early Republic." In *Native Americans and the Early Republic*, edited by Frederick E. Hoxie, Ronald Hoffman, and Peter J. Albert, 62–84. Charlottesville: University of Virginia Press, 1999.
———. *"It's Your Misfortune and None of My Own": A History of the American West*. Norman: University of Oklahoma Press, 1991.
———. *The Middle Ground: Indians, Empires, and Republics in the Great Lakes Region, 1650–1815*. New York: Cambridge University Press, 1991.
———. *The Organic Machine*. New York: Hill & Wang, 1995.
———. "Trashing the Trails." In *Trails toward a New Western History*, edited by Patricia Nelson Limerick, Clyde A. Milner II, and Charles E. Rankin, 26–39. Lawrence: University Press of Kansas, 1991.
Wiget, Andrew. *Native American Literature*. Boston: Twayne, 1985.
Williams, Michael. *Americans and Their Forests: A Historical Geography*. New York: Cambridge University Press, 1989.
Williams, Raymond. *Problems in Materialism and Culture: Selected Essays*. London: Verso, 1980.
Williams, Robert A., Jr. *Linking Arms Together: American Indian Treaty Visions of Law and Peace, 1600–1800*. New York: Oxford University Press, 2000.
Williams, Samuel. *The Natural and Civil History of Vermont*. Walpole, N.H., 1794.
Williams, William Carlos. *In the American Grain*. New York: New Directions, 1953.
Williamson, James R., and Linda A. Fossler. *Zebulon Butler: Hero of the Revolutionary Frontier*. Westport: Greenwood, 1995.
Wilson, Joan Hoff. "Dancing Dogs of the Colonial Period: Women Scientists." *Early American Literature* 7, no. 3 (1973): 225–35.
W. M. P. *A Poem on the Acquisition of Louisiana*. Charleston: Query & Evans, 1804.
Wood, Gordon S. *The Radicalism of the American Revolution*. New York: Vintage, 1993.
Wood, W. Raymond. "Contrastive Features of North American Trade Systems." In *For the Chief: Essays in Honor of Luther S. Cressman*, edited by Fred W. Voget and Robert L. Stephenson, 153–69. Eugene: University of Oregon Anthropological Papers, no. 4 (1972).
Worster, Donald. *Nature's Economy: A History of Ecological Ideas*. 2nd ed. New York: Cambridge University Press, 1994.
———. *The Wealth of Nations: Environmental History and the Ecological Imagination*. New York: Oxford University Press, 1993.
Wroth, Lawrence C. *An American Bookshelf, 1755*. New York: Arno, 1979.
———. "The Indian Treaty as Literature." *Yale Review* 17, no. 4 (1928): 749–66.
Young, Chester Raymond, ed. *Westward into Kentucky: The Narrative of Daniel Trabue*. Lexington: University Press of Kentucky, 1981.
Young, Mary. "The Cherokee Nation: Mirror of the Republic." *American Quarterly* 33, no. 5 (1981): 502–24.

INDEX

Adams, John, 218
Adoption: of whites by natives, 5, 68–70, 72, 169–70, 210–11
Albany Congress, 39, 47–48, 93, 234–35 (n. 16). *See also* Evans, Lewis; Franklin, Benjamin
American Philosophical Society, 138

Barlow, Joel, 29
Barton, Benjamin Smith, 125, 128, 233 (n. 3)
Bartram, John, 31, 40, 141, 143–44, 146; Onondaga journey of, 34–38, 52–55, 170, 173; southern tour of, 57, 151, 156 (ill.), 165; and William, 153, 163–65, 170, 201
Bartram, William, 19, 123, 149–73 passim, 184, 186, 208, 214; as artist, 149, 152, 160, 162 (ill.), 170–72, 171 (ill.), 172 (ill.); pastoral themes of, 150–51, 153, 158, 164, 177–79, 172–73; and composition of *Travels*, 151–58; in South Carolina, 152, 158–60; route of travels, 152, 158–60, 164–69; plants and animals described by, 152, 160–63, 166, 169; in Florida, 153–58, 160–61, 165–73; and Creeks, 155, 159–61, 173; and Seminoles, 158, 160–61, 163, 166, 169, 171; and Cherokees, 159–60, 62; in Georgia, 159–60, 165. *See also* Bartram, John
Battle of Wyoming (Wyoming Massacre), 78, 87–88, 94, 96. *See also* Crèvecoeur, Hector St. John de; Susquehanna River; Yankee-Pennamite War

Biddle, Nicholas, 128
Board of Trade, 39, 48–49, 79
Boone, Daniel, 61, 64–71, 83, 103. *See also* Filson, John
Boudinot, Elias, 219–25; education of, 219; and racism, 219; and *Cherokee Phoenix*, 220–21; and Cherokee removal, 220–21, 224; "Address to Whites," 221–24. *See also* Cherokees
Boundaries: disputes over, 9–13, 79, 97–101, 109–12, 180–81, 188–89; and native-white relations, 12, 15–17, 57–59, 79, 97–98, 101, 109–13, 221–22. *See also* Geography; Ohio ordinances; Proclamation Line; Space; Treaties; United States; Yankee-Pennamite War
Bradford, William, 112
Brant, Joseph (Thayendanegea), 87
Brown, Charles Brockden, 17, 247 (n. 6)
Bryan, Joseph, 171
Buffon, Georges Louis Leclerc, Comte de, 103–8, 163, 193. *See also* Jefferson, Thomas
Byron, George Gordon, Lord, 65

Cameahwait, 134, 136. *See also* Lewis and Clark Expedition; Shoshone Sioux
Canada, 43, 93, 122, 187, 217
Canasatego, 90–94. *See also* Treaties
Captivity. *See* Adoption
Cartographic text. *See* Boundaries; Geography; Place; Space
Catesby, Mark, 162
Charleston, 143–48, 152, 158

285

Cherokees, 24, 57–59; environmentalism of, 146–47; language of, 220; and removal, 220–21, 224; society and politics of, 220–22. *See also* Bartram, William; Boudinot, Elias
Chillaway (Delaware), Job, 82–83, 116
Civilization, Euroamerican ideas of, 2, 50–52, 88, 154; and environmental change, 14, 82–83, 194; and imperial expansion, 38, 189; and wilderness, 68, 172, 187; and race, 86, 98, 104, 107, 124, 218–19, 223. *See also* Environmental change; Native Americans; Race
Clark, George Rogers, 103, 246 (n. 24)
Clarke, William, 39
Coffee, John, 197
Colden, Alice Christie, 139, 145
Colden, Cadwallader, 109–10, 138–42, 144–45, 149, 181, 251 (n. 35), 254–55 (n. 5). *See also* Colden, Jane
Colden, Jane, 138–45, 161; education of, 138–39, 149; "Botanic Manuscript" of, 139–41, 140 (ill.); and collaboration, 142; publications of, 142; on herbal medicines, 251 (n. 35)
Collinson, Peter, 141, 143, 149
Condorcet, Marie Jean Antoine Caritat, Marquis de, 105
Conestoga massacre, 86
Cooper, James Fenimore: politics of, 195, 199–205, 211–12, 221; and geographic writing, 198, 202, 214–16; and "Indians," 199–200, 205–16 passim, 222, 224; and nature, 200, 203–6, 215; class anxieties of, 200–205, 208–15
Cooper, Susan, 216
Cooper, William, 200–201, 207
Creek Confederacy, 196–98. *See also* Bartram, William
Cresap, Michael, 111
Crèvecoeur, Hector St. John de, 74, 187, 189, 202; and Ohio Company, 3–4; *Voyage*, 3–4, 6, 170, 178–79, 208; *Letters from an American Farmer*, 3–5, 78; *Lettres d'un Cultivateur Américain*, 4; and Seven Years' War, 78; as mapmaker, 78–79; "Susquehannah," 78–89 passim, 193
Cutler, Manasseh, 14. *See also* Land companies; Northwest Territory; Ohio ordinances

Delaware River, 86, 90, 94. *See also* Crèvecoeur, Hector St. John de; Evans, Lewis
Delawares, 43, 45–46, 103, 211–16, 222; in Ohio Valley, 8, 58; and Iroquois, 79, 90–91; and Susquehanna Valley, 82–83, 88, 90–91, 94
DePauw, Cornelius, 104–5
Doddridge, Joseph, 179
Drowne, Solomon, 1–3, 108, 168
Dunmore's War, 111–13
Dwight, Timothy, 29, 201, 202; *Conquest of Canaan*, 186; *Greenfield Hill*, 186; *Travels*, 186–95; readers of, 187; and New York, 187, 192; and Vermont, 187–89; conceptions of progress, 187–89, 192, 194; and pioneering, 187–89, 193–95; politics of, 187–89, 194–95; on Connecticut River valley, 188, 256 (n. 19); pastoralism of, 191–95

Ecological (pastoral) criticism, 6–7, 18–21, 62–63, 123, 150, 162, 164, 179–80
Ellicott, Andrew, 125
Ellis, John, 141
Environmental change: and deforestation, 5, 104, 178, 189, 193–94, 201; theories of, 9, 103–8, 163, 178, 220; and social conflict, 17–18, 48, 94–95; and social change, 17–18, 66, 81, 202–3, 211; and overhunting, 58–59, 81, 203; and extinction, 178–79, 190, 194, 205
Evans, Lewis: and Benjamin Franklin, 30, 40–41; and John Bartram, 34, 36–37, 53–55; and Conrad Weiser, 34, 53–55; and "Map of Pensilvania," 34–38; and native Americans, 34–38, 43–45, 52–55, 214; and geographic writing, 36, 41–43, 202; and Albany Congress, 38–40; and "General Map," 38–45, 100, 215; revisions of work of, 47–48

Filson, John: and frontiers, 56, 59–60, 65–66; and *Kentucke*, 56, 60–74 passim; and natural history, 56, 63–64; and geography, 61, 62–64, 62 (ill.), 63 (ill.); as mythmaker, 61, 64–71; and environmental change, 61–62, 73; and American Revolution, 70, 72–74. *See also* Boone, Daniel
Florida. *See* Bartram, John; Bartram, William; Stork, William

Franklin, Benjamin: and Lewis Evans, 30, 38–41; and Albany Congress, 39, 234 (n. 16); on imperial expansion, 39–40; and land speculation, 49; and treaties, 90–91, 105, 109–10. *See also* Albany Congress; Evans, Lewis; Treaties
Franklin, state of, 59–60, 60 (ill.)
Frazier, Charles, 186
French-Indian War. *See* Seven Years' War
Freneau, Philip, 15–17, 98, 221
Frontier ("New Western") history, 7, 18–25, 202, 238 (n. 13)
Fry, Joshua, 100

Garden, Alexander, 139, 142, 149; and Cherokees, 146–47, 161, 163, 170
Geography: republican ideas of, 10–12, 79, 82, 97–99, 113; and narrative design, 23, 31–32, 41, 63–64, 78–79, 88, 97–101, 143, 198, 202, 221; and colonization, 29–31; and native Americans, 32, 36–38, 54. *See also* Boundaries; Place; Space
Grant, Anne (Macvicar): financial straits of, 180, 182; and Stamp Act, 180–81; and Schuyler family, 180–81, 183–86; and Vermont, 180–82; *Memoirs of an American Lady*, 180–86, 197, 213; pastoralism of, 180–86, 200–201; and American Revolution, 184–85
Greathouse, Daniel, 111
Gronovius, John Frederick, 139, 141

Handsome Lake, 217–18. *See also* Iroquois
Hanson, John, 96
Hawkins, Benjamin, 196
Henderson, Richard, 59
Hendrick, 38–39, 93
Hidatsas, 128–29
Humphreys, David, 8–9
Hutchins, Thomas: and Ohio survey, 12–14, 13 (ill.), 73; and geographic writing, 30, 37, 57

Imlay, Gilbert, 31
Iroquois, 110, 188, 211, 216; politics and diplomacy of, 33–34, 38–40, 43–49, 89–90, 217; and place, 36–37; and travel, 52–54; and treaties, 57, 79, 90–95; and warfare, 82, 87–89, 110–11; and religion, 217–18. *See also* Evans, Lewis; Native Americans; Treaties
Irving, Washington, 24, 196–98, 201, 221, 223–24

Jackson, Andrew, 196, 198, 219
Jefferson, Peter, 100, 102
Jefferson, Thomas, 1, 188; *Notes on the State of Virginia*, 2, 30, 98–117 passim, 123; spatial politics of, 10–11, 97–99, 112–13; and native Americans, 97–98, 103–4, 107–17, 177, 208, 214, 217–18; and geographic writing, 99, 100–102, 202, 221–22; and nature, 99–100, 103–8, 163, 193; and mastodon, 103, 105–6, 106 (ill.), 108; and exploration, 124–32 passim, 149–50
Johnson, William: and Iroquois, 38, 48–49; and native-white relations, 40, 79; and Iroquois "dependents," 48–49, 58, 82; political ascenscion of, 93; and Dunmore's War, 111, 113. *See also* Boundaries; Iroquois; Treaties

Kennedy, Archibald, 39
Kentucky. *See* Filson, John; Ohio River valley
King George's War, 34, 93
Knox, Henry, 98, 101, 116, 123–25, 155, 178, 208. *See also* Native Americans; United States

Land companies: in Ohio, 4, 10, 14–15, 100, 187; "Suffering Traders," 49; Susquehannah Company, 79, 97, 112
Leopold, Aldo, 19
Lewis and Clark Expedition, 121–38, 149; plants and animals described by, 121–22, 127, 136; and native Americans, 121–25, 126, 128–29, 132, 134–36; and Missouri River, 122, 125, 129–34; expectations of, 122, 125–26, 150; enlisted members of, 122, 129, 133–36; and sex, 122, 138; and Columbia River, 125; preparation of Lewis for, 125–26; and Lewis's mental state, 126, 132; *Journals* of, 127–28; and portable boat, 132–33; and food, 133–36; and Sacagawea, 134, 136. *See also* Louisiana Purchase

INDEX { 287

Linnaeus (Carl von Linnè), 106, 138–39, 141, 162
Little Turtle (Michikinikwa), 17–18, 219
Logan (Tahgahjute), 107, 109–17, 197. *See also* Jefferson, Thomas
Logan, James, 92, 111
Logan, Martha Daniell, 143–46
Louisiana Purchase: boundaries of, 122; debates over, 124, 150, 247 (n. 6); settlement of, 188
Lydius, John, 79, 82, 86–87

Madison, James, 112, 188
Mandans, 120, 128–29
Manifest Destiny, 15, 20
Marbois, François, 99, 125
Marietta, Ohio, 1–3, 14–15, 73, 107, 168
Masculinity, constructions of, 123, 138, 158
May, John, 3, 16
Mississippi River, 44, 102, 153
Monroe, James, 208, 218–19
Morse, Jedediah, 179, 255 (n. 11)
Morton, Sarah Wentworth, 30, 37
Mounds, Indian, 2, 107, 168, 254 (n. 25)

Native Americans: U.S. policies toward, 15, 73, 98–99, 116, 123–24, 155–58, 177, 179, 194, 208, 217–19; textual removals of, 16–18, 21, 24–25, 32–33, 44–45, 82–83, 89–90, 108, 114–17, 197–99, 208, 212–16, 219–25; literary representations of, 16–18, 107–8, 114–17, 214, 221–24; and environmentalism, 18, 20, 36–37, 53, 161; and agriculture, 18, 36–37, 82, 168, 184, 220, 223; and geography, 36, 38, 54, 129; and travel, 52–53; and disease, 213–14. *See also individual groups*
Natural history: as literary genre, 31; conventions of, 62–64, 100, 127, 139–41; and nationalism, 103–8, 163–64; collaboration in, 121–24, 142, 145–48; hierarchies in, 142–43, 153–54
Nature: as effacement, 7, 18–20, 81, 189, 256; and social order, 9, 14, 61–64, 99–100, 105–7, 167–68, 256 (n. 15). *See also* Environmental change; Natural history; Pastoral; Place; Wilderness
Neolin, 45–46, 49, 219

New England: emigration from, 1–3, 14–15, 79, 82, 85, 188; representations of, 28–30, 50, 181–82, 186–95 passim
Nez Perce, 121–22, 136–37
Northwest Ordinance. *See* Ohio ordinances: Northwest Ordinance
Northwest Territory, 1–4, 8–18 passim, 29, 73–74, 98–99, 219

Ohio ordinances, 1, 73, 108, 150, 158, 168; Ordinance of 1784, 11–12, 97, 113; Land Ordinance of 1785, 12–13, 13 (ill.), 73; Northwest Ordinance, 12–14, 15
Ohio River valley: representations of, 1–4, 8–9, 15–18, 29; conflicts in, 8–9, 12, 16–19, 49, 57–61, 70–74, 107, 110–11; settlement of, 8–9, 12–15, 72–74; mapping of, 13 (ill.), 40 (ill.), 42–44, 54–55, 62 (ill.), 63 (ill.), 73. *See also* Filson, John; Northwest Territory; Ohio ordinances
Oquaga, 87–89

Paine, Thomas, 84
Pastoral: as elegy, 7, 198, 210–12; and colonization, 21–23, 158, 193–95; and nature, 150, 180; as escape, 182–85, 207. *See also* Nature; Place; Wilderness
Patterson, Robert, 125
Paxton Boys, 85–86
Peck, William Dandridge, 31
Penn, William, 93
Pinckney, Eliza Lucas, 143–45, 187, 202, 221
Pioneering: and class tensions, 9, 181–82, 185, 189, 203–4, 229–30 (n. 24); and race, 15, 59, 86; and environmental change, 85, 189, 193–94, 201–5
Place: contested ideas of, 7, 57; and memory, 36, 188–91; and colonization, 50, 64, 83, 198; and conservation, 150–51, 180, 190–92; and social class, 179, 185, 197–98. *See also* Geography; Pastoral; Space
Pontiac, 47, 49, 219
Pownall, Thomas, 47–52, 187, 202
Price, Richard, 105
Proclamation Line (1763), 49, 57–59, 81, 113. *See also* Boundaries; Treaties
Puccoon, 147, 170

Race, 24–25, 86–87, 98–99, 104–5, 196–97, 210, 219, 221–25. *See also* Environmental change; Native Americans; Pioneering
Ramsay, David, 30
Raynal, Guillaume Thomas François de, the Abbé, 104–5, 107. *See also* Jefferson, Thomas
Records, Spencer, 72
Revolution, American, 8–9, 70–73, 77–89 passim, 96–97, 105, 111, 182, 217; backlash against, 179, 184–85, 189, 194
Rochefoucauld-Liancourt, François-Alexandre Frédéric, Duc de, 178
Royal Society, 138, 152–53
Rush, Benjamin, 125

St. Clair, Arthur, 15, 73–74, 189
Saint-Mémin, Charles B. J. F., 136, 137 (ill.)
Scalping, 3, 61, 72, 110–11, 190
Seven Years' War (French-Indian War), 30, 39–44, 56, 78–79, 151, 180
Shawnees, 8; and Iroquois, 43, 45; land claims of, 57–58; social organization of, 58; and warfare, 59, 110; and adoption, 65–66, 69–70, 170
Shickellamy, 34, 111
Shoshone Sioux, 134–36
Smith, James Edward, 31
Space: and place, 7, 20, 189–91; and conflict, 16, 48, 50, 57, 112; and narrative, 23, 29–30; vacating of, 36, 81, 83–84. *See also* Boundaries; Geography; Place
Stamp Act, 105, 180–81
Stockades, 1–3, 70, 72, 87–88
Stork, William, 30–31, 37, 56–57, 151
Susquehanna River, 34–37, 77–95 passim. *See also* Crèvecoeur, Hector St. John de; Yankee-Pennamite War
Susquehannocks, 81

Tecumseh, 18, 196, 219
Teedyuscung, 79, 85
Thomas, George, 93–94
Thoreau, Henry David, 19, 158, 190

Translation, 91–92, 109, 114–17, 199–200. *See also* Treaties
Transylvania, 59–60, 97
Treaties: Fort Stanwix (1768), 49, 57–59, 81, 110; at Albany Congress (1754), 79, 82, 86–87; Walking Purchase (1737), 90, 242–43 (n. 19); at Philadelphia (1742), 90–95, 109; and verbal arts, 90–95, 109–10; protocol of, 92–93, 109; New Purchase (1773), 159–60; New Echota (1835), 220. *See also* Translation
Trumbull, John, 65

United States: land ordinances of, 8–9, 10–12, 73–74; Indian wars of, 17–18, 196–97, 219; boundary conflicts of, 59–60, 96–97, 112, 182, 188–89; and Indian policies, 73, 98–99, 108, 155–56, 173, 177, 179, 194, 208, 217, 219, 224. *See also* Native Americans; Ohio ordinances; Revolution, American; Treaties

Vermont, 180–82, 188–89, 256 (n. 15). *See also* Dwight, Timothy; Grant, Anne
Volney, Constantin-François Chasseboeuf, Comte de, 17

War of 1812, 18, 188
Washington, George, 8
Weiser, Conrad, 34, 52–55, 91
Western history. *See* Frontier history
Wiandots, 43–44
Wilderness: as predeveloped land, 1–2, 7, 52, 62, 68–71, 88; romantic ideas of, 18–23; and religion, 61–62, 154, 187; and social conflict, 178, 180, 187. *See also* Ecological criticism; Nature; Pastoral
Williams, Samuel, 177, 187–89
Williams, William Carlos, 65
Wistar, Caspar, 125
"Wyoming Massacre." *See* Battle of Wyoming

Yankee-Pennamite War, 79–88 passim, 90, 96–97, 188–89. *See also* Crèvecoeur, Hector St. John de; Susquehanna River

www.ingramcontent.com/pod-product-compliance
Lightning Source LLC
Chambersburg PA
CBHW020057020526
44112CB00031B/201